The Foreign Policy
OF THE
European Union

The Foreign Policy
OF THE
European Union
ASSESSING EUROPE'S ROLE IN THE WORLD

FEDERIGA BINDI
editor

BROOKINGS INSTITUTION PRESS
Washington, D.C.

Library of Congress Cataloging-in-Publication data

The foreign policy of the European Union : assessing Europe's role in the world /
Federiga Bindi, editor.
   p. cm.
  Includes bibliographical references and index.
  Summary: "Explores European foreign policy and the degree of European Union
success in proposing itself as a valid international actor, drawing from expertise of
scholars and practitioners in many disciplines from North America, Europe, Australia,
and New Zealand. Addresses issues past and present, theoretical and practice-oriented,
and country- and region-specific"—Provided by publisher.
  ISBN 978-0-8157-0140-8 (pbk. : alk. paper)
  1. European Union. 2. European Union countries—foreign relations. I. Bindi,
Federiga M. II. Title.

JZ1570.F67 2010
341.242'2—dc22   2009042861

9 8 7 6 5 4 3 2 1

Printed on acid-free paper

Typeset in Minion

Composition by Cynthia Stock
Silver Spring, Maryland

Printed by R. R. Donnelley
Harrisonburg, Virginia

Contents

Foreword

In July 2008, *The Economist* headlined one of its issues "What a way to run the world."[1] It featured the tower of Babel on the cover, indicating that today the world is run by a Babel power, with everything in contradiction with everything else. The image of this new tower of Babel raises the question, what is the nature of the contemporary world? When asked to answer this question, most "experts" resort to the "in a rapidly changing world" explanation, according to which our world is one of perpetual change: the price of oil fluctuates wildly; climate conditions are rapidly shifting the world over; and the balance of power in the world is also rapidly changing.

Change is good, but change that is too rapid requires appropriate responses. Many things are needed in this "rapidly changing world." Above all, contradictory as it might seem, some stability is needed. This has become evident with the ongoing world financial crisis. It is worth noting that financial crises themselves seem to have gone through a "rapid change." In the past they have occurred in Japan, Argentina, and third world countries, while today the United States is the main source of the world's financial woes. In addition, support for the dollar has come for years not from the club of the G-7 countries, but from China. Financial resources worldwide now tend to go on a sort of equal footing to the United States and to the Far East, to China, to India, and to other eastern countries.

And while most people are not necessarily becoming wealthier, they certainly are less poor, by the thousands and hundreds of thousands. As a consequence, prices of food are rising. As more people eat rice and bread, the price of rice and bread goes up. As more people use electricity, the price of oil and natural gas goes up. By the same token, while many are less poor, the richest are much richer than ever. The distance between the few and the many has increased, despite the fact that the many are better off than they were in the past. According to Goldman Sachs, in the distribution of the produced wealth in the past fifteen to twenty years the share that has gone to what is called "capital" has been increasing, in contrast to the share that has gone to salaries, to jobs, and to employees. Because of worldwide competition, salaries are kept low in order to sell at competitive prices. If this strategy is successful, huge profits are obtained, but salaries remain low—otherwise prices would not be competitive anymore. How to achieve a better distribution of wealth between employers and employees is an open question for the future.

What are the other matters of concern? Climate change is one of them. It makes more production of electricity a hope for some, but at the same time a threat to all of us. Similarly, terrorist activities and extremist ideologies in various parts of the world are matters of concern, as well as outflows and inflows of migration. Migrations are generally the consequence of uneven distribution of global production and wealth, but in the future climate change is expected to be one of the main causes of population outflows from certain parts of the world. These are just sketches of several issues that need a new kind of governance. Here too we are coping with a rapidly changing world.

Only a few years ago, before the turn of the twenty-first century, it seemed that the world would be run by only one country, the only remaining military power. But the world is no longer unipolar, and other countries are becoming more and more relevant. Along with the increase in their number and influence has come greater interdependence, as well as more matters to cope with. Irrespective of whether globalization is a good or a bad thing, it is today's reality. Nation-states have too limited a jurisdiction to do the job. Supranational institutions are largely insufficient. There are several multinational agencies in the world, each of them taking care of one specific thing. To say the least, there is a problem of policy coherence in our global governance. But there is more than that.

Within this broad framework, the questions this book deals with are whether and what role Europe can play in this Babel power and what its relationship with the United States can be. Three basic issues have to be addressed: whether Europe has the resources to play a role; what Europe's limits are in using such resources; and what is being done, or can be done, to reduce the weight of these limits and to improve the European performance. At the start it is worth noting that, for the sake of brevity, the terms "Europe" and "European Union" are used interchangeably.

With regard to resources, Europe has already demonstrated that it has them. We actually speak of the transformative power of Europe and of its power of attraction vis-à-vis its neighbors. Understanding what we mean by these formulations is essential to appreciate what Europe has done up to now and what it can do in the future.

Well before the fall of the Berlin Wall, when the boundaries of the European Union were somehow set, Europe had already proven to have transformative power. The Union transformed its member states and their citizens, making armed conflict among them unthinkable for the future. Europe's very mission had been to stop the wars between its countries and to open a history of peace and cooperation. The European nation-states, responsible for the main wars of the previous centuries and for starting the two world wars of the twentieth century, inside Europe, successfully transformed themselves.

The notion of transformative power came to the fore after the fall of the Berlin Wall, when other countries historically belonging to Europe questioned who they were and why they were not in the Union. It is worth remembering that this latest wave of enlargement was also called the reunification of Europe. Despite the highly emotional value of this name, it had to tackle the sharp differences between the preexisting member states and countries that had communist regimes, economies, and institutions. Transforming a communist economy into a free-market one is a titanic job: it must be done not only through the establishment of new legal arrangements but also through the adoption of a new mental framework. It requires taking risks without relying on ministerial decisions, as well as allowing new (frequently unwritten) freedoms based on common interests to flourish. This transformation has happened, and the process of integration of the eastern European economies into the preexisting European market is progressing.

The second type of transformation in the central and eastern European countries (CEECs) was from communist institutions to democratic institutions. In practice, this meant different principles and rules for administrative officials, a different role for the police, and the creation of an independent judicial apparatus and independent antitrust authorities. Ultimately, this resulted in a new mentality in the administrative branches of the executive: not only deciding, but more frequently supervising, coordinating, and promoting. And this transformation took place in ten years, through financial programs, training programs, exchanges, and negotiations. The complexity of this transformation was grasped by a researcher now working for the European Commission, Heather Grabbe.[2] In her work she underlines that the strength of Europeanization goes far beyond the negotiations related to individual sectors of activity. Europe's power was a sort of transverse tide that affected the sociocultural realities of the new countries as well. The aim was the same for Europe and the accession countries. Therefore the interaction between them went beyond bureaucratic agreements on the so-called *acquis communautaire*. Its 80,000 pages of regulations contained the essential, but not the fascinating. One couldn't fall in love with Europe by reading and adopting the *acquis communautaire*.

But it is here that the second European resource, namely the power of attraction, enters the scene. Not unlike transformative power, it is actually a basket of resources. It produces its effects also without using the tools of transformative power, and even countries that will never join the Union are positively affected. Its impact is high on neighboring countries, beneficiaries of generous neighborhood policies. In some cases (at the eastern borders more easily than at the southern ones), these policies are the prelude to accession to the EU. For several reasons, these policies can also affect countries that are not immediate neighbors.

One is the status of international affairs. In times of insecurity, countries prefer to get closer to a military protector. Europe does not fill this role. In times of peace and in certain domains countries prefer to deal with a partner that is not a military power. Europe is the biggest donor of foreign aid worldwide, although its primacy is threatened by China. Europe brings both aid and companies that are less powerful and less dominating than the U.S. multinationals symbolized by McDonald's. In other words, other countries have a sense that a more even relationship can be established with Europe and the Europeans.

A second reason for Europe's attractiveness is its welfare system. Owing to that safety net, Europeans tend to be less protectionist than Americans. When a job is in danger in the United States, the holder of that job fears losing everything—income, health care, the ability to pay the mortgage—and will do almost anything to protect the job. This attitude results in support and demand for protectionist measures. In a similar situation the Europeans feel more protected. Consequently, their preexisting openness to foreign trade is safer.

Another growing reason for Europe's attractiveness is the euro. The euro is an important resource to play a positive role in the world. Today's reality shows that the weaker the dollar, the higher international inflation. This is true because it is the dollar, not the euro, that is the main currency in international trade. Although not used as often as the dollar in international transactions, the euro is increasingly becoming a reserve currency. This means that it is increasingly perceived as an anchor of stability. Against this background, unpredictable developments will depend on the credibility of Europe not just as a friendly market player, but also as a meaningful political player on the global scene.

The role of Europe as a political player is negatively affected by its well-known limits. One of those is its internal divisions. Although the notion is bizarre, Europe is expected to simultaneously have a single voice and multiple voices in international institutions. Imagine the scenario of a meeting of the UN Security Council in which the Union was invited to speak with its own High Representative; that single European foreign official, speaking to an audience of permanent members of the Security Council, would also speak to a French and a British representative.

At the same time, European states have distinct executive directors in both the International Monetary Fund (IMF) and the World Bank. By agreeing to merge their shares and have one director, the Europeans would be the primary shareholders in these institutions. The headquarters of the IMF would be not in Washington, but in London or Frankfurt. At the moment, Europeans apparently prefer those institutions to remain in Washington.

The second limitation of Europe is its organization, which makes its policies weak and frequently inconsistent. American scholars often describe the way Washington is organized as a mess. If they go to Brussels, they might discover that Washington has a comparatively harmonious system of government, much more harmonious than Europe's. The reason for this is simple: the European Community was conceived as an international organization. According to the patterns of international organizations, decisions are bestowed on national ministers, by sector. Europe has a council of agriculture ministers, a council of industry ministers, and a council of interior ministers, and each of these councils makes separate decisions. This never happens inside nation-states, where all interests in a political decision take part in the decisionmaking process. Therefore, if the minister for industry has an objection to the position of the minister for environment, they can consult before the decision is made.

The consequences of this European arrangement are illustrated by the following example. Transforming Kosovo into a state is not an easy task. Here the transformative power of Europe should play that role. An essential prerequisite is to have as much economic stability as possible. Kosovars at the moment have a crucial economic resource: the ability to migrate to western Europe for seasonal jobs. When the son of a peasant family reaches 18 or 19 years of age, his family accompanies him to the railway station to travel to Italy, Germany, or Austria (usually one of these three countries) for seasonal work. He saves some money and with that money buys the furniture with which he will furnish his future home. This has become a pattern in Kosovo.

In the view of ministers of foreign affairs, this practice should continue, as long as the economic structure of the country is not modified. But the ministers of the interior are now increasingly averse to migration, even of a temporary nature. Therefore they tend to restrict the inflow of seasonal workers from the western Balkans and elsewhere. Although these two sets of policies conflict with each other, both are European policies.

The third limit is the uncertainty of the possible role of the Union, also due to the uncertainty of its boundaries. Will enlargement stop with the reunification of Europe? If so, one could argue, it should stop with the western Balkans, for they have always been European countries. They have admittedly been the troublemakers in the family, as exemplified by the beginning of the First World

War, yet members of it nevertheless. But Turkey is also a candidate. Another important point of discussion is whether Ukraine and Georgia should be members or neighbors. Enduring doubts about the answers to these questions create uncertainties not only in the involved countries, but also in the wider world, where the role Europeans intend to play is not understood. The crucial issue of Europe as a regional or global power is linked to this unresolved issue.

A final limit is the current condition of the transatlantic relationship. Europe and the United States have historically been friends and allies. However, on both sides of the Atlantic discussions consider whether this traditional alliance still makes sense. On the American side, the increasing importance of East Asia as well as the end of the cold war and thus of the importance of Europe as one of its major "battlefields" has led to reduced U.S. interest in its European allies. The role of Europe is reduced to that of the rest of the world: to offer "the willing." Furthermore, in recent decades many of the new U.S. leaders have come from regions other than the traditionally Europe-oriented East Coast. On the European side the sharp division on Iraq was just a symptom of the diversity of approaches toward America. This diversity of approaches was enhanced by enlargement. France is now returning to a more cooperative approach, but the proximity of Russia is a reason for Europe and the United States to have different positions toward that country.

I have reached the closing question of this introductory essay, whether something can be done to overcome Europe's limits and enhance its role in the world. The correct assumption is that its role has to be global because the challenges that have to be faced are also global. The example of migration is enough to make clear that this global dimension is present everywhere. The immigrants who arrive by boat on the Italian coast are mainly Africans, but some come from Asian countries, such as Pakistan and Bangladesh. After they have entered Italy, they may become members of the national community, but they remain sensitive to what is happening in their homelands. Consequently, Italians also have to be sensitive to what is happening there. All of us, immigrants and nationals, have to get used to thinking globally.

In order to be credibly global, Europeans must improve their organization. Some of this improvement would be brought by the Lisbon Treaty. If we were to compare it to a movie, the Lisbon Treaty would be in black and white, not Technicolor. It brings streamlining, fine-tuning, and adjustments to remedy some shortcomings. If voters want more democracy they will have to approve the treaty; otherwise national parliaments will be able to play almost no role in the Union. If voters want a direct role for their citizens, they will have to approve the treaty. It will be a real paradox if the treaty fails because voters believe it deprives citizens of a bigger role. If Europe's citizens want to eliminate the sectoral policies that prevent interaction and coordination, they need the treaty. They need it because the treaty would give the General Affairs Council the specific task of coordinating the policies of the sectoral councils and give the new president of the European Council the mission to safeguard continuity, cohesion, and coherence in the policies of the Union. With these improvements, the internal divisions, inconsistencies, and uncertainties that currently weaken the Union should (at least) be reduced.

It is equally essential for Europe to reset its relationship with the United States. In order for our Tower of Babel to remain a tower but to be less Babel-like two things are needed. First, both the Americans and the Europeans have to accept that any future "world order" will not be a Western one as it was in the past. Today, people who traditionally obeyed the rules are eager to become rule makers; they have earned such a change and have the substantial power to obtain it. The only alternative would be a separate order of their own, which would make everyone's lives even more difficult. In this sense, some of the news coming from Asia is fine, but has to be read carefully: consider the newly established direct flights between China and Taiwan and agreements between China and Japan.

Second, the United States and Europe must contribute to the future order side by side. Up to now discussions have focused on transatlantic differences and sometimes divergences. But Europe and the United States have more in common with each other than either does with anyone else in the world. This is an asset that must be exploited for our impact on the future to be adequate to the principles and values we share. I am not advocating here a Christian West opposing the rest, a sort of nonsensical renewed crusade. Instead, Europeans and Americans have the common responsibility to support their vision of a world based on the rule of law, on the respect of human rights and the empowerment of the people, and on sustainable economic growth in the new multipolar arena. The best way to do this is by playing the same game.

Giuliano Amato
Vice President of the European Convention
Former Prime Minister of Italy

Notes

1. *The Economist,* July 5, 2008.
2. Heather Grabbe, *The EU's Transformative Power: Europeanization through Conditionality in Central and Eastern Europe* (London: Palgrave Macmillan, 2006).

FEDERIGA BINDI *and* IRINA ANGELESCU

Introduction

Is the concept of a European Union (EU) foreign policy paradoxical, as Jan Zielonka claims?[1] According to Zielonka, the EU wants to become a powerful international actor without becoming a superstate in the process; it hopes to have a strong impact on Europe and the rest of the world, without basing these aspirations on a well-defined and consistent strategy. Its numerous aims include the prevention and management of conflicts, but little has been done to incorporate a military dimension into its foreign policy.

The history of European integration makes it clear that the European Economic Community/European Union (EEC/EU) has always struggled to acquire a substantial external dimension. The Treaty of Rome (1957) opened the way for external relations of the European Communities (EC) based on economic considerations. The Pleven Plan in 1950, the creation of the Western European Union in 1954, and the Fouchet Plan proposed in 1961 subsequently attempted to expand the external economic competencies the EC had acquired with a diplomatic and military capacity. The aim was to turn the EC into an autonomous actor. All these attempts failed to achieve their purpose, but the logic of the European integration process eventually led to a progressive evolution toward closer cooperation in foreign policy.

In the 1970s, a first measure undertaken on this long path was the creation of the European Political Cooperation (EPC). As a precursor of the Common Foreign and Security Policy (CFSP), the EPC came to symbolize the need for dialogue at the European level. The member states had to understand that, on the international stage, their interests were best defended if they worked together. The EC already conducts an autonomous economic foreign policy in international forums such as the World Trade Organization (WTO). The EU itself is directly involved in significant cases of international negotiations such as the four-party negotiations over the settlement of the Israeli-Palestinian conflict.

However, the balance is counterweighted by the individual membership of EU member states in international organizations. The permanent status of France and Great Britain on the United Nations Security Council is probably the most prominent example. Furthermore, individual member states continue to engage in bilateral negotiations with third parties. As illustrated in recent years by the Georgia crisis, the conflict in Gaza, or the Russian-Ukrainian gas crisis, Europe could benefit from more cooperation and a single, unified voice to counter the third parties' policies of *divide et impera.*

This volume aims to explore the state of European foreign policy and the degree of EU success in proposing itself as a valid international actor. The complexity of this subject demanded bringing together the foremost experts on the different aspects of EU foreign policy. The book draws on an international conference held in Rome in July 2008 organized by the University of Rome Tor Vergata in collaboration with the Center for American Studies in Rome and the Brookings Institution. The participants included some of the best-known academic experts and practitioners in EU affairs from North America, Europe, Australia, and New Zealand. To unravel the myths associated with European Union foreign policy, this volume examines it in its entire complex dimension. The contributors come from different disciplinary backgrounds. This is one of the few volumes of its kind, inasmuch as it addresses individual issues both past and present, theoretical and practice-oriented, and country- and region-specific.

This volume also deals with both "horizontal" and "vertical" issues. Vertical issues focus on particular geographic regions; horizontal issues explore themes relevant to the EU's external affairs. Vertical analyses are based on the EU's relations with the rest of the world, from its neighbors to Oceania, passing by North America, the Middle East, Latin America, and the Far East. Horizontal issues include the EU's foreign policy tools, ranging from the CFSP to Justice and Home Affairs (JHA) to competition policy and the European Neighborhood Policy (ENP). They also include human rights, peace and democracy, the influence of the European integration model, and the perception of the EU by the international public.

In more specific terms, the volume addresses the following questions:

—How have relations between the EC/EU and the rest of the world developed historically?

—What are the instruments the EC/EU has set up to deal with different parts of the world?

—What are the main objectives that the EU wants to pursue in other areas of the world? How have they changed over the years?

—Is it possible to say that there has been a shift of attention by the EU in its foreign policy, from economic issues to political ones?

—Has the EU contributed to the development of human rights, peace, and democracy?

—Has the EU contributed to the economic development of specific areas of the world?

—Does the EU foreign policy contribute to creating a European identity? Are foreign populations aware of that the EU has a foreign policy? If so, is the EU considered a useful and reliable partner?

—Has the EU contributed to the promotion of regional integration in other areas of the world? How is the European integration process similar to and different from integration models pursued in other regions?

The book's foreword is by Giuliano Amato, the vice president of the European Convention and a former prime minister of Italy. Bringing to the discussion both his theoretical knowledge and practical experience in European affairs, he identifies the European approach as unique among those of the other parts of the world. He points out the advantages and limits of the European approach in dealing with the rest of the world and suggests measures Europe could adopt to improve its influence and power. While praising the merits of European power, he warns against internal divisions, against goals that are too modest for the EU's potential, and against the danger of breaking the connection with the other important global power, the United States of America.

Part I of the volume is devoted to the EU's foreign policy tools. First Federiga Bindi provides a short history of European foreign policy. Then Nicola Verola focuses on the new tools that the EU would acquire should the Lisbon Treaty be adopted and compares them with those listed under both the Constitutional Treaty and the founding treaties of the European Community. He notes an evolutionary crescendo, with the Lisbon Treaty as the climax, from the granting of a unique judicial personality to the EU to the creation of the EU Presidency and the High Representative for the Common Foreign and Security Policy.

The following chapter is dedicated to what Stephan Keukeleire calls the "spearhead" of the European Union: the European Security and Defense Policy (ESDP). His analysis centers on the history that led to the development of this policy. He notes that the ESDP is a result of a long series of failed attempts by the EU to develop autonomous defense capabilities. However, it was only because of the post–cold war scenario and the precedent of the Balkan wars that the ESDP gathered momentum at the end of the twentieth century. Although the ESDP represents a significant transformation in the EU's struggle to obtain its own military capability, Keukeleire warns that the ESDP has a long way to go before achieving this aim.

The chapter by Francesca Longo highlights the link that has emerged between two former pillars of the EU: the CFSP and the JHA, with the creation of the

Area of Freedom, Security, and Justice (AFSJ). She argues that the EU has been and essentially remains a "civilian power" and a "normative power." The evolution of the military capacity of the EU, with the creation of the European Security and Defense Policy, further confirms this fact. She uses the case of the 2003 European security strategy and the EU's relations with the Mediterranean countries to present her case.

Alberto Heimler analyzes the links between the European economic policy and its foreign policy. His underlying argument is that the latter evolved from the former both through intentional measures and because of unintended consequences of certain economic policies. He examines the evolution of competition rules as his case study.

Finally, Tom Casier addresses the nature of one of the newest mechanisms the EU has implemented for dealing with its neighbors, the European Neighborhood Policy (ENP). He argues that, in the post–cold war world, the ENP was created to ensure stability in the wider Europe and therefore to avoid a new security vacuum and new dividing lines. The ENP also represents a shift in the EU's strategy of creating stability across its borders through means other than membership conditionality. Ultimately, the success or failure of the ENP will be determined by the outcomes of the social learning process and the ability of the EU to consistently put forward a coherent voice when dealing with its eastern and southern neighbors.

Part II of the volume is dedicated to the EU and its neighbors. Lara Piccardo offers insight into the relations between the EU and its biggest and most powerful Eastern neighbor: Russia. She argues that their relations are governed by ideological differences and misunderstandings that have been present since the creation of the European project. With the fall of the Berlin Wall, the attitude of the Russian people and Russian leaders shifted positively and many began to look to Europe as a model for rebuilding and reintegration. However, actions undertaken by the EU (mainly its enlargement to the east) have led to another shift in the attitude of the Russian leaders toward a "bipolar logic." They see contemporary Europe as either a competitor or an enemy, not as a friend. The Georgian crisis, the antiballistic missiles in eastern Europe, NATO enlargement, and the more recent Russian gas crisis are all important events that demonstrate that many differences must still be overcome for a harmonious relationship to emerge.

In another case study, Serena Giusti and Tomislava Penkova examine the EU policy toward Ukraine and Belarus. In looking at these two countries and their interactions with the EU, the United States, and Russia, the authors challenge many of the conventional views on the subject. While emphasizing the differences and points of disagreement between the EU and the United States on the one hand and Ukraine and Belarus on the other, they also explain how relations between Russia and Belarus, for example, are less close than commonly thought.

Addressing another "hot" region in Europe's neighborhood, the Balkans, Luca Gori assesses the impact of the EU in the region. He finds that the glass is both half empty and half full, depending on one's viewpoint and the region at issue. He argues that while the EU's merits should not be exaggerated, neither should its shortfalls be downplayed. Given that the EU did not decide on a consistent strategy toward the Balkans until 2003, more efforts should be undertaken in order to make up for the lost time.

Moving south, Joseph Joseph addresses one of the most contentious issues in the history of EU enlargement: the possible membership of Turkey. Aiming to provide an overview of the challenges and opportunities that Turkey presents to the EU and vice versa, he concludes that at present the only ambivalent opinion comes from the EU side. He predicts that the heated debate on this argument will continue for years and concludes that accession negotiations will be not so much a matter of contention over the *acquis communautaire* as a mission of diplomatic maneuvers and negotiations.[2]

In a chapter about the EU and the Mediterranean nonmember states, Alfred Tovias returns to the mechanisms of the ENP discussed previously by Tom Casier. He looks at a specific case: the ENP and the Arab countries of the Mediterranean basin. Tovias argues that the EU should pay special attention to this region because, with the rise of China and India, it will likely become more dependent on the Mediterranean region for the import of energy supplies. Tovias argues in favor of a rational and reasonable approach and a sober calculation of the impact of the ENP on the Arab countries, as well as the interests of the other key superpower in the region: the United States.

On a similar note, Stefania Panebianco explains the ENP and its impact on the Mediterranean area from a historical perspective. Looking at the evolution from the Barcelona process to the ENP, she observes that although for the past fifty years the European integration model has been the model of reference, the ENP illustrates that security issues have recently overridden all other considerations.

Noting that despite its geopolitical and geostrategic importance and the increased European interest in the region since the 1970s, the Mediterranean region remains mired in conflict, Khalid Emara brings another possible EU solution into the discussion. His interest lies in the proposal put forward by the French Presidency of the EU: the creation of a Mediterranean Union. Khalid Emara argues that, just as in the ENP, security issues dominate in the Mediterranean Union proposal, and that, in order to be effective, a Mediterranean Union should be modeled along the lines of the Marshall Plan.

Part III of the volume discusses the relations of the EU with the other continents. Andrew Moravcsik begins this part by challenging the "conventional view" of transatlantic relations. According to this view, the golden age of transatlantic relations ended with the cold war. Iraq emerged as symbol of a clash of visions and values (multilateralism vs. unilateralism), and the EU undermined the chances of stronger transatlantic ties because of its own internal divisions and lack of consensus. Looking at concrete examples from both the past and the present, Moravcsik dismisses each of the three presuppositions underlying this view. His analysis points to the opposite conclusion: that transatlantic relations are now closer and more promising than ever. With Europe as a splendid "quiet superpower" and the United States as a military superpower, the two can form a very strong and long-lasting team in the international arena, but only if they start working on the small individual problems plaguing the relationship.

In a chapter dedicated to the economic cooperation between the EU and the United States, Marta Dassù and Roberto Menotti look at the legacy of the George W. Bush administration. They argue that despite the declining importance of the strategic and military relationship during the Bush years, the economic relationship has remained very strong. They identify the economic relationship as the backbone of EU-U.S. relations. Because of its strength, they predict that the current financial crisis may lead to a paradoxical result: despite the best efforts of the new administration of Barack Obama to burnish the United States' image abroad, the economic slowdown may inflict further serious damage and weaken the perception of U.S. leadership. The solution proposed by the two authors is that in order to refurbish America's image in Europe, emphasis should be put not only on diplomatic measures, but also on the creation of a "transatlantic economic area." Given the enormous economic capabilities and potential of both players, such an entity would benefit them and the rest of the world as well.

In a chapter dedicated to the EU's relations with Latin America and the Caribbean, Joaquin Roy recalls that it was only after Spain and Portugal joined the Union that relations with Latin America and the Caribbean increased in saliency. Roy argues that the relationship between the EU and the region is unequal but beneficial, inasmuch as the EU is the biggest donor in the region and offers a model for integration.

The shadow of the United States is also present in Finn Laursen's chapter dedicated to EU-Canadian relations. The asymmetry favors the EU, with Canada relatively more interested in developing freer trade and greater cooperation with the EU. This interest is partly determined by Canada's close historical and economic ties with the United Kingdom. Laursen puts EU-Canadian relations into broader perspective, describing their development alongside and through (other) international organizations such as the General Agreement on Tariffs and Trade (GATT)/World Trade Organization (WTO), the United Nations, the North Atlantic Treaty Organization (NATO), the Organization for Security and Cooperation in Europe (OSCE), and others. Laursen proposes stronger ties between the two actors. In the absence of more free trade ties with the EU, he warns, Canada may become more and more dependent on the North American Free Trade Agreement (NAFTA) and then, as an alternative to the EU, shift its attention toward other regions of the globe, such as East Asia.

In his chapter dedicated to the relationship between the EU and Africa, Maurizio Carbone says that Africa has always played a major role in European foreign relations. He critically analyzes the provisions of the series of three major agreements between the EU and Africa: the Yaoundé Convention, the Lomé Convention, and the Cotonou Agreement. He argues that there has been a shift in the tone of these agreements that was determined by the European side and driven by its interests—that is, the security dimension that has been added is to the detriment of weaving closer ties among equal partners. The chapter warns against the shortcomings of the European approach toward its southern neighbors and suggests ways to redress them by changing European rhetoric and by implementing a more coherent and unitary approach to the region.

In a chapter on relations with East Asia, Philomena Murray argues that there is increasing common ground between the EU and East Asian countries through multidimensional engagement in trade, investment, development, market access, and various aspects of foreign policy. These positive relations are determined by the EU's soft power, perceived as a beneficial alternative to the American approach. So, Murray argues, while the interest of the EU is to promote a "global Europe," East Asian countries mainly want to counterbalance the U.S. influence in the region. This may be one explanation for the ineffectiveness of EU–East Asian initiatives such as the Asia-Europe Meeting (ASEM), as well as for a call for further concrete actions to improve them.

Mara Caira analyzes the evolution of the EU's foreign policy with the emerging (super)power in the region: China. She argues that EU-Chinese relations evolved slowly and were driven by different interests. In the 1970s, when formal relations began, they were guided by the Chinese interest in gaining international recognition and in the unique European project. In the 1990s the Europeans were the main promoters of closer relations for their economic benefits. Caira also points out that relations remain limited to sectoral dialogues, given the existence of areas of contention (Taiwan, Tibet, an arms embargo) and, in general, by the Chinese lack of understanding of the nature of the EU project. Furthermore, as in the case of the other vertical issues, the relationship between the EU and China is almost triangular, with the United States always present in the background.

Part IV presents a horizontal approach and discusses the EU's promotion of its values and models abroad. Bernard Yvars returns to one of the core elements of the EU's soft power: its integration model. He observes that the deepest regional integration by far has been undertaken by the European Union. It is such a complex and specific process that it is important to characterize it in order to see to what extent it can serve as a model for other integrative efforts in the world (such as the Common Market of the South, Mercosur; the Caribbean Community, Caricom) or in regions that have established monetary unions (the Western Africa Economic and Monetary Union, Waemu; the East Caribbean Currency Union, Eccu). In comparing the EU with Mercosur, Yvars argues that although many significant elements of its model can be exported, the EU model as a whole is inapplicable; it must be adapted to local conditions.

Laura Ferreira-Pereira argues that for the EU to be able to promote peace, democracy, and respect for human rights in the world, politics is not enough. In order to profile itself as a model on the basis of "what the EU is" and the values it espouses it needs to be a "model power." This requires the Union to play a proactive role and to act in a consistent way at the international level.

In the following chapter, Elena Baracani compares the EU and U.S. approaches to foreign policy. She argues that "democracy promotion" lies at the heart of both actors' foreign policy agendas and that they are united by a series of similarities. She also points out that while the United States has a long history of democratic promotion, the EU has only recently become a promoter of democracy.

Finally, Martin Holland and Natalia Chaban focus on an element that is often forgotten in the study of EU affairs and international relations: public opinion and perceptions. This factor counterbalances the "Euro-dominant" perspective by incorporating visions of the EU from outside its borders and by featuring external views of the EU's foreign policy. They say that systematic inquiries into the external views of the EU will inform both the EU's citizens and its policymakers. All could gain valuable information about how outsiders' perceptions might influence the EU's external actions and subsequently how they could affect foreign policy discourse within the Union.

In their conclusion, Federiga Bindi and Jeremy Shapiro assess the present state of EU foreign policy and discuss its most immediate international challenges. Bindi and Shapiro sum up the findings of the book and place them in a broad historical and international context. They argue that despite the opinion of many skeptics, the EU has developed its own foreign policy, which, like the EU itself, is *sui generis*. Therefore, any attempts to assess EU foreign policy according to the criteria used for nation-states or international organizations will fail. This, however, is far from saying that the EU's foreign policy has achieved its full potential, and they welcome all further evolution on this path.

Notes

1. Jan Zielonka, "Introduction—Constraints, Opportunities and Choices in European Foreign Policy," in *Paradoxes of European Foreign Policy*, edited by Jan Zielonka (The Hague: Kluwer Law International, 1998), p. 11.

2. The *acquis communautaire* is the entire body of legislation of the European Communities and Union. Applicant countries must accept the *acquis* before they can join the EU.

The European Union's Foreign Policy Tools

FEDERIGA BINDI

1   *European Union Foreign Policy: A Historical Overview*

In the words of Walter Hallstein, "One reason for creating the European Community [was] to enable Europe to play its full part in world affairs. . . . [It is] vital for the Community to be able to speak with one voice and to act as one in economic relations with the rest of the world."[1] However, the early European Community did not have a coherent foreign policy *stricto senso*. The European Economic Community (EEC) treaty did, however, contain important provisions in the field of external relations that evolved and became increasingly substantive as the years went by. The purpose of this chapter is to provide a comprehensive view of the evolution of European foreign policy (EFP) in its various forms and stages. The chronological description presented here links the different actions and decisions taken by the EEC with the external and domestic events facing the member states at that time.

The European Defense Community

During the negotiations for the Schuman Plan (1950), on which the agreement to form the European Coal and Steel Community (ECSC) is based, concerns emerged about a possible German rearmament. German disarmament after World War II had created a sort of power vacuum in the heart of Europe, which was dramatically emphasized after the Korean War. The United States suggested creating an integrated operational structure within the sphere of the Atlantic alliance within which a German army could participate under direct American control. This arrangement was to become the North Atlantic Treaty Organization (NATO). The French government rejected this proposal and offered as an alternative the so-called Pleven Plan (1950), named after French prime minister René Pleven. The Pleven Plan called for the creation of a European army that would be placed under the control of a European ministry of defense. The soldiers were to come from the participating countries, including Germany. The plan, nevertheless, discriminated against Germany in that the future of the German army would have been entirely—not partially, as in the other countries—embedded within the European army.

The French proposal included all the members of the North Atlantic alliance, as well as Germany. However, only Germany, Italy, Belgium, and Luxembourg, besides France, met in Paris on February 15, 1951, to start negotiating a possible new treaty. Holland joined on October 8, while the United States, Great Britain, Canada, Norway, and Denmark sent observers. The outcome was the European Defense Community (EDC) agreement signed on May 27, 1952. As Jean Monnet's brainchild, the European Defense Community differed from the Pleven Plan and proposed a supranational structure along the lines of the ECSC. The EDC also implied a certain degree of economic integration, necessary considering that military integration in many ways called for a standardization of industrial-war capabilities.

Between 1953 and 1954, the EDC treaty was ratified by Germany and by the Benelux countries (Belgium, the Netherlands, and Luxembourg). The treaty was approved by the competent parliamentary commission in Italy, but the parliament as such did not take a vote, waiting for France's lead instead. In the meantime, in Paris, Robert Schuman had been replaced by Georges Bidault as minister of foreign affairs in a new government led by Pierre Mendès-France that also included the Gaullists. Public opinion was divided between the *cédistes* (who favored ratification) and the *anticédistes* (opposed), and as a consequence the treaty failed to pass a vote in the National Assembly on August 30, 1954.

The problem of German rearmament remained open. A new initiative came this time from the English foreign secretary, Anthony Eden. This initiative benefited from U.S. support. Throughout 1954, a number of agreements were signed allowing for Germany's membership in NATO, Italian and German membership in the Brussels Pact, the creation of the Western European Union (WEU), Germany's assurance that it would not engage in the creation of atomic arms, and a British agreement to station two British divisions in Germany. The question of European defense thus became a transatlantic issue and a taboo in Europe for decades to come.

The European Economic Community

As a consequence of the EDC's failure, the Treaties of Rome did not deal with foreign policy. However, the treaty establishing the European Economic Community (EEC) did foresee some degree of foreign competence in the EEC's external relations. These included: a common external trade tariff (as a complement to the customs union) and external trades; the possibility for other states to join the EEC; the establishment of a free trade area with the French, Belgian, Dutch, and Italian territories; and the creation of a European Fund for Development, as stipulated in article 131 of the treaty. Similarly, articles 110–16 dealt with commercial policy, in relation both to third states and to international organizations. The treaty affirmed in article 110 that, by establishing a customs union, the member states aimed to contribute "to the harmonious development of world trade, the progressive abolition of restrictions on international trade, and the lowering of customs barriers." To that extent, they were to create a common commercial policy based "on uniform principles, particularly in regard to changes in tariff rates, the conclusions of tariff and trade agreements."[2] The member states were "in respect of all matters of particular interest to the common market, [to] proceed within the framework of international organizations of an economic character only by common action."[3]

The Commission was given a leading role in the field of commercial policy. Not only was the Commission entrusted with the power to submit proposals to the Council of Ministers for the implementation of the common commercial policy, it also had the ability to "make recommendations to the Council, which shall authorize the Commission to open the necessary negotiations" if agreements with third countries needed to be negotiated.[4] For a member state facing economic difficulties, the Commission could authorize the Council to take the necessary protective measures as foreseen in article 115 TEEC. In article 228 the treaty also entrusts the Commission with the power to negotiate agreements between the EEC and one or more states or international organizations. Agreements such as those based on tariff negotiations with third countries regarding the common customs tariff were to be concluded by the Council, after consulting with the National Assembly where so required by the treaty.[5]

Articles 131 to 136 of the treaty dealt with the associations of non-European countries and territories having special relations with the EEC countries.[6] The possibility of enlarging the EEC was addressed in article 237, which established that "any European State may apply to become a member of the Community. It shall address its application to the Council, which shall act unanimously after obtaining the opinion of the Commission." Last but not least, article 210 TEEC established that the Community had legal "personality" or status. Even today, only the Community possesses such legal personality. As Nicola Verola explains in the next chapter, it is only with the adoption of the Lisbon Treaty that legal personality will be attributed to the European Union.

The Fifth (French) Republic

In the spring of 1958, following the Algerian crisis, General Charles de Gaulle was called to lead the French government. He accepted on the condition that a new national constitution would be prepared. The new constitution, approved by a referendum in September 1958, marked the beginning of the Fifth Republic. In November 1958, Charles de Gaulle became its first elected president. Contrary to pessimistic expectations that he would destroy the newborn EEC, de Gaulle quickly adopted the financial and monetary measures necessary to implement the common market in France.

Yet de Gaulle had a rather contradictory personal view of Europe and of France's role within it. On the one hand, he wanted a "European Europe," able to counterbalance the United States and the USSR. On the other hand, he was eager to keep Europe as a "*Europe des Etats*," a community in which the member states would retain their full national sovereignty. This contradiction came to characterize the French approach to the process of European integration and constitutes one of the major contradictions of a European foreign policy today.

De Gaulle instinctively averted any institutional shift toward greater European integration, while at the same time pushing for stronger coordination between the six member states ("the Six") in the field of foreign policy. With this in mind, in 1958 he proposed regular meetings between the EEC foreign ministers. This proposal was approved on November 23, 1959. The first meeting was held in January 1960 and is the basis for today's CAGRE (the Conseil Affaires Générales et Relations Extérieures), an essential element of the EFP. De Gaulle further reiterated his support for European cooperation and the need for meetings at the level of heads of state and government. The first summit of this kind was held in Paris, on February 10–11, 1961, with the assistance of the foreign ministers; it was the precursor to the European Council. The Dutch foreign minister, Joseph Luns, however, rejected the idea of regular meetings and was even less fond of the idea of creating an ad hoc secretariat. Hence the EEC leaders decided to create the so-called Fouchet Committee, which would be responsible for developing proposals for political cooperation. The Fouchet Committee's report was presented on October 19, 1961. It proposed a union of states with the aim of developing a common foreign and defense policy. Unsurprisingly, these proposals faced resistance by a number of member states, and after several modifications the report was ultimately put aside despite de Gaulle's rage.

The Origins of the European Union's Development Policy

In the early 1960s, the EEC took its first steps to form a development policy. In 1963 the Yaoundé Convention was signed by the EEC and the eighteen former colonies of the Six. In 1969 the convention was renewed for a period of five years. Initially, it was essentially a policy toward (francophone) Africa. Following the 1973 EEC enlargement it was then extended to cover the African members of the British Commonwealth and other former colonies in the Caribbean and the Pacific. The Yaoundé Convention (1963–75) maintained the system introduced by the Treaty of Rome: an aid allocation for five years, channeled through the European Development Fund (EDF), and a trade regime based on reciprocal preferences.

The Kennedy Round

As mentioned, the EEC treaty established that the EEC should represent its members in external trade matters. The General Agreement on Tariffs and Trade (GATT) negotiations were clearly part of this category. The Kennedy Round (1964–67) marked the first round of negotiations in which the six member states were represented by the EEC.

During the GATT meetings held in Geneva, the EEC could negotiate from a position of strength. It had signed a number of important commercial agreements with Greece (1961), Turkey (1963), Israel (1964), Lebanon (1965), and the Saudi Arabian Monetary Agency countries (1963) and was about to further expand its commercial relations to the Mediterranean, central Asia, and Africa. In ten years EEC exports had soared by 265 percent within the free trade area and by 113 percent with third countries. In 1962, under President John F. Kennedy, the United States had passed the Trade Expansion Act, allowing the United States to bargain for lower tariffs on whole families of products instead of negotiating item by item. Yet two years later the United States had to accept the principle of "unequal cuts," consisting in a cut of tariffs by 50 percent for the United Kingdom and the United States and a cut by 25 percent for the EEC countries. The Kennedy Round was thus an important first test for the EEC and its foreign policy and an important step forward for the Europeans as they sought to reduce the commercial gap with the United States.

Soon afterward, in 1968 and ahead of schedule, the EEC's customs union for goods became a reality with the removal of tariffs and quotas among the Six. With internal tariffs eliminated, the Common External Tariff (CET), also known as the Common Customs Tariff (CCT), was introduced for goods coming from third countries.

The United Kingdom-France Problem

In 1961, the English conservative government led by Harold Macmillan introduced a request to join the EEC. Negotiations thus began with the UK, alongside Ireland, Denmark, and Norway. The conditions set down by the English were uncompromising. To make matters worse, at least from the point of view of de Gaulle, on July 4, 1962, President Kennedy launched his Grand Design, an idea aimed at enhancing the cooperation of an enlarged European Community with the United States. The situation further deteriorated when, on December

18, 1962, at Nassau, Kennedy offered Polaris missiles to Great Britain. The same offer was made to France but was rejected. De Gaulle viewed the American proposal as a way for the United States to dominate Europe with respect to nuclear weapons. Moreover, in his eyes, Britain's acceptance of the proposal was a clear indication of the UK's true allegiance.

De Gaulle thus abruptly ended all negotiations with the United Kingdom and offered it an Association Agreement instead, a move that was taken as an insult by the British, as it would have put the United Kingdom on the same level as Greece and Turkey.[7] Finally, on February 21, 1966, de Gaulle announced that France would reassume full sovereignty over the armed forces on its territory and withdraw formally on March 7 from the operative structures of the Atlantic pact (NATO), although not from the Atlantic alliance.

In 1967, Harold Wilson's Labor Party won the elections in Great Britain. Wilson soon announced that the United Kingdom would once again apply for EEC membership on May 2, 1967. De Gaulle again vetoed the accession on November 27, 1967. After having lost a referendum on the reform of the Senate and of the French regional framework on April 27, 1969, de Gaulle resigned and Georges Pompidou was elected president of France on June 15.

The Origins of the Pact on European Political Cooperation

In a press conference on July 10, 1969, Pompidou presented his ideas for the future of Europe in what is commonly known as Pompidou's *Triptique*. The summit in The Hague took place on December 1–2, 1969, and approved these ideas. They consisted of three principles: completion, deepening, and enlargement. More specifically, the *Triptique* called for the completion of the Common Market by January 1, 1970, with particular attention to the financing of the Common Agricultural Policy (CAP) through the resources of the Community; the deepening of the Community, especially in the field of economic and monetary policy; and enlargement to include Great Britain and other countries, with the condition that the Community would adopt a common position before negotiations. The Hague Summit Declaration mentioned the establishment of the Common Market as "the way for a united Europe capable of assuming its responsibilities in the world."[8]

With respect to deepening, Etienne Davignon, then political director of the Belgian Foreign Ministry, was charged with studying potential future steps down the path of European integration. The Davignon Report, adopted by the foreign ministers on October 27, 1970, in Luxembourg, was especially important with regard to policymaking and European foreign policy. It established the principle of regular meetings among the EEC foreign ministers, eventual meetings of the heads of state and government, regular consultations on matters of foreign policy among member states, and regular meetings of the political directors of the Six. What emerged from the report was the so-called European Political Cooperation (EPC), which institutionalized the principle of consultation on all major questions of foreign policy. The member states would be free to propose any subject for political consultation. The European Commission would be consulted if the activities of the European Community were affected by the work of the foreign ministers, and the ministers and the members of the Political Affairs Committee of the European Parliament would hold meetings every six months.

The subsequent Copenhagen Report of July 23, 1973, further specified the EPC's role and mechanisms. According to the report, the EPC established "a new procedure in international relations and an original European contribution to the technique of arriving at a concerted action."[9] It resulted in an institutional framework "which deals with problems of international politics, is distinct and additional to the activities of the institutions of the Community which are based on the juridical commitments undertaken by the member States in the Treaty of Rome."[10] The Copenhagen Report established that the ministers of foreign affairs would meet four times a year and whenever they felt it was necessary. It stressed the role of the Political Committee as the body entrusted with the preparation of the ministerial meetings and created the "Group of Correspondents" and the system of European telex (COREU). The Copenhagen Report also emphasized the importance of subcommittees and working groups. The first ones were to deal with the Commission on Security and Cooperation in Europe (CSCE), the Middle East, the Mediterranean, and Asia. They established the principle that ambassadors accredited to countries other than members of the EEC could consult with each other.

The First Enlargement

Last but not least, the Hague Declaration called for the enlargement of the European Community. The negotiations with the United Kingdom, Denmark, Ireland, and Norway were divided into two phases, based on French demands. The first set of negotiations took place among the Six, during the first semester of 1970. The second took place with the four candidates beginning on June 30, 1970. The country holding the Presidency represented the general position of the Six. The Council also gave the Commission the mandate to research a solution for various problems that emerged during the negotiations by working with the candidate countries.

When the treaty was signed on January 22, 1972, the United Kingdom, Denmark, and Ireland became members of the Community starting January 1, 1973. It became known as the "Europe of the Nine." In Norway, despite the positive conclusion of the negotiations and a clear yes vote in the Storting, a referendum on September 25, 1972, rejected EEC membership with 53.5 percent of the votes.

A free trade agreement was thus signed with the remaining member countries of the European Free Trade Association (EFTA), including Norway.

The United Kingdom was to thank the EEC several times in its first years of membership. The United Kingdom was not left to deal alone with the civil war in Rhodesia in the mid-1970s or when Argentina invaded the Falkland Islands in April 1982. The immediate response and solidarity of the Community in imposing sanctions on Argentina (April 10, 1981) was in fact much stronger than that of the United States. Despite gaining much from their support, the UK did at times oppose the EEC's common positions on foreign policy. For example, in 1985, when violence broke out in South Africa and the government declared a state of emergency, it took several months for the UK to agree to sanctions against South Africa. It eventually agreed only on the condition that these measures would be implemented nationally.[11]

The Birth of the European Council

In 1974 another (potentially) important actor in European foreign policy emerged: the European Council. On April 2, 1974, Pompidou passed away. Valéry Giscard d'Estaing was elected president on May 19, 1974. In Germany, Helmut Schmidt had replaced Willy Brandt as chancellor. Giscard d'Estaing's motto was "l'Europe est ma priorité," and although he was not a supporter of supranational institutions, he was convinced of the need to revive the process of European construction. Following Jean Monnet's advice, on September 14, 1974, Giscard d'Estaing organized a meeting with the other heads of government and with the (French) president of the European Commission, François-Xavier Ortoli. An agreement was reached to organize such gatherings every three or four months. At the subsequent Paris summit in December 1974 the European Council was born under the slogan "The Summits are dead, vive les Conseils Européens!" The European Council was composed of heads of state or government and their foreign ministers, with the participation of the president of the European Commission. They were to meet three times a year, and any other time deemed necessary, within the framework of European Political Cooperation.

Also in 1974 the first meeting of what was to become the "Gymnich formula" was held at Gymnich Castle in Germany's Rhineland region. The formula referred to the informal meeting of the foreign ministers to consult on matters of foreign policy.

Troubled Relations with the United States and the World in the 1970s

By the beginning of the 1970s, the EEC had begun to feel pressure from the international community to engage further in international affairs. The Arab-Israeli wars, the oil crises, and the Vietnam War were all external events pushing the Europeans together. Later, the Soviet invasion of Afghanistan (December 1979) and the Iranian revolution and hostage crises (1980) underlined the need for a common European response. Other events affecting the EPC included the establishment of martial law in Poland, the Argentinean invasion of the Falklands, and the Israeli invasion of Lebanon. Germany also wished to give a European hat to its Ostpolitik.

Transatlantic relations became strained in the 1970s. Until the end of the Kennedy administration, the United States had been generally supportive of the European integration process.[12] That started to change in the late 1960s. By the 1970s, the United States perceived the EEC as an economic competitor and held it responsible for the deficit that the United States experienced in its balance of payments. U.S. behavior vis-à-vis the EEC became rather contradictory. The United States insisted that Europe should contribute more to NATO expenses while the U.S. president, Richard Nixon, affirmed the principle of American leadership over the organization. Similarly, Secretary of State Henry Kissinger called 1973 the "year of Europe." Yet the idea was essentially that the United States had global responsibilities and interests while Europe's interests were and could only be regional.

In response, on December 14, 1973, the EEC foreign ministers adopted in Copenhagen a "Declaration on European Identity." Its objective was to better define the EEC's relations and responsibilities to the rest of the world and the place they occupied in world affairs. In the declaration, the Nine affirmed that "European Unification is not directed against anyone, nor is it inspired by a desire for power. On the contrary, the Nine are convinced that their union will benefit the whole international community. . . . The Nine intend to play an active role in world affairs and thus to contribute . . . to ensuring that international relations have [a] more just basis. . . . In pursuit of these objectives the Nine should progressively define common positions in the sphere of foreign policy."[13] It was also decided on June 11, 1974, that the country holding the Presidency should consult with the United States on behalf of its partners.

In any event, the United States continued to disagree with the Europeans on a number of foreign policy issues, including the Middle East. The Europeans themselves were divided until the Six-Day War in 1967. October 1973 brought a new war and the subsequent OPEC oil embargo on the United States and the Netherlands. Between October and November of that year, the Nine agreed on a common view and on a common declaration regarding the legitimate rights of the Palestinians. The Nine greeted the Camp David peace talks (1977–79) without any noticeable enthusiasm. In the Venice Declaration of June 12–13, 1980, they reaffirmed the Palestinians' right to self-determination and for the

Palestinian Liberation Organization (PLO) to be included in peace negotiations. The election of U.S. president Ronald Reagan, who was resolutely against any European initiative outside Camp David, and the Israeli invasion of Lebanon (June 6, 1982) put an end to European activism in the area. Still, the EEC took action in favor of the Palestinians and became gradually more critical of Israel.[14]

A similar story took place in the neighboring Iran. When on November 4, 1979, the U.S. embassy in Tehran was seized and sixty-three hostages were taken, the United States immediately responded with a boycott on imports of Iranian oil and froze Iranian assets in the United States. While the EEC called several times for the release of the hostages, it did not support the U.S. call for sanctions. Only on April 22, 1980, did the EEC agree to sanctions, although only if implemented by the individual states.[15]

Relations with Eurasia were also a matter of contention in transatlantic relations. The EEC and the United States clashed over the question of Poland when martial law was declared on December 13, 1981. While the United States imposed sanctions both on the USSR and Poland and pushed the Europeans to do likewise, the Europeans agreed on March 15, 1982, to only a limited number of restrictions on the USSR (on imports). This was the first time they had used article 113, referring to commercial policy, for political purposes.

In the case of the USSR, it took three weeks for the EPC to formulate a response to the Soviet invasion of Afghanistan in December 1979. Moreover, the Europeans disagreed with the U.S. decision to boycott the 1980 Moscow Olympics. The United Kingdom supported the U.S. position, but France and Germany stood opposed, worried that it would undermine deterrence.[16] As a consequence of the slow EEC response to these events, in 1981 it was decided that three member states could call for an emergency meeting of the EPC.

Finally, Europe's relations with Asia during the 1970s and 1980s proved somewhat less problematic. In 1975, China was the first socialist country to recognize the EEC, and in 1978 a first agreement was signed, followed in 1985 by an agreement on trade and economic cooperation. In 1978, a co-operation agreement was also signed with ASEAN.

Democratization in Southern Europe: Toward the Community of the Twelve

Meanwhile, the geography of Europe had changed with the end of the dictatorships in Greece, Portugal, and Spain. The "regime of the colonels" came to an end in Greece in 1974, the same year that the long dictatorship of Antonio Salazar in Portugal was overthrown by the Carnation Revolution. In 1975, with Franco's death, Spain also started its démarche toward democracy. All three countries quickly introduced a request for EEC membership. It was politically impossible for the EEC to close the door on these new democracies, which needed institutional support to consolidate, especially politically and economically.

For France, enlargement in the South would have balanced the EEC, reinstating it at the center of the Community. However, the three candidate countries were characterized by low wages, high inflation rates, unstable currencies, low-cost agriculture products, and underdeveloped industrial sectors. The EEC dealt with each one differently: Greece, mainly owing to heavy French and U.S. pressure, was admitted into the EEC on January 1, 1981. This quick action soon proved to be a major mistake as the new Greek government led by the Socialist Andreas Papandreou rose to power and asked for special economic benefits for Greece. In 1985 he obtained the creation of the Integrated Mediterranean Program.

As a consequence, negotiations with Spain and Portugal stalled, and those two countries did not become members until January 1, 1986. With their membership, the EEC became more interested and involved in Latin America. In subsequent years, relations were established or further developed with subgroups in the region. The San José dialogue (with Costa Rica, Guatemala, Honduras, Nicaragua, and Panama) was particularly important as European foreign ministers decided to send a strong signal to the United States (which was at the time involved in several Central American countries) by attending in full the first meeting in San José de Costa Rica, in September 1984. In 1990 a dialogue with the Rio Group was institutionalized.[17] The Treaty of Asunción was signed in 1991 with the Common Market of the South, Mercosur (Argentina, Brazil, Paraguay, and Uruguay), followed by the Interregional Framework Cooperation Agreement in 1995. The year 1996 marked the beginning of a political dialogue with the Andean Community (Bolivia, Columbia, Ecuador, Peru, and Venezuela).

The 1980s and the Need for EEC Reforms

With the second enlargement, the EEC reached a format ("the Twelve") that it believed would endure for a long time. Attention shifted to the need for internal reforms in order to complete the internal market. The internal market was one of the original goals of the EEC treaty that had remained unachieved. Member states also pushed for the reform of the EPC in order to make it more effective and ensure more active participation of the European Community in international affairs.

On October 13, 1981, the then ten member states adopted the London Report, further outlining the functions of the EPC domestically and abroad. For instance, it established regular consultations with EEC ambassadors in third countries and elaborated on the function of the Gymnich meetings and potential emergency meetings of the ministers of foreign affairs. The subsequent Stutt-gart Solemn Declaration of June 19, 1983, enlarged the EPC's scope of action to include "the political and economic aspects of security" (point 3.2). The decla-ration also called for the "progressive development and definition of common principles and objectives [and] the possibility of joint actions in the field of for-eign policy" (point 3.2), while stressing the need for consistency between action taken by the EPC and the Community. Last but not least, the declaration, also known as the Gensher-Colombo plan, called for concerted action on "interna-tional problems of law and order"—what came to be called Justice and Home Affairs (see discussion of the Maastricht Treaty below).

On February 14, 1984, the European Parliament, under Altiero Spinelli's leadership, approved a "draft treaty," calling for a new European Union that would be given legal personality and allow for greater coordination of the EPC and external relations. According to the draft treaty, the European Council would also have the authority to extend foreign policy coordination to defense and arms trade questions. Although the draft treaty was not endorsed by the member states, they did, in 1985, undertake the first major reform of the treaty with the so-called Single European Act (February 17 and 28, 1986).

The Single European Act

With regard to foreign policy, the major effect of the Single European Act (SEA) was the codification of the European Political Cooperation and the European Council. The SEA formalized intergovernmental cooperation in foreign policy without changing its existing nature or methods of operation. Title III of the SEA specifically dealt with the treaty provisions on European cooperation in the sphere of foreign policy and affirmed that the member states should inform and consult reciprocally "to ensure that their combined influence is exercised as effec-tively as possible through coordination, the convergence of their positions and the implementations of joint action" (article 30.2.a), and that "common princi-ples and objectives are gradually developed and defined" (article 30.2.c). In codi-fying what had been informally established over the years through a number of different texts and treaties, the SEA defined the role of the European Council, the European Commission, and the Parliament within the EPC. A leading role was given to the first; the possibility to assist in all matters was given to the second; and the minimal right to be informed was granted to the third. Coordination on matters of European security was mentioned, specifically on the political and economic aspects of security, as well as the development of a European identity in external policy matters. Member states were asked to define common posi-tions within international institutions and conferences and to mutually assist and inform each other. The SEA also codified the role of the Presidency and of the troika (the High Representative for the Common Foreign and Security Policy, the foreign minister of the country holding the EU Presidency, and a senior representative from the European Commission) in the EPC, as well as of the different decision-making levels (European correspondents, the Political Committee and related working groups, the Council of Ministers). A secretariat based in Brussels was established to assist the Presidency in dealing with the EPC. Last but not least, member states' missions and the European Commission's delegations were asked to intensify their cooperation with third countries.

The SEA also substantially increased the role of the European Parliament, to which it gave the power of assent both in future enlargements of the Community (as foreseen in new article 237 of the treaty establishing the EEC), and in agreements with either third states or international organizations involving "reciprocal rights and obligations, common actions and special procedures" (new article 238 of the treaty). The latter became what are essentially the present-day Association Agreements.

The End of the Cold War

As mentioned, in the late 1980s the member states were convinced that the EEC's membership would remain stable for the long run. However, dramatic changes were to take place that would profoundly affect both the Community and the world. The year 1989 brought great changes in Eastern Europe. In June, Solidarity won the elections in Poland and the Iron Curtain separating Austria and Hungary fell. During the summer, an increasing number of Eastern Europeans arrived in Western Europe through Austria, aiming for the most part to reach the Federal Republic of Germany. In autumn, massive demonstrations took place in the rest of Eastern Europe. In Czechoslovakia the protesters, led by Vaclav Havel and Alexander Dubček, obtained the resignation of the entire Communist Party. In December, Havel was elected president of the republic. In Bulgaria, Todor Živkov was forced to resign in November; the reformist foreign minister Petar Toshev Mladenov took his position and quickly announced liberal elections before May of the following year. In Romania, the opposition forces had taken control of the entire country by December. Nicolae Ceausescu was captured in his attempt to escape and was immediately tried and shot. The true symbolic event among these dramatic changes, however, took place on the evening of November 9, 1989, when the gates between East Berlin and West Berlin were reopened with the fall of the Berlin Wall.

All of these changes brought both hope and fear about the prospect of a united Germany. The solution of the European leaders was to have a united Germany in a stronger Europe. On December 8–9, 1989, the European Council in Strasburg approved the idea of German reunification. Germany would be reunified and the four eastern *Länder* would be incorporated without needing to revise the EEC treaties.[18] At the same time, the EEC leaders decided to summon an intergovernmental conference to establish the European Monetary Union (EMU). As the president of the European Commission, Jacques Delors declared in front of the European Parliament: "We need an institutional structure that can withstand the strains."[19]

On April 18, 1990, François Mitterrand and Helmut Kohl proposed to complete the monetary union with a political union that would ensure democratic legitimacy, institutional efficiency, the EEC's unity, and coherence in the economic, monetary, and political sectors and eventually a common foreign and security policy. The European Council endorsed Mitterrand and Kohl's proposal in Dublin on April 28, 1990, with the United Kingdom and Portugal dissenting. In June 1990, the European Council in Dublin decided to convene two intergovernmental conferences (IGCs) before the end of the year: one to discuss the monetary union and the other to discuss the political union, which was to include a common foreign policy. In the meantime, Germany reunified and the four eastern *Länder* were incorporated into Federal Republic of Germany and the EEC, again without any formal modifications of the treaties.[20] The two IGCs lasted for all of 1991. On February 7, 1992, the Maastricht Treaty, or Treaty on the European Union (TEU), which created the new European Union, was signed.

The Treaty on the European Union, or the Maastricht Treaty

The Maastricht Treaty established a Common Foreign and Security Policy (CFSP) for the European Union. The Iraqi invasion of Kuwait in August 1990 was a source of friction among EEC partners, in particular between Prime Minister Margaret Thatcher's government in the United Kingdom and the others. It led to disagreement over issues of security, majority voting, how to integrate foreign policy into the Community, and whether the philosophical distinction made between security and defense could be abandoned. Different views were also expressed over whether the WEU should be merged with the EU. The United States and the more pro-NATO member states were extremely worried about this possibility and what they saw as an impediment to NATO and Western security.[21]

In the end, the European Political Cooperation was replaced by the Common Foreign and Security Policy, which constituted the second pillar of the new three-pillared European Union, according to Title V and associated declarations. The CFSP was to safeguard the common values, the fundamental interests, and the independence of the Union; to strengthen its security and its member states in all ways; to preserve peace and strengthen international security; to promote international cooperation; to develop and consolidate democracy and the rule of law, respect for human rights and fundamental freedoms, as spelled out in article J.1.2 of the TEU. Articles J.1.3 and J.3 stipulated that such objectives were to be pursued through systematic cooperation between member states and by "joint actions." Member states were to act in a "spirit of loyalty and mutual solidarity," refraining from "any action which is contrary to the interest of the Union or likely to impair its effectiveness as a cohesive force in international relations."[22] Member states were also to inform and consult with each other and define "common positions" around which to conform their national policies. They were also to coordinate in international organizations and international conferences. The WEU was to be closely associated with the CFSP, acting as a bridge to NATO, and the CFSP was finally permitted to address the previously taboo question of "defense," with the possibility of gradually moving toward a common defense system.[23]

The Presidency was to represent the EU in CFSP matters. Abroad, member state diplomatic missions and European Commission delegations were to cooperate, and the European Parliament was to be consulted. The general guidelines concerning the CFSP were to be defined by the European Council, to which the TEU granted the proper status of EU institution, and implemented by the Council, both acting on the basis of unanimity, as stipulated by the article J.8. Foreign policy was to be discussed in the Council of Ministers, while the European Commission received a (joint) right of initiative and became associated with the CFSP. Extraordinary meetings of the Council of Ministers could be convened as needed in the event of an emergency. Finally, the EPC Secretariat in Brussels was to be enlarged, and it was also agreed that the European Community budget should pay for the CFSP's administrative expenditures. Different, though, was the question of who would pay for operational or nonadministrative expenditures. This topic had not come up with the EPC because it was assumed that in the spirit of intergovernmentalism, each member government would pay individually. Title V did not create a budget for the CFSP. Rather, it created a system for charging operational costs to the EC budget and letting the Council decide whether to charge the EC budget of member governments for operational expenditures associated with joint actions, thus opening the door to endless procedural battles.[24]

At the European Council on June 26–27, 1992, before the implementation of the TEU, the Lisbon Report specified what areas would be of interest to the EU (the so-called "Lisbon goals"). These areas were defined geographically, as, for example, central and eastern Europe (including Eurasia); the Balkans; Maghreb and the Middle East; transatlantic relations (the United States and Canada); the North-South dimension (Africa, Latin America, the Caribbean, and Asia); and

Japan. They were also defined with respect to horizontal issues such as security issues (the CSCE process and the policy of disarmament and arms control in Europe, including confidence building measures); nuclear and nonproliferation issues; and the economic aspect of security, in particular control of the transfer of military technology to third countries and control of arm exports.

Between November 1993 and May 1995, eight joint actions were pursued. These actions included observing elections in Russia and South Africa, supporting measures to enhance stability and peace in the central and eastern European countries (CEECs) and the Middle East, providing humanitarian aid to Bosnia, promoting the indefinite extension of the Non-Proliferation Treaty (NPT), controlling the export of dual-use (civil and military) goods, and strengthening the review process of the anti-personnel landmines. During the same period, fourteen common positions were also adopted, mainly concerning economic sanctions against third parties.[25]

The TEU also modified the articles of the treaty dealing with the common commercial policy. It had become urgent to clarify the relationships between proper trade policy and the new CFSP.[26] New article 228a of the TEU specified that in the event that the CFSP generated a need for sanctions, the Council would decide this based on qualified majority voting (QMV) on a proposal from the Commission. The new wording of the EU commercial policy increased the European Parliament's power of assent regarding all agreements in the field of external trade. As stipulated in article 228 of the TEU, this field concerned policy areas covered by the co-decisionmaking procedure in domestic matters, as well as in areas likely to have important budgetary implications for the Community.

Last but not least, the new treaty established the steps and the conditions needed to create an economic and monetary union by 1997, or 1999 at the latest.[27] Also, in response to fear about crime from the East after the fall of the Berlin Wall, the Maastricht Treaty established means of cooperation among member states in the field of internal security. This cooperation fell under the jurisdiction of Justice and Home Affairs (JHA), as stipulated by article K.

The Maastricht Treaty set up a system based on three "pillars": two intergovernmental pillars (the CFSP and the JHA) and the supranational EC pillar. The treaty also foresaw the possibility to "communitarize" step by step the JHA through the so-called *passarelle* mechanism—that is to say, without having to further review the treaty.

The Fourth Enlargement

A new enlargement to the north was now appearing on the horizon. By the end of the 1980s, the relationship between the EC and the European Free Trade Association (EFTA) had become a priority for both parties. Formal negotiations between the two organizations started in December 1990 and ended in October 1991. The European Economic Agreement (EEA) was signed on May 2, 1992, In Porto. Yet, as the fall of USSR had opened new scenarios, a number of EFTA countries also introduced requests for EEC membership: Austria on July 17, 1989; Sweden on July 1, 1991; Finland on March 18, 1992; and Norway on November 22, 1992. On January 1, 1995, the EU grew to encompass fifteen member states. Once again, in a Norwegian referendum a negative vote prevented Norway from entering.

Changing Patterns in Transatlantic Security Relations

The events of 1989 had first and foremost a relevant impact on ideas about European security. In 1991, both the Warsaw Pact and the Council for Mutual Economic Assistance (Comecon) among eastern European nations ceased to exist. In November of the same year, the North Atlantic Cooperation Council (NACC) was set up in order to enable security consultations with the eastern European states. In 1992 a "forum of consultation" was created within NATO, including only the CEECs, but not Russia. In 1994 they were offered the status of "associate partners" by the WEU: that meant that they could eventually participate in Petersberg-like operations but were not offered the WEU's security guarantee. In January 1994, NATO set up the Partnership for Peace to allow consultation and cooperation at the politico-military level between all the CSCE member states. In the light of events in the former Yugoslavia, it was becoming clear that NATO, the EU, the WEU, and the *constituenda* OSCE needed to cooperate to the greatest possible extent. Peacekeeping in particular emerged as a central concept in European security discussions. At the July 1992 Helsinki summit the CSCE decided to launch peacekeeping operations and other crisis management operations. The previous month the WEU had issued the "Petersberg Declaration" showing its willingness to engage in humanitarian, peacekeeping, and crisis management tasks. In December 1992, NATO also joined the mainstream by agreeing to participate in UN operations on a case-by-case basis, thus ending its formal ban on out-of-area engagements. In fact, NATO had already started to cooperate with the UN and the WEU in the Balkans.[28]

For their part, the Europeans had begun to talk of a European security and defense identity (ESDI), once again alarming the United States, which was eager for the Europeans to bear more of the burden, but not to rival NATO. The United States was determined to locate any such entity firmly within the boundaries of transatlantic relations. The resulting decision to create combined joint task forces, ratified in the Berlin Council of June 1996, made NATO's facilities and forces available to the WEU when it wanted to act but could not sustain action with its own forces. NATO's enlargement, a process that paralleled the

EU fifth enlargement, at times created serious transatlantic antagonism."[70] On July 8, 1997, the North Atlantic Council in Madrid invited the Czech Republic, Hungary, and Poland to begin accession talks with a view to joining NATO by its fiftieth anniversary in 1999. The EU followed in December of the same year by deciding to open negotiations with the ten CEECs and Cyprus.

Dealing with the Central and Eastern European Countries

The USSR did not recognize the EEC until 1988, the same year Comecon and the EEC signed a trade agreement. Just one year later, however, the USSR's former satellites aimed to become part of the EEC. The Community was fast in responding: economic and trade agreements were signed in 1988 (with Hungary and Czechoslovakia), 1989 (with Poland), and 1990 (with Bulgaria and Romania) and then replaced with Association Agreements (the so-called Europa agreements) in 1992 (Hungary and Poland) and 1993 (the Czech Republic, the Slovak Republic, Bulgaria, and Romania) and Slovenia (1996). The Europa agreements provided a framework for political dialogue, promoted trade and economic relations between the CEECs and the EEC (virtually eliminating trade barriers), and provided the basis for financial and technical assistance and for the gradual integration of the CEECs into a wide range of EU policies and programs. In addition, the EU set up programs to assist countries with their preparations for joining the European Union. For the first time, Europe was to be united on the basis of common ideals and principles, and the EEC put all its weight into using agreements to positively influence the democratic and economic development of the CEECs. The Copenhagen European Council in June 1993 specified the criteria to be fulfilled by prospective candidates (the so-called Copenhagen criteria): a working democratic system; the rule of law; respect for human rights and protection of minorities; a functioning market economy; and the ability to take on the obligations of membership (economically and politically). In 1994 the Essen European Council approved a pre-accession strategy. As part of this, the associated countries would participate in an enhanced political dialogue on CFSP matters and also become associated with the WEU. In 1995 the Madrid European Council added a fourth condition: the implementation of and adaptation to the *acquis communautaire* (the entire body of legislation of the European Community and Union). This condition was determined by a view that considered enlargement "a political necessity and a historic opportunity for Europe," which would "guarantee stability and security for the Continent." According to the decision of the European Council in December 1997, negotiations with the Czech Republic, Estonia, Hungary, Poland, Slovenia, and Cyprus began on March 31, 1998. A year later Latvia, Lithuania, Malta, Slovakia,

Bulgaria, and Romania were also invited to join. The successful transformation, democratization, stabilization, and incorporation of the neighboring countries has been one of the most significant foreign policy achievements of the EU.[30]

Relations with Russia in the 1990s

After the fall of the Soviet Union in 1991 the EEC reacted quickly and strongly. Relations with Russia were less successful than hoped, despite the decision in 1993 to have joint meetings twice a year and the 1995 adoption by the Council of a strategy on Russia. A strategic partnership agreed to in Corfu on June 25, 1994, was not enforced until 1997 because of the first Chechen War (1994–96). In Vienna a report on the "northern dimension" of EU policies was approved in December 1998, and in June 1999, at Cologne, a new common strategy toward Russia also got the green light.

The disintegration of the USSR also raised the tricky issue for the EU of whether to recognize the constituent republics of the dissolved federation. This problem was presented by (the former) Yugoslavia. Two of the main former USSR republics, Ukraine and Belarus, have antagonistic relations with the EU. The founding pillar of the EU-Ukraine relationship is the 1998 Partnership and Cooperation Agreement (PCA) from which the European Neighborhood Policy (ENP) followed in 2004. Thus the EU has since then tried to offer a carrot-and-stick approach, which does not, however, contemplate the possibility of membership. As for Belarus, the EU decided to resort to "negative conditionality," suspending contractual agreements after 1997.

Relations with the Balkans in the Early 1990s

The disintegration of the former Yugoslavia was a very good illustration of European disunity. In the midst of the debates, Germany (and the Vatican) announced the unilateral recognition of Slovenia and Croatia (December 23, 1992). The rest of the Europeans had no choice but to follow suit. The war in the former Yugoslavia, which had started in June 1991, is also a textbook case of the failure of European foreign policy. In the first year of the conflict the EU futilely tried to negotiate an agreement. Only through the intervention of the United States and its hosting of the series of negotiations did the war come to an end with the Dayton accords (1995). An EU "regional approach" to the western Balkans was elaborated, but it was not until the spring of 1999, with the Kosovo crisis, that the EU seemed to opt for a clear "accession strategy" for the (new) countries in the area.[31] In June 1999 the Stability Pact for South Eastern Europe was launched. One year later, the Feira European Council (June 2000) declared the Balkans to be "potential candidates," and in November of that year the first summit between the EU and the Balkan heads of state and government was held in Zagreb. In June 2003 the "Salonika Agenda" gave concrete substance to the membership promise.

In contrast, the Albanian case, with so-called operation Alba, was a lost opportunity for Europe. Under the pressure of events in Albania in March 1997, Italy asked the EU to use the tool of "reinforced cooperation"—that is, an action organized by a reduced number of member states—to address the crisis. When the Nordic states refused, the rather successful operation Alba was then transformed into a multinational force organized by the Italian government under the auspices of the UN and the OSCE.

Relations with the Middle East and the Mediterranean in the Early 1990s

As mentioned, the Middle East has been an issue of division between Europe and the United States. In 1986, for instance, there was a major crisis involving Libya. After terrorist attacks at the airports in Vienna and Rome in December 1985, the EEC foreign ministers agreed to intensify their cooperation in several areas linked to security. The United States, however, insisted that Libya should be singled out as responsible for terrorism in Europe. While the divided Europeans were discussing the issue, the United States took action and, informing only the United Kingdom (and using their bases), launched a punitive raid on Libya. This act was strongly criticized by the rest of the Europeans, and after a tense investigation in the European Parliament the UK was forced to admit that, in violation of its EPC obligations, it had failed to warn its European partners of the U.S. action.

The First Gulf War in 1991 was also initially an issue of disagreement both with the United States and among Europeans (eventually British, French, and Italian forces took part in the war under U.S. leadership). The disagreements were not as strong as those over the Second Gulf War, when France and Germany came down on one side and the members of the "coalition of the willing" on the other side.

The southern shore of the Mediterranean Sea has always been a priority interest for Europe. Beginning in the 1970s, the EEC signed a number of trade and cooperation agreements with Mediterranean countries. Agreements on agriculture, energy, industry, distribution trades, infrastructure, education and training, health, environment, and scientific cooperation exist with the Maghreb countries (Algeria, Morocco, and Tunisia), the Mashreq countries (Egypt, Jordan, Lebanon, and Syria), Israel, the PLO (formerly with the Gaza Strip and the West Bank), and the Gulf states. In 1991 the Renewed Mediterranean Policy created a new financial instrument and indicated new fields of cooperation. A major attempt to revitalize and develop a framework for relations with the Mediterranean countries came in November 1995 with the Barcelona Euro-Mediterranean Conference (also known as Barcelona Process). Comprising twenty-seven participants, including the PLO, it set up regular meetings and launched the idea of a EuroMed free trade zone, which is, however, still far from being achieved.

Relations with the Rest of the World in the Mid-1990s

The first half of the 1990s witnessed a relaunch of the foreign ambitions of the European Community. With the United States, the relationship continued on its ambiguous path. On the one hand, both sides claimed to attach great importance to closer cooperation and to stronger relations; on the other hand, they have been involved in petty disputes, threats, retaliation measures, and counter-retaliations. In November 1990 a transatlantic declaration was adopted in which both parties affirmed their determination to strengthen their partnership, by informing and consulting with each other, strengthening the multinational trading system, and cooperating in fields such as medical research and environmental protection. The transatlantic declaration also affirmed the principle of biannual meetings between the U.S. president and the EU president in office (and the European Commission). In one such meeting in Madrid in 1995, Bill Clinton, Jacques Santer, and Felipe Gonzales set out a framework for action with four major goals: promoting peace, stability, democracy and development around the world; responding to global challenges (including fighting international crime, drug trafficking and terrorism; and protecting the environment); contributing to the expansion of world trade and closer economic relations; and building bridges across the Atlantic (working with business people, scientists, and others). The main objective of the so-called New Transatlantic Agenda was the establishment of a transatlantic marketplace designed to eliminate trade barriers, expand trade and investment opportunities, and create jobs on both sides of the Atlantic. Following that, in November 1995 a transatlantic business dialogue (TABD) was also launched. In 1996 a joint declaration and an action plan were also signed with Canada.

In 1994 a white paper outlining a "new Asia strategy" was approved during the German Presidency. The EU had meanwhile also ratified a number of trade agreements with India, Pakistan, Sri Lanka, Bangladesh, Macao, Mongolia, Thailand, and China. A framework for a cooperation agreement was agreed in October 1996 with South Korea, while a joint declaration between the EC and Japan was adopted in 1991, establishing cooperation on trade, environment, industry, scientific research, social affairs, competition policy, and energy.

With Latin America the European Union has enjoyed a strategic partnership since the first biregional summit held in Rio de Janeiro in 1999. EU–Latin America summits have since been held every other year.

As for Africa, in 1990 the Lomé IV Convention was signed. Since 1997 it has also included South Africa. One of the first CFSP joint actions was to send observers to South Africa to help prepare for and monitor the April 1994 elections. In December 1995 the European Council declared that it would support Organization of African Unity (OAU) efforts at preventive diplomacy and peacekeeping. In June 2000 the Cotonou Agreement replaced Lomé.

The events of the early 1990s led the Community to incorporate the principle of political conditionality into its external relations. Human rights considerations were made an explicit part of the Community's development policy with the November 1991 declaration on human rights, democracy, and development. The possibility of human rights clauses in agreements with third countries was then envisaged. In May 1995 the European Council decided that *all* agreements signed by the EC would include respect for human rights and democratic principles as founding elements.

The Amsterdam Treaty

With another enlargement in sight, a decision was taken in Corfu in June 1994 to hold a new intergovernmental conference. For that purpose the Spanish minister of European affairs, Carlos Westendorp, was asked to lead a reflection group, which concluded that the main objectives of the treaty revision should be: (a) to make Europe more important in the eyes of its citizens; (b) to make EU decisionmaking more efficient; and (c) to provide the EU with greater responsibility and power in addressing foreign relations. The IGC was launched in Turin on March 29, 1996; the new treaty was adopted by the European Council of Amsterdam on June 16–17, 1997, to enter into force on May 1, 1999.

The Amsterdam Treaty substantially revised some of the CFSP provisions. Articles 11 to 28 of the Treaty on the European Union are devoted specifically to the CFSP. The most important decision in terms of improving the effectiveness and the profile of the Union's foreign policy was the decision to appoint the secretary general of the Council to the office of High Representative for the CFSP. The High Representative, together with the foreign minister of the country in the EU Presidency and a senior representative from the European Commission would now form a new troika (article J.8, TEU). In his job, the High Representative would support the newly created Policy Planning and Early Warning Unit (or Policy Unit). For the first time EU foreign policy was to have a name and a face. The impact of this innovation was not initially clear, as several member states thought that a low-profile figure would be suitable for the new job.[32] Following the EU debacle in Kosovo, the 1999 Cologne European Council opted for the high-profile political figure of Javier Solana Madriaga, who as secretary general of NATO had just led NATO military operations in Serbia. Solana took up the post on October 18, 1999, for a period of five years, a term that was then twice renewed. The Presidency was given the power to negotiate international agreements in pursuit of both the CFSP and the JHA, assisted by the European Commission when appropriate (article J.14, TEU).

A second innovation of the Amsterdam Treaty was the creation of a new "common strategies" instrument. In 1999–2000, three common strategies were adopted, toward Russia, Ukraine, and the Mediterranean. However, because they offered no real added value to the strategies and partnerships the EU had been developing since the mid-1990s, this new instrument was quickly dropped.[33] The treaty also introduced a slight relaxation of the voting requirements in the European Council. As foreseen by article J.13 of the TEU, there are more possibilities for qualified majority voting once a joint action or a common position has been agreed on, as well as the possibility of "constructive abstention" by one or more member states. However, since the Council hardly ever votes, this provision did not have a real effect on CFSP decisionmaking.

Amsterdam also strengthened the relationship between the EU and the WEU, with a view toward possibly integrating the WEU into the EU. The EU gained access to the WEU's operational capabilities for humanitarian and rescue tasks, peacekeeping, and tasks of combat forces in crisis management (the so called "Petersberg tasks" that were approved in 1992 by the WEU). Finally, the financing of CFSP was clarified, with the EC budget becoming the default setting, apart from military and defense operations. The European Parliament thus gained a larger control over financing. The new treaty also made the possibility of a EU defense policy seem more likely by replacing the word "eventual" with "progressive" in article J.7.[34]

The possibility to negotiate internationally in the field of external economic relations was extended by Amsterdam to services and intellectual property with new article 113(5) of the TEU. The new treaty also foresaw in its article 228(2) the possibility to suspend the application of an international agreement.

Last but not least, Amsterdam called for the development of an area of freedom, security, and justice (AFSJ). It incorporated the *acquis* of the Schengen agreements of 1985 and 1990 into the EU, thus locating asylum, immigration, and border control measures under pillar 1 (new Title IV, TEU), while police and judicial cooperation in criminal matters remained under pillar 3.

Toward the Fifth Enlargement: The Treaty of Nice

The fifth enlargement was to be far more complex than the previous ones, given the institutional, political, and socioeconomic differences of the CEECs. The number of candidates was thirteen, more than all the former candidate countries added together. Without considering Turkey, the enlargement would increase the Union's geographic territory by 30 percent, its population by 29 percent, and its GNP by 10 percent. Therefore, the enlargement to the countries of central and eastern Europe and to the south shore of the Mediterranean had significant institutional implications. Protocol n. 23, attached to the Treaty of Amsterdam, introduced a revision in two stages: the first for a Union with twenty member states or fewer, and the second for successive enlargements.[35] Meeting in Cologne on June 3–4, 1999, the European Council decided to convene one more inter-governmental conference at the beginning of 2000 with the aim of resolving the institutional questions that had to be solved before enlargement. The European Council of Helsinki (December 10–11, 1999) further set the aims of the IGCs, namely the so-called leftovers: the organization of the European Commission, the reweighing of the votes in the European Council, and the extension of the qualified majority voting system. The result was the Nice Treaty, agreed upon in December 2000 in a besieged Nice. Among the issues of interest, it modified the conditions for setting up enhanced cooperation in the CFSP by reducing to eight the minimum number of participating member states and simplifying the procedure for authorization. Because of British opposition, this coopera-tion was not extended to matters of defense. The new Treaty of Nice entered into force on February 1, 2003, and contained new CFSP provisions. Notably, it increased the areas that fall under qualified majority voting and enhanced the role of the Political and Security Committee in crisis management operations.

Toward a European Security and Defense Policy

Meanwhile, domestic changes took place in the United Kingdom and in France, now led by Tony Blair and Jacques Chirac. The two countries negotiated secretly on matters of European defense. The result was the Saint-Malo Declaration of December 4, 1998, which stated that the EU needed to be in a position "to play its full role on the international stage." Because of this, it needed "the capacity for autonomous action, backed by credible military forces, the means to use them, and a readiness to do it, in order to respond to international crises." To many people's surprise, it thus announced that the WEU would be, after all, folded into the EU and then disappear. This was heralded at an informal Euro-pean Council meeting at Portschach under the Austrian Presidency. The United States had no option but to accept the ESDP. However, this came with the condi-tion that the EU avoid the "three Ds": no decoupling (of ESDP from NATO); no duplication (of capabilities); no discrimination (against non-NATO members).

The so-called Berlin Plus arrangements of December 2002 now govern relations between the EU and NATO in crisis management.[36]

Meanwhile, at the fiftieth anniversary of NATO summit (April 25, 1999), the idea of European defense cooperation was endorsed. It noted its compatibility with the alliance, while at the same time enlarging NATO to include the Czech Republic, Hungary, and Poland.

The European Council meeting in Cologne in June 1999 announced the end of the WEU by the start of 2001 and the arrival of a legitimate EU defense policy. The EU would take over the WEU institutions and personnel. Javier Solana was appointed WEU secretary-general in addition to his role as High Representative for the CFSP. In response to the events in Kosovo, at the Helsinki European Council in December 1999 it was agreed that by 2003 the EU would be able to deploy up to 60,000 troops within sixty days for at least one year to deal with Petersberg task operations. New permanent political and military bodies would be established under the European Council. Two months later they were already holding their first meetings. In May 2003 the Council agreed that the EU had operational capabilities across the full range of Petersberg tasks.

A European security strategy (ESS) entitled "A Secure Europe in a Better World" was approved by the European Council in Brussels on December 12, 2003. It was drafted under Javier Solana and considered a counterpart to the U.S. security strategy. While affirming that "Europe has never been so prosperous, so secure or so free," the ESS concludes that "the world is full of new dangers and opportunities." Thus, in order to ensure security for Europe in a globalizing world, multilateral cooperation within Europe and abroad was to be the imperative, because "no single nation is able to tackle today's complex challenges." The ESS also identified a list of key threats Europe needed to deal with: terrorism; proliferation of weapons of mass destruction; regional conflict; failed states; and organized crime. It indicated as a strategic priority for Europe the neighbors (Balkans, Eurasia, Russia), the Mediterranean, and the resolution of the Arab-Israeli conflict. The EU was to promote regional governance in Europe and beyond and needed to become more capable and more coherent. The European Defense Agency was created in July 2004.

The EU at Twenty-Seven

On May 1, 2004, the Czech Republic, Estonia, Hungary, Poland, Slovenia, Cyprus, Latvia, Lithuania, Malta, and Slovakia joined the EU, followed on January 1, 2007, by Bulgaria and Romania. The EU had reached a membership of twenty-seven countries. One of the major external policies bolstered by the last rounds of enlargement was securing the new external borders of the EU. The 2004 Hague Program set the course for the EU's action in the area of freedom, security, and justice for the years 2005–09, and in 2005 a strategy for external dimensions of the JHA was approved. The Schengen Information System (SIS) was upgraded, and in 2005 the European Agency for Management at the External Borders (Frontex) became operational.

Since then, the EU has incorporated AFSJ issues into its cooperation and Association Agreements with third countries and organizations in several agreements, such as the 2003 agreement with the United States on extradition and mutual legal assistance.

Another issue of concern became the fight against terrorism after the 9/11 attacks in the United States and the 2004 and 2005 bombings in Madrid and London. If before these attacks the action undertaken by the EU was mainly directed at fighting terrorism internally, later action was also taken abroad. In 2001 the EU governments agreed on an EU action plan on counterterrorism, which was then revised and adopted by the European Council in 2004 as the EU Plan of Action on Combating Terrorism. By this point, external relations had become increasingly relevant. Among the main objectives of the plan of action are actions towards countries where counterterrorist capacity or commitment to combating terrorism must be enhanced. The EU also initiated a political dialogue on counterterrorism with the United States, Russia, India, Pakistan, Australia, and Japan. In 2005 the EU adopted a counterterrorism strategy composed of four strands: prevention, protection, pursuit, and response. The EU was heavily engaged in formulating and adopting the 2005 UN Convention against Nuclear Terrorism and the 2006 UN Counter-Terrorism Strategy. It encouraged third states to ratify existing UN conventions and protocols.[37]

Notes

1. Walter Hallstein, *United Europe: Challenge and Opportunity* (Harvard University Press, 1962), p. 79.

2. Treaty establishing the European Economic Community, art. 113.

3. Ibid., art. 116.

4. "The Commission shall conduct these negotiations in consultations with a special committee appointed by the Council to assist the Commission with this task and within the framework of such directives and the Council may issue to it." Ibid., art. 113, 3.

5. Ibid., art. 114.

6. In particular, the treaty established that the Community could negotiate Association Agreements with a union of states or an international organization giving birth to "reciprocal rights and obligations, common action and special procedure."

7. The Association Agreement with Greece was signed on July 9, 1961, and became effective on November 1 of the following year. The agreement with Turkey was still under negotiation.

8. The Hague Summit Declaration, December 2, 1969, point 3.

9. The Copenhagen Report, July 23, 1973, Part I.

10. Ibid., point 12(a).

11. Not until 1986, when the ANC refused to meet with the United Kingdom's foreign secretary and Council president Sir Geoffrey Howe, did the UK finally change its position and agree to Community sanctions on September 16, 1986.

12. Federiga Bindi and Palma D'Ambrosio, *Il futuro dell'Europa* (Milan: Franco Angeli, 2005).

13. "Declaration on European Identity," December 14, 1974, point II.9.

14. C. Hill and K. E. Smith, *European Union Foreign Policy: Key Documents* (London: Routledge, 2000), p. 299.

15. Ibid., p. 317.

16. Ibid., p. 259.

17. Established in 1986 with an initial membership of six, the Rio Group now comprises twenty-three countries: all of the Latin American countries plus the Dominican Republic, Jamaica, Belize, Guyana, and Haiti. Cuba joined the Rio Group in November 2008. The other Caribbean countries are represented by one of the full Caribbean members (presently Jamaica).

18. Such a decision was in fact made in Dublin on April 28, 1990.

19. Jacques Delors, *Le nouveau concert Européenne* (Paris: Editions Odile Jacob, 1992).

20. As far as the treaties of the Community are concerned, the only modifications concerned the number of members in the European Parliament. Of course, the main consequence was that Germany, which was a clear contributor to the Community budget in the past, would receive substantial financial aid for the new *Länder*.

21. Hill and Smith, *European Union Foreign Policy*, pp. 151–52.

22. Treaty on the European Union (TEU), art. J.1.4.

23. Ibid., arts. J.2. and J.4.

24. B. White, *Understanding European Foreign Policy* (New York: Palgrave, 2001), p. 105.

25. Ibid., p. 103.

26. Hill and Smith, *European Union Foreign Policy*, pp.158–59.

27. On January 1, 1994, the so-called "second phase" of the EMU began (the first phase having been the freedom of circulation for capital accomplished under the single market). The European Central Bank (ECB) was thus created. Prospective EMU members had to comply with four criteria related to interest rates, the public deficit, and inflation rates. On May 2, 1999, the heads of state and government decided that eleven countries qualified to join the EMU: Portugal, Spain, France, Luxembourg, Belgium, Holland, Ireland, Italy, Germany, Austria, and Finland. The United Kingdom and Denmark opted not to participate; Greece was eventually accepted to join as of January 1, 2001.

28. Hill and Smith, *European Union Foreign Policy*, p. 195.

29. Ibid., pp. 194–95.

30. S. Keukeleire and J. MacNaughtan, *The Foreign Policy of the European Union* (London: Palgrave Macmillan, 2008), p. 259.

31. See Luca Gori's chapter in this volume.

32. Keukeleire and MacNaughtan, *Foreign Policy*, pp. 54–55.

33. Ibid., p. 55.

34. TEU, art. J.7, reads: "The common and security policy shall include all questions relating to the security of the Union, including the progressive framing of a common defense policy."

35. "At least a year before the number of member states exceeded twenty, a conference for the representatives of government was summoned with the aim of reexamining the dispositions of the Treaties, in particular, the composition and the performance of its institutions," Protocol n. 23, attached to the Treaty of Amsterdam.

36. Keukeleire and MacNaughtan, *Foreign Policy*, p. 176.

37. Ibid., pp. 227–38.

NICOLA VEROLA

2

The New EU Foreign Policy
under the Treaty of Lisbon

The Common Foreign and Security Policy (CFSP) was undoubtedly one of the "hottest areas" of the constitutional process in the European Union between 2002 and 2007. The final balance remains ambiguous. The Lisbon Treaty introduces important CFSP innovations, but it limits them through a series of prerogatives. It is worth focusing on these elements in order to better understand their implications. In so doing, this chapter first defines the position of the CFSP in the communitarian policies. It then focuses on the substantial innovations brought to the CFSP and concludes by addressing the pros and cons of the Lisbon Treaty's institutional architecture.

The CFSP in the Context of EU Policies

Following the legacy of the Constitutional Treaty (CT), an important innovation of the Lisbon Treaty is the introduction of the EU legal personality. At present, the European Community (EC) has a legal personality, whereas the EU has an uncertain international status. With the Lisbon Treaty, there will no longer be a distinction between the two, as it creates just one international actor: the European Union. An important consequence of this fact is the absorption into the "single pillar" of communitarian policies of the so-called "second pillar" of the CFSP, created by the Maastricht Treaty. However, a series of prerogatives minimizes this "normalization." All of them emphasize the special nature of the CFSP compared to other policies. According to the Lisbon Treaty, all aspects of the CFSP are drawn from the modified Treaty on the European Union (TEU), whereas all other policies are drawn from the Treaty on the Functioning of the European Union (TFEU).

The new Title V of the TEU will become Chapter 1, referring to the "horizontal" general provisions on the Union's external action, and Chapter 2, on the specific provisions on the Common Foreign and Security Policy. Provisions related to the other external aspects of the Union (such as the commercial policy, the signature of international treaties, development cooperation) will be included in Title 5 of the Lisbon Treaty. A significant difference from the CT is the new text in paragraph 1 of article 24 of the new TEU.

The first line of the new paragraph basically reiterates article 17 of the TEU, according to which "The common foreign and security policy shall include all questions relating to the security of the Union, including the progressive framing of a common defense policy, in accordance with the second subparagraph, which might lead to a common defense, should the European Council so decide."[1] It is important to note here that the formulation of the CT was less hypothetical: "The common security and defense policy shall include the progressive framing of a common Union defense policy. This will lead to a common defense when the European Council, acting unanimously, so decides."[2]

The second paragraph mentions the special procedures the CFSP needs to follow. First and foremost, it is defined and enacted by the European Council by unanimity and is enacted by the high representative of the member states, using the means of the member states and of the Union. It is worth noting here that article I-41 of the Constitution seemed to leave larger room for maneuver for the minister of foreign affairs. The European Council is assigned the task of elaborating a common defense and security policy and adopting the necessary decisions. However, it granted the Union's minister of foreign affairs the task of enacting them. The special role of the European Parliament and the European Commission in the CFSP is also mentioned here, as well as the role of the European Court of Justice in this area.[3]

These provisions and caveats were present to a certain extent in the CT as well, but it is impossible not to deduce from their enumeration right after the part on the CFSP the intention to separate this EU policy from other EU policies. In this sense, a declaration (no. 13) was attached to the final act of the conference. It was directly related to article 24, paragraph 1, and it emphasized that the CFSP provisions do not limit the competencies of the member states in foreign policy matters. They do not grant power of initiative to the European Commission and do not affect the specific nature of the common and security policy of the member states.

In addition to these matters, which were, after all, present in the CT as well, the Treaty of Lisbon, amending the Treaty on the European Union, introduces a series of new provisions. Article 39 introduces an ad hoc judicial basis for the legislation on data protection in the field of the CFSP. It will now follow specific procedures of the other EU policies. Consequently, decisions in the field of CFSP data protection will not be taken on the basis of co-decision with the

Parliament, but, following the provisions of article 24, only by unanimous vote of the Council.

Furthermore, in order to prevent the risk of progressive interpretations, a special mention was inserted in article 352 of the TFEU clarifying that the "flexibility clause" inherited from the old Treaty on the European Community cannot be used to pursue CFSP objectives. The flexibility clause has to respect the limits fixed by article 40 of the TEU.

As if the message were not clear enough, an additional declaration (no. 14) in the final act emphasizes that "In addition to the specific rules and procedures referred to in paragraph 1 of Article 11 of the Treaty on the European Union, the Conference underlines that the provisions covering the Common Foreign and Security Policy including in relation to the High Representative of the Union for Foreign Affairs and Security Policy and the External Action Service will not affect the existing legal basis, responsibilities, and powers of each Member State in relation to the formulation and conduct of its foreign policy, its national diplomatic service, relations with third countries and participation in international organizations, including a Member State's membership of the Security Council of the United Nations."[4] The same declaration says that the provisions governing the CFSP do not prejudice the specific character of the security and defense policy of the member states.

The Lisbon Treaty emphasizes that the member states will remain bound by the dispositions of the United Nations (UN) Charter and, in particular, by their responsibilities to the Security Council and its members in order to maintain international peace and security. From a certain point of view, this declaration only repeats *ad abundantiam* the explicitly formulated concepts in the articles of the treaty or already mentioned on other occasions, such as the declaration in article 24. This declaration is based on distrust, reticence, and commitment to national prerogatives. It seems that the EU's real problem is not getting truly efficient instruments for its CFSP, but rather curbing the potential evolutionary elements of the CFSP.

In this sense, the reference to the primary responsibility of the UN Security Council (UNSC) members is symbolic. Apart from the fact that the UN Charter makes no reference to the responsibilities of the individual UNSC members, it is worth noting the regressive nature of the declaration as compared to article 34 of the TEU. This article is already in effect, and it stipulates that "member states which are members of the Security Council will, in the execution of their functions, defend the positions and the interests of the Union, without prejudice to their responsibilities under the provisions of the United Nations Charter."[5] However, the Treaty of Lisbon ads to this provision an innovation introduced by the CT in its article III-305. Here it was mentioned that when the Union has defined a common position on a subject that is also on the UNSC agenda, then those EU member states that are also part of the UNSC shall request that the Union's minister of foreign affairs be present to present the Union's position.[6] It is important to note here that the term used was "shall request," and not "may request."

So, whereas article 34 unsuccessfully attempted to ensure greater coordination among the EU member states that also had an important weight in international organizations, and especially in the UNSC, this declaration of the Lisbon Treaty tried to resolve this matter. It did so by emphasizing that it did not aim to limit the possibility of the EU member states to autonomously determine and enact their own positions on foreign policy matters, especially in the UNSC. This is another example of the fact that, beyond the judicial effect (since, as is well known, the declarations are not binding), one main obstacle to the creation of a true CFSP are the privileges in matters of foreign policy already possessed by (some) of the EU member states.

The Substantial CFSP Innovations Brought by the Lisbon Treaty

One innovation of the Lisbon Treaty is that it provides for the CFSP the same institutional changes stipulated by the Constitutional Treaty. Thus the Lisbon Treaty creates the office of EU minister of foreign affairs. It combines the responsibilities, the "two hats," of the existing CFSP High Representative and the EU commissioner for external relations. However, the title has been modified to a form thought to ease some of the EU member states' fears about losing national sovereignty. The new title is "High Representative for Foreign Security and Defense." The High Representative is to be nominated by the European Council on the basis of qualified majority voting, with the endorsement of the president of the European Commission. She or he becomes a full member, and vice president, of the Commission. However, his or her responsibilities will vary depending on whether the office acts in matters pertaining to external relations with nations that are not members of the EU or in matters that fall under the CFSP umbrella. In the first case, the High Representative acts according to the collegiality principle, as an integral part of the European Commission. In the second case, the High Representative acts as a "representative" of the European Council, with the right of initiative. Furthermore, the High Representative is the president of the Foreign Affairs Council, with duties to ensure the coherence of all aspects of EU foreign policy, assisted by the European External Action Service, which is made up of national diplomatic services personnel and personnel from the European Council's Secretariat and the European Commission.[7]

As in the Constitution, the position of High Representative comes with some ambiguities. For example, although the High Representative will have no formal authority over the other commissioners, as president of the External Relations Committee he or she will be expected to ensure the coherence of the Council. In fact, this authority is attributed to the General Affairs Council, whose presidency rotates among all the member states. However, the High Representative will have a central political role and administrative resources that should make it possible to exert de facto leadership of all external actions by the Union.

The High Representative's success will depend on the ability to take advantage of all these instruments and relate with the other commissioners and the member states. In a meeting on June 29, 2004, a declaration was adopted entitled "The Declaration of the Heads of States or of Government on the Transition towards the Nomination of the Future Minister of Foreign Relations of the European Union."[8] The declaration nominated Javier Solana as the minister of foreign affairs of the Union after the entry into force of the Constitution. A new decision will have to be made in the future, probably together with the decision on the nomination of the future president of the European Commission and the future president of the European Council. It is hoped that the person nominated will possess the authority, prestige, and "coalition building" capacity necessary to fulfill this complicated task.

The characteristics of the European External Action Service will be vital for the success of the High Representative's mission. According to Declaration 24 of article III-296, the secretary general of the European Council, the High Representative for the Common Foreign and Security Policy, the European Commission, and the member states should begin preparatory work on the European External Action Service as soon as the Constitution is signed.[9]

The High Representative and the president of the European Commission presented a joint report of the European Council in June 2005. However, all actions on this matter were halted after the negative outcome of the French and Dutch referendums on the Constitution. Consideration of these matters needs to resume now. In particular, it is necessary to find solutions to a series of issues: whether the External Action Service needs to be a global and integrated structure or rather a simple unit of coordination; whether the European Commission has to encompass most of this service or only some of its parts; whether it has to encompass all the services of the Council in charge of external relations; what relations it should have with the EU Joint Situation Center (SitCen) and the European Union Military Staff (EUMS); how many diplomats from the member states it should have; whether it should also deal with consular protection matters; whether it should have financial autonomy; and other matters.

With regard to the CFSP, the innovations introduced by the Lisbon Treaty refer, on the one hand, to the extension of the majority vote and, on the other hand, to enhanced cooperation. With regard to the extension of the majority vote, the Lisbon Treaty preserves in practice all of the CT innovations. In the case of the CFSP, the same general provision applies, which permits the European Council to unanimously decide whether to adopt qualified majority voting in areas where unanimity is still foreseen.[10] Theoretically, this provision would lead to a "normalization" of the CFSP (but not of the European Security and Defense Policy [ESDP], which is explicitly mentioned) and to its transfer into the communitarian policy area without the intervention of an intergovernmental conference (IGC).

A special provision is foreseen for the CFSP, according to which the European Council can unanimously make decisions based on majority voting in cases other than the ones explicitly mentioned in article 31 of the TEU.[11] So, this special wording would introduce qualified majority voting not for the whole CFSP, but only for specific matters.

One of these instances is introduced directly by the Lisbon Treaty. In its article 31, para. 2 (or, subsequently, III-300, para. 2) it introduces an innovation to article 23 of the TEU. It stipulates that the European Council can approve, with a majority of votes, the proposals of the minister of foreign affairs following a request from the European Council. The innovation is diminished by the following provision, which stipulates that should a member of the European Council oppose the adoption of qualified majority voting based on national interests, the vote will not take place. Only a qualified majority of the Council can demand that the European Council make a decision unanimously. This mechanism is probably meant for situations in which none of the member states has particularly strong preferences or when there are no divisions within the Council. It these cases, it is reasonable to assume that: (a) the heads of state and government easily reach the consensus necessary to request a proposal by the minister of foreign affairs; (b) no member state considers that its interests are so vital that they require the "emergency break" mechanism stipulated in para. 2. On particularly sensitive issues it is unlikely that the heads of state and government would risk asking for a proposal from the High Representative. Furthermore, there is an increased risk that, at a later stage, a member state "in the minority" will decide to use the "emergency break."

As for enhanced cooperation, the objective of the Constitution was to harmonize as much as possible managing affairs in the CFSP with that of the first pillar. However, unlike the "ordinary" communitarian policies, the authorization to proceed to enhanced cooperation within the framework of the CFSP can only be given by a unanimous vote of the Council of Ministers.[12] This limitation was not a result of the 2007 IGC, because the unanimity provision had already been introduced by the 2004 IGC, as a significant step backward from the European Convention. On the positive side, the 2007 IGC confirmed the right of the

members to unanimously decide to make a decision based on qualified majority voting in the case of enhanced cooperation, or to introduce the ordinary
legislative procedure in cases where special legislative procedures are foreseen.[13]
However, this does not apply to military or defense matters.

Defense Policy

Most of the measures discussed in relation to the Common Foreign and Security Policy are also applicable to the European Security and Defense Policy. The
new article 24, the two declarations, and the content of most of the new provisions of the Lisbon Treaty aim at creating a "safety belt" around it. That goal
was not well hidden, since it focused on preventing evolutionary interpretations
of the treaty norms. This logic is also reflected in TEU article 4 on relations
between the Union and its member states. Using the same formulation as the
CT, it stipulates that the European Union shall respect essential state functions,
including ensuring the territorial integrity of the state, maintaining law and
order, and safeguarding national security. It goes on to emphasize that national
security remains the sole responsibility of each member state.

These provisions do not diminish the innovations that the Lisbon Treaty
inherits from the CT. Compared to the present situation, they are significant.
The Lisbon Treaty borrows from the CT a series of important innovations in
the field of defense, which by now is considered an integral part of the Common Foreign and Security Policy.[14] First, the role of the Petersberg tasks (a set of
security and defense priorities) is enhanced. The Union can now use both civil
and military means to accomplish them.[15] It is also stipulated that the Council
can decide, based on unanimous voting, to grant the responsibility of managing
these missions to a group of states.[16]

Second, the possibility is envisaged that the member states that want to assume
a larger role in this field can create among themselves a permanent structured
cooperation after a decision of the Council. This decision needs to be agreed to
by a majority vote and after consultation with the minister of foreign affairs.[17]
The criteria for access to the permanent structured cooperation are defined in
an ad hoc protocol. Its first article stipulates that the structured cooperation is
open to any member state that wants to enhance its defense capacity. It can do
so by increasing its national contribution to the main European programs of
equipment providers and by participating in, for example, multinational task
forces and the activities of the European Agency in developing defense capacity, research, acquisition, and armaments. It should be able to provide combat
units for any foreseen missions, as a national force or as part of a multinational
task force, all of them organized as combat forces, with the elements of support, transport, and logistics and the capacity to pursue the above-mentioned

missions as stipulated by TEU article 44.[18] These combat units were to be provided by 2007 at the latest, and they would be deployed within five to thirty days, in particular following a demand from the United Nations. They would be deployed for a varying period, from 30 to 120 days. TEU article 46 (CT, ex art. III-312) stipulates that any member state can request participation in an existing structured cooperation. It should first notify its intention to the European Council and to the minister of foreign affairs of the Union. The Council can then adopt a European decision confirming the participation of the interested member state that corresponds to the criteria and commits to the duties entailed in the protocol.

At the same time, it is stipulated that member states will commit to a reciprocal defense.[19] While showing consideration for the specific conditions in certain member states, this formulation introduces an obligation to provide mutual assistance should a member state be the victim of military aggression on its territory. This aspect is particularly important in the light of creating an authentic European defense community, compatible with the framework of NATO and the UN. The Lisbon Treaty uses the same provisions here as the Constitutional Treaty, and it stipulates the creation of an agency with arms, research, and military capacity. These provisions were unanimously adopted by the Council on July 12, 2004.

With regard to the decisionmaking process, it should be noted here that the unanimity rule is even stronger here than in the CFSP. Both the Lisbon Treaty and the CT stipulate a series of limited but important cases when the unanimity rule can be replaced by qualified majority voting. This is the case, for example, for the determination of the statute, headquarters, and functioning of the European Defense Agency, for the beginning of a permanent structured cooperation, and for the creation of an initial budget for financing certain preparatory missions of the ESDP. An important innovation here is the possibility to use enhanced cooperation, although, unlike the CFSP, the special passage of TEU article 333 does not apply.

Conclusions

The Lisbon Treaty has deepened a series of provisions of the CT in the CFSP field, without upsetting the important aspects. Some will attempt to resurrect the old pillars, having as a starting point the positioning of the CFSP in a different regime than the other policies. The complex formulation of the new TEU and the TFEU and, above all, the sole judicial personality should constitute a sufficient protection against this risk.

The crucial factor that will determine the success or failure of the "new CFSP" will be the capacity of the High Representative to create a common European political will on the main international issues. Beyond the nominal issues, the High Representative retains the important prerogatives granted by the CT.

It is discouraging, however, to see the diffidence and reluctance at the basis of the new demands by some of the member states. The institutional negotiations sometimes appeared to create "shields" of protection against the other member states and the European institutions, rather than to promote common interests. It is clear, therefore, that until these countries' reservations are overcome, the European integration process will not make significant progress, at least not with twenty-seven member states.

Therefore, the "security exits" introduced by the European Constitution and kept by the Lisbon Treaty should be positively evaluated. This is especially true for the dispositions on the permanent structured cooperation and the ad hoc dispositions in the field of defense policy, which permit some member states to proceed more rapidly on the integration path. It is now left to the leaders of the member states and of the European institutions to use the tools offered by the Lisbon Treaty to develop a genuine European foreign and security policy.

Notes

1. Treaty on the European Union (TEU), art. 17 (http://eur-lex.europa.eu/en/treaties/dat/11997M/htm/11997M.html#0145010077 [September 2008]).

2. The Treaty Establishing a Constitution for Europe, art. I-41, part 2 (http://eur-lex.europa.eu/LexUriServ/LexUriServ.do?uri=OJ:C:2004:310:0011:0040:EN:PDF [September 2008]).

3. This was not an innovation of the Constitution. The same provision was already mentioned in art. III-376 of the CT, following the tradition that decisions made in the field of foreign affairs are considered to be "acts of a political nature."

4. "Declaration Concerning the Common Foreign and Security Policy" (http://eur-lex.europa.eu/en/treaties/dat/12007L/htm/C2007306EN.01025502.htm [September 2008]).

5. TEU, art. 34 (cur-lex.europa.eu/LexUriServ/LexUriServ.do?uri–OJ:C:2008:115:0013:0045:EN:PDF [September 2008]).

6. Art. III-305 of the CT (eur-lex.europa.eu/JOHtml.do?uri=OJ:C:2004:310:SOM:EN:HTML, [September 2008]).

7. TEU, art. 27.

8. Council of the European Union 10995/04 (Presse 214) (http://ue.eu.int/ueDocs/cms_Data/docs/pressData/en/misc/81278.pdf [November 2008]).

9. See http://eur-lex.europa.eu/LexUriServ/LexUriServ.do?uri=OJ:C:2004:310:0420:0464:EN:PDF [November 2008].

10. See art. 48, para. 7, of the new TEU, and former art. IV-444 of the CT.

11. See art. 31, para. 3, and ex art. I-40-7. This provision was already present in the CT, ex art. III-300.

12. Art. 329 of the TFEU and ex art. III-419 CT.

13. Art. 333 of the new TEU, ex art. IV-422 of the CT.

14. TEU, art. 42; CT, ex art. I-41.

15. TEU, art. 43; CT, ex art. III-309.

16. TEU, art. 42, para. 5, and art. 44; CT, ex art. III-310.

17. TEU, art. 46; CT, ex art. III-312.

18. CT, ex art. III-309.

19. TEU, art. 42; CT, ex. art. I-41.7.

STEPHAN KEUKELEIRE

3

European Security and Defense Policy: From Taboo to a Spearhead of EU Foreign Policy?

Quite surprisingly, the European Security and Defense Policy (ESDP) has emerged in the past decade as one of the spearheads of the EU's foreign policy and a main asset in the EU's foreign policy toolbox. Even more, the ESDP has become one of the rare recent success stories of European integration. This came at a time when the integration process seemed to be in disarray, with growing divergences between the twenty-seven member states, a weakened institutional framework and European leadership, and serious hurdles to getting the 2007 Lisbon Treaty ratified. In the space of merely a few years, the EU managed to translate the first ideas on the ESDP into concrete operational capabilities, leading to the first ESDP operation in early 2003 and more than twenty operations on most continents by 2009. The emergence of the ESDP as a light in the darkness is quite remarkable, particularly as the military and security dimension has been one of the major taboos in the European integration process for several decades. This fundamental change was made possible because for the first time in some fifty years of European integration the member states managed to sufficiently overcome two major areas of tension that had paralyzed EU foreign policy: the cleavages between European integration and Atlantic solidarity and between civilian power and military power.

This chapter discusses the historical background, explaining the long-standing taboo on military and security issues; analyzes the establishment of the ESDP and of the EU's military and civilian crisis management instruments and operations; and concludes with some general assessment and warnings, particularly on the danger of an increasingly active ESDP, without the ESDP being sufficiently matched by and embedded within a clear European foreign policy.[1]

Historical Background

After World War II, the resulting Western European military weakness, American military superiority, and the perceived Soviet threat meant that for most

Western European states the Atlantic alliance and the American guarantee were the essential prerequisites for security.[2] In April 1949, the signing of the North Atlantic Treaty sealed America's commitment to providing a security guarantee for its Western European allies. However, it was not clear at that time what kind of military structures would be established to organize Western Europe's collective defense and what the position of West Germany would be. Whereas the Europeans pushed for greater American leadership and the continued presence of American soldiers, the United States initially expected Western European countries themselves to assume more responsibility for guaranteeing Europe's defense.

The escalation of the East-West conflict and the outbreak of the Korean War in 1950 transformed this context, and half a year later the North Atlantic Treaty was upgraded, becoming the North Atlantic Treaty Organization (NATO). An integrated military alliance, including a heavy commitment of American troops with an American supreme allied commander, directed the territorial defense of Western Europe and reflected U.S. leadership as well as America's direct role in managing European affairs.[3] This dependency on the United States also largely defined and restricted the parameters of member states' national foreign and security policies and attempts to initiate European cooperation and integration in the field of security and defense. Practically every proposal was, and still is, reviewed by a major part of the member states against what has been labeled the "what do the Americans think?" test.[4] The appropriateness and feasibility of an EU security and defense policy initiative came to be measured not solely in terms of its importance for European security or European integration, but also or often even in the first place for its impact on transatlantic relations and acceptability in Washington.

The logic of the Atlantic choice was confirmed in the early 1950s and 1960s by the failure of French attempts to bring defense within the scope of European integration: first through the Pleven Plan and the failed European Defense Community, next through the rejected Fouchet plans. In October 1950, the French launched the Pleven Plan, under which military units from the member states would be integrated to create a European army, which would operate under the direction of a council of member states' ministers. Following the example of the European Coal and Steal Community (ECSC), the creation of a supranational European Defense Community (EDC) meant that German soldiers could operate within a European army without having to create a new German army. This was unacceptable to most European states, which barely five years earlier had been the victims of German aggression. Negotiations over the Pleven Plan finally resulted in the EDC Treaty, which was signed in May 1952 by the six member states of the ECSC (France, West Germany, Italy, the Netherlands, Belgium, and

Luxembourg). However, the treaty was less "common" and "European" than its title suggested. The French had been forced to accept that the project would be more intergovernmental and more linked to NATO than foreseen. By mid-1954, improvements in the East–West relationship had lessened the urgency to create a European army and, amid growing concerns about the loss of national sovereignty in security and defense, the French Assembly refused to ratify the EDC Treaty.[5]

Following the failure to establish the EDC, an alternative method was needed to address the question of German rearmament. The solution was the creation of the Western European Union (WEU) through the signing of the Modified Brussels Treaty of October 1954. This treaty allowed West Germany and Italy to enter a six-year-old military assistance pact among France, Great Britain, and the Benelux countries. Interestingly, the treaty's article IV foreshadowed the arguments and concerns that forty-five years later would also be at the heart of the debate on ESDP: "Recognizing the undesirability of duplicating the military staffs of NATO, the Council [of the WEU] and its Agency will rely on the appropriate military authorities of NATO for information and advice on military matters."[6] In practice, responsibility for military affairs was de facto passed to NATO. When the WEU was stripped of its potential as a site for independent European defense cooperation, the Europeans also lost the opportunity to use their own military capabilities in pursuit of their own foreign policy choices.

The second French attempt to get the Six to act as one in foreign policy and defense also failed. With the Fouchet plans of 1960 and 1962, Paris proposed creating a "European Union" with a common foreign and defense policy on the basis of purely intergovernmental cooperation outside the framework of the existing ECSC and European Economic Community (EEC). The subsequent negotiations broke down because the other EEC partners feared that the French plans were aimed at undermining both the Atlantic Alliance and the EEC and its supranational method of integration. In 1965, President de Gaulle withdrew France from the military structures of NATO after America and Britain rejected its request to be on an equal footing with the United Kingdom in NATO's military command structure. The French withdrawal and decision to follow its own military and nuclear doctrine led to a fundamental breach between France and the other EEC countries, making European cooperation or integration in the field of security and defense virtually impossible. This would only be reversed through the Franco-British Saint-Malo Declaration of December 1998, which launched the ESDP process, and through the gradual rapprochement between France and NATO, leading to the decision of French president Nicolas Sarkozy to reintegrate France into the military organization of NATO in 2009.

The fundamental choice between organizing security and defense policy within the Atlantic framework or within a purely national setting (for France) turned military security into a taboo in European integration and set the parameters for attempts in the following decades to pursue cooperation and integration in the field of foreign policy. When the EC member states in the early 1970s initiated the first informal cooperation in the field of foreign policy within the framework of the European Political Cooperation (EPC), it was clear that the EC/EPC would manifest itself exclusively as a "civilian power."[7] The EPC lacked both military and civilian crisis managements instruments, which made it impossible for the European countries to give substance to its declarations and initiatives. The constraints of being "a civilian power in an uncivil world" became painfully obvious during the several military conflicts in the 1970s and 1980s.[8] European military impotence during the Yugoslav wars in the 1990s would be the painful consequence of the choices made in the early 1950s. This was particularly painful as neither NATO nor Washington was willing to be involved in the conflict in the initial stage of the Yugoslavia conflict, during the Bosnia war, or in the subsequent Kosovo war. They intervened only later, when tens of thousands of people had already been killed or injured.

These various crises made it impossible for member states to continue to ignore the military dimension of security when negotiating the new Treaty of Maastricht and the new Common Foreign and Security Policy (CFSP), which was to replace the EPC. However, whereas France, Germany, and some other countries were pleading for a "common defense," the Atlantic-oriented and neutral countries opted for minimal changes. Several ambiguous formulas allowed them to overcome this paralysis and to sign the new treaty text in 1992. First, they agreed that "the common foreign and security policy shall include all questions related to the security of the Union, including the eventual framing of a common defense policy, which might in time lead to a common defense," as stated in article J.4(1) of the Treaty on the European Union (TEU). According to article J.4(2) of the same treaty, the Council of Ministers could ask the WEU "to elaborate and implement decisions and actions of the Union which have defense implications." In article J.4(4), the text also incorporated safeguards for neutral and NATO-oriented states, indicating that the new arrangements "shall not prejudice the specific character of the security and defense policy of certain member states and shall respect the obligations of certain member states under the North Atlantic Treaty and be compatible with the common security and defense policy established within that framework."

A closer look at the treaty made it clear that the United Kingdom and other member states had conceded much on words and symbols, but nothing on substance and practice. The TEU included the term "defense" and referred to "all areas of foreign and security policy," but the member states had not provided the EU with its own instruments and institutions to allow it to become active in the field of crisis management or conflict prevention. Also, the intended more intensive cooperation with the WEU proved illusory. This reflected the fundamental rejection by the United Kingdom (and also the United States) of any involvement by the EU or the WEU in military security matters. Not surprisingly, also after the entry into force of the Maastricht Treaty the EU demonstrated impotence in the Balkans, which further discredited the CFSP.[9]

The Amsterdam Treaty of 1997 strengthened the relationship between the EU and the WEU. The EU gained access to the WEU's operational capability for humanitarian and rescue tasks, peacekeeping tasks, and tasks of combat forces in crisis management, including peacemaking (the "Petersberg tasks"). The EU was also to "foster closer institutional relations with the WEU with a view to the possibility of the integration of the WEU into the EU." However, the new provisions on EU-WEU relations were quickly overtaken by a new dynamic, leading to the European Security and Defense Policy.

The Establishment and Development of the ESDP

In the space of a few years, the military dimension, which had for decades been taboo in the process of European integration, became one of the spearheads of EU foreign policy. This was made possible because the member states managed to sufficiently overcome two areas of tension that had paralyzed EU foreign policy: European integration versus Atlantic solidarity and civilian power versus military power.[10] The first area of tension was tackled through intensive high-level negotiations among Paris, London, Berlin, and Washington, while the second was overcome by carefully balancing the NATO states and the EU's neutral states and by complementing new *military* crisis management tools with *civilian* crisis management tools.

This new-found flexibility in the mindset of member states was mainly triggered by the Kosovo crisis, which increased frustration in the capitals of the three largest EU member states and in Washington over Europe's military impotence and dependence on the United States. Most European countries, particularly the United Kingdom and France, recognized that Europe had to take more responsibility for security in Europe and that the EU had to become more than merely a civilian power. The British government, under Prime Minister Tony Blair, adopted a more pro-European attitude than the previous British government. It recognized that strengthening Europe's military capacities was essential to rebalance transatlantic relations and thus to safeguard the future of NATO. In Paris, after the debacle in Kosovo, political leaders assumed a more pro-Atlantic attitude and demonstrated a greater willingness to cooperate with NATO.

These moves were sealed in several agreements between the main capitals and within the context of the EU with all partners. The Saint-Malo Declaration of December 1998, signed by President Jacques Chirac of France and Prime Minister Tony Blair of the United Kingdom, provided the political basis for the establishment of ESDP. This Franco-British declaration was less a meeting of vision than a compromise between two opposing views on European security. Nevertheless, getting Britain and France to move toward common ground was the fundamental prerequisite for the start-up of the ESDP. In their "Joint Declaration on European Defense" adopted in Saint-Malo, Blair and Chirac agreed that "the Union must have the capacity for autonomous action, backed up by credible military forces, the means to decide to use them, and a readiness to do so, in order to respond to international crises." It was emphasized that Europe would be "contributing to the vitality of a modernized Atlantic Alliance which is the foundation of the collective defense of its members."[11] These two sentences in the Saint-Malo Declaration perfectly reflected the traditional priorities of Paris and London, thereby bringing them together in one text and paving the way for further progress within the EU context.

Only half a year after the Franco-British declaration, the EU member states at the Cologne European Council of June 1999 adopted the goal to establish a European Security and Defense Policy in the EU.[12] In their conclusions, the EU member states repeated practically verbatim the two sentences cited above, as well as other crucial parts of the Saint-Malo Declaration. This set a pattern that would be followed in other important ESDP steps, with London and Paris (as well as Berlin and, from behind the scenes, also Washington) effectively pre-cooking decisions that were subsequently also accepted by the other member states.

The quick succession of new steps in the following years demonstrated that the EU member states took the new ESDP objective quite seriously and were willing to move beyond the declaratory level. Half a year after the Cologne summit, the European Council in Helsinki in December 1999 made the commitment to develop the capacity to deploy military forces (known as the "Helsinki Headline Goal"; see below), as well as decisions on the institutional setup of the ESDP. Within the framework of the Council, a standing Political and Security Committee (composed of national representatives at the ambassadorial level), an EU Military Committee (composed of the member states' chiefs of defense), and an EU Military Staff (which provides the requisite military expertise) were to be created.[13]

On the initiative of Sweden and Finland, the EU member states also agreed to develop civilian crisis management capabilities. After the experience in Bosnia, the situation in Kosovo had again strengthened their arguments that civilian crisis management was an essential complement to military crisis management in order to achieve stability over the longer term.[14] The European Council of June 2000 in Feira defined four priority areas for the EU to develop civilian capabilities: police, rule of law, civil administration, and civil protection, with security sector reform and monitoring missions being added to the priorities in a later stage. Reflecting the fact that the member states were serious in establishing the ESDP, the member states started a series of capability commitment conferences in order to evaluate the available military and civilian capabilities immediately after the Helsinki and Feira meetings. They were meant to assess shortfalls and to set out concrete targets and pledges regarding military and civilian personnel and crisis management instruments.[15]

The ESDP, NATO, and the United States

One of the most difficult aspects of establishing the ESDP was clarifying the relationship with NATO and the United States (as well as with Turkey). The administration of U.S. president Bill Clinton had called for increased European military efforts and in principle had a positive attitude toward the development of the ESDP. It thereby reversed the historic U.S. opposition to the Europeans developing autonomous military capabilities. However, this was on condition that the EU avoided the "three Ds," as formulated by Secretary of State Madeleine Albright: no decoupling (of ESDP from NATO); no duplication (of capabilities); and no discrimination (against non-EU NATO members).[16] The thorny issue of EU access to NATO military assets and command structures was resolved by the December 2002 Berlin Plus arrangements, which would govern relations between the EU and NATO in crisis management. Under these arrangements, the EU can either conduct an operation autonomously by making use of the operational headquarters of one of the member states or use NATO assets and capabilities. If it opts for the second alternative, the EU can ask for access to NATO's planning facilities, can request that NATO make available a NATO European command option for an EU-led military operation, and can request the use of NATO capabilities. The Berlin Plus arrangements were both pragmatic and symbolic: pragmatic because the Europeans lacked the core equipment and logistics necessary to conduct major military operations within the ESDP framework, symbolic because it also institutionalized for many member states the essential interlinking of the EU with NATO.

The December 2002 agreement on the Berlin Plus arrangements came just in time for the EU to take over the NATO operation Allied Harmony in the former

Yugoslav Republic of Macedonia (FYROM) in January 2003 (through the EU's first-ever military operation, Operation Concordia), followed in 2004 by the takeover of the NATO-led Stabilization Force (SFOR) in Bosnia-Herzegovina (through the then 7,000-strong EU Force Althea [EUFOR Althea] mission of the EU). In 2003, the EU's first military operation under the Berlin Plus arrangement was followed quickly by the first military operation conducted through the "Europeanized" national operational headquarters of a member state, which was also the first operation outside the European continent (Operation Artemis, in the Democratic Republic of the Congo, with France providing the operational headquarters) and the first civilian crisis management operation (the EU police missions in Bosnia-Herzegovina and in the former Yugoslav Republic of Macedonia). In short, less than three years after the decision of the European Council in Cologne to establish an ESDP and to break the forty-five-year-old taboo on defense, the EU had not only created the necessary institutional and instrumental apparatus, but had also moved to operational action.

These first operations were followed in fairly rapid succession by other military and civilian operations in the Balkans, the Caucasus, Africa, the Middle East, and Asia (see table 3-1). By May 2009, the EU had conducted (or was still conducting) twenty-three ESDP operations, including six military crisis management operations and seventeen civilian crisis management operations, nine operations in Europe (mainly the Balkans), nine in Africa, and five in the Middle East and Asia.[17] These ranged from rather small operations such as the EU border assistance mission in the Palestinian Territories (with a staff of only twenty) to very extensive missions, such as EUFOR Althea in Bosnia-Herzegovina (which still has 2,200 soldiers) and the European Union Rule of Law Mission (EULEX) in Kosovo (with 1,700 international staff and 800 local staff).

Remarkably, the establishment of the ESDP and its subsequent development were possible despite the open conflict between the EU member states (and between some EU member states and the United States) during the Iraq crisis and the invasion in Iraq in 2002–03. Progress in the field of security and defense might have been expected to be impossible in view of the painful disagreement between those member states that actively participated in the American-led military invasion of Iraq (led by the United Kingdom and including most central and eastern European countries) and the countries that actively opposed the war, which they considered both illegitimate and detrimental to global and Western security (led by France and Germany).[18] Instead, the dramatic events provided new impetus to the ESDP.

First, the wars in Afghanistan and Iraq painfully demonstrated the limitations of European military capabilities, leading to new commitments within the ESDP to tackle some of these shortfalls through new Headline Goal (including

Table 3-1. *Overview of ESDP Operations, 2003–09*

Operation	Type of Mission	Scope
BALKANS		
Operation Concordia (Former Yugoslav Republic of Macedonia, FYROM, 2003)	Military (Berlin Plus)	400 forces
EUPM (Bosnia-Herzegovina, 2003–09)	Police	166 international police officers, 35 international civilian staff, and 220 Bosnia-Herzegovina staff
Operation Proxima (FYROM, 2003–05)	Police	200 police experts
EUFOR Althea (Bosnia-Herzegovina, 2004–)	Military (Berlin Plus)	2,200 forces
EUPAT (FYROM 2005–06)	Police	30 police advisers
EULEX KOSOVO (Kosovo, 2008–10, open to extension)	Police/Rule of law	1,710 international and 825 local police officials, judges, prosecutors
CAUCASUS		
EUJUST Themis (Georgia, 2004–05)	Rule of law	10 international civilian experts
Border Assistance Mission to Moldova and Ukraine (2005–07)	Border assistance mission	69 experts and 50 local support staff
EUMM Georgia (Georgia, 2008–09, open to extension)	Monitoring mission	340 staff (personnel in headquarters and field offices, monitors)
AFRICA		
Operation Artemis (DR Congo, 2003)	Military autonomous (EU Operational HQ in France)	1,700 forces
EUPOL Kinshasa (DR Congo, 2005–07)	Police	Approx 30 staff
EUFOR RD Congo (DR Congo, 2006)	Military autonomous (EU Operational HQ in Germany)	Over 1,000 forces; a rapid force available
EUSEC RD Congo (DR Congo, 2005–09)	Security sector reform	60 staff
DARFUR EU support to Amis II (Sudan, 2005–06)	Civilian-military	31 police officers, 17 military experts, and 10 military observers

(table continues)

Table 3-1 (*continued*)

Operation	Type of Mission	Scope
EUPOL RD Congo (DR Congo, 2007–10)	Police	53 international and 9 local staff
EUFOR TCHAD/RCA (Chad, 2008–09)	Military autonomous (EU Operational HQ in France)	3,700 troops
EU SSR Guinea-Bissau (Guinea-Bissau, 2008–09)	Security sector reform	19 international and 13 local staff
EU NAVFOR Somalia (operation Atalanta) (Somalia, 2008–)	Military autonomous maritime operation (EU Operational HQ in the United Kingdom)	1,500 forces
MIDDLE EAST		
EUJUST LEX (Iraq, 2005–09)	Rule of law	800 judges and police officers
EUBAM Rafah (Palestinian Territories, 2005–09)	Border assistance mission	20 EU staff and 7 local staff
EUPOL COPPS (Palestinian Territories, 2005–10)	Police	41 EU staff and 16 local staff
ASIA		
Aceh Monitoring Mission (AMM) (Aceh, 2005–06)	Monitoring mission	Approx. 80 unarmed personnel
EUPOL Afghanistan (Afghanistan, 2007–10)	Police	225 international and 123 local staff

Source: Council of the European Union, *European Security and Defence Policy: Operations, 2009* (www.consilium.europa.eu/showPage.aspx?id=268&lang=en).

Note: Situation as of May 2009. For a more comprehensive and continuously updated version of this table, see the Online Resource Guide "Exploring EU Foreign Policy" (www.exploring-europe.eu/foreignpolicy).

the decision to develop the EU Battlegroup Concept). Second, and more important, with its new military engagements in Iraq and Afghanistan and its new "war on terror," it became clear that the United States would be unable and unwilling to maintain its extensive military presence in the Balkans, implying that the Europeans should prepare to assume these responsibilities. Washington also wanted NATO and its NATO partners to gradually shift attention to the new security challenges that it considered more important than the situation in the Balkans. In this sense, it was not by chance that the Berlin Plus arrangements were adopted and that the EU for the first time took over a NATO operation in the months preceding the invasion of Iraq in March 2003.

As a sign of the member states' willingness to proceed with the ESDP, progress was not hampered by the French and Dutch rejection of the 2004 European Constitution or the Irish rejection of the 2007 Lisbon Treaty. Despite the rejection of the Constitutional Treaty, new ESDP operations were launched and the European Defense Agency was established. Nor did the difficulty getting the Lisbon Treaty of December 2007 ratified stop the EU from launching its largest civilian crisis management operation (EULEX Kosovo) and its first military autonomous maritime operation, EU Naval Force (NAVFOR) Somalia in 2008. The new Lisbon Treaty, if entered into force after a positive Irish referendum, will in the first place institutionalize the existing setup of ESDP.[19] It will thus not fundamentally alter the basic rules of the game of the ESDP.[20]

Military Crisis Management Instruments and Operations

This section and the next look in more detail at the military and civilian crisis management instruments available to the EU and the nature of ESDP operations.

The 1999 Helsinki Headline Goal is at the basis of the EU's military capabilities. The Helsinki European Council decided that, in "cooperating voluntarily in EU-led operations, member states must be able, by 2003, to deploy within 60 days and sustain for at least one year military forces of up to 50,000–60,000 persons capable of the full range of Petersberg tasks."[21] These tasks include humanitarian and rescue activities, peacekeeping, and the tasks of combat forces in crisis management, including peacemaking (with joint disarmament operations and support for third countries in combating terrorism and security sector reform added to this list in 2004). This formulation of the Helsinki Headline Goal implicitly points to two fundamental principles of ESDP, which together underline the parameters and also limitations of ESDP. The first principle is related to the objectives of ESDP: in contrast to what its title might indicate, the ESDP is not at all involved in the territorial defense of the EU member states. On the contrary, it focuses on various dimensions of crisis management. And it is also clear that the ESPD is not conceived for large-scale military operations (such as those in Iraq or Afghanistan). The second principle is related to methodology: European military capabilities are not achieved by creating permanent European forces, and even less by establishing a permanent European army, but are based on the voluntary and temporary contribution of member states to operations conducted in the framework of the ESDP.

Whereas the 1999 Helsinki Headline Goal was largely inspired by the context of the Balkan wars, the New Headline Goal 2010 (HG2010), adopted by the European Council in June 2004, reflected the new security context after 2001 and the experience with the rapid reaction force used in Operation Artemis in the Democratic Republic of the Congo (DRC).[22] With HG2010, the member states endorsed a list of high-profile initiatives aimed at reducing the remaining shortfalls in military capability, including the establishment of a European Defense Agency and the goal to increase capacity in strategic lift. In terms of soldiers, attention shifted from the capacity to deploy 50,000–60,000 troops (the Helsinki Headline Goal) to the Battlegroup Concept. The Battlegroup Concept implied a more limited number of troops but was meant to increase the capacity for rapid reaction.[23] For the EU, a battlegroup consists of 1,500–2,000 troops with appropriate support at a high state of readiness (deployable within fifteen days) and capable of high-intensity operations. On paper, the EU should be able to concurrently deploy two battlegroups for a period of between 30 and 120 days. They can be formed by one nation or a group of nations, with two battlegroups being on standby for a six-month period. For instance, in the first half of 2010 a Polish-led battlegroup (with troops from Poland, Germany, Lithuania, Latvia, and Slovakia) and a British-Dutch battlegroup are on standby, with two other battlegroups taking over in the second half of the year.

From the start, doubts have been raised about the effectiveness of the Battlegroup Concept, in view of the operational challenges of the half-yearly rotation system, the different capabilities of the various battlegroups, problems of financing, and dependence on the agreement of the countries that take part in the multilateral battlegroups that are on standby. The latter proved to be a major stumbling block, as countries on several occasions were unwilling to use their battlegroup for an envisioned operation or could not reach a consensus about the modalities. This was the case with Germany with regard to a military mission in the DRC in 2006, with the Nordic battlegroup in the discussion of a mission in Chad in 2007, and with the British and the Spanish-Italian battlegroups in 2008–09 in the discussion about sending troops to the DRC. By the spring of 2009, the battlegroup had not yet been used in any ESDP military operation.[24]

The result is that several ESDP operations could not be launched because the member states were not willing to battle in risky contexts (such as the DRC in 2008), preferred other multilateral frameworks for crisis management operations (such as the UN for the intervention following the Israel-Lebanon crisis in 2006), or continued to be established on an ad hoc basis, depending on a "coalition of the willing and able" to contribute troops and to use one of the multilateralized operational headquarters (see below).[25] This "ad hocism" also explains why the EU was often not able to provide a "rapid response." For example, half a year or more was needed to deploy the operation for the DRC election in 2006 and in Chad in 2008. On the other hand, the deployment of EU NAVFOR Somalia indicates that the EU in some circumstances is able to react rather swiftly and that flexible ad hoc solutions, with contributions from countries that can make a real difference in a specific context, can be more appropriate than predetermined battlegroups.

The limited "European" and "integrated" nature of military crisis management also becomes clear from the three options available for the military headquarters of ESDP operations. The first option, under the Berlin Plus arrangements, is to make use of NATO's operational headquarters located at SHAPE (Supreme Headquarters Allied Powers Europe) in Belgium, with NATO's Deputy SACEUR (Supreme Allied Commander Europe) being the operation commander. This option was used for only two operations in the Balkans: Operation Concordia in the former Yugoslav Republic of Macedonia (with 400 forces) and Operation Althea in Bosnia-Herzegovina (initially 7,000 forces, reduced to 2,500 in 2007). As indicated before, the EU in both cases took over responsibility from NATO, which meant in practice that the majority of the soldiers replaced their NATO badges with EU badges, and that the Deputy SACEUR, not the SACEUR, was the operation commander.

The second option, for "autonomous" ESDP operations, is to use facilities provided by one of the operational headquarters made available by five EU member states (France, the United Kingdom, Germany, Italy, and Greece). These are then "multinationalized" for the EU operation. In this case, the operational commander is also provided by the member state providing the headquarters. This option was chosen for Operation Artemis in the DRC and EUFOR Chad/Central African Republic (both using the French headquarters), for Operation EUFOR DRC (using the German headquarters), and most recently for EU NAVFOR Somalia (using the British headquarters). Operation Artemis in 2003, with some 1,700 forces involved, was aimed at the stabilization of security conditions and the improvement of the humanitarian situation in Bunya in the northeastern part of the DRC, awaiting UN troop reinforcements (from MONUC, the French acronym for UN Mission DR Congo). Operation EUFOR DR Congo in 2006, with 1,000 forces and an additional rapid reaction force in reserve, helped to secure the region during the elections in Congo (again in support of MONUC). EUFOR Chad/RCA in 2008–09, including 3,700 troops, was a bridging operation for the UN mission in the Central African Republic and Chad. It protected civilians in danger and the UN staff, and facilitated humanitarian aid. EU NAVFOR Somalia or Operation Atalanta, with 1,500 forces, started in late 2008, with the objective of protecting vessels off the Somali coast against acts of piracy.

The third option is to command operations of up to 2,000 troops and civilian experts from Brussels through an integrated Civil-Military Operations Center (OpsCen) within the EU Military Staff (EUMS) under the command of a designated operation commander. This EU Operations Center is not a standing headquarters, but can be activated through the small joint Civilian-Military Cell

(Civ-Mil Cell) that has been established within the EU Military Staff.²⁶ An EU operations center would consist mainly of "double-hatted" personnel from the EUMS and from member states, implying that virtually no extra personnel were provided to the EU. As such, in its final form, the civilian-military cell was far from the autonomous military headquarters originally proposed by France and Germany, but went beyond London's original position. By mid-2009, this third option had not yet been used, reflecting the continuing reluctance of member states to allow the EU to have its own operational headquarters.

Civilian Crisis Management Instruments and Operations

As noted earlier, the June 2000 European Council in Feira defined four priority areas in which the EU should develop civilian capabilities (police, strengthening the rule of law, civil administration, and civil protection), with two additional priority areas defined later (monitoring missions and generic support capabilities). The Civilian Headline Goal 2008, which was adopted in 2004, included clear objectives for these six agreed priority areas.[27] The EU aimed to be capable of carrying out any police operation, from strengthening missions (advisory, assistance, and training tasks) to substitution missions (where the international force acts as a substitute for local police forces). From a pool of more than 5,000 police officers, 1,400 are to be deployable in less than thirty days. Rule-of-law missions, similar to police missions, were to be capable of both strengthening and temporarily substituting for the local judiciary or legal system. The member states committed 200 judges and prosecutors, some portion of whom were to be deployable within thirty days. Under the civilian administration rubric, a pool of more than 500 experts had to be created, capable of carrying out civilian administration missions to provide basic services that the national or local administration is unable to offer (covering fields such as elections and taxation). In civil protection, the objective was to develop assessment and/or coordination teams of ten experts that could be dispatched within seven hours, as well as intervention teams of up to 2,000 people and additional specialized services. More than 500 experts have been committed to establish a monitoring capability, with possible missions including border monitoring, human rights monitoring, and observing the general political situation. Finally, the generic support capabilities to support the work of EU special representatives or form part of multifaceted ESDP missions are to consist of a pool of 400 personnel, including experts in fields such as human rights, political affairs, mediation, media affairs, security sector reform (SSR), and disarmament, demobilization, and reintegration (DDR).

In quantitative terms, member states managed to substantially exceed their targets, at least on paper. However, shortfalls were identified in mission and planning support capability, financing, the ability to deploy on short notice, common training and exercises, institutional memory, partnerships with other international and local actors, procurement, and capability requirements (particularly judges and staff with financial expertise). The EU's civilian capacity was less integrated than expected, and the capacity goals for 2008 in fact quickly seemed to be unattainable, with progress afterwards also very limited.[28] In November 2008, the EU member states agreed to develop new strategies for civilian crisis management and also adopted a declaration of strengthening capabilities.[29] In this declaration they indicated that the EU should be able to conduct "two major stabilization and reconstruction operations, with a suitable civilian component," as well as "around a dozen ESDP civilian missions" of varying formats, "together with a major mission (possibly up to 3,000 experts) which could last several years." However, these goals reflected more the existing situation than they did a clear strategy for the future.

Institutionally, on the political level the Committee for Civilian Aspects of Crisis Management (CIVCOM) was established to give advice to the Political and Security Committee and Committee of Permanent Representatives (COREPER) and to ensure follow-up on civilian crisis management capabilities and operations. On the operational level, the joint Civilian-Military Cell served as the locus for the civilian crisis management operations. The EU's capacity to conduct civilian operations and to integrate capabilities can be expected to further improve as a result of the establishment within the Council's General Secretariat of the new Civilian Planning and Conduct Capability (CPCC), which since late 2008 is responsible for planning, deployment, conduct, and review of civilian crisis management.

However, on the institutional and administrative level the civilian component of the ESDP remains hindered by several specific problems. First, in quantitative terms, the number of people working for the civilian side of the ESDP is markedly smaller than its military counterpart, which is paradoxical since there are many more civilian operations than military operations and because the number of civilian ESDP operations is growing. Furthermore, while the military has the possibility of recourse to NATO or national headquarters for planning and operational control, the EU staff working on civilian operations cannot rely on backup from external planning entities.

Second, problems of consistency and coordination follow from the relationship between the ESDP's civilian capabilities and the civilian crisis management instruments of the EU's first pillar, which are largely managed by the European Commission. These partially complementary, partially overlapping competencies of the EC and the ESDP can be positive when the various initiatives indeed complement and strengthen each other, but can also undermine the consistency and effectiveness of the EU's crisis management policy if they give rise to turf

battles between ESDP actors and the European Commission and to an ineffi-
cient use of resources. Third, civilian crisis management implies that a wider set
of national actors is becoming involved in the ESDP. This makes the preparation
and management of civilian operations much more complicated and leads to
major challenges for consistency and coordination among actors. In addition to
foreign and defense ministers, ministries of interior affairs, justice, finance, and
others are also involved, each with its own bureaucracy, procedure, and culture.
Moreover, most of these actors had no or only limited traditional experience
in extracting judges, police, and civilian experts from their domestic duties to
undertake foreign missions.

The two main areas of EU civilian crisis management are the Balkans and
the DRC, which complement the military-civilian crisis management operations of the EU in these two areas. The most important, comprehensive, and visible civilian operation is EULEX Kosovo, with 1,800 European police officials,
judges, prosecutors, and other specialists involved since 2008 in assisting and
supporting the Kosovo authorities in three major areas of the rule of law: police,
the judiciary, and customs.

Since 2003, the EU has also conducted the EU Police Mission in Bosnia-
Herzegovina, with around 500 police officers and other staff supporting the
local police, to develop independence and accountability, to create capacity
and institutions and, increasingly important, to fight organized crime. By mid-
2009, the only other mission on the European continent was the EU Monitoring
Mission in Georgia, with a staff of 340 personnel who monitor the stabilization process and the compliance of the parties to the six-point agreement of
August 2008.[30] Following two more modest civilian operations in that country,
the main civilian crisis management operation in DRC is EUPOL RD Congo,
which since 2007 has assisted the Congolese authorities in its security sector
reform with around fifty international staff.[31] Other active ESDP missions outside the European continent in the spring of 2009 were: the rule of law mission
EUJUST LEX, which since 2005 has provided training for judges, magistrates,
and senior police (mainly outside Iraq); the police mission EUPOL Afghanistan,
which since 2007 has mentored, advised, and trained a sustainable and effective
civilian police force under Afghan ownership; and the rather modest mission in
Guinea-Bissau, which since 2008 has provided advice and assistance on security
sector reform in Guinea-Bissau.[32]

Assessment

How can we evaluate these various crisis management operations and the ESDP
in general?[33] Looking first at the operations, it is clear that the assessment will be

different depending on the criteria used and the perspectives adopted. From a historical perspective, some clear trends can be detected, which together testify to the growth of the ESDP. Nicoletta Pirozzi and Sammi Sandawi see the following operational trends: globalization of the operational area (from an initial focus on the Balkans to the eastern part of the European continent, the Middle East, Africa, and even Asia); the expansion of the operational spectrum and objectives (from military crisis management to a widening spectrum of civilian crisis management); an increasing interaction between civilian and military operations and blurring of this divide; a growing intertwining of the first and second EU pillars; and an evolving capability development process.[34]

However, growth in the range of ESDP operations is paralleled by a series of shortcomings and related challenges. Beside those already mentioned, there is a need to pay more attention to quality, since in the past the main concern was often quantitative, centered on finding enough soldiers and civilians for the missions; the need to envisage the possibility of more risky operations; the need to increase the efficiency of interaction with other (local and international) actors involved in a conflict; and the need to tackle the increasingly complex interventions that cover the entire crisis management cycle, including issues such as institution building and security sector reform.[35] The latter also points to one of the innovative developments in the civilian crisis management operations of the ESDP and of the EU at large: the increasing focus on structural crisis management as part of a broader structural foreign and security policy, a policy that seeks to influence or shape sustainable political, legal, socioeconomic, security, and mental structures on various levels.[36]

When assessing ESDP operations from the perspective of the effectiveness, efficiency, and added value provided by these missions, the story becomes even more complicated. For instance, a large military operation such as that in Bosnia-Herzegovina can seem to be effective, but this may be mainly the result of the close link to NATO and the remaining security guarantee of the United States. Missions such as Operation Artemis in the DRC and the mission in Aceh might have been rather limited in time and terms of mandate, but can nevertheless have been important and valuable.

With the exception of the missions in the Balkans, it is clear that the scope of most ESDP operations was or is too limited to make a real difference. And in some of the main conflict areas in the world like the Middle East, Darfur, and Afghanistan, the contribution of the ESDP is at best symbolic, although it is fair to say that the sometimes more robust interventions of other international actors were not more successful in these areas. In this context, it is also important to take into account that, for many member states, the purpose of launching ESDP operations is not primarily about having an impact on a crisis, but also about proving that European integration is progressing (despite all the problems in the EU) and about managing and balancing the different interests among member states (or between the European Union and the United States).[37]

Looking at the ESDP at large, a historical perspective also leads to different conclusions based on criteria such as relevance, legitimacy, visibility, and coherence. Considering that the military dimension was a taboo in the preceding decades, that ESDP operations only started in 2003, and that civilian crisis management is a fairly new domain of conflict management, it is fair to say that the speed of change in the ESDP has been rather impressive. The ESDP has been able to move forward while being increasingly perceived by the member states as a positive-sum game in which the added value of military and civilian ESDP missions, in addition to acting unilaterally and/or interventions through NATO or the UN, is recognized in a growing number of situations. The time lag between the rhetoric and the reality of civilian and military operations has indeed been relatively small. Moreover, from this perspective, it is also inevitable that such a process is accompanied by the problems, ambiguities, and shortcomings that have been discussed.

However, there is also a paradox in this evolution, which is mainly related to the relationship between the ESDP and the CFSP. One the one hand, the ESDP qualitatively changed the nature of CFSP and resulted in an "upgrade" of the EU's foreign policy. It allowed the CFSP to move from a declaratory foreign policy focused on diplomacy to a more action-oriented foreign policy focused on proactive crisis management. For the first time, the member states succeeded in developing a framework to effectively pool national resources within the CFSP. And although still limited in scope, the EU finally had boots on the ground. This strengthened both the credibility of the High Representative and other EU negotiators when dealing with third parties or mediating conflicts. It also increased the EU's potential effectiveness in its foreign policy on specific issues, as it now has a bigger toolbox.

On the other hand, there is real risk inherent in an enhanced ESDP without a sufficiently developed European foreign policy. The development of the ESDP and military and civilian crisis management operations has not been matched by parallel efforts on a common foreign policy. The ESDP operations can indeed be misleading, giving the impression that the EU has an agreed, clear, coherent, and comprehensive policy toward the issues at stake and in foreign policy in general. Agreement on ESDP operations is sometimes a surrogate for a coherent common foreign policy on specific issues. Even Kosovo and Central Africa are examples of areas where the EU member states were able to agree to ESDP operations, but where they nevertheless have major political disagreements on the fundamentals of these crises.[38] Moreover, with the exception of the operations in the Balkans, no other ESDP operation really answers the urgent strategic needs of the European Union.

The European security strategy adopted in 2003 and slightly adapted by late 2008 does not provide clear clues about when, where, and under what conditions the EU should initiate ESDP operations.[39] This political and strategic ambiguity can also be considered the Achilles' heel of the ESDP. It might become particularly apparent when an ESDP operation runs into real trouble, for example as a result of an escalation of violence and geographic spread of a conflict, including a high number of casualties. Within this context, even though the ESDP has emerged as one of the spearheads of EU foreign policy, it may prove to have been mainly a symbolic spearhead, which does not pass the test when confronted with "real" violent crises.

Notes

1. This chapter draws to a major extent on the analysis in S. Keukeleire and J. Mac-Naughtan, *The Foreign Policy of the European Union* (London: Palgrave Macmillan, 2008), as well as on a series of interviews with diplomats and civil servants of the EU and EU member states conducted in April 2009. For recent comprehensive studies of ESDP, see J. Howorth, *Security and Defence Policy in the European Union* (Basingstoke, UK: Palgrave Macmillan, 2007); M. Merlingen and R. Ostrauskaite, eds., *The European Security and Defence Policy: Operationalisation, Impact and Context* (London: Routledge, 2007); M. Merlingen and R. Ostrauskaite, eds., *European Security and Defence Policy: An Implementation Perspective* (London: Routledge, 2007); F. Merand, *European Defence Policy: Beyond the Nation State* (Oxford University Press, 2008). For other sources, see www.exploring-europe.eu/foreignpolicy.

2. For a comprehensive analysis of the evolution from the European Defense Community (EDC) to the creation of the Common Foreign and Security Policy (CFSP), see S. Duke, *The Elusive Quest for European Security: from EDC to CFSP* (Basingstoke: Palgrave Macmillan, 1999).

3. See D. P. Calleo, "Early American Views of NATO: Then and Now," in *The Troubled Alliance: Atlantic Relations in the 1980s*, edited by L. Freedman (London: Heinemann, 1983), pp. 7–27; D. Cook, *Forging the Alliance: NATO, 1945–1950* (London: Secker and Warburg, 1989).

4. Keukeleire and MacNaughtan, *Foreign Policy*, p. 10.

5. For a comprehensive analysis of the EDC, see E. Fursdon, *The European Defence Community: A History* (London: Macmillan, 1980). For the basic documents, see C. Hill and K. E. Smith, *European Foreign Policy: Key Documents* (London: Routledge, 2000), pp. 16–32.

6. Hill and Smith, *European Foreign Policy*, pp. 40–41.

7. F. Duchêne, "Europe's Role in World Peace," in *Europe Tomorrow: Sixteen Europeans look Ahead*, edited by R. Mayne (London: Collins, 1972), pp. 32–47.

8. A. Pijpers, "The Twelve Out-of-Area: A Civilian Power in an Uncivil World?" in *European Political Cooperation in the 1980's*, edited by A. Pijpers, E. Regelsberger, and W. Wessels (Dordrecht: Martinus Nijhoff, 1988), p. 143. For a detailed analysis of the EPC, see Pijpers, Regelsberger, and Wessels, *European Political Cooperation in the 1980's*, and S. Nuttall, *European Political Co-operation* (Oxford: Clarendon Press, 1992).

9. For an analysis of the genesis and first years of the CFSP, see S. Nuttall, *European Foreign Policy* (Oxford University Press, 2000); M. Holland, ed., *Common Foreign and Security Policy: The Record and Reforms* (London: Pinter, 1997); E. Regelsberger, P. de Schoutheete de Tervarent, and W. Wessels, eds., *Foreign Policy of the European Union: From EPC to CFSP and Beyond* (Boulder, Colo.: Lynne Rienner, 1997).

10. For an analysis of these and other cleavages and areas of tension in determining EU foreign policy, see Keukeleire and MacNaughtan, *Foreign Policy*, pp. 8–19.

11. See the full text of the Saint-Malo Declaration in M. Rutten, "From St-Malo to Nice: European Defence: Core Documents," Chaillot Paper 47 (Paris: European Union Institute for Security Studies, 2001), pp. 8–9.

12. European Council, *Presidency Conclusions* (Cologne, June 1999).

13. For an analysis of the institutional framework, see J. Howorth, *Security and Defence Policy in the European Union* (Basingstoke: Palgrave Macmillan, 2007), pp. 61–91. On the role of the PSC in the ESDP, see S. Duke, "The Linchpin COPS: Assessing the Workings and Institutional Relations of the Political and Security Committee," European Institute for Public Administration Working Papers 5, no. 35 (Archive of European Integration, 2005); A. E. Juncos and C. Reynolds, "The Political and Security Committee: Governing in the Shadow," *European Foreign Affairs Review* 12, no. 2 (2007): 127–47.

14. On the role of Sweden and Finland, see H. Ojanen, "Participation and Influence: Finland, Sweden and the Post-Amsterdam Development of the CFSP," Occasional Paper 11 (Paris: European Union Institute for Security Studies, 2000), pp. 1–26.

15. B. Schmitt, "European Capabilities: How Many Divisions?" in *EU Security and Defense Policy: The First Five Years (1999–2004)*, edited by N. Gnesotto (Paris: European Union Institute for Security Studies, 2004), pp. 89–110; E. J. Stewart, "Capabilities and Coherence? The Evolution of European Union Conflict Prevention," *European Foreign Affairs Review* 13, no 2 (2008): 229–53.

16. M. Rutten, "From St.-Malo to Nice," pp. 10–12.

17. For more detailed information and formal documents on all ESDP operations, see the website of the Council of the European Union (European Security and Defense Policy: Operations): www.consilium.europa.eu/showPage.aspx?id=268&lang=en. For regular updates and analysis of ESDP operations, see the bimonthly "European Security Review" of ISIS Europe (www.isis-europe.org).

18. P. Van Ham, "The EU's War over Iraq: The Last Wake-Up Call," in *European Foreign Policy: From Rhetoric to Reality?* edited by D. Mahncke, A. Ambos, and C. Reynolds (Oxford: Peter Lang Verlag, 2004), pp. 209–26.

19. A second referendum is planned in Ireland in the second half of 2009.

20. The implications of the Lisbon Treaty are discussed in this book in the chapter by Nicola Verola. See also the comprehensive analysis in B. Angelet and I. Vrailas, "European Defence in the Wake of the Lisbon Treaty," Egmont Paper 21 (Ghent: Royal Institute for

International Relations, 2008), pp. 1–62; S. Biscop and F. Algieri, "The Lisbon Treaty and ESDP: Transformation and Integration," Egmont Paper 24 (Ghent: Royal Institute for International Relations, 2000), pp. 1–53, R. Whitman and A. Juncos, "The Lisbon Treaty and the Foreign, Security and Defence Policy: Reforms, Implementation and the Consequences of (Non-)ratification," *European Affairs Review* 14, no 1 (2009): 25.

21. European Council, *Presidency Conclusions—Helsinki Headline Goal* (Helsinki, December 2009), pp. 10–11. These tasks were labeled the "Petersberg tasks" because they were initially defined in a WEU meeting in 1992 in Petersberg, Germany.

22. See European Council, *Presidency Conclusions—Headline Goal 2010* (Brussels, June 17–18, 2004).

23. G. Lindstrom, "Enter the EU Battlegroups," Chaillot Paper 97 (Paris: European Union Institute for Security Studies, 2007), p. 97.

24. C. Mölling, "EU Battlegroups 2007: Where Next?" *European Security Review* 31 (December 2006): 7–10; Lindstrom, "Enter the EU Battlegroups," pp. 57–61; Jean-Yves Haine, "Battle Groups: Out of Necessity, Still a Virtue?" *European Security Review* 39 (2008): 1–5.

25. M. Dembinski, "Europe and the UNIFIL II Mission: Stumbling into the Conflict Zone of the Middle East," *CFSP Forum* 5, no. 1 (2007): 1–4.

26. European Council, *European Defense: NATO/EU Consultation, Planning and Operations. Annex to the Presidency Conclusions* (Brussels, December 12–13, 2003).

27. European Council, *Presidency Conclusions—Civilian Headline Goal 2008* (Brussels, December 17, 2004).

28. P. Viggo Jakobsen, "The ESDP and Civilian Rapid Reaction: Adding Value Is Harder Than Expected," *European Security* 15, no. 3 (2006): 299–322; Giji Gya, "Tapping the Human Dimension: Civilian Capabilities in ESDP," *European Security Review* 43 (2009): 2–4.

29. *Council Declaration of 8 December 2008 on the Enhancement of the Capabilities of the European Security and Defense Policy* (16840/08).

30. Completed missions in Europe include: the police missions Operation Proxima and EUPAT in Macedonia (with 200 and thirty advisers respectively); the rule of law mission EUJUST Themis in Georgia to support the reform of the criminal justice system (with around ten experts); and the Border Assistance Mission to Moldova and Ukraine to help prevent smuggling, trafficking, and customs fraud by providing advice and training (with seventy experts).

31. These are: EUPOL KINSHASA to monitor, mentor, and advise the integrated police units (with thirty staff) and EUSEC RD Congo, which was an advisory and assistance mission for security reform (with eight experts).

32. Completed missions outside Europe were located in Indonesia and the Palestinian Territories. In 2005–06, after the tsunami, the Aceh Monitoring Mission monitored the implementation of the peace agreement. The police mission EUPOL COPPS provided support to the Palestinian Authority in establishing effective policing arrangements, while the border assistance mission EUBAM RAFAH monitored the operations at the border crossing at Rafah in Gaza. In 2005–06, the EU also conducted a mixed civilian-military operation in Sudan: Darfur EU support to Amis II, with sixty police

officers and military experts supporting the African Union in its efforts to address the crisis in Darfur.

33. For recent evaluations of the ESDP, see also A. Menon, "Empowering Paradise? The ESDP at Ten," *International Affairs* 85, no. 2 (2009): 227–46; A. J. K. Bailes, "The EU and a 'Better World': What Role for the European Security and Defense Policy?" *International Affairs* 84, no. 1 (2008): 115–30.

34. Nicoletta Pirozzi and Sammi Sandawi, "Five years of ESDP in Action: Operations, Trends, Shortfalls," *European Security Review* 39 (2008): 14–17.

35. Ibid. On SSR, see D. Spence and P. Fluri, eds., *The European Union and Security Sector Reform* (London: John Harper, 2008).

36. Keukeleire and MacNaughtan, *Foreign Policy*, pp. 25–28; Stephan Keukeleire, Robin Thiers, and Arnout Justaert, "Reappraising Diplomacy: Structural Diplomacy and the Case of the European Union," in "Special Issue: The European Union and Diplomacy," edited by Brian Hocking and Jozef Batora, *Hague Journal of Diplomacy* 4, no. 2 (2009): 143–65.

37. Keukeleire and MacNaughtan, *Foreign Policy*, pp. 189–91. On the difference between "external" objectives and "internal" (integration, identity, and interrelational) objectives, see pp. 12–14.

38. EULEX Kosovo is the largest civilian crisis management mission of the EU, but the member states did not manage to agree on the fundamental issue of the formal recognition of an independent Kosovo. And the DRC is, after the Balkans, the location of most ESDP missions, but the member states still fundamentally disagree on issues related to the Great Lakes Region at large and the relationship between and with Rwanda and the DRC in particular.

39. European Council, *European Security Strategy—A Secure Europe in a Better World* (Brussels, December 12, 2003); Council of the European Union, *Report on the Implementation of the European Security Strategy—Providing Security in a Changing World* (17104/08) (Brussels, December 10, 2008); see also S. Biscop, *The European Security Strategy: A Global Agenda for Positive Power* (Hants, UK: Ashgate, 2005); S. Biscop, ed., "Special Issue—The European Security Strategy 2003–2008: Review and Implementation," *Studia Diplomatica* LXI, no. 3 (2008).

FRANCESCA LONGO

4

Justice and Home Affairs as a New Tool of European Foreign Policy

The European Union was established with the aim of bringing peace to Europe by creating economic interdependence among European countries. Military cooperation was excluded from the original objectives of integration because the military defense of Western European countries was provided by NATO and the United States. The notion of Europe as a "civilian power" was theorized in 1972 by François Duchêne, and it refers broadly to the use of non-military, primarily economic means by the EU in exercising its international role.

Since the 1970s, the European Union has developed several types of policies toward third states. They range from economic policies to foreign policy and security. Even if the institutional arrangements and actors are different from policy to policy and the EU is not a traditional unitary actor with a stable set of preferences and interests, it has a stable set of formal and informal rules and procedures for decisionmaking in the fields of foreign, security, and defense policy. It has developed the "habit of working together," limiting the member states in their autonomy and promoting the convergence of competing interests.[1] The nature of external European action turns out to be not a temporary convergence of member states' interests, but a continuous process of redefining the member states' interests in light of existing institutional structures. Even if the involved actors, the decisionmaking process, and the efficiency of the policy instruments depend on the issue and the relevant pillar,[2] it is possible to say that institutions, rules, and procedures strengthen the EU's ability to promote a convergence of interests and to define collective policy strategies toward external actors.

In 1999 the European Council of Cologne decided to provide the EU with the capacity for autonomous military action, backed by military forces, as well as the means to decide to use them in responding to international crises. From 1999 to 2001 a military and political structure was established to implement that declaration. This new military complex has added the issue of "EU security actorness" to its common foreign policy and has changed the perception of the EU as a "civilian power."

More recently the notion of the EU as a "normative power" emerged. The idea of normative power draws the attention of analysts because it captures the main characteristic of EU international action.[3] The EU has developed a domestic model for conflict resolution based on shared values and peaceful negotiation. It exports these values and this model to the outside world, influencing both the structuring of global cooperative processes and the issues relating to soft security.

A new theoretical perspective has emerged recently, aiming to link the concept of the EU as an international political actor with the study of the European model of governance. The bridge between the European Union's international actorness and European governance is based on the idea that "the EU is emerging as a key regional actor in certain global affairs, particularly in such areas as finance, trade, the environment and development, and the current policy is directed towards enhancing the role of the European Union in the global governance system."[4] The research agenda of this new perspective is focused on the role of Europe in the world, the possible application of European governance in external relations, and the relevance of the European model of governance for international and global governance. A relevant research question is the EU's ability to provide security to its member states and to contribute to the European and global security governance. In sum, is the European Union a *security provider*?

If the Franco-British joint statement issued in Saint-Malo in December 1998 has opened the way for a European Security and Defense Policy (ESDP), and has permitted the establishment of the military complex called the Common Defense and Security Policy, there is less consensus on theorizing the EU as a traditional security actor. European military capabilities remain modest, and the operational activities of the European Rapid Reaction Forces remain small-scale military operations. Moreover, Europe remains absent from important conflicts and dependent on NATO and U.S. forces for its military security.

Nevertheless, criticism of European security actorness fails to consider two sets of arguments. The first is related to the fact that even though the European Union is far from having a military capability comparable with that of the United States, over the past decade it has made progress in the field of military cooperation that would have been unthinkable a few years earlier.

The development of the ESDP is a multifaceted undertaking. For decades security and defense were taboo subjects for European integration, but since the Cologne European Council in 1999 the European Union has developed a complex institutional and political organization, beginning with the Rapid

Reaction Force (RRF). The RRF consists in the capability of member states to deploy within sixty days and sustain for at least one year military forces up to 50,000–60,000 persons capable of the full range of military tasks. The RRF is politically and militarily dependent on common institutions: at the political level, on the Council of the European Union; at the level of foreign and defense ministers and the Committee of Permanent Representatives (COREPER) on the European Union military staff (EUMS), the only permanent integrated military structure of the European Union; on the European Union Military Committee (EUMC), composed of the chiefs of defense of the member states; and on the Political and Security Committee (PSC), formed by national experts at the ambassadorial level.

The PSC has a focal role in the ESPD. First, the PSC oversees the "political control and strategic direction" of the EU's military response to crises and, day by day, it keeps track of the international situation in the areas falling within the Common Foreign and Security Policy. It issues guidelines to the Military Committee and receives its opinions and recommendations. In the event of a crisis, the PSC is the European Council body that deals with crisis situations and examines all the options that might be considered in response. In preparing the EU's response to a crisis, the PSC outlines the Union's political objectives and recommends options aimed at contributing to the settlement of the crisis. In particular, it may draw up an opinion recommending to the Council that it adopt a joint action.

In December 2001, at the European Council of Laeken, the ESPD was declared partly operational. The activities of the Rapid Reaction Force are part of the "Petersberg tasks." They include humanitarian action, peacekeeping, and peacemaking operations. In May 2002 the first joint military exercise was launched and served as a first test of the decisionmaking procedures and of procedures for improving the pre-decisionmaking phase of crisis management.

The change in the European attitude toward defense cooperation can be analyzed as an effect of the Balkan crisis. Despite the sensitiveness of the Balkans for European security, the lack of internal consensus among members on the Balkan crisis and the need to ask for military intervention by the United States made it clear that the cooperation network of the second pillar was not effective in managing crises.

Nevertheless, improving the CFSP by abolishing the requirement that votes be unanimous and adopting qualified majority voting was not inserted in the agenda of the European Union. After the EU's failure to engage in international action in the former Yugoslavia, Kosovo, and Bosnia, the member states preferred to debate the issue of military capability. Their discussion was focused on the need for a common military force. After the September 11 attacks on the

United States made credible the hypothesis that the United States was no longer willing to intervene in a crisis at the periphery of Europe, the establishment of military capabilities to manage crises was perceived as an urgent need to safeguard European security.

The second area to be considered in evaluating the security actorness of the European Union is the nature of its security needs. The EU's security characteristics have changed dramatically since the early 1990s. From Kosovo to Iraq, new dimensions of security emerged, such as soft security, human security, and comprehensive security. These new concerns required security guarantees that cannot ignore military capabilities but that consider highly relevant other security tools, such as dialogue, confidence building, and civilian cooperation in crisis management.

In this context, Europe desires to develop a new security strategy that is multidimensional. In that sense, the European security strategy (ESS) drafted by the High Representative for Common Foreign and Security Policy, Javier Solana, and approved by the European Council in December 2003 is a first attempt to define a common vision of the EU's role in international security environment underpinning the military tools created from 1999 to 2001.

Solana's security strategy starts from the new security situation: the end of a direct military threat to Europe's security, the rise of a new form of inter- and intrastate armed conflict on the European periphery, the diffuse threat posed by international terrorism, and new menaces such as organized crime, illegal immigration, socioeconomic underdevelopment, regional conflicts, lack of democratic institutions and respect for human rights, failed states, failing multilateral institutions, and environmental problems.

Stressing the new multidimensional nature of security, the ESS document emphasizes that, "as a union of 25 states with over 450 million people producing a quarter of the world's Gross National Product (GNP), the European Union is, like it or not, a global actor" that "should be ready to share in the responsibility for global security," while noting at the same time that in recent years "European forces have been deployed abroad more often than in any previous decade." The document focuses on the main threats to international security and identifies a three-way strategy for dealing with the new security environment. First, it suggests "address[ing] the threats" with a strategy of "preemptive engagement" since "conflict prevention and threat prevention cannot start too early." Nevertheless, preemptive engagement is a concept based not on the preventive use of military force but on the preemptive use of "a mixture of instruments," for "none of the new threats is purely military; nor can any be tackled by purely military means." This mixture comprises a menu of different tools, such as the promotion of the rule of law and respect for human rights; trade and development, in combination with "conditionality" (meeting certain specified conditions); and the readiness to act when multilateral commitments are not lived up to or when states place themselves outside international society.[5]

Second, Solana urges the European Union to "build security in our neighborhood," to stress the validity of the collective security approach, and to establish "a ring of well-governed countries . . . with whom we can enjoy close and cooperative relations": the Balkans, Ukraine, Moldova, and Belarus, the countries of the southern Caucasus and the Mediterranean. The third aspect of Solana's strategy is strong and active European support for an effective multilateral system and for "a stronger international society based on the central role of international institutions, well functioning international institutions and a rule-based international order." At the end the ESS calls for European measures aimed at strengthening the decisionmaking mechanisms of the EU and providing it with standby forces in order to create an effective crisis management capacity; contributing to the building of local conflict prevention mechanisms and crisis management capabilities in key regions; reinforcing the verification mechanisms of the non-proliferation treaties; exporting control regimes and establishing a counter-proliferation committee under the UN Security Council to monitor compliance with relevant agreements and resolutions.

Solana's strategy represents the first attempt of the Union to replace the "civilian power approach" with a "multidimensional power" equipped with a set of useful tools for confronting the multidimensional nature of actual threats. In this framework, the establishment of the Area of Freedom, Security, and Justice (AFSJ) is part of a security strategy based on the project of developing regional stability abroad. The issues covered by the AFSJ such as respect for human rights, respect for the rule of law, guarantees of personal freedom, the right of defense, and freedom of movement make the AFSJ one of the more value-based policies of the EU. The process of "externalizing" this policy, either by including JHA objectives in the foreign and security policy agenda or by tackling the "new" security challenges of organized crime, illegal immigration, and terrorism by developing a specific external dimension, is considered a tool for securing the European near abroad..[6] The Mediterranean is the first neighborhood area to be the focus of the new stabilization "mission" of the AFSJ because of its high relevance for EU foreign policy.

AFSJ and the Mediterranean

The relevance of the AFSJ in stabilizing relations between the EU and the Mediterranean countries can be analyzed from two different perspectives: the EU domestic security perspective and the EU foreign policy perspective. The domestic perspective considers internal security to be connected with the security relationships between the EU and all the countries that are perceived as potential sources of instability and threats.

From the foreign policy perspective it is to be noted that, over the past decade, the promotion of the international actorness of the EU has been one of the declared objectives of the European Union. In particular, conflict management has become a growing priority. More emphasis is placed on preventing conflicts through political engagement and constructive dialogue. Military action is seen as a measure of last resort. In this perspective, the inclusion of the AFSJ issues among the variables that influence the structure of the political and security relationships of the Union with non-EU states is the key point for developing an approach based on the convergence of security and democracy and human rights promotion policies.

The Mediterranean area has been one of the EU's main external relations concerns since the establishment of the European Political Cooperation. From the EU domestic security perspective, the Mediterranean is perceived as a source of threat because it is the world's greatest producer and exporter of oil, terrorism, and migration. The main interests of the EU in the region are security interests: access to energy supplies, prevention of mass emigration from the region to the EU, and prevention of international terrorism and drug trafficking.

From the perspective of EU foreign policy, the Mediterranean is one of the hottest areas of global politics and one of the largest sources of conflict. Relations with the Mediterranean region are focused on the prevention of conflict by promoting not only economic development, but also democracy, good governance, judicial reform, and respect for human rights. As one of the main pillars of EU external relations with the Mediterranean, the AFSJ seeks to foster domestic security policy, manage cooperation in combating terrorism, organized crime, and illegal immigration, and play the role of promoter and supporter of respect for human rights, fundamental freedoms, and good governance worldwide, especially with its near neighbors.

In 1995, the EU established a "Mediterranean policy" with the Barcelona Process. It was initiated with the Barcelona Declaration of November 1995, proclaiming a three-pronged Euro-Mediterranean Partnership (EMP) based on (1) political and security partnership; (2) economic and financial partnership; and (3) partnership in social, cultural, and human affairs. The broad aim is to promote peace, stability, and prosperity in the Euro-Mediterranean region where political, economic, and social issues are perceived as common challenges. In 2003 the EU presented the European Neighborhood Policy (ENP), framing EU politics toward the Mediterranean as part of a larger foreign policy strategy to secure its neighboring areas.[7] In both the "old" Mediterranean partnership and the "new" ENP, the issues dealt with by the AFSJ were and are both political and financial.

In the past, the Mediterranean policy was based on three instruments: a regional strategy paper, the Euro-Mediterranean Association Agreements, and the Mediterranean Agreements (MEDA). The first establishes a multilateral strategic framework for allocating resources in the Mediterranean region. The second are political agreements governing bilateral relations between the EU and each Mediterranean country involved in Mediterranean politics. The MEDA program is the financial instrument implementing the Euro-Mediterranean Association Agreements. MEDA has been replaced by the new European Neighborhood and Partnership Instrument (ENPI).

Since 2000 the Mediterranean documents (both regional strategy papers and bilateral Association Agreements and Action Plans) have emphasized issues related to the prevention of terrorism and the management of migration flows that deserve special funding in Justice and Home Affairs (JHA) policies. The regional strategy paper of 2002–06 stated that a Justice and Home Affairs program, covering justice, the fight against drugs, organized crime, and terrorism, and cooperation on the social integration of migrants, migration, and movement of people, deserves special funding of €6 million.

The ENPI regional strategy paper for 2007–13 lists three priority objectives to be implemented at the regional level from 2006 to 2009. The first is the establishment of a common Euro-Mediterranean area of justice, security, and migration cooperation. The JHA program is financed with €15 million from 2007 to 2009. These issues were also at the center of the November 2005 Mediterranean summit. The summit marked the tenth anniversary of the Barcelona Declaration and agreed on a five-year work program to develop a partnership and a code of conduct to combat terrorism.

The strategy documents outline the EU's capability to use political and financial instruments to influence the environment of its Mediterranean partners. Nevertheless, all the scholars involved in the analysis of the Barcelona Process agree that the ENP has failed to promote democracy, good governance, and respect for human rights in the area. Some endogenous factors in Mediterranean politics are to blame, aside from the difficulties related to international politics.

Mediterranean politics reflect a delicate balance between the EU's strategy to promote respect for human rights and fundamental freedoms and the will to promote cooperation on security issues—namely counterterrorism and migration. As Rosa Balfour has noted, to be credible, a human rights promoter should practice what it preaches.[8] In that sense the EU should offer reciprocity that requires it and its member states to address the issues that concern their

Mediterranean partners. Respect for the rights of migrants in the EU, even in the counterterrorism policy and in the migration and asylum policy of the European states, is an example of the lack of EU coherence between practice and theory.

Even though Euro-Med relations are based on negative conditionality (punishment or sanctions when specified conditions are not met), the EU has been unable to translate its policies into action. The ENP introduced a new approach and some new arrangements that may reflect the EU's recognition of shortcomings in its former cooperation initiatives. The EU's weak record in promoting human rights in the Mediterranean could be considered a result of its choice to use conditionality coercively, through negative means. The new approach is based on a differentiation approach. It creates incentives for those Mediterranean partners that are most willing to demonstrate their respect for human rights, fundamental freedoms, and good governance.

Conclusion

While stating the importance of a standard and coherent approach, the European Commission recognizes that there are big differences in the regional commitment to economic cooperation, in countries' administrative and institutional capacities, and in the willingness of its neighbors to participate. The way to pursue the neighborhood policy is no longer through political conditionality, but rather with benchmarks: clear and public definitions of the actions that the EU expects its partners to implement. Both political and economic benchmarks may be used, depending on which targets and reforms are desired. In shaping this new Mediterranean policy, the European Commission has drawn on its experience with the political transitions in new member states and candidate countries. However, since the Mediterranean policy does not foresee the possibility of full EU membership, the differentiation approach should be enriched with incentives to help carry the process forward.

In this sense it would be useful to introduce positive conditionality in the framework of the differentiation approach. There should be incentives for trade cooperation and in some relevant sectoral policies, such as agriculture. As a powerful instrument, the EU should make the conclusion of Association Agreements dependent on progress in human rights. The EU should set clear benchmarks on the progress expected through the use of incentives, on the basis of commonly agreed objectives, and consider the activation of sanctions if those conditions are not met.

In conclusion, the AFSJ in the framework of Euro-Med relations is one of the main instruments for fostering the role of the EU as a democracy promoter and managing the EU's domestic security policy. Even if the AFSJ is part of the EU's Mediterranean policy, the ability of the Euro-Mediterranean Partnership to promote political change will be limited in the authoritarian regimes of the Mediterranean. Even if the Barcelona Process formally rewards progress on democracy and human rights, in practice the EU has never used the conditionality clause to apply sanctions against a country that violates human rights and democratic principles. A European Neighborhood Policy that balances incentives with sanctions could encourage states to further pursue a political reform agenda.

Notes

1. S. Bulmer, "Analyzing European Political Cooperation: The Case for Two-Tier Analysis," in *The Future of European Political Cooperation: Essays on Theory and Practice*, edited by M. Holland (London: Macmillan, 1991).

2. In the EU glossary, the term "pillar" identifies each different area of policy as follows: the first pillar is the group of policies included in the Treaty of the European Community; the second pillar is the Common Foreign and Security Policy; the third pillar is the Justice and Home Affairs policy.

3. I. Manners, "Normative Power Europe: A Contradiction in Terms?" *Journal of Common Market Studies* 40, no. 2 (2002): 235–58; and I. Manners, "Normative Power Europe Reconsidered," *Journal of European Public Policy* 13, no. 2 (2006): 182–99.

4. M. Farrell, "EU External Relations: Exporting the EU Model of Governance?" *European Foreign Affairs Review* 10 (2005): 451–62.

5. "The European Security Strategy," December 12, 2003 (http://consilium.europa.eu/uedocs/cmsUpload/78367.pdf [January 2009]).

6. The term "externalize" in this chapter refers to the international dimension of the AFSJ and the relevance of this policy for the political and security relationships of the Union with third countries. F. Longo, "Il Ruolo della Politica Europea di difesa e di sicurezza comune," in *L'Occidente Diviso. La Politica e le Armi*, edited by A. Colombo (Milan: Egea Bocconi Editore, 2004), pp. 69–101.

7. In addition to the ten Mediterranean partners grouped under the EMP, the ENP partners are: Armenia, Azerbaijan, Belarus, Georgia, Moldova, and Ukraine.

8. R. Balfour and A. Missiroli, "Reassessing the European Neighbourhood Policy," EPC Issue Paper no. 54 (Brussels: European Policy Centre, June 2007).

ALBERTO HEIMLER

5

Competition Policy as a Tool of EU Foreign Policy: Multilateralism, Bilateralism, and Soft Convergence

Signed in Rome on March 25, 1957, the treaty establishing the European Economic Community (hereafter the "Rome Treaty") was designed to achieve a unified market across the six founding member countries. The belief was that after two world wars that originated in Europe, economic integration would be the most effective way to avoid wars and conflicts. A solution briefly discussed after the end of the war was to force Germany to become an agricultural country. The influence of Hans Kelsen, a professor of international law and one of the most important legal scholars of the twentieth century, prevailed and led to the construction of a system that would pursue integration with a combination of political and legal instruments.[1] A free trade zone was not considered to be sufficient. The ambition of the founders of the European Community (EC) was to create an institutional setting governed by the rule of law, so as to constrain member countries and make sure that the objectives of the Rome Treaty would not be set aside. The treaty established the European Commission as its guardian and the European Court of Justice as the supreme court of the unified market.

This articulated institutional setting was necessary because, together with the elimination of tariff and nontariff barriers, the Rome Treaty introduced a system of legal obligations.[2] They were designed to discipline the regulatory power of the member states and accompanied trade liberalization, ensuring that the objective of market integration would be achieved. Competition rules were meant to impede private restraints aimed at segmenting national markets that could prevent the creation of the common market. Additional provisions stopped governments from maintaining or introducing protectionist regulations or from helping firms with anticompetitive state subsidies. No other international organization (or for that matter, any other country) had a similar portfolio of instruments aimed at achieving an integrated single market.

One of the objectives of the Rome Treaty, together with the creation of the internal market, was to maintain fair and undistorted competition in Europe.[3] After the entering into force of the Lisbon Treaty, this may no longer be the case. In fact, in the Lisbon Treaty, competition was downgraded and is no longer explicitly cited among the objectives of the treaty. The change was justified by a desire to create greater clarity and better articulation between objectives and instruments. In fact, there was a political desire to downgrade competition. The process started with the question "What has competition done for Europe?" posed by the newly elected French president, Nicolas Sarkozy.[4] It is true that Protocol 27 on the internal market and competition acknowledges that the internal market includes a system ensuring that competition is not distorted. Politically, the fact that once the Lisbon Treaty enters into force competition will no longer be in article 3 but in Protocol 27 must have a long-term effect. Legally, however, nothing has changed.

Competition has been the driving force of European integration, but it also had a foreign policy dimension, a standard to be imposed on candidate countries and on the world at large. For the new members, competition has been a discipline imposed on them and an important criterion for membership. As for international antitrust, the European Commission first attempted to suggest a multilateral approach to antitrust enforcement, but the international community was not ready. The Commission then contributed to the founding of the international competition network, a soft convergence exercise. This chapter first addresses the role of competition internally and then describes the major initiatives the Commission took internationally.

The Role of Competition in the EC

The development of Europe was driven by market integration objectives, but this did not imply disregarding the usual benefits of competition (lower prices, increased quantities, enhanced technical progress, wider product differentiation, and others). An internal market and competition have been interpreted as being the same thing, as reflected in the wording of Protocol 27 of the Lisbon Treaty.

The important role competition has played in the treaty was not anticipated. Like the internal market, a competitive regime is also hampered by protectionist regulation and by private restrictive conduct. With its provisions and institutions, the Rome Treaty has been the right response to these challenges from a political-economy perspective. As the economist Mancur Olson observed, stable societies with unchanged boundaries are particularly prone to accumulating protectionist provisions and private associations aimed at promoting collusion over time.[5] The political process by which such an evolution takes place is strictly dependent on a concentration of special interests that gain substantially from any restriction of competition. Losers created by such restrictions are scattered across societies. Each loss is minimal, so that, individually, they do not have much incentive to publicly oppose the efforts of special interest organizations. Only by organizing their own coalitions might they be able to counterbalance the activity of the other lobbies. Such coalitions are difficult to bring about, since the interested participants change depending on the issue involved. The organizational cost of coalition formation may be so burdensome as to make the effort not worthwhile. Furthermore, special interests have a dominant interest in one subject, while the rest of the society pursues differentiated goals. This is why the voice of consumers is seldom heard in the political debate, and more important, why special interests receive such great attention.

In Olson's analysis there is a series of events that tend to eliminate existing distributional coalitions, making it easier for competition to operate to the benefit of consumers and of society at large. They include free trade, the opening of markets, changes in the social order, political upheavals, war and destruction. Except for free trade, the problem with these structural shocks is that they are exceptional and cannot be relied upon as a disciplining device. Furthermore, free trade, which at a first glance seems to be a broad instrument, is not in itself neutral with respect to existing protectionist coalitions. For example, a free trade policy would affect only markets open to import competition, but would not exercise much influence on purely local markets. In order to foster and maintain competition in all markets, free trade is not enough.

In a 1993 Australian report on national competition policy Frederick Hilmer suggests that the best way to gain support for competition-oriented legislation is to adopt a constitutional norm of a general nature.[6] Special interests do not have sufficient incentive to organize themselves to contest a rule that does not seem likely to affect them directly. Everyone would like to become at the same time a monopoly seller and a customer of a competitive industry. This is why the incentive to form a global alliance against a constitutional constraint based on the principle of competition is quite weak.

At the time of the signing of the Rome Treaty, the only vocal opponents were manufacturers who in some countries were protected by tariffs as high as 50 percent. They reached consensus by referring to the larger market that the treaty would create and the greater business opportunities associated with it. Every other stakeholder was silent then, but over the course of the years took a stand whenever a specific protectionist rule that affected it was under threat of being eliminated. Given the strong opposition to every liberalization measure the Commission undertook, a more realistic explanation for the lack of opposition by the business community to the signing of the treaty was that it expected the EC to be abstract and distant and generally not able to make much difference.

At the start, EC competition was not widely viewed as an important policy tool. This was probably the main reason governments did not find it necessary to strictly control the enforcement of competition rules. They left their application to the European Commission, not to the Council of Ministers. Probably because the importance of antitrust was not fully appreciated, the Rome Treaty insulated its enforcement from political control and put the decisionmaking of the Commission under the jurisdictional control of the Court of Justice. Consequently, the Court took upon itself the task of becoming the key player for enhancing European integration. It did not limit itself to a narrow view of competition policy. Following the Commission, the Court promoted a very broad interpretation of the rules of the treaty, setting the foundations for the important developments that competition policy would have in the Community, with respect to both liberalization measures and antitrust enforcement.[7]

Developments at the European level have also influenced the evolution of the member states' institutional settings. Fifty years after the signing of the Rome Treaty all member states have a competition law and an institutional structure very similar in substance (and in the followed procedures) to the European one. The imitation of a very successful model was the major driving force of such positive developments. The need for better cooperation within the network of European competition authorities played an additional reinforcing role. In the antitrust field, consensus on substantive provisions and institutional design originated primarily from the deliberate choice of an efficient model. Member states equipped with a competition regime aligned with the European one were able to play a more influential role in European decisionmaking on competition matters, thereby reinforcing the drive to conform to the European model.

Rules of Competition, the New Member States, and the Role of the European Commission

Right after 1989, the European Commission began providing bilateral short-term technical assistance to the former Eastern European countries. The program was costly, but quite ineffective. The Commission relied on outside consultants, most of them university professors with some knowledge of the state apparatus. Since the projects were short term, consultants developed, at best, only a very general understanding of the specific circumstances of the beneficiary.

As a result of these shortcomings the Commission launched the "twinning projects" in 1998. These projects (around 1,000 in number) covered all areas of Community interest and addressed different sectors, including agriculture, customs, police cooperation competition, and state aid. So far, thirteen projects on competition policy have benefited Bulgaria, Croatia, Estonia, Lithuania, Macedonia, Malta, Romania, Poland, and the Czech Republic (some of these countries more than once). Their aim was to provide training for the administration of a beneficiary country with the help of the administration of a member state. Over the long term, the recipient administration would be brought to the "European standard." In practice this meant convergence on "hard" law, which was easier to achieve, and also on soft law–organizational matters and the application of the law. While the bilateral short-term programs used before 1998 were a one-shot exercise and did not provide many benefits outside of the planned events, the relationships developed between sister administrations were long term and quite successful. The provided assistance was tuned to the needs of the beneficiary, and policy suggestions originated from a strict coordination between the beneficiary and member it was paired with. The program's success was due to its demand-driven nature. When a country expressed the need for technical assistance, member states competed to offer the services. A contract was then written with all the details of the project, including the precise results to be achieved, and signed by the administrations of the two countries together with the Commission.

The successful conclusion of these projects was quite important for countries eager to acquire EU membership. It signaled to the Commission that in a specific area that country had reached the European standard and was ready for accession. There was a risk that in some cases demand for technical assistance was driven by a strategic rather than a modernization objective and that the beneficiary would try to comply only formally with the European standard. However, this was a risk that the twinning exercises were well organized to minimize, since the advisory teams, having operated in the accession country for two years or more, had enough information to evaluate the seriousness of the accession country's determination to reform.

In the field of competition the prime objective of these twinning programs was not only to put in place the right substantive provisions, but also to promote an effective application of antitrust law. This meant ensuring that legal provisions were interpreted according to the European standard and in a way that would reduce the possibility of mistakes, either by prohibiting competitive behavior or letting anticompetitive practices go unchecked. Procedural and organizational matters were also important, such as guaranteeing the right of companies accused of an antitrust violation to defend themselves, ensuring transparency, obtaining and maintaining high-quality staff, organizing the authority in a way that would guarantee an efficient decisionmaking process, and making sure that there were enough resources for the most serious cases.

While twinning projects were the major instruments for achieving convergence in accession countries, through partnership and free trade agreements the Commission has encouraged the adoption of the EC competition rules outside the geographic area of its traditional or historical influence. An OECD survey of eighty-six regional agreements incorporating provisions on competition policy identified two broad "families" of such agreements, one associated with the EC and one with North American (NAFTA-style) approaches.[8] While Robert Anderson and Simon Evenett suggest that this characterization is simplistic, it is nonetheless clear that the EC has effectively used its partnerships and other agreements as a vehicle to promote the adoption of EC-style rules internationally.[9] As a result, the rules encountered by EC businesses operating abroad are more likely to be familiar—an important benefit in a globalizing economy.

The WTO Effort to Incorporate Competition in Trade Agreements

In the international community, the number of jurisdictions that have adopted a competition law has increased substantially in recent years. Today there are more than one hundred. The importance of antitrust law enforcement worldwide caused the European Commission to launch a number of initiatives in the mid-1990s. Their objective (not always explicit) was to make sure that all national administrations follow an effect-based approach (that is, adopt a consumer welfare standard) when enforcing their domestic antitrust laws and do not protect their national champions.

Picking up on a proposal by the European Commission, the 1996 World Trade Organization (WTO) intergovernmental conference in Singapore created a working group to study issues relating to the interaction between trade and competition policy raised by members. The mandate of the group was open, but speeches by representatives of the Directorate General for Competition (DG Competition) made it clear that the agenda was ambitious. In a speech delivered in Rome in 1995, Jean-François Pons, the deputy director general of DG Competition at the time, referred to the possibility to negotiate a plurilateral agreement on competition within the WTO.[10] Countries would commit themselves to adopting a minimum set of antitrust rules and be subject to a dispute settlement mechanism. Pons did not go further, but in his intervention in Rome he cited several times the 1995 report "Competition Policy in the New Trade Order: Strengthening International Cooperation and Rules" drafted by a group of three external and five Commission experts.[11] That report made clear reference to the possibility that the proposed plurilateral agreement on competition would also deal with controversies over the way a jurisdiction would decide on specific antitrust cases. This matter would raise a lot of concerns over the following years.

These concerns were not only theoretical or ideological. In a controversy initiated in 1996 and concluded in 1998, the U.S. government accused Japan of impeding access by Kodak films to the Japanese market in favor of Kodak's Japanese rival, Fuji.[12] According to the complaint, Japan failed to enforce Japanese antitrust laws against Fuji and allowed exclusive distribution agreements between Fuji and most retail shops in Japan. The U.S. government further argued that "Japan's entire retail system puts foreign competition at an unfair disadvantage."[13] The report of the dispute settlement panel is based mostly on fairness, equity, and antitrust considerations, and in particular on comparisons between Kodak's market share in Japan and Fuji's market share in the United States. The panel concluded that Japanese rules (including antitrust law) did not discriminate against foreign companies since they applied equally to domestic and foreign firms.

The substance of the matter—that is, whether a nation was in violation of the GATT/WTO rules because it failed to enforce its antitrust laws against private practices that might foreclose its domestic market—never made it into the Kodak-Fuji dispute. If the panel had addressed the antitrust issues, it would have had a number of difficulties because exclusive distribution agreements are considered restrictive by modern antitrust only in fact-specific circumstances. In particular, the WTO panel would have had to prove that Japanese consumers were actually hurt by the disputed practice, evidence that would require a lot of technical expertise to evaluate.

The debates stirred by the Kodak-Fuji case and the discussions within the WTO working group on competition were not able to eliminate all concerns. Thus, in the WTO meeting in Doha in 2001, ministers further clarified the group's mandate:

> 23. . . . we agree that negotiations will take place after the Fifth Session of the Ministerial Conference on the basis of a decision to be taken, by explicit consensus, at that session on modalities of negotiations.
>
> 24. . . . we shall work in cooperation with other relevant intergovernmental organizations, including UNCTAD, and through appropriate regional and bilateral channels, to provide strengthened and adequately resourced assistance to respond to these needs.
>
> 25. In the period until the Fifth Session, further work in the Working Group on the Interaction between Trade and Competition Policy will focus on the clarification of: core principles, including transparency, non-discrimination and procedural fairness, and provisions on hardcore cartels; modalities for voluntary cooperation; and support for progressive reinforcement of competition institutions in developing countries

through capacity building. Full account shall be taken of the needs of developing and least-developed country participants and appropriate flexibility provided to address them.[14]

As Clarke and Evenett note, paragraph 25 of the declaration shifts the focus away from market access issues and demands that the WTO's Working Group on the Interaction between Trade and Competition Policy focus on hard-core cartels, a previously largely ignored area.[15] As Pons had indicated, the original objective of the Commission was directly linked to access issues in domestic antitrust cases, especially restrictions of competition originating from vertical restraints and abusive unilateral conduct. Given the judicial nature of antitrust decisions and the case law approach so common in antitrust, in the course of the discussions within the WTO working group and the OECD it had become clear that such results would have been impossible to achieve.

Even this major reduction in the objectives to be pursued in multilateral negotiations led to no support, and the WTO General Council "July package" of 2004 put the whole subject of trade and competition in limbo. As Anderson and Jenny suggest, the WTO General Council decision leaves open the possibility of resuming this work following the conclusion of the Doha Round.[16]

Already in 1948 the Havana Charter required nations to address restrictive transnational business practices by authorizing the proposed International Trade Organization to "take every possible remedial action" against them.[17] The Havana Charter was never adopted because of the lack of support by the U.S. government. Very similar developments have characterized the more recent attempt to launch negotiations on antitrust matters. Fox argues that "although strongly supported by the EU, the antitrust proposal lacked support from the United States, which feared a transfer of powers to a global bureaucracy and a lowest-common-denominator law, and it was opposed by developing countries because they feared a Trojan horse that would open floodgates to imports and disarm them from protecting their nations' interests."[18]

It can be concluded that this result was a defeat for the Commission. The issue was not so much that the United States was not enthusiastic about the original project. The U.S. criticism was easy to handle, and over the course of the years the objectives accommodated most of the problems that the United States had identified. The major U.S. criticism of the original project of the EU was that antitrust laws were enforced by judges and it would have been contrary to any principle of law to make governments responsible should a judgment (not a legal provision) be considered unsatisfactory by a foreign nation. The 2001 Doha declaration rightly allows only national laws to prohibit hard-core cartels.

What led to the defeat of the trade and competition dossier was the opposition of developing countries. They argued that any negotiation on antitrust would only help the developed world and its multinationals. If the Commission (and member states as well) had started with a much less ambitious but feasible agenda, aimed at helping developing countries in their efforts to introduce a domestic competition law system (as the Doha declaration implicitly acknowledges), there would have been a greater chance for the trade and competition dossier to flourish.

The International Competition Network and the Cooperation Agenda

The lack of consensus in support of a WTO-led negotiation on antitrust did not impede further developments in cooperation on antitrust. In February 2000 the International Competition Policy Advisory Committee (ICPAC) published its final report. It set forth recommendations to competition agencies around the world, designed to enhance merger enforcement and to improve cooperation to address private restraints on competition that impede market access. On the subject of the intersection of trade and competition policy, the Department of Justice press release stated:

> The report recommends further development of bilateral agreements with "positive comity" provisions (which allow a nation affected by anti-competitive practices to request that the nation in which the alleged conduct is occurring initiate an appropriate enforcement action) as well as the use of extraterritorial enforcement tools where necessary. Further, the report argues that new multilateral approaches are also needed, although it does not see the WTO as the natural home for all global competition policy initiatives. Instead, it proposes a new Global Competition Initiative for addressing the broad global competition agenda.[19]

In particular, the report recommended that "the United States explore the scope for collaborations among interested governments and international organizations to create a new venue where government officials, as well as private firms, non-governmental organizations (NGOs), and others can consult on matters of competition law and policy."[20]

Speaking in Brussels at the tenth anniversary of the EC merger regulation in September 2000, Joel Klein, at that time U.S. assistant attorney general for antitrust, took the ICPAC recommendations forward, suggesting that "whatever happens on antitrust at the WTO . . . we should move in the direction of a Global Competition Initiative." More specifically, he suggested that "interested jurisdictions along with the international bodies already thinking about these issues, e.g., the OECD, WTO, UNCTAD, World Bank, and others might establish a joint working group—first for exchanging information and views (e.g., about ongoing and planned activities, common challenges, approaches each are taking to support sound enforcement practices, areas that are most vexing, greatest opportunities for cooperation, etc.) and then for fully exploring a Global Competition Initiative along the lines laid out in the ICPAC report."[21] Speaking at the same conference, Mario Monti, at the time the EC commissioner for competition, endorsed Klein's suggestion to create a new forum addressing the international challenges of antitrust enforcement.

Meeting at the Fordham conference on international antitrust in New York City in October 2001, a group of top antitrust law officials from fourteen jurisdictions created the International Competition Network (ICN).[22] Its objective was to become "an informal network of antitrust agencies from developed and developing countries that will address antitrust enforcement and policy issues of common interest and formulate proposals for procedural and substantive convergence through a results-oriented agenda and structure."[23]

The ICN quickly became the world forum for convergence of antitrust law enforcement practices. In 2008 the ICN had more than 100 members, a sign of its success. Within the ICN there are three working groups whose mandate is to identify best practices in merger control, in the identification of cartel behavior, and in addressing the anticompetitive practices of dominant companies. Furthermore, there is a working group, the Competition Policy Implementation Group, that aims to overcome the challenges developing countries face in building up an efficient antitrust authority and effective enforcement.

The ICN is an organizationally efficient virtual organization that operates without a secretariat. Every report is written by members or by nongovernmental advisers who work for ICN on a voluntary basis. Discussions are held via conference calls, and any agency that so desires may participate. Decisions are made only by members (that is, antitrust authorities) and must be reached by consensus.

Of course, the larger agencies, such as the U.S. Department of Justice, the U.S. Federal Trade Commission, and the European Commission, have more resources than the others and therefore can put more people to work on ICN issues than the other agencies. However, the fact that decisionmaking relies on consensus is an important safeguard that allows even very small agencies to count. And in many instances the veto power of small agencies has been successfully used. As time goes by, more difficult issues will be taken up by the ICN, raising the barriers to entry for small agencies. In this sense, the risk of being excluded from decisionmaking increases. However, the fact that the ICN was created to ensure convergence in antitrust enforcement especially in developing countries will maintain the right incentive on the part of the most developed agencies to engage the smaller ones and to make sure that they actively participate.

Since its establishment in 2001, the ICN has issued more than 100 recommended practices to member agencies on issues such as merger control, cartels, abuse of dominance, banking, telecommunications, and advocacy. These practices are nonbinding, and it is left to governments and agencies to implement them as appropriate. These recommendations have increasingly become the benchmark that agencies and the private sector use to evaluate the appropriateness of laws and policies; and in that respect there can be pressure for agencies to adopt regimes that conform to them. Three recent examples highlight the influence of the recommended practices on merger procedure and review.

The first example is that of South Korea which, in 2007–09, made significant changes to its merger notification thresholds. In doing so, it indicated publicly its desire to bring national law into line with the Recommended Practices for Merger Notification and Review Procedures. Second, India adopted a merger regime in the summer of 2007 that was at odds with one of the most important recommended practices for mergers. Immediately thereafter there was widespread complaint from the private sector, within and outside India, with the majority using the ICN recommendations as a benchmark for their complaints. In February 2009, the Indian agency proposed implementing regulations that would bring the regime into greater conformity with the ICN recommendations. Third, in countries that are just adopting merger control regimes, such as China, the ICN has been cited many times by outside bodies commenting on various proposals. There was considerable interest by the Chinese government in understanding and incorporating the ICN recommendations into their merger control regime.

As these examples show, the influence of the ICN on compliance with recommended practices has been so far limited to rules and regulations. There is no experience with applying ICN recommendations to actual cases. It might be difficult to do so for an organization that relies on consensus decisionmaking.

Is the ICN Sufficient to Guarantee Convergence in International Antitrust? The Microsoft Example

The flurry of cases in various jurisdictions involving the Microsoft Corporation clearly has had repercussions in international markets. Different approaches to the assessment of liability and the imposition of different remedies can have spillover effects: measures adopted in one jurisdiction can affect commercial decisions and/or the welfare of consumers in another jurisdiction.

In many cases, the spillover will be positive in the sense that measures taken to protect competition in one market will also benefit consumers in other markets and will have no adverse effects. Negative spillover can also arise. To take an extreme example, the breaking up of a large international corporation that has abused its dominant position in one jurisdiction might be deemed negative in another jurisdiction in which behavioral remedies for the alleged abuses are considered sufficient. Yet once a corporation is broken up for the sake of one jurisdiction it may well, for practical purposes, be broken up in the rest of the world.

The recent example of remedies implemented by various jurisdictions with respect to practices by Microsoft illustrates the extent of concerns that may arise in transnational abuse or monopolization cases where different jurisdictions impose differing remedies for similar practices. In the course of numerous related cases the competition authorities of the United States and the European Communities have taken different positions toward Microsoft's conduct. A key aspect of the 2004 European Commission decision against the Microsoft Corporation concerned the refusal by Microsoft to provide competitors with information relating to its operating system source code, which allegedly was necessary for the development of competing software products in the group server market.[24] Furthermore, in the same decision the EC Commission required Microsoft to sell two versions of its Windows operating system, one with Windows Media Player and one without it. In reviewing that decision, the Antitrust Division of the U.S. Department of Justice issued the following statement:

> The U.S. experience tells us that the best antitrust remedies eliminate impediments to the healthy functioning of competitive markets without hindering successful competitors or imposing burdens on third parties, which may result from the EC's remedy. . . . Sound antitrust policy must avoid chilling innovation and competition even by "dominant" companies. A contrary approach risks protecting competitors, not competition, in ways that may ultimately harm innovation and the consumers that benefit from it. It is significant that the U.S. district court considered and rejected a . . . remedy [similar to that imposed by the EC] in the U.S. litigation.[25]

In early December 2005, the Fair Trade Commission of Korea made public an order for Microsoft to sell in Korea a version of its Windows operating system that included neither Windows Media Player nor Windows Messenger functionality. It required Microsoft to facilitate consumer downloads of third-party media player and messenger products selected by the commission and prohibited Microsoft from selling in Korea a version of its server software that includes Windows Media Services. In response, the Antitrust Division of the

U.S. Department of Justice issued a press release similar in tone to the one quoted above.[26]

Without taking a position here on the substantive merits of the three jurisdictions' approaches (those of the United States, the EC, and Korea), the foregoing exchanges illustrate clearly the potential for conflict among jurisdictions in addressing transnational abuses of a dominant position (or monopoly). As emphasized by Campbell and coauthors, a minimum requirement to avoid conflicts in such cases is adherence to the well-known principle of national treatment (one of the founding principles of the WTO).[27] The principle broadly requires countries not to impose burdens on foreign producers or products that they do not impose on their own firms or products.[28] However, it is not clear that this, by itself, will answer all possible concerns, as the results of the Kodak-Fuji dispute have already shown, particularly where differences in the remedies imposed by particular jurisdictions result not from discrimination as such but from substantive differences in enforcement philosophies and approaches.

There are no simple solutions to such issues. It may well be that the answers will be found in further international discussions. However, the potential for conflict when abuse of a dominant position affects multiple jurisdictions raises the possibility that a system of international coordination will eventually be needed.

In 2004, Fox reproposed the international antitrust code she contributed to developing back in 1993.[29] She recalled that, together with professor Lawrence Sullivan, she had prepared an alternative proposal.[30] It set out fifteen principles that would discipline the behavior and the powers of the International Antitrust Authority that the group had proposed. Principle 11 is particularly relevant to the issues raised by the Microsoft case:

> 11. Contracting nations should be invited to assert in a proper case, that another nation's enforcement will impair competition, efficiency or technological progress so as to undermine an important national or world interest. If the complaining nation has been unable to obtain satisfaction from the enforcing nation, it should be entitled to seek an order of non-interference from a panel of the International Antitrust Authority. The enforcing nation should be obliged to respect an order of non-interference.[31]

Commenting on principle 11, Fox adds: "The main aspect of competition policy is: people have the freedom to compete and invent. Overbroad prohibitions can undermine competition. If proscribing jurisdictions always win out over authorizing jurisdictions, competition is impaired. If one jurisdiction proscribes conduct that another determines is good for competition, progress, markets and consumers, this constitutes a clash. . . . The proposal is that the IAA (the International Antitrust Authority) resolve the clash . . . by reasoned analysis. . . . Legitimate and respected resolutions will require a panel with expertise, impartiality and credibility."[32]

This is the type of clash that the ICN might avoid through a process of substantive convergence. Should it fail to do so and the problem of diverging decisions becomes serious, the need for a multilateral agreement on competition might well arise again. In this respect the creation of an International Antitrust Authority may then become a workable solution, avoiding the pitfalls of the generalist WTO dispute settlements panels.

Conclusions

In recent policy debates, the role of competition in economic policy has been widely questioned. The uncertainties associated with competition have taken precedence over the opportunities that competition offers. This chapter has described the contribution of competition policy to European prosperity and welfare, which originated with the prominent place of competition in the 1957 Rome Treaty. In particular, competition provisions were needed to facilitate efficient market integration and break down barriers to internal trade. From this perspective, competition policy in the treaty clearly has an international trade origin. Over the fifty years since the treaty entered into force, the role of competition has been greatly enhanced, becoming one of the founding policies of an integrated Europe, extending far beyond the traditional boundaries of international trade. Competition policy and related institutions and expertise have played an important role in the accession of central and eastern European states to the European Community, with technical assistance helping to ensure substantive and procedural convergence.

Competition policy was not only an instrument of European integration, but also a strategy for international relations. The 1948 Havana Charter was never completed and the competition discipline that was to accompany trade liberalization in international markets never materialized. The Commission strongly pushed the trade and competition agenda within the WTO, proposing competition as one of the four new issues over which the 1996 WTO Singapore intergovernmental conference should begin negotiations. The Commission's (not always explicit) strategy was to use international constraints on antitrust enforcement to force market access. The opposition to this project by the United States led to the Doha declaration that greatly restricted the scope for negotiations. In 2004 the whole dossier was put aside, this time because of the opposition of developing countries.

In 2000, understanding that the WTO option was difficult or at best slow in leading to positive results, the Commission accepted the U.S. proposal to create the International Competition Network. This virtual organization became in only a few years a very important and successful center for the creation of convergence on substantive and procedural issues in antitrust enforcement worldwide. The need to adopt more binding trade instruments has not necessarily been eliminated by the ICN. Soft voluntary convergence may indeed eliminate all the problems of contradictory decisions by several jurisdictions, but that is not guaranteed. Should the need come up again, the WTO option will return from the limbo where it has been parked since 2004.

Notes

1. Hans Kelsen, *Peace through Law* (University of North Carolina Press, 1944). Kelsen proposed a very similar system to the one adopted in Europe for the whole world.

2. Nontariff barriers were eliminated with the completion of the internal market in January 1993.

3. Art. 2f of the Rome Treaty and art. 3g of the Maastricht Treaty.

4. For example, at the EC summit in June 2007, Sarkozy reportedly asked, "Competition as an ideology, as a dogma, what has it done for Europe?" See "EU Leaders Strike Deal on 'Reform' Treaty," *Financial Times,* June 22, 2007 (http://search.ft.com/ftArticle?sortBy=gadatearticle&queryText=sarkozy+competition+done+for+Europe+&y=7&aje=true&x=9&id=070622011560&page=3 [October 2007]).

5. Mancur Olson, *The Rise and Decline of Nations: Economic Growth, Stagflation and Social Rigidities* (Yale University Press, 1982).

6. See full report at www.australiancompetitionlaw.org/reports/1993hilmer.html [September 2009].

7. See David Gerber, *Law and Competition in Twentieth-Century Europe: Protecting Prometheus* (Oxford University Press, 1998).

8. Oliver Solano and Andreas Sennekamp, *Competition Provisions in Regional Trading Agreements*, OECD Trade Policy Working Paper 31, 2006.

9. Robert D. Anderson and Simon Evenett, "Incorporating Competition Elements into Regional Trade Agreements: Characterization and Empirical Analysis," 2006 (www.evenett.com/working/CompPrincInRTAs.pdf [September 2008]).

10. Jean-François Pons, *Règles, Institutions et Relations internationales: Politique de concurrence et développement des échanges: pour un renforcement significatif de la coopération*, Rome, November 20–21, 1995.

11. The three external experts were Ulrich Immenga, Fréderic Jenny, and Ernst-Ulrich Petersmann. The Commission experts were Claus-Dieter Ehlermann, Roderick Abbott, François Lamoureux, Jean-François Marchipont, and Alexis Jacquemin.

12. See World Trade Organization, "Japan—Measures Affecting Consumer Photographic Film and Paper," Dispute Settlement (www.wto.org/english/tratop_e/dispu_e/cases_e/ds44_e.htm [September 27, 2008]).

13. Emily Nelson, "Presentation of Data in Kodak's Case against Japan and Fuji Delayed by U.S.," *Wall Street Journal*, September 20, 1996, Sec. B, p. 4.

14. The Doha 2001 Ministerial Declaration, WT/MIN(01)/DEC/1 (http://www.wto.org/english/thewto_e/minist_e/min01_e/mindecl_e.htm [February 2009]).

15. J. L. Clarke and S. J. Evenett, "A Multilateral Framework for Competition Policy?" in *The Singapore Issues and the World Trading System: The Road to Cancun and Beyond* edited by State Secretariat of Economic Affairs and Simon Evenett (World Trade Institute, June 2003).

16. See R. D. Anderson and F. Jenny, "Competition Policy, Economic Development and the Possible Role of a Multilateral Framework on Competition Policy: Insights from the WTO Working Group on Trade and Competition Policy," in *Competition Policy in East Asia*, edited by Erlinda Medalia (London: Routledge, 2005).

17. See Havana Charter for an International Trade Organization, chap. 13 (www.worldtradelaw.net/misc/havana.pdf [September 2008]).

18. E. Fox, "The WTO's First Antitrust Case—*Mexican Telecom*: A Sleeping Victory for Trade and Competition," *Journal of International Economic Law* 9, no. 2 (2006): 271–92.

19. See the Department of Justice press release (http://www.usdoj.gov/atr/icpac/4272.htm [September 2008]).

20. See ICPAC report, p. 282 (www.usdoj.gov/atr/icpac/finalreport.htm [September 2008]).

21. See Joel Klein, "Time for a Global Competition Initiative?" talk at the EC Merger Control 10th Anniversary Conference Brussels, Belgium, 2000 (www.usdoj.gov/atr/public/speeches/6486.htm [September 2008]).

22. The founding authorities of the ICN were from Australia, Canada, the European Union, France, Germany, Israel, Italy, Japan, Korea, Mexico, South Africa, the United Kingdom, the United States, and Zambia.

23. See the "Memorandum on the Establishment and Operation of the International Competition Network" (www.internationalcompetitionnetwork.org/index.php/en/about-icn/operational-framework [September 2008]).

24. European Commission Case No COMP/37.792 Microsoft of 24.3.2004.

25. U.S. Department of Justice, press release, March 24, 2004.

26. "The Antitrust Division believes that Korea's remedy goes beyond what is necessary or appropriate to protect consumers, as it requires the removal of products that consumers may prefer. The Division continues to believe that imposing 'code removal' remedies that strip out functionality can ultimately harm innovation and the consumers that benefit from it. We had previously consulted with the Commission on its Microsoft case and encouraged the Commission to develop a balanced resolution that addressed its concerns without imposing unnecessary restrictions. Sound antitrust policy should protect competition, not competitors, and must avoid chilling innovation and competition even by 'dominant' companies." (U.S. Department of Justice, July 12, 2005).

27. See A. N. Campbell, J. W. Rowley, and M. J. Trebilcock, "The Role of Monopoly Laws in the International Trading System," *Proceedings of the Symposium on Competition Policy in a Global Economy* (Taipei: Pacific Economic Cooperation Council, April 1995), pp. 5–51. Revised version published in *International Trade Law and Regulation* 1 (1995): 167–80.

28. The application of the principle of national treatment in the WTO varies in the relevant agreements. See "The Fundamental WTO Principles of Transparency and Non-discrimination" (WT/WGTCP/W/118).

29. International Antitrust Code Working Group, Draft International Antitrust Code as a GATT-MTO-Plurilateral Trade Agreement (published on July 10, 1993), BNA Antitrust & Trade Regulation Report, Special Supplement 64, no. 1628 (August 19, 1993).

30. E. Fox, "The Alternative DIAC (Draft International Antitrust Code) in Light of the Twenty-First Century," *Festschrift für Ulrich Immenga* (Munich: Verlag C. H. Beck, 2004), pp. 149–56.

31. Ibid., p. 154.

32. Ibid.

TOM CASIER

6

The European Neighborhood Policy:
Assessing the EU's Policy toward the Region

On the eve of eastern enlargement in 2004, the European Union was confronted with a double fear. On the one hand, enlargement brought a security challenge, with the EU closer to more unstable areas. On the other, the big enlargement created a major paradox. While it included ten former communist countries in the process of European integration, it risked creating new dividing lines by leaving others out. Enlargement would inevitably affect trade relations or human mobility between the new member states and their neighbors. The danger was that of creating a two-speed Europe, with a firmly integrated, stable, and affluent Europe in the West and a less stable, much poorer, and possibly less democratic Europe in the East. This possibility ran counter to the founding commitments of European integration.

Driven by concerns about a two-speed Europe and by fears of instability, several new policies toward the eastern neighbors were proposed.[1] In May 2002 the British foreign secretary Jack Straw sent a letter to the Spanish Presidency of the European Council, in which he proposed new policies toward Ukraine, Moldova, and Belarus that would offer them incentives to reform. Straw's rationale was: "We must not create a new dividing line of 'haves and have not's on the continent."[2] This gave rise to a debate on how a security vacuum and new dividing lines could be avoided by projecting stability and prosperity in the wider Europe.

The EU's new regional foreign policy was born when EU High Representative Javier Solana and European Commission member Chris Patten launched the "Wider Europe" initiative in August 2002. The initiative was developed into a full-fledged policy, first renamed the Neighborhood Policy, then the European Neighborhood Policy (ENP).[3] The European Commission published its strategy paper on the topic in May 2004.[4] While Straw's original concerns were about the countries of eastern Europe, the policy was extended to the countries of the Mediterranean. This was done mainly for internal political reasons, as the southern countries of the EU were afraid that too much attention would go to the East.

This chapter looks at the ENP as a specific form of regional foreign policy. The first part of the chapter describes the nature of the ENP. The analysis departs from the peculiar position of the EU in international relations as an actor with a strong unintended impact on its neighborhood inter alia, in terms of its economic power and the attraction it exerts. The ENP can therefore be regarded as a specific type of foreign policy that tries to manage this unintended impact. Against this background the paper looks at the core strategic objectives of the ENP: creating stability and avoiding new dividing lines. The ENP signifies a shift in the EU's strategy to create stability across its borders by extending the Union, to a strategy of actively exporting its rules and norms while excluding the option of membership.

The second part attempts to explain how the ENP functions and what determines success or failure in the transfer of the EU's rules, norms, and practices to the target countries. The chapter concludes that the ENP is fundamentally different from the enlargement process. Conditionality, or offering rewards to non-EU countries for meeting certain specified requirements, is not the key to understanding the variation in the adoption of EU rules. The EU's regional foreign policy needs to be understood as a complex social learning process, which is highly determined by interplay between the domestic agenda in the target country and the subjective perception of potential accession to the EU, even if this is formally excluded under the ENP.

The Nature of the European Neighborhood Policy: (Un)like Enlargement Policy

The ENP is essentially a regional foreign policy with the aim of developing "privileged relations" with the new neighbors of the enlarged EU, without giving them the prospect of accession. As defined in the European Commission's strategy paper of May 2004: "The objective of the ENP is to share the benefits of the EU's 2004 enlargement with neighboring countries in strengthening stability, security and well-being for all concerned. It is designed to prevent the emergence of new dividing lines between the enlarged EU and its neighbors and to offer them the chance to participate in various EU activities, through greater political, security, economic and cultural co-operation."[5]

The interpretation of "privileged relations" in initial statements was quite far-reaching. The Commission's president, Romano Prodi, said that the ENP countries would share "everything but the institutions."[6] Early documents referred to participation in the four freedoms of movement: of goods, persons, services, and capital. Later, strong commitment was replaced by vague and conditional references to visa facilitation.[7] In practice, most of the benefits awarded so far consist of assistance and financial support (through the ENP instrument), preferential trade measures, and participation in certain Community programs.

There are sixteen ENP target countries, which can be roughly divided into four geographic areas: the southern Mediterranean (Morocco, Algeria, Tunisia, Libya, Egypt), the eastern Mediterranean (Jordan, Israel, Lebanon, the Palestinian Territory, Syria), eastern Europe (Moldova, Ukraine, and Belarus), and, since 2004, the southern Caucasus (Armenia, Georgia, Azerbaijan). In the case of Libya full participation is subject to the acceptance of the commitments following from the Barcelona process. As to Syria, the ENP can only be activated upon the ratification of the Association Agreement.[8] Belarus will benefit from the ENP only once it has established a democratic form of government. The western Balkan states are not included because they have the prospect of EU membership at some point in the future. For these countries the EU has developed the Stabilization and Association Process.

Russia, although originally included in the blueprints, is not part of the ENP. Moscow has always been lukewarm to the initiative, which it considered to be too EU-centric. Outside the ENP framework the Russian Federation has been granted special status as a "key partner of the EU."[9] The strategy paper recognizes that "Russia and the enlarged European Union form part of each other's neighborhood," thus acknowledging the equivalence of both.[10] By acknowledging explicitly that the EU and Russia belong to *each other's* neighborhood, Russia is recognized as a fully equal partner of the EU.[11] It needs to be recognized that the relationship between the EU and Russia is of a fundamentally different nature. This is, among other things, the result of the size of the country, its ambitions to play a prominent international role, and the fact that its economy is not heavily dependent on the EU, unlike the economies of most ENP countries. Of the EU's neighboring states, Russia is the only country with whom the EU has a trade deficit (65 billion euros in 2006).[12]

At first glance, the ENP seems to be modeled on the enlargement policy of the EU. Both policies are based on agreements, negotiations, and monitoring. In both policies the EU stipulates conditions for the partner states and provides financial and other incentives. The instruments used have different names but look highly similar. For the ENP they include country reports, prepared by the European Commission, which assess the political, institutional, and economic situation in a country and, at the next stage, tailor-made ENP Action Plans set up for each country. They outline the priorities and serve as a point of reference for the next three to five years. The Action Plans are proposed by the European Commission, negotiated with the target country, and agreed by both. They define an agenda of political, social, and economic reforms in the target country and provide incentives for successful implementation (for example, better access to the internal market, increased assistance, participation in European programs). Although in principle they are bilateral, they mainly reflect the strong asymmetry that characterizes relations between the EU and its neighbors. Action Plans were agreed in 2005 with Israel, Jordan, Moldova, Morocco, the Palestinian Authority, Tunisia, and Ukraine; in 2006 with Armenia, Azerbaijan, and Georgia; and in 2007 with Egypt and Lebanon. There is no Action Plan yet for Algeria. The implementation of reforms is monitored through subcommittees and is evaluated in the EU's Progress Reports.

The neighborhood and enlargement policies also share a structural approach. In contrast to conventional foreign policy, the goal of "structural foreign policy" is to create a favorable or stable external environment by socializing third countries to one's way of doing things.[13] In contrast to a conventional, possession- and goal-oriented foreign policy, the timeframe is long term. The EU, in other words, shapes its immediate external environment in its own image. It is an explicit attempt to structure the immediate neighborhood along the dominant principles and norms of the EU.

Despite appearances, the ENP differs from the enlargement policy in a few fundamental ways. First and most obvious, it *excludes membership*. Unlike enlargement, the ENP does not envision a transition from EU external governance to full integration. Instead it aims at reshaping the neighboring countries in its own image without leaving the door open for membership. Second, the ENP is a *framework policy*. It is based on a number of common principles, but consists of differentiated policies toward the different target states. The "one size fits all" approach of the accession process has been replaced by a tailored approach for each country. Considering the diversity of the countries involved, this is not surprising. Third, the ENP is a *dynamic policy*. It provides a flexible framework for developing privileged relations with the new neighbors. Not only do the relations develop at different speeds, depending on the progress made, but the outcome of the process itself is undetermined. Finally, the ENP *functions in a fundamentally different way* from enlargement. The success or failure of rule transfer from the EU to the ENP countries cannot be explained in terms of conditionality.

Analytical Framework: The ENP as a Policy to Mitigate Unintended Side Effects

All players on the international scene have an impact on their environment. Each country affects other countries, first of course its immediate neighbors. It creates certain opportunities and certain constraints. Part of this impact is unintentional, the natural result of a country's geopolitical position, its domestic policies, its economic capabilities, its ideological attractiveness, and other factors. But there is also a deliberate, intentional impact. A country develops a proactive foreign policy through which it tries to achieve certain objectives.

Intended and unintended impacts are strongly related. A foreign policy will seek to structure the unintended impact in such a way as to be used to achieve certain objectives. Theoretically, this may take two forms. Either a foreign policy will try to reinforce and even exploit the existing impact or it will seek to reduce certain negative unintended effects.

What makes the EU a unique actor on the international scene is first the balance between its intended impact (or proactive foreign policy) and its unintended impact. As an economic giant, the EU has a considerable impact, not least on its direct neighbors. Many ENP countries export around 30 percent of their goods to the EU, with peaks over 60 percent, as in the case of Morocco.[14] They find themselves in a strong position of dependence, which leaves them little choice but to adapt to certain EU standards and practices. Moreover, the EU enjoys a high level of legitimacy in wider Europe and exerts a magnetic force or "gravitational pull" on its direct neighbors.[15] The intended, structured impact of the EU, however, is more limited than that of a classic state. The Common Foreign and Security Policy (CFSP) is relatively young and heavily constrained by institutional characteristics, not least its predominantly intergovernmental nature. Therefore one can state that the EU is characterized by a large gap between its relatively limited intended impact and its (regionally) considerable unintended impact.

A second contested issue is the nature of the relation between intended and unintended impact. Is the way in which EU foreign policy deals with the Union's own unintended impact fundamentally different from that of other actors, such as states? In the simplest terms, the relation may take different forms: the foreign policy may try to reinforce the existing unintended impact, or conversely may try to mitigate the negative effects thereof.

It is in particular in this respect that the ENP forms an interesting case. As one of its central objectives is to prevent new dividing lines in Europe that could result from the 2004 and 2007 enlargements, the ENP has a founding commitment to mitigate the negative consequences of the enlarged EU. The question investigated below is whether the EU puts relatively more emphasis on mitigating its (negative) impact for the benefit of its neighbors than on reinforcing it.

Balancing Two Structural Objectives

In order to answer this question, we need to look at the two core strategic objectives of the ENP: creating regional stability and preventing new dividing lines.

Creating Stability

Romano Prodi, the former president of the European Commission, summarized the core objectives of the ENP as creating "a ring of friends" around the Union.[16] In the European security strategy "building security in our neighborhood" is declared to be a strategic priority.[17] The ENP would allow neighboring countries that had made specified progress to share the benefits of European integration without including them in the European Union. This is a fundamental shift in strategy. On one hand, the EU confirms its founding commitment to create stability and conditions for structural peace. On the other, it changes the method for reaching this objective. While in the enlargement process stability is created by extending the EU, the ENP seeks to create stability by exporting the rules, practices, and norms of the EU to its new neighbors. It attempts to project the EU's model of stability and prosperity rather than open it to new members. The goal is to escape the problem that, confronted with "enlargement fatigue," the EU would feel morally compelled to keep on enlarging in order to create stability.[18]

The shift in the EU's policy of stability creation from extending the organization to exporting its norms and practices is a fundamental one. Although the outcomes are far from certain, the strategic shift implies a fundamental change in both the political instrument of conditionality and the mechanisms of social learning.

Preventing New Dividing Lines

The second core objective of the ENP was to "prevent the emergence of new dividing lines between the enlarged EU and its neighbors."[19] Enlargement would inevitably produce certain negative effects for the neighboring countries, especially in the East. Accession, for example, implies that the EU's external tariffs apply to trade between the neighboring countries and the new member states. Moreover, as the new member states had to accept the Schengen *acquis*, border crossing became subject to often lengthy and expensive visa procedures, thus affecting people's mobility and cross-border trade.[20] President Leonid Kuchma of Ukraine warned that Schengen would replace the "old Iron Curtain with a different, more humane but no less dangerous Paper Curtain."[21] This reveals a crucial paradox of the enlargement process. While the process of European integration makes borders increasingly irrelevant, enlargement creates new external borders, which are more strongly secured and more difficult to cross than before. Ruben Zaiotti has described this as the "gated community syndrome."[22]

Rephrasing the quotes above, the ENP's goal was to prevent a new curtain from descending over Europe, this time along the borders of the European Union. It had to mitigate the negative, unintended impact of enlargement on the neighboring states. To what extent does the ENP agenda reflect this goal? Surprisingly little research has been done to answer this question.[23] A study of the Action Plans for Ukraine, Moldova, and Morocco indicates that they mainly reflect the EU agenda.[24] Although these documents are formally bilateral, they appear to be strongly EU-centric. The priorities listed in the Action Plans mainly represent the concerns of the European Union. Most of the objectives listed aim at approximating the legal and institutional framework of the ENP target countries to that of the European Union.

The demands put forward by the neighboring countries themselves are largely absent, and the EU makes few concrete commitments. The ENP target countries would mainly like to gain more access to the Single European Market and be free to travel across borders without a visa. Neither of those goals is part of the Action Plans. However, the reforms proposed in the European Commission's 2007 "Communication" on the ENP reflect some of the major concerns of the neighboring states: greater political commitment to economic integration and market access; the facilitation of legitimate short-term travel, as well as more ambitious longer-term developments in managed migration; further engagement with the ENP partners in tackling frozen conflicts and using the full range of instruments at the EU's disposal to stabilize conflict and post-conflict areas; intensified EU support for partner countries' sectoral reforms in areas such as energy, climate change, fisheries, transport, maritime policy, research, information society, education, employment, and social policy.[25]

These proposals for reforming the ENP may indicate a willingness to mitigate the negative side effects of enlargement on the part of the European Commission. However, they are unlikely to win much support from the member states, especially a more relaxed visa policy. Even if the Commission is committed to softening the negative impact of enlargement, the member states will play a crucial role in taking concrete decisions that lead there. The member states are guided by very different motivations, be it national interest or "irrational" support for a particular neighboring state.

In sum, the ENP reflects the asymmetric relations between the EU and its partner states. Even if the process is formally bilateral, in terms of both agenda-setting and results achieved, the EU is the dominant power. This may seem logical, taking into account the considerable dependence of most member states on the EU. It does, however, risk contradicting one of the central objectives of the ENP, namely avoiding new dividing lines in Europe. The mobility of persons, access to the single market, and the solution of frozen conflicts in particular are EU neighborhood demands that go largely unheard. Though further research is needed, currently the ENP process seems to fall short in mitigating the negative impact of enlargement.

Exporting Stability: What Determines Success and Failure?

There is a large degree of variation in the achievements of the ENP. Which, then, are the factors that account for the variation? When is the EU successful in exporting its rules, norms, and practices to the target countries? Studies of enlargement have suggested that conditionality is important in triggering reforms in the candidate member states: that the reward of membership is a strong incentive for a country to implement reforms and to integrate the *acquis* into its national system. Does the same incentive also facilitate rule transfer to the ENP countries?

Explaining the ENP through Conditionality?

In their influential study of EU enlargement, Frank Schimmelfennig and Ulrich Sedelmeier present three models of external governance that explain the effectiveness of rule transfer from the EU to the candidate member states.[26] They define rule transfer as "the adoption of EU rules in non-member states, i.e. their institutionalization at the domestic level."[27] The authors conclude that the variation in the effectiveness of rule transfer in the accession process is best explained by the "external incentives model." This is a rationalist bargaining model that starts from the assumption that the actors involved are rational utility-maximizers who will be led by cost-benefit calculations. EU conditionality, a strategy based on "reinforcement by reward," affects the domestic equilibrium and may change the cost-benefit balance. In an enlargement context, the authors expect that a candidate member state "adopts EU rules if the benefits of EU rewards exceed the domestic adoption costs." This cost-benefit calculation is determined by four factors: the determinacy of conditions, the size and speed of rewards, the credibility of threats and promises, and the size of adoption costs.[28]

In the same study the authors present two alternative models of EU external governance. One is the "social learning model." This is a constructivist approach, assuming that candidate member states adopt the EU rules if they consider them appropriate or legitimate. The other is the "lesson-drawing model," in which "domestic dissatisfaction with the *status quo*" is the ground for approximating domestic legislation to the EU legislation. Candidate states adopt EU rules because they expect "these rules to solve domestic policy problems effectively."[29]

The conditionality of the ENP is outlined in the formulation of the Action Plans.[30] The EU-Morocco Action Plan states that "the rate of progress on this ambitious plan will depend on the efforts and concrete achievements in meeting jointly agreed priorities."[31] Considering that, according to Schimmelfennig and Sedelmeier, the external incentives model has the highest explanatory value for rule transfer from the EU to the candidate member states, we could expect the model to have a high explanatory value for the ENP as well.

However, when we apply the external incentives model to the ENP, there are a number of striking differences. While enlargement was characterized by clear and explicit conditionality, this is less evident in the case of the ENP. The comparison made here is based on a study of the Action Plans for Ukraine, Moldova, and Morocco.

When looking at the conditions side, differences between enlargement policy and the ENP do not at first seem to be tremendous. The Action Plans contain a long list of conditions that partner countries have to fulfill, even more detailed than the list required for accession partnership. What is lacking in the ENP, however, is the explicit broader framework in which macro-conditions were set for accession. Since the European Council in Copenhagen in 1993, a country that wants to qualify for membership needs to fulfill three sets of conditions, widely known as the "Copenhagen criteria."

Some of the Copenhagen criteria are reflected to different degrees in the ENP. The Action Plans for Ukraine and Moldova refer to the strengthening of "the stability and effectiveness of institutions guaranteeing democracy and the rule of law."[32] In the case of Morocco there is only a reference to "pursuing legislative reform and applying international human rights provisions."[33] This omits the condition of democracy. This may be explained both on the basis of the "joint ownership" of the Action Plans and by fear on the EU's side that too much insistence on democratization might lead to instability in some Mediterranean countries. In all Action Plans we find partial references to the second Copenhagen criterion and the establishment of a competitive market economy, mainly in terms of liberalization of the market and improving the investment climate. The third Copenhagen criterion, the obligations of membership, obviously does not feature in the ENP Action Plans. However, most of the technical conditions in the Action Plans are about the approximation of rules to those of the EU. They therefore reflect a selective adoption of the *acquis communautaire*.

On the rewards side, the difference is striking. First, the rewards promised by the ENP are vague. While in the case of enlargement membership was the big bonus, the rewards under the ENP are less clear. The phrase saying that the ENP would lead to "privileged relations" between the EU and its new neighbors is revealing. What exactly these privileged relations entail is not clear. The formulations in the Action Plans do little to clarify this. References are made to "the perspective of moving beyond cooperation to a significant degree of integration" and to "a stake in the EU's Internal Market."[34]

Moreover, the rewards are uncertain. While the conditions imposed on the partner country tend to be specific and clear, the rewards are formulated in a very careful and open-ended way. A good example is visa facilitation, a crucial demand by the partner countries. The potential reward is only "a constructive dialogue on visa facilitation between the EU and Ukraine, with a view to preparing for future negotiations on a visa facilitation agreement."[35] The EU clearly does not commit itself. Moreover, the reward is made dependent on the signing of a readmission agreement. As the ENP is a dynamic policy without agreement on its finality, the rewards are subject to case-by-case decisions by the member states.[36]

Finally, the link between conditions and rewards is very unclear. From the official documents, it is unclear which conditions need to be fulfilled in order to obtain a specific reward. Overall the Action Plans read like a wish list of the EU, with the EU amply stipulating detailed conditions with only a limited number of vague and uncertain rewards in return.

This may lead us to think that the EU is tougher in applying conditionality to the ENP states than it was toward the candidates for EU membership. However, as Gwendolyn Sasse argues, the ENP conditionality is weaker and more vague on both sides. The ENP conditions are easier to bypass than those required for accession, and the rewards promised are vague and uncertain. "Rather than presenting the ENP as a case of weak incentives and high adoption costs, it should be thought of as being vaguely defined on the side of the incentives as well as the adoption costs." She speaks in this respect of "conditionality-lite" as a form of "conditionality without clear commitments and rewards."[37]

We may take this one step further and wonder to what extent it makes any sense to speak of conditionality in the case of the ENP. The eastern enlargement of the EU was mainly a collective process in which all member states agreed on the rules of the game: the conditions, rewards, incentives, and process. Drawing on a comparison made by a Commission official, conditionality under enlargement involved one single exam for all, with identical criteria (the Copenhagen criteria) and the same bonus if successful (accession). The preparation for the exam (the accession process) was a collective process.[38]

The ENP does not apply one single exam, but different exams with different criteria and different rewards. As a result, it is a much more political process, driven less by collective considerations at the EU level than by the preferences of different member states.[39]

Differentiation within the neighborhood policy may thus undermine conditionality, which can function well only if it is applied in a fairly consistent way: "If international organizations were perceived to subordinate conditionality to other political, strategic or economic considerations, the target state might either hope to receive the benefits without fulfilling the conditions or conclude that it will not receive the rewards in any case."[40]

Before dismissing conditionality altogether we need to make a distinction between different levels of conditionality. Strict political conditionality at the macro level (that is, conditionality involving the big principles of democracy, rule of law, or a liberal market) is largely absent from the ENP, whereas it played a prominent role in setting the benchmarks for accession. At the micro level, when it comes to negotiating more technical and specific aspects of approximating rules to the EU standards or getting specific concessions, conditionality does play a role. A good example is the Commission's decision to recommend to the member states granting autonomous trade preferences to Moldova. This was done on the basis of clear conditions, namely that Moldova would reform its customs practices and guarantee respect for the rules of origin (avoid allowing goods subject to preferential trade measures from other destinations to enter the EU via Moldova). In the event of considerable fraud, Moldova would lose the autonomous trade preferences.[41]

To summarize, the issue is not so much that the ENP is characterized by conditionality, but rather that conditionality is lacking altogether at the macro level: there are no major political rewards for fulfilling major political conditions. At the micro level conditionality does play a role because of specific technical issues.

Understanding the ENP Differently

The absence of strict political macro-conditionality suggests that the external incentives model has limited explanatory value for the ENP: "The attempt to capture the effects of the ENP based on a model informed by positivist notions of causality is . . . inappropriate."[42]

My interviews with officials from the European Commission indicate that they consider the domestic agenda in the target country to be the most important factor for success or failure of rule transfer under the ENP. Of central importance is whether a country realizes the utility of reforms. The Action Plans may then serve as an agenda for domestic reforms, or at least a menu for choice, as adoption of the EU rules is often selective. It should be noted that this does not necessarily mean that the ruling elite (which in many ENP countries has not been democratically elected) accepts the need for reforms. Public opinion or opposition may use the Action Plan as a platform to mobilize against domestic veto players, actors who are powerful enough to block certain reforms.[43] This suggests that the "alternative" models of Schimmelfennig and Sedelmeier have a higher explanatory value for the ENP: rule transfer appears to be highly determined by lesson-drawing and social learning.[44]

Another important but neglected factor in understanding the variation in rule transfer from the EU to its partner countries is of a subjective nature. One of the countries with the most apparent achievements is Ukraine. After the Orange Revolution protesting the official results of the 2004 Ukrainian presidential elections, Ukraine received extensive support from the EU for political reasons, rather than as a reward for its compliance with the Action Plan. In March 2007 the EU and Ukraine opened negotiations on a New Enhanced Agreement. After the Orange Revolution, the new regime revived the older "European choice" of Ukraine.[45] The EU political support for these pro-European choices triggered hopes in Ukraine that the ENP would be a first step in the direction of membership.

Statements by politicians and policymakers at that time reinforced those hopes. External Relations Commissioner Benita Ferrero-Waldner appeared to leave the door ajar for membership in stating: "The question of Ukrainian entry into the EU is not on the agenda. But it is clear we are not closing any doors."[46] Political support from within the EU for Ukraine's new regime thus triggered hopes that it could move closer to the target of membership and increased the willingness in Ukraine to comply with the Action Plan. The prospect of accession over the mid- or longer term is another factor in whether rule transfer under the ENP is successful. Political support, the domestic agenda, political preferences, and dependency are parts of an ongoing constitutive process of interaction between the EU (and its member states) and the ENP partner countries.

Thus the EU's gravitational pull is another example of "unintended impact" (as discussed earlier). It is not simply a function of "objective" factors, such as economic dependence, but also a matter of subjective factors, such as perception. It can be argued that the perception of potential accession to the EU is very important in explaining selective rule transfer. Table 6-1 compares enlargement and the ENP in terms of subjective attraction and conditionality.

The prospect of accession sets the eastern European countries apart from the other ENP countries, where membership is not an issue.[47] Although the ENP does not offer a formal prospect of EU membership, eastern European countries hope that a successful ENP process will eventually lead to an accession process. Several scholars share the expectation that successful reform under the ENP will increase pressure to open the door for the accession of the eastern European countries.[48]

An ENP country may actively seek legitimacy with the EU by adopting the rules stipulated in the Action Plans, hoping to increase its chance for membership in the longer term. Rule adoption and institutional change as the result of an active quest for legitimacy with a dominant organization, such as the EU, have been insufficiently researched in the study of the EU's relations with its neighbors. In an innovative study, Lien Verpoest uses the theory of institutional isomorphism developed by Walter Powell and Paul DiMaggio to explain the variation in institutional change in Russia, Belarus, and Ukraine.[49] In Ukraine,

Table 6-1. *The Effects of Enlargement Policy and the European Neighborhood Policy on the Adoption of Changes in Non-EU Member States*

Policy	Unintended impact	Intended impact
Enlargement—a strategy to *extend* the model of democracy and stability	Strong "gravitational pull" because of the prospect of accession to the EU over the short term	Strong political conditionality (Copenhagen criteria)
European Neighborhood Policy (ENP)—a strategy to *export* democracy and stability	"Gravitational pull" dependent on the prospect of accession to the EU over the medium term	Weaker and more ambiguous conditionality: (1) little political macro-condition-ality; (2) technical micro-conditionality

Source: Author's summary.

Verpoest considers the 2004 enlargement and the Orange Revolution as a critical juncture: "Initially applauded by the European institutions, Ukraine felt encouraged; this gave a new impetus to its European membership drive. Yushchenko quickly acted upon this by appointing a Deputy Prime Minister for European Integration, and developing an extensive institutional support structure for Ukraine's European bid."[50] Verpoest says that at this point Ukraine shifted from "mimetic isomorphism" to "normative isomorphism" toward the European Union.[51] In the first case, Ukraine tried to gain legitimacy by (selectively) imitating EU institutions. Mimetic isomorphism is rooted in uncertainty: as a country in transition, Ukraine modeled itself (partly) after the EU as a response to uncertainty. For Powell and DiMaggio "the motivation for isomorphism is legitimacy rather than efficiency."[52] After the revolution, "normative isomorphism" became dominant. In this case the modeling is mainly the result of the professionalization that follows from the institutional structures of cooperation set up between the EU and Ukraine through which new models diffuse rapidly.[53]

A better understanding of EU external governance may be furthered by studying how perception in non-EU countries affects their quest for EU membership. Such studies may also prevent the analysis of successful rule transfer from being considered either rationalist and causal or constructivist and constitutive. Incentives may play an important role in rule transfer, but they are always perceived within a context that affects their interpretation and meaning.[54]

It is unlikely that the Eastern Partnership, launched in May 2009, will fundamentally change the dynamics of active legitimacy seeking. Its multilateral aspect may even reinforce it.

Conclusion

The first part of this chapter analyzes the nature of the ENP as a policy offering privileged relations with the neighbors of the enlarged EU but without the prospect of membership. Through the ENP the EU intended to mitigate the negative side effects of its considerable unintended impact on its direct neighbors. In this policy the EU has to find an uneasy balance between the aim of creating a stable and secure environment and preventing new dividing lines in Europe by partially integrating its neighbors. By excluding membership, the EU has made a substantial strategic shift from creating stability through extending the Union to creating stability by exporting the EU model. As a result of the separation of stability and integration in the EU's new regional strategy, we can expect the ENP to follow a different logic from enlargement.

The second part highlights the absence of conditionality from the ENP at the political macro level, although it does play a role at the technical level. The external incentives model, according to which a third country adopts EU rules if the cost-benefit calculation (domestic adoption costs versus EU rewards) is positive, cannot explain success and failure of rule transfer under the ENP. It was suggested that the variation in successful rule transfer is rather the result of a complex social learning process, in which the domestic agenda, political support from individual member states, and the perceived prospect of accession in the longer term interact.

This approach opens perspectives for filling some of the gaps in current research. First, the focus has been too much on the EU. More efforts should be undertaken to investigate how the ENP is received in the target countries. Second, research should focus on how the EU's unintended impact on its neighborhood and its deliberate policy toward the same area interact. To what extent does the ENP reinforce or mitigate the effects of the EU's presence? Does economic dependence foster the acceptance of the ENP priorities? Finally, the subjective factor deserves more attention, in particular the role of perception in the target countries. Bringing these three lines together, one research track that needs to be further explored is how the subjective attraction of the EU leads certain ENP states to proactively seek legitimacy with the EU. Such approaches will allow research to move beyond a one-sided analysis of the ENP as a utilitarian reaction to the incentives provided by the EU.

Notes

1. Karen Smith, "The Outsiders: The European Neighborhood Policy," *International Affairs* 81, no. 4 (2005): 757–73; Geoffrey Edwards, "The Construction of Ambiguity

and the Limits of Attraction: Europe and Its Neighborhood Policy," *Journal of European Integration* 30, no. 1 (2008): 45–62.

2. Jack Straw, "A New Mission for Europe," speech at the Auswärtiges Amt, Berlin, 2002.

3. Commission of the European Communities, COM (2003) 104 final, "Communication from the Commission to the Council and the European Parliament. Wider Europe—Neighborhood: A New Framework for Relations with Our Eastern and Southern Neighbors" (Brussels, March 11, 2003).

4. Commission of the European Communities, COM (2004) 373 final, "Communication from the Commission. European Neighborhood Policy. Strategy Paper" (Brussels, May 12, 2004).

5. Ibid., p. 3.

6. Romano Prodi, "A Wider Europe—A Proximity Policy as the Key to Stability," speech at the Sixth ECSA-World Conference, December 5–6, 2002 (http://europa.eu/rapid/pressReleasesAction.do?reference=SPEECH/02/619&format=HTML&aged=1&language=EN&guiLanguage=en [September 2006]).

7. On the toning down of conditionality, see Judith Kelley, "New Wine in Old Wineskins: Promoting Political Reforms through the New European Neighborhood Policy," *Journal of Common Market Studies* 44, no. 1 (2006): 29–55. See also Gwendolyn Sasse, "The European Neighborhood Policy: Conditionality Revisited for the EU's Eastern Neighbors," *Europe-Asia Studies* 60, no. 2 (2008): 301.

8. Association Agreements are cooperation agreements between the EU and nonmembers establishing a closer relationship—for example, through extensive free trade or preferential treatment.

9. Commission, COM (2004) 373 final, p. 4.

10. Ibid., p. 6.

11. Ibid., p. 4.

12. European Commission, Directorate General for Trade, "Bilateral Trade Relations—Russia" (http://ec.europa.eu/trade/issues/bilateral/countries/russia/index_en.htm [June 2008]).

13. Stephan Keukeleire and Jennifer MacNaughtan, *The Foreign Policy of the European Union* (Basingstoke, UK: Palgrave Macmillan, 2008).

14. European Commission, DG Trade, "Bilateral Trade Relations" (http://ec.europa.eu/trade/issues/bilateral/countries/index_en.htm [June 2008]).

15. Hanns Maull, "Europe and the New Balance of Global Order," *International Affairs* 81, no. 4 (2005): p. 782.

16. Prodi, "A Wider Europe."

17. European Council, "A Secure Europe in a Better World. European Security Strategy," p. 8. Approved by the European Council held in Brussels on December 12, 2003, and drafted under the responsibilities of EU High Representative Javier Solana (http://ue.eu.int/uedocs/cmsUpload/78367.pdf [February 2009]).

18. Smith, "The Outsiders," p. 758; Tom Casier, "The New Neighbors of the European Union: The Compelling Logic of Enlargement," in *The Boundaries of EU Enlargement.*

Finding a Place for Neighbors, edited by Joan DeBardeleben (Basingstoke, UK: Palgrave Macmillan, 2008), pp. 19–20.

19. Commission, COM (2004) 373 final.

20. Judy Batt, "The EU's New Borderlands," Working Paper (London: Centre for European Reform, 2003), pp. 12 and 14–15.

21. Kuchma in 1999, quoted in Sandra Lavenex and Emek Uçarer, "The External Dimension of Europeanization: The Case of Immigration Policies," *Cooperation and Conflict* 39, no. 4 (2004): 433–34.

22. Ruben Zaiotti, "Of Friends and Fences: Europe's Neighborhood Policy and the 'Gated Community Syndrome,'" *Journal of European Integration* 29, no. 2 (2007): 144.

23. A few authors have contributed to the research on this; see, for example, Zaiotti, "Of Friends and Fences"; Edwards, "The Construction of Ambiguity."

24. Comparative study by the author of the Action Plans between the EU and Ukraine, Moldova, and Morocco.

25. Press release, Commission of the European Communities, COM (2007) 774 final, "Communication from the European Commission: A Strong European Neighborhood Policy" (Brussels, December 12, 2007).

26. Frank Schimmelfennig and Ulrich Sedelmeier, "Governance by Conditionality: EU Rule Transfer to the Candidate Countries of Central and Eastern Europe," *Journal of European Public Policy* 11, no. 4 (2004): 661–79.

27. Ibid., p. 662.

28. Ibid., pp. 663, 664ff.

29. Ibid., p. 668.

30. See Edwards, "The Construction of Ambiguity," p. 48.

31. EU/Morocco Action Plan 2005, p. 1 (http://ec.europa.eu/world/enp/pdf/action_plans/morocco_enp_ap_final_en.pdf [January 2009]).

32. EU/Ukraine Action Plan 2005 (http://ec.europa.eu/world/enp/pdf/action_plans/ukraine_enp_ap_final_en.pdf [February 2009]) and an identical formulation in the EU/Moldova Action Plan 2005 (http://ec.europa.eu/world/enp/pdf/action_plans/moldova_enp_ap_final_en.pdf [February 2009]).

33. EU-Morocco Action Plan 2005.

34. Identical formulations appear in EU/Ukraine 2005 and EU/Moldova 2005 Action Plans.

35. EU-Ukraine Action Plan 2005, p. 4.

36. Though one could argue that although the accession process is characterized by a considerable degree of uncertainty, most notably in the case of Turkey, there is at least agreement on the principles and the outcome it should lead to.

37. Sasse, "The European Neighborhood Policy," pp. 303 and 301.

38. Author's interview with a Commission official from DG External Relations, June 2008.

39. It remains of course true that compliance with the Copenhagen criteria in the case of enlargement is subject to political interpretation. See, for example, Heather Grabbe, "How Does Europeanization Affect CEE Governance? Conditionality, Diffusion and Diversity," *Journal of European Public Policy* 8, no. 6 (2001): 1020.

40. Schimmelfennig and Sedelmeier, "Governance by Conditionality," p. 666.

41. Author's interview with a Commission official from DG External Relations, June 2008.

42. Sasse, "The European Neighborhood Policy," p. 303.

43. Ibid.

44. Schimmelfennig and Sedelmeier, "Governance by Conditionality."

45. Paul Kubicek, "The European Union and Democratization in Ukraine," *Communist and Post-Communist Studies* 38 (2005): 274ff.

46. Benita Ferrero-Waldner, "Situation in Ukraine," speech at the Plenary Session of the European Parliament, December 1, 2004 (http://ec.europa.eu/comm/external_relations/news/ferrero/2004/speech04_506_en.htm [September 2006]).

47. According to the treaties, "any *European* country can apply for membership." Morocco saw its application for membership in 1987 turned down on the ground that it was not a European country.

48. See concepts such as "procedural entrapment" in Sasse, "The European Neighborhood Policy," p. 296; or "the compelling logic of enlargement" in Casier, "The New Neighbors of the European Union," p. 20.

49. Lien Verpoest, "State Isomorphism in the Slavic Core of the CIS: A Comparative Study of Post-communist Geopolitical Pluralism in Russia, Ukraine and Belarus," Ph.D. dissertation, Katholieke Universiteit Leuven, 2008 (unpublished).

50. Ibid., p. 391.

51. Ibid., pp. 390–91. For the distinction between mimetic, normative, and coercive isomorphism, see Paul DiMaggio and Walter Powell, "The Iron Cage Revisited: Institutional Isomorphism and Collective Rationality in Organizational Fields," *American Sociological Review* 48 (April 1983): 147–60.

52. Verpoest, "State Isomorphism," p. 35.

53. Ibid., pp. 35 and 391.

54. One of the crucial factors in Schimmelfennig and Sedelmeier's external incentives model, for example, is "the credibility of the EU's threat to withhold rewards in case of non-compliance and, conversely, its promise to deliver the reward in case of rule adoption" (Schimmelfennig and Sedelmeier, "Governance by Conditionality," p. 665). However, credibility itself is not a purely rational factor, as the model suggests, but also a matter of perception.

*The European Union
and Its Neighbors*

LARA PICCARDO

7

The European Union and Russia: Past, Present, and Future of a Difficult Relationship

The collapse of the USSR, the dissolution of the Eastern bloc, and the fifth enlargement of the European Union have radically changed the political map of the "old continent." Today, "political Europe" consists of the enlarged EU, taking in three former Soviet republics and seven central European "satellites"; a few additional countries, which in some cases are candidates or potential candidates for EU membership (such as Croatia, the former Yugoslav Republic of Macedonia, Turkey, Albania, Bosnia-Herzegovina, Montenegro, Serbia, and Kosovo); and Russia, which has not made clear to what degree it views itself as a European power.

Following the admission of twelve new countries into the EU, Russia's neighbors Ukraine and Belarus now share borders with the EU, and Kaliningrad is completely encircled by EU member states.

In modifying the geopolitical map of the "old continent" so radically, the completion of the fifth enlargement of the EU (which had two phases, one in 2004 and one in 2007) was greeted with dismay in Moscow. The Kremlin's disappointment is rooted in history, which shows how the "new" Russia shares with the "old" Soviet Union some aspects of its foreign policy. The Soviet/Russian policy toward the European Economic Community (EEC)/EU is a case in point.

Since the beginning of the European construction process, by focusing on the ideological prophecies of capitalist contradictions, communist authorities did not understand the potential significance of the efforts of people like Jean Monnet,[1] directed at economic, financial, and cultural integration.[2] And although the Soviet bloc economy needed economic relations with Western Europe, its political rulers rejected the idea of any European federation or confederation on the old continent.[3]

The European Integration Process and the Soviet Union

In August 1915, before the "Red Revolution," Lenin wrote an article about the economic incorrectness of the "United States of Europe" slogan.[4] "A United States of Europe, under capitalism," he wrote, "is either impossible or reactionary."[5] This position became the ideological basis for Soviet rejection of the European integration process.

During World War II, on January 11, 1944, Ivan Maisky, the Soviet ambassador in London, and Maxim Litvinov, the Soviet ambassador in Washington from 1941 to 1943, delivered a memorandum to Stalin. In their view, it was "not in the interests of the Soviet Union, at least in the first period after the war, to foster the creation of various kinds of [European] federations."[6] The consensus was that the USSR should remain an unchallenged land power in Europe, without even a shadow of countervailing power represented by another state or a group of smaller states.[7]

When the Schuman Plan and the Pleven Plan were launched at the beginning of the 1950s, Stalin evaluated them only in the context of the militarization process of the Federal Republic of Germany (FRG). Moscow thought that the plans would create an "aggressive" bloc against the USSR and its allies.

Under Khrushchev, the Soviet leadership developed a new diplomacy. Despite the initial rejection of the Stalinist ways, as soon as the Rome Treaties were signed on March 25, 1957 (establishing the European Economic Community and the European Atomic Energy Community), Khrushchev and his diplomats expressed strong opposition to the new European Community.[8]

The week before the treaties were signed, Moscow submitted a proposal to the United Nations Economic Commission for Europe that included a draft treaty for all-European economic cooperation. Attached to the proposal was a Soviet Foreign Ministry statement warning of the dangers of the EEC to the peace and stability of the world.[9] In 1957 and 1962, two papers by a number of experts of the Soviet Academy of Sciences[10] accused the EEC of being the economic ground of the North Atlantic Treaty Organization (NATO) and a form of neocolonialism, formed for the exploitation of the working class, based on the expansionist dreams of Germany.[11]

The same view of the EEC prevailed in the Brezhnev period,[12] when the goal of the Soviet Union became the fragmentation of Western Europe and its separation from the United States.[13] The Soviets used propaganda again, and in 1971–72 the Muscovite review *La vie internationale* (published in Russian, but also in French and English for a Western audience) dedicated eight articles to bitterly criticizing the European integration process. Another four articles expressed the Soviet position against the first enlargement of the European Communities and denounced China's openings to the EEC.

In the 1980s the Soviet position changed radically, mainly because of Mikhail Gorbachev.[14] In 1985–86, the new Soviet leadership for the first time conceded the enormity of its economic problems and sought a global solution. Gorbachev called for a completely new approach to international relations, which he called "New Thinking."[15]

Three practical ideas emerged from this new approach: peaceful coexistence had to be cooperative, true security had to be mutual, and the USSR and the United States had to promote the concept of "reasonable sufficiency" in their strategic thinking.[16] These principles resulted in a resumption of dialogue between the Americans and the Soviets on nuclear arms, as well as the end of Soviet involvement in many parts of the world (including, first, the Soviet withdrawal from Afghanistan).

In his address to the 43rd UN General Assembly session on December 7, 1988, Gorbachev talked of a "new world order," and on July 6, 1989, addressing the Parliamentary Assembly of the Council of Europe, he outlined his idea of "a Common European Home."[17] At that time there was still an opportunistic dimension to Gorbachev's proposals: since political and economic relations between the USSR and its eastern satellites had become increasingly difficult, the Kremlin had a clear economic incentive to develop trade and exchanges with Western Europe.

But Gorbachev's perception of Europe was becoming more global and ambitious. In his mind, the "Common European Home" could contribute to ridding the world of its bipolarity and thus bring security to the continent; and it could provide a framework for a reformed USSR and its reformed eastern satellites to grow. This framework would be based on a "socialism with a human face," a socialism that would be tolerant and respectful of others' values, of the principle of renunciation of force, and of freedom of choice.[18]

Although the concept of a "Common European Home" was little more than an idea, rather than a concrete political strategy, the rest of the Soviet leadership still hated it.

The European Union and the Russian Federation: The Partnership and Cooperation Agreement and EU Enlargement

Immediately after the collapse of the Soviet Union in 1991, the relationship between the "new" Russia and the West looked like a romance. Having cast aside the basic premises of communist propaganda along with communism itself, Moscow now considered the West (divided into two "levels," the Atlantic and the communitarian) to be a friend and a role model. The Russian people trusted the West and believed that Russia's integration into the Western world was desirable and inevitable. A substantial part of the new Russian elite and the public shared this view.

At the same time, the EU was pursuing a patient and determined long-term strategy aimed at integrating Russia into Europe.[19] The Partnership and Cooperation Agreement (PCA) was signed in 1994 and entered into force in 1997.[20] In December 1997, following an initiative of the prime minister of Finland, Paavo Lipponen, the European Council of Luxembourg asked the European Commission to prepare an interim report on the "Northern Dimension" in the policies of the European Union, which was presented in Vienna on December 12, 1998.[21] On June 4, 1999, the European Council of Cologne adopted a "Common Strategy towards Russia," a challenging program of long-term engagement by the EU with Russia.

The cornerstone of EU-Russian relations remained the PCA, which defined the EU and Russia as strategic partners. It was signed on June 25, 1994, in Corfu by the heads of state and government of the then twelve member states of the EU; the president of the European Commission, Jacques Delors; and the president of the Russian Federation, Boris Yeltsin. The PCA was ratified by the EU member states (and signed by the acceding countries of Austria, Finland, and Sweden thereafter) and entered into force on December 1, 1997. It took so long to enter into force because of the Chechen War, which began on December 11, 1994, and lasted until August 1996.[22] In the meantime, an "interim agreement on trade and economic relations" entered into force on February 16, 1996.

The PCA was based on core principles shared by the parties, ranging from the promotion of international peace and security to the support for a democratic society based on political and economic freedoms. Through the PCA, the intention of the EU and Russia was to create an "economic co-operation of vast scope" (art. 56, para. 1) in the framework of a well-functioning political and institutional dialogue evidently inspired by the suggestions of the so-called institutionalist approach.[23] The PCA proved to be an important milestone in relations between the two partners; its extensive provisions provided a foundation for further possible deepening and elaboration that never took place.

Indeed, at the end of the 1990s the relationship between Russia and the West worsened. The first cause was the Washington Declaration on April 23, 1999, stating that the Atlantic organization "remains open to all European democracies, regardless of geography, willing and able to meet the responsibilities of membership, and whose inclusion would enhance overall security and stability in Europe."[24]

The declaration posed a serious dilemma for Russia. Its rejection of previous ideological schemes to create a partnership with the EU was accompanied by a geopolitical distancing of Russia from the West, which originated with the NATO enlargement. On the one hand, during the 1990s Russia had become the main commercial and economic partner of the EU. On the other, by the end of the 1990s Russian foreign policy toward the West had begun to regress.

NATO's enlargement preceded the European one, so two different opinions were expressed by Moscow.[25] It considered NATO enlargement to be a threat to Russian security and accepted EU enlargement only because "European political space" represented an alternative to NATO expansion. Nevertheless, the integration into the EU of three former Soviet republics and seven central European "satellites" created in Moscow an intense debate between two opposing theses.[26]

According to the first one, Russia should not be afraid of the establishment of a wider and stronger EU guided by the West, since this evolution could produce political and economic benefits. Politically, the new EU could be seen as "containing" those members with anti-Russian inclinations. Economically, greater proximity and common borders with the EU would decrease transaction costs between Russia and its most important economic partner and market area. Russia's economic foothold in the EU market would be reinforced and expanded by the accession of countries with traditionally strong trade ties with Russia, and the unification of rules and regulations by new EU members would benefit Russian business interests throughout the region.[27]

The second thesis descended in a direct line from the cold war period: the integration into the EU of the central and eastern European countries (CEECs) was considered a danger for Russia, which would remain on the geographic—but also political and economic—borders of Europe. Moreover, from a political point of view, the EU would be ruled by members that had anti-Russian feelings. And from an economic point of view the eastern market, so important for Russia, would be absorbed by the EU.

This second thesis prevailed. Not only was there great resentment in Russia that its former allies were joining "the West," but Russia also made excessive demands from the EU in light of enlargement, only to have to backpedal later on highly sensitive issues such as transit to Kaliningrad.

The matter of the Kaliningrad enclave was experienced by government authorities as a threat to the country's territorial integrity and an insult to Russian residents of Kaliningrad.[28] An agreement was reached quite quickly, safeguarding major Russian interests. It is essentially a technical solution: Russian citizens could cross Lithuania or Poland with a special transit document adapted to the means of transport used (rail or road) and free of charge in some cases.[29] This agreement, however, does not provide complete satisfaction to Russia. Moscow believes that the optimal solution for Kaliningrad would be to implement broad free movement between the EU and Russia. This topic is therefore discussed at every Russia-EU summit.[30]

Russia has also denounced the treatment of Russian-speaking minorities, who cannot easily gain citizenship in the state in which they live (language tests are required, especially in Estonia) and who at the same time do not have sufficient means to maintain their cultural identity. They are considered to be non-citizens and likened to stateless persons. That being the case, the two new EU member states (Estonia and Latvia) have eased their citizenship requirements somewhat. The Baltic Republics refuse, however, to declare Russian an official language in their states. This is what Russia secretly wants.[31]

Subsequently, the Kremlin has attempted to play the role of "old Europe" against new members. It favored interstate diplomacy to the detriment of relations with the EU as a whole. In early July 2005, President Vladimir Putin invited only the French president and the German chancellor to the Russia-Europe mini-summit in Kaliningrad, conspicuously neglecting the Polish and Lithuanian presidents. A few weeks later he went to Finland, while the Russian foreign affairs minister praised Finnish tolerance for authorizing all permanent residents to take part in elections, without condition of citizenship, in obvious reference to and criticism of Estonia and Latvia. It is interesting to note that his personal representative to the EU, Sergej Yastrzhembsky, has never explicitly held the position of ambassador to the European Union.[32]

Moscow was also reluctant to agree to the extension of the PCA with the EU to the first ten new member states.[33] A deal was only reached at the last moment. Finally, Moscow did not renew the PCA, which expired in December 2007.

So it could be said that, starting with the intention of breaking with the past, the Russian political elite has instead returned to a "bipolar" logic, looking at the West as a competitor or an enemy but not as an ally. In the early twenty-first century, Russian society's view of the West has also deteriorated sharply. The United States ranks first as the object of hostility, followed by the European states. Opinion polls show that there is little trace of benevolence toward the West, and fear and disagreement have replaced friendly feelings.[34] Now the talking point is the intention of the West to ruin and destroy Russia and eternal European hostility toward Russia and the Russians. Such paranoia is highlighted by the mass media and by allegedly scientific conferences. In rural areas as well as capitals, it is shared by both the well educated and the less well educated, the young and the old. For its part, the West speaks of traditional Russian hostility and Russian imperialism, referring to peculiarities inherent in Russia and its people that have not changed for centuries.

A Difficult Scenario

Since their accession, many of the new EU member states have urged the Union to take a more robust approach toward Moscow, arguing that Russia only understands a strong partner.

Adopted by the European Parliament on May 4, 2005, the Malmström Report is highly critical of Russia and calls on the European Commission and the Council of Ministers to agree on a consistent approach.[35] Moscow has to understand that dealing with the EU means dealing not only with Berlin and Paris, but also with Tallinn and Warsaw.[36] Political relations are particularly tense.

From the start of his term in 2001, President Putin went to great lengths to (re)establish state control over all institutions and practices with the intention of consolidating the emerging democracy in Russia. This political situation makes it difficult to ensure the free operation of institutions and has led to management problems for Russia's European partners as they attempt to reconcile democratic values with economic pragmatism. With the gas crisis in Ukraine that began in early 2005 casting considerable doubt on the reliability of Russian supplies, Russian-European tensions have spread to the strategic energy sector.[37]

In this new scenario the options seem to be two: the separation of Russia from the rest of the continent or cooperation between the two parts. Russia's isolation would be a defeat of both Russian democracy and the West, and its separation from Europe could constitute a new "Berlin Wall." It would be better to implement and/or change the cooperation mechanisms between Russia and the EU.

All of the European assistance tools developed during the 1990s and early 2000s do not really correspond to EU-Russia relations as they have developed in the meantime. When Technical Assistance to the Commonwealth of Independent States (TACIS), for example, was no longer sufficient,[38] it was replaced with a more ambitious program, the European Neighborhood and Partnership Instrument (ENPI).[39] Its aim is to provide the framework for the execution of the road map elaborated for each common cooperation space.

New impetus for cooperation came from the EU-Russian summit held in the Siberian city of Khanty-Mansiysk on June 26–27, 2008. On that occasion the new Russian president, Dmitry Medvedev, and top EU officials announced the start of talks on a new strategic partnership agreement, whose negotiations Putin had long delayed. The talks formally began in Brussels on July 4, 2008.

Talks focus primarily on trade, since Russia is the EU's third-largest trading partner and half of all Russian exports go to the EU. The new agreement is meant to replace the previous PCA, which will continue to govern relations until the new text comes into force.

During the summit, some objections arose. Medvedev said Russia was alarmed by what he called a tendency to use European solidarity to promote the interests of individual members in bilateral disputes with Russia. He also harshly criticized U.S. plans to site missile defense facilities in Europe and warned the EU against relying on others to ensure European security. Indeed, Russia proposed a new treaty covering security across the European continent, a suggestion it said was warmly welcomed. Despite these openings, in the following weeks the relationship between the EU and Russia seemed to worsen again. Two important events took place.

While the G-8 summit was taking place in the northern mountain resort of Lake Toyako (Hokkaido, Japan) July 7–9, 2008, Prague signed an agreement with Washington on an anti-ballistic missile system. The Russian foreign minister, Sergey Lavrov, declared that Russia would be forced to respond militarily if the United States went forward with constructing the system in the Czech Republic. Russian officials added that a missile shield would severely undermine European security balances by weakening Russia's missile capacity. If the agreement is ratified "we will be forced to react not with diplomatic but with military-technical methods," the ministry said, without giving specifics.[40]

The second dramatic event was the South Ossetian conflict, fought between Georgia, on one side, and the separatist regions (South Ossetia and Abkhazia) and Russia, on the other.[41] Ongoing occasional skirmishes escalated into war early on August 8, 2008, with a Georgian artillery attack on Tskhinvali, the capital of the breakaway Georgian province of South Ossetia. The attack killed a large number of civilians as well as several Russian peacekeepers, prompting Russia to invade Georgia and push its forces out of South Ossetia. Russian forces also entered another breakaway province, Abkhazia, occupied several towns in Georgia proper, and briefly appeared to threaten the Georgian capital, Tbilisi. A preliminary ceasefire was signed by Georgia and Russia on August 15, 2008. Russia announced a ten-day withdrawal from advance positions, while Georgian authorities expressed discontent with the rate and extent of the pullback, and with the continuing Russian presence in the towns of Gori and Poti.

On August 26, 2008, Medvedev formally recognized the independence of South Ossetia and Abkhazia. Georgia denounced this move as an annexation of its territory. The unilateral recognition by Russia was condemned by some members of the international community and other members of the United Nations, NATO, the Organization for Security and Co-operation in Europe (OSCE), and the European Council. The Shanghai Cooperation Organization issued a joint statement voicing support for Russia's "active role" in "assisting in peace and cooperation in the region" without explicitly backing Russia's recognition policy.[42] On September 13, Russian troops began withdrawing from Georgia.

Two days later, the Council of the European Union decided to establish an autonomous civilian monitoring mission in Georgia. The mission was deployed on October 1, in accordance with the arrangements set out in the agreement of September 8.

The European Union Monitoring Mission (EUMM) in Georgia is an autonomous mission led by the EU under the European Security and Defense Policy (ESDP). Its objectives are to contribute to stability throughout Georgia and the surrounding region and, in the short term, to contribute to the stabilization of the situation in accordance with the six-point agreement and subsequent implementation measures. Its main tasks will include monitoring and analyzing both the stabilization process, centered on full compliance with the six-point agreement leading toward normalizing relations and the return of internally displaced persons and refugees. The tasks will also include contributing to the reduction of tensions through liaison, facilitation of contacts between parties, and other confidence-building measures. On September 17, the German ambassador, Hansjörg Haber, was appointed the head of EUMM Georgia.

The EU has provided €6 million in humanitarian aid for people affected by the recent conflict in Georgia. An international donors' conference to assist Georgia's economic recovery was held in Brussels on October 22, 2008.[43] The conference was co-chaired by the European Commission and the World Bank and co-hosted by the French Presidency and the incoming Czech Presidency of the Council of the European Union.

The purpose of the conference was to mobilize a critical mass of external assistance to support the country in the reconstruction of its damaged infrastructure, to reintegrate internally displaced people, and to accelerate Georgia's economic recovery. Over the past five years, Georgia has pursued a challenging program of institutional and policy reforms, which have resulted in a sustained high level of economic growth and in the strengthening of key institutions. Tbilisi will have the opportunity to confirm its strong commitment to furthering this agenda to ensure the country's rapid and sustained development in the years ahead. Donors will also discuss delivery mechanisms and principles of donor coordination.

Despite the coordinated institutional response to the war, it should be said that the Georgian conflict divided the EU instead of uniting it. Some member states condemned Russia and gave (nonmilitary) aid to the Georgian government; others accused Tbilisi of provoking the war. Their reactions suggest that the EU capitals make different assumptions about Moscow's goals and intentions toward countries on Russia's borders and about Europe's interests in those countries. These differences will thwart Europe's attempts to craft a common Russia policy. But they should not prevent Europe from rethinking the EU's policy toward its eastern neighborhood. In response to the war in Georgia, the EU should take a more active role in defusing "frozen" conflicts in eastern Europe, and it should accelerate the integration of countries between the EU and Russia into the European Union.[44]

During the war, the EU governments developed sufficient consensus to pursue a two-pronged policy. With partial success, they made strong statements discouraging Russia from expanding the war beyond South Ossetia. More successfully, the French president, Nicolas Sarkozy, in his capacity as the holder of the EU's rotating Presidency, brokered the ceasefire agreement that halted the fighting. Sarkozy has continued to talk to both sides about the exact terms of peace.

At the moment, there is little hope for a common policy on Russia. While Germany, France, and other like-minded countries say that what Moscow really dislikes is not Western influence in general but a U.S. military presence in its backyard (pointing out that Russian criticism focuses on NATO enlargement and U.S. missile-defense plans), the Czechs, the Poles, and other like-minded states think that Russia wants to control the foreign policies and economies of its neighbors.

As a result, the EU's leverage is limited, but it does have some influence. Russia is not a rogue state; it wants to be an accepted member of the international community, and it wants the EU and NATO to treat it as a privileged partner. This Russian desire for recognition as a member of the "civilized" international community allows the EU to play on Russian sensitivities about its role and status in the world.[45] But this influence is subtle and cannot be turned on and off to suit the needs of individual crises. It stems from what Europe is (a respected, rich community) rather than what it does.

Notes

1. The Frenchman Jean Monnet is one of the founding fathers of the United Europe. From 1950, he played an active role in the establishment of the European Coal and Steel Community (ECSC), serving as president of the High Authority in Luxembourg from 1952 to 1955. On his life and activities see Jean Monnet, *Mémoires* (Paris: Fayard, 1976); François Duchêne, *Jean Monnet, the First Statesman of Interdependence* (New York: Norton, 1994); Clifford Hackett, ed., *Monnet and the Americans, the Father of a United Europe and His U.S. Supporters* (Washington: Jean Monnet Council, 1995); Gérard Bossuat and Andreas Wilkens, eds., *Jean Monnet, l'Europe et les chemins de la paix* (Paris: Publications de la Sorbonne, 1999).

2. Alla Sergeevna Namazova and Barbara Emerson, eds., *Istorija evropejskoj integratsii (1945–1994)* (Moscow: RAN, 1995). In the Gorbachev era the expression "European integration" was never used in mass media or in scientific reviews. The word "integration" always had to be written in quotation marks and preceded by the adjective "imperialist."

3. For the Soviet view of European integration, see, for example, Andrej M. Aleksandrov-Agentov, *Ot Kollontai do Gorbačëva* (Moscow: MGU, 1994); Vladislav Zubok, "The Soviet Union and European Integration from Stalin to Gorbachev," *Journal of European Integration History* 2, no. 1 (1996): 85–92; Franco Soglian, "L'integrazione europea e il blocco sovietico," in *Storia dell'integrazione europea*, edited by Romain H. Rainero (Rome: Marzorati, 1997), vol. 1, pp. 525–59, and vol. 2, pp. 573–615.

4. The article, "On the Slogan for a United States of Europe," was published in the review *Sotsial-Demokrat* 44 (August 23, 1915). It is now published in *Lenin Collected Works* (Moscow: Progress, 1974), vol. 21, pp. 339–43. Lenin presented a thesis against the position expressed by Leon Trotsky one year earlier. In October 1914, in *The War and the International*, Trotsky affirmed that socialists should fight for a democratic peace, without annexation or compensation. On this topic see also Renato Monteleone, "Le ragioni teoriche del rifiuto della parola d'ordine degli Stati Uniti d'Europa nel movimento comunista internazionale," in *L'idea dell'unificazione europea dalla prima alla seconda guerra mondiale*, edited by Sergio Pistone (Turin: Einaudi, 1975), pp. 77–95.

5. *Lenin Collected Works*, p. 339.

6. *Majskij Molotovu*, AVPRF (*Archiv vnešnej politiki Rossijskoj Federatsii*), fond [collection] 06, opis' [inventory] 6, papka [folder] 14, delo [file] 145, list [page] 5, quoted in Zubok, "The Soviet Union," p. 85.

7. Ibid.

8. On this topic, see David F. P. Forte, "The Response of Soviet Foreign Policy to the Common Market, 1957–63," *Soviet Studies* 19, no. 3 (January 1968): 373–86.

9. "Soviet Proposals for All-European Economic Cooperation," *International Affairs*, no. 4 (1957): 156.

10. The first paper became famous as "The Seventeen Theses" ("On the Creation of the Common Market and of Euratom," *Kommunist*, no. 9 [1957]: 88–102), the second one as "The Thirty-Two Theses" ("On the Imperialist Integration in Western Europe," *Pravda*, August 1962).

11. Bernard Dutoit, *L'Union Soviétique face à l'intégration européenne* (Lausanne: Centre de Recherches Européennes, 1964), pp. 41–42.

12. Soglian, "L'integrazione europea," p. 594.

13. Hannes Adomeit, "Capitalist Contradictions and Soviet Policy," *Problems of Communism*, no. 3 (May–June 1984): 9.

14. Marie-Pierre Rey, "From Fulton to Malta: How the Cold War Began and Ended," p. 1 (www.gorby.ru/imgrubrs.asp?img=file&art_id=25031 [October 2008]).

15. "New Thinking" was Gorbachev's slogan for a policy based on shared moral and ethical principles to solve global problems rather than on Marxist-Leninist concepts of irreconcilable conflict between capitalism and communism. The "New Thinking" was applied both in foreign and domestic policy under three programs, whose names became household words: *perestroika* (rebuilding), *glasnost* (transparency, openness), and *uskorenie* (acceleration). Mikhail Gorbachev, *Perestroika: New Thinking for Our Country and the World* (London: Collins, 1987). See also Michael Barratt Brown, *The Challenge: Economics of Perestroika* (London: Hutchinson, 1988); Peter J. Boettke, *Why*

Perestroika Failed: The Politics and Economics of Socialist Transformation (London: Routledge, 1993).

16. Rey, "From Fulton to Malta," p. 2.

17. *CWIHP Bulletin*, no. 12–13 (Fall–Winter 2001): 29.

18. Rey, "From Fulton to Malta," p. 6.

19. On the relationship between Russia and the EU, see Tanguy de Wilde and Laetitia Spetschinsky, eds., *Les relations entre l'Union Européenne et la Fédération de Russie* (Louvain-la-Neuve: Institut d'études européennes, 2000); Michael Emerson, *The Elephant and the Bear: The European Union, Russia and Their Near Abroad* (Brussels: Centre for European Policies, 2001); Gabriella Meloni, "Russian Federation towards an Enlarged Europe," Working Paper no. 5 (Rome: CIDEM, 2002); John Pinder and Yuri Shishkov, *The EU and Russia: The Promise of Partnership* (London: The Federal Trust, 2002); Oksana Antonenko and Kathryn Pinnick, *Russia and the European Union: Prospects for a New Relationship* (London: Routledge, 2005); Eberhard Schneider, "The European Union and Russia," *Bulletin. World Public Forum Dialogue of Civilizations*, no. 1 (2005): 51–56; Roderic Lyne, "Russia in the EU? We Should Never Say Never," *Europe's World*, no. 2 (2006): 38–41; Sabine Fischer, "The EU and Russia: Conflicts and Potentials of a Difficult Partnership," Research Paper 1 (Berlin: SWP, 2007); Roberto Gualtieri and José Luis Rhi-Sausi, eds., *L'Europa e la Russia a vent'anni dall'89. Rapporto 2009 sull'integrazione europea* (Bologna: Il Mulino, 2009).

20. "Agreement on Partnership and Cooperation Establishing a Partnership between the European Communities and their Member States, of one part, and the Russian Federation, of the other part—Protocol 1 on the establishment of a coal and steel contact group—Protocol 2 on mutual administrative assistance for the correct application of customs legislation—Final Act—Exchanges of letters—Minutes of signing," *Official Journal of the European Union*, no. L 327 (November 28, 1997): 0003–0069 (eur-lex.europa.eu/LexUriServ/LexUriServ.do?uri=CELEX:21997A1128(01):EN:HTML [October 2008]). PCAs are legal frameworks based on the respect for democratic principles and human rights, setting out the political, economic, and trade relationship between the EU and its partner countries. See Michel Dubisson, *Les accords de cooperation dans le commerce international* (Paris: Lamy, 1989); Kenneth R. Simmonds, ed., *The European Community, the Soviet Union and Eastern Europe* (New York: Oceana, 1991). On the Russian side, see *Dokumenty, kasajuščiesja sotrudničestva meždy ES i Rossiej* (Moscow: Pravo, 1994).

21. See the Presidency Conclusions of the Vienna European Council, December 11–12, 1998 (www.consilium.europa.eu/ueDocs/cms_Data/docs/pressData/en/ec/00300-R1.EN8.htm [October 2008]).

22. On May 12, 1997, Chechen president Aslan Maskhadov traveled to Moscow, where he and Yeltsin signed a formal treaty "on peace and the principles of Russian-Chechen relations." On this, see, for example, Anna Politkovskaia, *Voyage en enfer: journal de Tchetchenie* (Paris: Robert Laffont, 2000); Tracey C. German, *Russia's Chechen War* (London: Routledge, 2003); Valery Tishkov, *Chechnya: Life in a War-Torn Society* (Berkeley: University of California Press, 2004).

23. See Mark Aspinwall and Gerald Schneider, eds., *The Rules of Integration: The Institutionalist Approach to European Studies* (Manchester: Manchester University Press, 2001).

24. "The Washington Declaration. Signed and Issued by the Heads of State and Government Participating in the Meeting of the North Atlantic Council in Washington, D.C., on 23rd and 24th April 1999," Press Release NAC-S (99) 63 (www.nato.int/docu/pr/1999/p99-063e.htm [October 2008]).

25. See, for example, Konstantin Vasiliyevich Totskiy, "Le relazioni tra la Russia e la NATO," *Affari esteri*, no. 146 (2005): 356–59; Alexandr Viktorovich Grushko, "Lo sviluppo dei rapporti tra la Russia e la NATO," *Affari esteri*, no. 149 (2006): 45–50; Hannes Adomeit, "Inside or Outside? Russia's Policies towards NATO," Working Paper 1 (Berlin: SWP, 2007).

26. The Russian sociologist Boris Kagarlitsky wrote: "In my country the general tendency is now the one that idealizes the EU. . . . The Americans are bad, while the Europeans are good." B. Kagarlitsky, *Dove va la Russia* (Rome: Di Renzo, 2004), p. 52 (translation by Lara Piccardo).

27. Urpo Kivikari, "EU Enlargement and Russia—A Win-Win Situation," *Economic Trends* (Russian edition, 2000): 27–28.

28. Laurent Vinatier, "EU-Russian Relations: Moscow Lays Down Its Conditions," Policy Paper 20 (Paris: Notre Europe, March 2006), p. 11.

29. Brussels summit, November 11, 2002 (http://europa.eu/rapid/pressReleasesAction.do?reference=MEMO/02/228&format=PDF&aged=1&language=EN&guiLanguage=en [October 2008]).

30. On this topic see, for example, Simon Petermann and Geoffroy Matagne, *Cahier n. 1, The EU Enlargement and Russia: The Case of Kaliningrad* (http://popups.ulg.ac.be/csp/document.php?id=65#tocto6 [October 2008]).

31. Vinatier, "EU-Russian Relations," p. 12.

32. Ibid., p. 12.

33. The "Laeken Group" (Cyprus, Estonia, Latvia, Lithuania, Malta, Poland, Czech Republic, Slovakia, Slovenia, and Hungary) acceded to the EU on May 1, 2004; Romania and Bulgaria entered the Union on January 1, 2007.

34. According to an opinion poll carried out by the Russian Public Opinion Research Center (WCIOM, http://wciom.com/ [October 2008]) and published in May 2005, 55 percent of Russians believed that the country's military bases in former Soviet republics should not be closed and only 6 percent regarded them as unnecessary. Fifty percent of respondents were in favor of putting pressure on the "near abroad" countries and only 42 percent wanted to conduct a dialogue with them. Among those who favored a tough stance, the majority preferred the introduction of economic sanctions (31 percent favored an increase in energy prices/supplies), 9 percent preferred political sanctions, and 11 percent would opt for military intervention. Such attitudes are strongly criticized in the West.

35. "P6_TA(2005)0207. EU-Russia Relations. European Parliament Resolution on EU-Russia Relations (2004/2170(INI))," May 4, 2005 (136.173.159.21/sides/getDoc.do?pubRef=-//EP//NONSGML+TA+P6-TA-2005-0207+0+DOC+PDF+V0//EN [October 2008]).

36. Fraser Cameron and Jarek M. Domański, "Russian Foreign Policy with Special Reference to Its Western Neighbors," Issue Paper 37 (Brussels: EPC, July 13, 2005), p. 17.

37. On this topic see, for example, Jonathan Stern, *The Future of Russian Gas and Gazprom* (Oxford: Oxford Institute for Energy Studies, 2005); Jonathan Stern, *The Russian-Ukrainian Gas Crisis of January 2006* (Oxford Institute for Energy Studies, 2006).

38. "Technical Assistance to the Commonwealth of Independent States" (TACIS), Council Regulation (EC, Euratom) no. 99-2000, December 29, 1999. See European Commission, Directorate-General for External Relations, "Guide to TACIS Small Project Programmes and Other Support Structures. What They Are, and How to Benefit from Them" (Brussels: European Communities, 2000). On the Russian side, see *Evropa v menjajuščemsja mire* (Moscow: Pravo, 1995).

39. Michele Comelli, "The Challenges of the European Neighborhood Policy," *International Spectator*, no. 3 (2004): 97–110; Roland Dannreuther, ed., *European Union Foreign and Security Policy: Towards a Neighborhood Strategy* (London: Routledge, 2004); Roberto Aliboni, "The Geopolitical Implications of the European Neighborhood Policy," *European Foreign Affairs Review*, no. 1 (2005): 1–16; Paul Duta, "European Neighborhood Policy and Its Main Components," *Romanian Journal of International Affairs*, nos. 1–2 (2005): 229–46; Nicolas Hayoz, Leszek Jesien, Wim van Meurs, *Enlarged EU–Enlarged Neighborhood: Perspectives of the European Neighborhood Policy* (Bern: Peter Lang, 2005). See also the official website of the European Commission (ec.europa.eu/world/enp/index_en.htm [October 2008]).

40. David Charter, "Russia Threatens Military Response to U.S. Missile Defense Deal," *Timesonline*, July 9, 2008 (www.timesonline.co.uk/tol/news/world/europe/article4295 309.ece [October 2008]).

41. "Russia vs. Georgia: The Fallout," Report no. 195 (Tbilisi-Brussels: International Crisis Group, August 22, 2008) (www.crisisgroup.org/home/index.cfm?id=5636 [October 2008]).

42. See the website of the Directorate-General "Enlargement" of the European Commission, ec.europa.eu/enlargement/index_en.htm [October 2008].

43. Georgia Donors' Conference, Brussels, October 22, 2008 (http://ec.europa.eu/external_relations/georgia/conference/index_en.htm [October 2008]).

44. Tomas Valasek, *What Does the War in Georgia Mean for EU Foreign Policy?* (London: Centre for European Reform, August 2008) (www.cer.org.uk/pdf/briefing_georgia_15aug08_tv.pdf [October 2008]), p. 1. See also the website of the International Crisis Group, www.crisisgroup.org/home/index.cfm [October 2008].

45. Valasek, *What Does the War in Georgia Mean?* p. 3.

SERENA GIUSTI *and* TOMISLAVA PENKOVA

8 | *EU Policy toward Ukraine and Belarus: Diverging Paths?*

This chapter investigates the role of the European Union in Ukraine and Belarus.[1] Despite sharing a Soviet past, the two countries have taken different paths since the disintegration of the Soviet Union. While Ukraine has opted for transformation and modernization, looking increasingly westward, Belarus has remained the only truly communist country in Europe, maintaining close links with Moscow and reluctantly espousing Europeanization. Although both countries are included in the European Neighborhood Policy (ENP), the EU's leverage is very limited. This is the case not only because the EU has excluded for the moment the prospect of membership, but also because the EU member states have different perceptions and preferences for the ENP participants.[2] The rewards provided by the EU have been unattractive so far, and thus Brussels has had only a minor influence on the politics of the two countries. In contrast, both countries' dependence on Russian oil and gas gives Moscow something resembling blackmail power over them. A significant share of the gas exported from Russia to the EU (about 25 percent of the gas consumed in the EU) runs through Ukrainian and Belarusian territory, making the countries strategic to Moscow.

The picture is incomplete without surveying the U.S. strategy toward the two countries. Washington has condemned the Belarusian president Alexander Lukashenka's undemocratic regime and extended its economic sanctions against Belarus, intensifying at the same time programs promoting civil society and supporting opposition movements. The U.S. role has been decisive for the success of the Orange Revolution in Ukraine, with President George W. Bush's doctrine of democracy promotion. The political crisis was "Europeanized" only after Washington took a tough stance on it. The U.S. decision to deploy an anti-missile defense system in Poland and the Czech Republic risks helping Belarus and Russia overcome their temporary disagreements.

Minsk initially turned a cold shoulder to Russia's intervention in Georgia, but, under pressure from the Kremlin, eventually supported Moscow. The U.S. insistence on accepting Ukraine as NATO's next member also induces Russia to play assertively against Kiev. There is a risk that NATO's enlargement may further downgrade the EU's role as a guarantor of democracy and security.

A range of factors will affect the already confused picture of Belarus's and Ukraine's future, which differ in legitimacy, power resources, and the leverage they can wield. This chapter argues that the key actors in the area should cooperate in view of the two countries' efforts at stabilization and modernization. In particular, Russia should be involved in the Western attempts to reshape the post-Soviet area. Finally, any plan for Belarus and Ukraine should not overlook their internal dynamics, especially their declining sense of European identity.

The chapter is divided into two parts. The first scrutinizes Ukraine's position toward NATO and the EU, and the second one considers Belarus's tense relations with Brussels and its deteriorating friendship with Moscow. The conclusions assess the EU strategy toward both countries and advance some policy recommendations.

Ukraine's Path to the Euro-Atlantic Community

Since the 2004 Orange Revolution in protest of the 2004 Ukrainian elections, Kiev's political elite has exploited the country's geographic location and its historical origins to claim Ukraine's Europeanness and to embark on the course of Euro-Atlantic integration. However, a deep internal geographic division strains Ukraine's advancement toward Western structures. The population in eastern and southern Ukraine aspires to integrate with Russia. The western and central parts strive for integration with the EU and NATO. This division is also reflected in politics, where parties defend their respective ambitions. As a result, Ukraine has become a battlefield between the West and Russia, and the domestic reform process required to come closer to EU standards has slowed down. However, both President Viktor Yushchenko and Prime Minister Yulia Tymoshenko are seeking to integrate the country as much as possible with the EU and NATO. The August 2008 conflict in Georgia and the consequent dissolution of the Orange Coalition in early September 2008 showed Ukraine's fragility. The path of Westernization will depend mainly on whose view prevails in setting the domestic and foreign policy agenda: Tymoshenko's pragmatic approach, open to a dialogue with Russia, or Yushchenko's firm anti-Russian stance.

Since the birth of the Ukrainian state, the EU has always approached its economic integration gradually because of its geographic proximity to Russia and the presence of pro-Russian political forces. The founding pillar of EU-Ukraine relations is the 1998 Partnership and Cooperation Agreement (PCA), which expired in 2008. The PCA determined the first normative framework of bilateral relations in a number of sectors, but it fell short of providing "a tool for modernization of Ukraine's economy (or facilitating its) democratic transformation. A membership perspective was excluded, while the major carrot, a free trade area, was foreseen only upon full implementation of the agreement."[3]

In 2004 the European Neighborhood Policy was inaugurated. In 2005 the ENP's Action Plan for Ukraine, the three-year working instrument on economic and political progress of the ENP, was adopted, and in 2008 its duration was extended until April 2009. For the first time the ENP conceived Ukraine as an autonomous actor in the European geopolitical project, abandoning the previous policy of "Russia's interests first."[4] The ENP responded to two goals: to guide Ukraine toward adopting a Western-style market democracy and defense structure such as NATO, and to expand the EU zone of stability and security beyond its borders, without incurring excessive costs and commitments.[5] However, the implementation of the ENP was mainly characterized by economic incentives. EU membership was not envisioned since the ENP was viewed as an alternative to membership. Ukraine is, however, trying to obtain EU membership, and the Orange Revolution was also meant to demonstrate its Europeanness. There is growing frustration among Ukrainians, who believe that Ukraine "belongs to Europe and not to its neighborhood (and therefore) the ENP is perceived as a fall back option" to exclude its membership.[6]

Furthermore, owing to the differentiated approach toward each EU eastern neighbor, the ENP did not establish a base for regionalism. A possible explanation is the overbearing Russian factor.[7] The EU has missed an occasion to affirm itself as an important regional factor and to elaborate a coherent strategy toward Russia. During its 2007 EU Presidency, Germany tried to upgrade the eastern neighborhood by introducing the ENP Plus concept, embracing the ENP countries, Russia, and Central Asia. Contrary to the EU Commission's preference for a holistic approach toward the EU neighborhood, the initiative made a clear distinction between eastern and southern ENP partners. The aim was to transform the EU into an active player in the East. A binding agreement would have imposed the implementation of as much as possible of the *acquis communautaire* (the body of EU law) in these states. At the same time, it would have boosted the countries' modernization. The initiative also aspired to integrate the states into the EU decisionmaking process and to strengthen regional cooperation. Unfortunately, this *Neue Ostpolitik* was fully carried out only in Central Asia.

In 2008, Poland and Sweden elaborated further on this idea, proposing an eastern partnership between the EU and its eastern neighbors, Armenia, Azerbaijan,

Belarus, Georgia, Moldova, and Ukraine. The initiative was welcomed by the European Council, which invited the Commission to present in early 2009 a proposal for its implementation. According to the proponents, the eastern partnership should be developed within the structures of the ENP, with the Commission playing a coordinating role. No additional institutional arrangements would be created, nor extra EU funds allocated. The areas of deeper cooperation should include a visa-free regime, a free trade zone for services and agricultural products, people-to-people contacts, transport infrastructure, border control, and the environment. The initiative does not explicitly advocate membership, but it prevents the EU from ruling it out.

Furthermore, the proposal hints at a division of commitments between the EU member states. Germany and Poland would take the lead in managing the eastern dimension. Developing an EU eastern policy has always been a priority in Polish foreign policy, which has long advocated being a "bridge" between the western EU and the post-Soviet states. A statement by the Polish minister of foreign affairs, Radosław Sikorski, urging the EU eastern neighbors to follow the example of the Visegrad group, confirms these ambitions.

In the meantime, Ukraine-EU relations are embedded in the debate over a new type of agreement, called the New Enhanced Agreement (NEA), to replace the expired PCA. The NEA represents a unique occasion to consolidate the EU's credibility and its role in the East. At present, the major difficulty with NEA is deciding whether it should open up the path toward EU membership for Ukraine. Progress in this direction will depend on EU members like the Czech Republic, France, Germany, Poland, and the United Kingdom. It will also depend on Kiev's capacity to raise its quality of governance, to curb the corruption phenomenon, establish a feasible system of checks and balances, reduce the power of oligarchs in the economy, and establish a constructive dialogue among the leaders of the Orange Coalition.

Along with negotiations over the NEA, the parties began discussions on a deep and comprehensive free trade agreement (FTA), which is deemed to be the NEA's core component. The FTA talks were conditioned on Ukraine's accession to the World Trade Organization (WTO) in May 2008. According to analysts, stronger economic ties are expected to boost agricultural, chemical, and metals exports and to have a positive impact on the Ukrainian economy. The EU being one of the biggest trading partners of Ukraine, an FTA might attract third-country investors in Ukraine.[8]

Although the EU's leverage on Ukraine appears ineffective, Russia still exerts a significant influence on the country. Moscow's attitude toward Ukraine changed over the years. After adopting a power politics approach in the aftermath of the USSR disintegration, when Ukraine oriented itself toward the EU,

Russia now favors a pragmatic approach.[9] It no longer seeks to adjust the political course in Kiev, but it does not tolerate policies that clash with the Kremlin's.[10] These tactics, associated with the presence of the pro-Russian Party of Regions of Viktor Yanukovich and of the Russian Black Sea Fleet in Crimea, constitute a guarantee for Russia in influencing Ukraine's development.

There are four factors linking Russia to Ukraine, which Brussels should not ignore when approaching Kiev. The first one is the economy. Moscow is keen to maintain the Ukrainian economy, once an essential part of the Soviet military-industrial complex, within its reach. It tried to attract Ukraine to the Commonwealth of Independent States (CIS) economic union, envisioning not just a free trade area but a deeper cooperation, but Kiev preferred the status of CIS associate member. And sharing an economic space with Russia would have been incompatible with Ukraine's WTO membership. The EU FTA project and Kiev's accession to the WTO challenge Russia's economic regionalism. And Ukraine's WTO membership reinforces its implementation of the Western economic model.

The second factor is gas and energy geopolitics. Although Ukraine has large untapped oil and gas reserves, it continues to import nearly all of the natural gas it consumes either from or through Russia. This explains why the state-owned Gazprom's primary aim is to control as much of the Ukrainian domestic gas market as possible, as well as its transit routes, for which Russia pays a transit fee. In April 2008, Premier Tymoshenko annulled the country's only hydrocarbon production sharing agreement, signed by her predecessor and opponent Yanukovich, owing to fears of murky relations with Moscow. The move not only tightens dependence on Russia's gas imports and politics, but it may also discourage foreign investors from developing the Ukrainian gas sector.[11]

Ukraine has benefited from low Russian gas prices, taking advantage of being a former Soviet republic and a transit country on the gas route to the EU.[12] This favorable status ceased when Russia started redefining its contractual obligations with gas prices running up from $50 per 1,000 cubic meters in 2005 to $179 per 1,000 cubic meters in 2008.[13] The latest gas crisis occurred in early 2008 and 2009, but new ones are expected by 2011, when the prices Russia charges Ukraine for gas are expected to equal Europe's. Kiev's incapacity to pay such prices, as well as to convince Central Asian countries to reduce the cost, may incite social unrest ahead of the 2010 presidential election and slow down the reforms necessary for EU integration.[14] The lack of agreement between Russia and the EU on an energy charter does not favor Ukraine. Russia's projects on the South and North Stream gas pipelines, designed to circumvent the Ukrainian territory (see figure 8-1), will gradually limit Moscow's dependence on transit countries. This scheme may further undermine Ukraine's importance for the EU in the energy sector.

Figure 8-1. *The Russian Pipeline Plans*

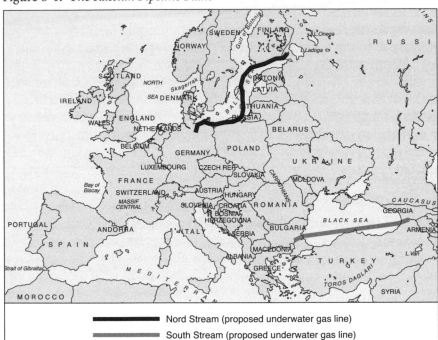

Source: Peter Zeihan, "The Unravelling of Russia's Europe Policy," Stratfor (Strategic Forecasting, Inc.), January 22, 2008.

The third factor is security and Russia's aspiration to safeguard its status as a major regional actor. Ukraine's NATO aspirations are perceived as a direct threat to Russia's security and its foreign policy goal to revise the post–cold war order and international institutions.

The fourth factor is the future of the autonomous region of Crimea. For Ukrainian nationalists the Russian presence there endangers national sovereignty. After Moscow's recognition of South Ossetia and Abkhazia in August 2008, Kiev fears the same fate may befall Crimea, but that scenario appears unrealistic, at least in the short term. Crimean nationalists, who are ethnic Russians, insist instead on joining Russia. Thus the ban on some Russian citizens from entering Crimea, the plans to end the Treaty of Peace and Cooperation stipulating the inviolability of territory and borders, and the anti-NATO demonstrations during NATO military exercises in 2008 are all evidence of the strained relations. The issue of Crimea is also linked to the presence in Sevastopol of the Russian Black Sea Fleet, as convened under an agreement that expires in 2017.[15] Unlike Moscow, Kiev is determined to remove the fleet by that date.

Russia suspects that a stable settling of NATO in the Black Sea region, crossed by its key energy routes to the EU and a fundamental area for its naval forces, may jeopardize the stability of the region. It thus aims to maintain Ukraine as a buffer zone, while trying to control as much as possible of its energy transit routes.

When assessing the EU's policy toward Ukraine, one should also consider the role of NATO.[16] Ukraine aspires to be admitted to the Membership Action Plan (MAP), a preliminary step in anticipation of NATO membership. Ukraine's MAP was expected to be approved at the NATO summit in Riga in 2006, but it was dropped because of political unpreparedness. The 2006 Universal Declaration of National Unity stressed, however, that NATO, EU, and WTO membership are Ukraine's foremost foreign policy objectives. At the NATO summit in Bucharest in April 2008, the MAP decision was once again postponed for further consideration in December 2008, but this time the decision was due to a division on the issue among NATO members.

The United States and some of the EU newcomers such as Poland, the Baltic states, and the Czech Republic strongly supported Ukraine's MAP, echoing U.S. fears that because of geographic and geopolitical "vulnerability" in the post-Soviet space the EU will not be able to safeguard the "demarcation line" of independence of the countries there or offer them alternatives to integration projects led by Russia. Germany and France, however, backed by Italy, pointed out the need to respect Russia's security concerns. As of now, Ukrainian membership in NATO seems highly unlikely. The "old" EU members will remain opposed, while the new U.S. administration of Barack Obama will have to take into account Russia's regional role as advanced with the August 2008 conflict in Georgia. The declining reputation of President Yushchenko, the strongest advocate of immediately accepting Ukraine's MAP, combined with the recent openness of Premier Tymoshenko toward Russia and the continuing low popular support for NATO membership, have downgraded the issue of NATO accession from Ukraine's short-term agenda.

Along with NATO's internal disputes, Kiev will have to address some major challenges. First, Ukraine does not enjoy full domestic support for its efforts to join NATO. This was used as the main reason for delaying the MAP decision.[17] The 2006 Universal Declaration of National Unity stipulates that a referendum on NATO membership should take place before the country's admission. Second, Ukraine's NATO aspirations should be considered within the wider framework of U.S.-Russia relations in the security sector. Ukraine's future "goes to the heart of both sides' perceptions of the nature of international affairs," as Henry Kissinger put it.[18] Russia regards NATO enlargement to include Ukraine as a geopolitical shift that would shatter the equilibrium of the post-Soviet space. This position was also stressed in July 2008 in "The Foreign Policy Concept ot the Russian Federation" approved by President Dmitry Medvedev.[19] Third, Ukraine has to assess the pros and cons of NATO membership.[20] Moreover, Ukraine should take into account that NATO, like the EU, may be experiencing "enlargement fatigue," being both politically and militarily incapable of welcoming a new member bordering Russia, such as Ukraine.

Belarus: Remote from Brussels and Yet Not So Close to Moscow

Unlike Ukraine, Belarus has never declared its desire to join the EU or to move toward a Western path of modernization. On the contrary, Belarus is unwilling to change, and its president, Alexander Lukashenka, "Europe's latest dictator," has shoved the country back into the worst of Soviet times. According to Freedom House, Belarus is a "consolidated autocracy," like Kazakhstan, Uzbekistan, and Turkmenistan.[21] Consequently, the traditional EU instruments, which are based on the principle of conditionality and gradual rapprochement, have been largely ineffective with Minsk. The EU is facing a player that not only disapproves of its economic and political model, but it is also linked to a resurgent power such as Russia, considered by the West almost an antagonist. Nevertheless, Minsk-Moscow relations have been increasingly ambiguous. Despite the project of the Commonwealth of Russia and Belarus, Moscow cooled its friendship with Minsk.[22] This change came in line with a cynical, "de-ideologized," and mercantilist foreign policy.[23] Does the new course of Russian-Belarusian relations leave some space for the EU to be proactive?

Following a referendum in 1996, Lukashenka replaced the first post-Soviet legislature with a National Assembly appointed by himself and has progressively created an authoritarian regime where electoral competition is de facto eliminated by harassment, the banning of opposition parties and leaders, and pressure on the media and the judiciary, as well as heavy restrictions on outside observers. In a referendum in 2004 a constitutional amendment lifted the restriction on the number of terms the president can serve, opening the way for Lukashenka to stay in power indefinitely.

Ukraine's Orange Revolution, unfolding only five weeks after the Belarusian constitutional referendum, raised the regime's concerns that a similar protest movement could occur in Minsk. Lukashenka boosted the law enforcement agencies in 2005 and purged their ranks of potential dissenters. Amendments to the Law on the Interior Troops introduced in February 2005 allowed for the discretionary use of firearms against protesters on orders from the president. The March 19, 2006, presidential elections, in which Lukashenka won a third term, were neither free nor fair, and the OSCE declared that the voting did not meet democratic standards. Although four candidates competed, Lukashenka's victory was clear from the start. The government took harsh repressive measures against the opposition, detaining and beating many campaign workers, including Alyaksandr Kazulin, one of the opposition candidates. A divided opposition that shares only an anti-Lukashenka credo has not been able to present an alternative project or to channel the popular criticism against the regime into a unified political action.

According to the OSCE, despite some minor improvements (such as the slightly greater access of opposition representatives to election commissions and being allowed to conduct meetings in authorized locations without interference), the September 28, 2008, parliamentary elections also did not fulfill the organizational commitments for democratic elections, and none of the seventy-eight opposition candidates won seats in the Parliament. Nevertheless, the election was freer than the previous one in 1994, when no opposition candidates were allowed to run.

The EU has reacted to the deterioration of democracy in Belarus by reverting to negative conditionality (punishments and sanctions) since Belarus does not aspire to EU membership. In September 1997, the EU suspended contacts and contractual agreements with Belarus and its assistance in support of civil society.[24] Since 1997, EU policy has sought to isolate the regime in Minsk and to induce positive changes through the prospect of renewed ties. Belarus has been included in the ENP, but so far no official negotiations have been opened on that dossier. In June 2007 the EU also withdrew Belarus's trade preferences under the Generalized System of Preferences (GSP), after the International Labor Organization voiced concern over the curtailing of the rights of trade unions in the country. Belarus also faces one of the most restrictive trade regimes with the EU in the textiles sector.

The EU pressure has not had much effect on the course of the country's domestic politics. The main reason resides in the country's strong economic dependency on Russia. As a result, Brussels cannot seriously affect Belarus's economy with sanctions or other restrictive measures. On the contrary, the way the West has exerted pressure on Lukashenka's regime risks being counterproductive. Generally, interference from abroad is depicted as a challenge to Belarusian sovereignty, while Lukashenka presents himself as the only bulwark against such threats, consolidating his internal legitimacy. Moreover, the more the West ostracizes Belarus the more the latter seeks partners among "deviant" countries such as Venezuela or "rogue states" such as Iran and North Korea.[25]

In general the EU is not palatable to the Belarusian political elite: representing a menace to Lukashenka's undemocratic regime, the EU is seen as a postmodern state (in contrast to the traditional modern state embodied by both Belarus and Russia). In addition, the EU is considered unreliable because it is a divided actor whose ENP is challenged by competing EU national interests while its effectiveness rests on intergovernmental initiatives. Finally, the ENP has proved unable to prevent crises, as illustrated by Russia's recognition of the independence of Georgia's breakaway regions of South Ossetia and Abkhazia in August 2008.

Looking at public opinion, the picture is also not promising. According to national surveys conducted between 2000 and 2006, there is a declining sense of European identity in Belarus, Ukraine, and Russia. Attitudes toward the EU and the possibility of becoming members are broadly supportive, but a substantial proportion of respondents have no view or say they are poorly informed about European matters. In Belarus only 16 percent of those interviewed in 2008 were strongly in favor of EU membership (in 2004 the figure was 25 percent) and 28 percent had no view.[26]

The EU must also be aware that Lukashenka's positive signs toward the West are mainly for appearances. Lukashenka is trying to re-brand his country and has launched a public relations campaign to improve its image abroad. The president also signed a memorandum on March 27, 2008, to establish a permanent mission of the European Commission in Minsk. However, this was not followed by any change in the established pattern of domestic political oppression. When the main opposition parties organized street demonstrations on March 25, 2008, to commemorate the ninetieth anniversary of the foundation of the Belarusian People's Republic, the short-lived independent Belarusian state, the authorities responded with preemptive arrests of activists and then sent riot police to disperse the demonstrators. Furthermore, in early August 2008, the president signed a decree equating the Internet with TV and printed materials, enabling him to gag opposition publishing activity. As for the conflict in Georgia, Lukashenka at first refrained from taking Russia's side, but then after a meeting with Russian president Dmitry Medvedev affirmed that Russian forces behaved "perfectly, in a very calm, wise, and beautiful manner."

But the real reason for the EU's failure in Belarus is the country's economic system and its dependence on Russia. This was illustrated, for example, on January 1, 2007, when Russia raised the price of its gas supplies to Belarus to $100 per 1,000 cubic meters from $46.70 in 2006. The price of gas paid by Belarus is to gradually increase to the European market level by 2011. However, the price paid by Belarus remains among the lowest of the former Soviet states thanks to its 2007 deal with Gazprom, which bought 50 percent of the country's pipeline monopoly company, Beltransgaz.[27] The tension between Moscow and Minsk also had effects on the West: on January 7, 2007, the Russian state-owned company Transneft stopped oil transport through the Druzhba (Friendship) pipeline, which carries Russian supplies via Belarus to Poland and then western Europe, on the grounds that Belarus had been illegally taking oil equal to the value of the transit duty that Minsk had imposed. Since then, Russia has planned to have sufficient energy transit capacity at its own Baltic ports.[28]

The Russian decision to raise gas prices for Belarus opened up a new phase in the relations between the two countries. Why did Moscow take such an unexpected and controversial decision? There are two main explanations: one is market driven, the other politically driven. The most rational explanation was offered by Moscow itself: a gradual transition to market relations with Belarus in accordance with the WTO's veto on favoring neighbors. Russia also sought to increase its energy trade value, along with the strategy of the former president Vladimir Putin to raise state income through export duties on energy.[29] Russia's political elite is not willing to divert the country's strategic resources to recreate the failed Soviet empire. This would imply paying to modernize the former republics and providing for the social welfare of their citizens. As a result, Russia has no objection to other Eurasian states developing political and economic ties with other states, as long as Russia's vital interests are not compromised. Russia's plan is rather to build up a Eurasian economic and political zone where Moscow sets the overall agenda.[30]

In the West, the decision triggered accusations that Moscow is using oil and gas as a political weapon. But it could be argued that if Moscow had not raised the price of its gas supplies to Minsk, then Russians were buying Belarus loyalty. In this way and in the pursuit of its own national interests, Russia was giving Minsk an opportunity to be more politically autonomous.

For those who favor a change in Belarusian domestic politics, Russia's decision should be applauded for undermining the government's statist economic model. The stability of Lukashenka's regime was guaranteed by huge profits ensured by oil and gas from Russia, which guaranteed full employment and equitable income distribution.

In addition, the restructuring of the fuel sector could reduce the influence of the highly corrupt elite, who are a serious obstacle to the modernization of the country. The government is already strained by the higher prices now being paid for Russian energy supplies. In Belarus, energy consumption is high because of the very low energy efficiency of buildings and in key sectors such as the metallurgical and chemical industries.[31] Through cheap energy supplies and the re-export of oil products alone, Minsk has earned about $6,500 million per year. The government has started shifting away from its statist and populist policies, acknowledging the need for more privatization in the major industries, reform of the country's collective farming system, and a reduction in subsidies to producers and consumers.[32] More economic freedom could mean more political freedom, gradually leading to a democratic regime. Contrary to the process of democratization in central and eastern Europe, the pattern in Belarus might be reversed and economic liberalization could anticipate and boost political reforms.

Final Remarks

EU policy toward Ukraine and Belarus needs to be revised. The Ukraine-EU relationship has a twofold dimension. On the one hand, there is a turbulent domestic political situation due to external competing influences; on the other hand, there is a weak ENP, requiring some revisions. Ukraine's Euro-Atlantic integration ambitions appear incompatible with continuous government rotations and poor institutional governance. Although some scholars and Ukrainian politicians argue that democratic consolidation is unlikely to occur without a clear prospect of EU membership, the country should try to elaborate a genuine national development pattern combining Western integration with a specific national policy. The latter should stem from a mature awareness of Russia's influence and economic strength, and a well-pondered use of national economic bargaining tools. As of now, Ukraine is not exploring its potential to engage both its eastern (Russia) and western (EU) neighbors and is not trying to mediate their relations. On the EU side, negotiations on the future bilateral legal framework (the NEA) should take into consideration the Polish-Swedish proposal as well as the French president's proposal to define it as an Association Agreement.

As for Belarus, which does not aspire to become a EU member, the only way for Brussels to make it an open market and a transitional democracy is to cooperate with Moscow. When dealing with Russia the EU confronts two alternatives: either compete or cooperate. The first option is very risky and unfit for a "civilian power." In addition, the EU is largely dependent on Russia's energy supplies. The second option is more realistic and suitable for a number of reasons. Only Russia has the capacity to destabilize the centralized Belarusian economy and its political regime. The EU doesn't have the economic means to sustain Belarus's transition to a market economy considering, in particular, the high social costs this process implies in a socialist country. Moreover, Lukashenka's sporadic overtures to the West have not been the outcome of a successful Western strategy but rather the consequence of the shifting dynamics of his relationship with Russia. The EU is still poorly known for representing an alternative to the current political stagnation or an incentive for change. The United States as well has little leverage, as the imposition of sanctions has shown. The case of Belarus should not be tackled separately from other issues confronting Brussels and Moscow. In particular, it should be part of a broader package deal (such as that discussed in negotiations to renew the Partnership and Cooperation Agreement).

The cases of Ukraine and Belarus cast doubts on the ENP's efficacy and on the whole Western strategy of democratizing contiguous areas when EU membership is not on the table. The external actors seem too confident in the success of the usual paths of democratization and have neglected countries' structural differences. A sense of realpolitik should be injected in the EU's Ostpolitik. So far, too much institutionalism has restricted the EU's efficacy in the area. The European diplomatic capacity to deal with Moscow should also be used to sort out the critical situations in the area. But the weak and unattractive ENP only creates disenchantment among beneficiary countries and exacerbates Russia's aggressive tone. Brussels should try to create regional conditions for a win-win situation and to avoid any initiative that insults Moscow's sensibilities.

Notes

1. This chapter was completed in September 2008 during a very unstable phase in Ukraine's domestic politics. By the time of publication some facts and considerations might have changed.

2. See the French plan for a Mediterranean Union or the Polish-Swedish proposal to strengthen the EU's ties with its eastern neighbors.

3. Olga Shumylo, "The Debate on the EU Membership Prospects of Ukraine," Polish Institute of Public Affairs Policy Brief, January 2007.

4. Vsevolod Samokhvalov, "Relations in the Russia-Ukraine-EU Triangle: 'Zero-Sum Game' or Not?" ISS Occasional Paper 68 (Paris: EU Institute for Security Studies, September 2007).

5. Kataryna Wolczuk, "Ukraine and Its Relations with the EU in the Context of the European Neighbourhood Policy"; and Sabine Fischer, Rosaria Puglisi, and Pawel Wolowski, "Ukraine: Quo Vadis?" both in Chaillot Paper 108 (February 2008), pp. 99–100.

6. Rob Boudewijn, Evelyn Van Kampen, and Jan Rood, "Overview Paper of EU Policy Seminar: Exploring the Scope of the European Neighbourhood Policy towards New Forms of Partnership?" EN Paper (The Hague: Clingendael Institute, April 11, 2008), p. 7.

7. Kerry Longhurst, "Injecting More Differentiation in European Neighbourhood Policy: What Consequences for Ukraine?" *Russie. Nei. Visions* no. 32 (Paris: IFRI, July 2008), p. 12.

8. "Ukraine Economy: WTO Entry Secured," *Economist Intelligence Unit*, April 11, 2008.

9. Samokhvalov, "Relations in the Russia-Ukraine-EU Triangle."

10. Fyodor Lukyanov, "Good Policies Should Make Good Neighbours," *Moscow Times*, March 19, 2008.

11. "Mugging Energy Investors," *Economist Intelligence Unit*, May 16, 2008.

12. Roughly 120 billion cubic meters of Russian natural gas transit Ukraine directed toward the EU.

13. The Kremlin's strategy under the Yanukovich government was to exploit the gas pricing dispute with Ukraine and the consequent suspension of gas deliveries to Europe

as a way to force Brussels to back Yanukovich's policies, thus strengthening Russia's influence in the country against the Orange Coalition.

14. In order to remedy a hike in gas prices at the beginning of 2009 (largely due to the increase in Central Asian gas prices), in October 2008 Premier Tymoshenko and her Russian counterpart, Vladimir Putin, signed a Memorandum of Understanding foreseeing a three-year transition to European pricing for Ukrainian gas imports and a parallel increase in gas transit fees payable by Russia to Ukraine.

15. The fleet, consisting of approximately 14,000 Russian Navy personnel, is a means for Russia to prevent Ukraine from entering the alliance, since NATO rules prohibit accession of new members when there are nonmember states' troops deployed in their territories.

16. Launched in 1991, Ukraine-NATO relations developed through different initiatives: the Partnership for Peace in 1994; the Charter on a Distinctive Partnership between Ukraine and NATO in 1997; the adoption of the NATO-Ukraine Action Plan in 2002; and, following the Orange Revolution, the launching of the "intensified dialogue" on membership.

17. A February 2008 poll by the Razumkov Centre Survey Institute found that only 25 percent of the Ukrainian population, concentrated mainly in western Ukraine, supports NATO membership. In the period 2004–07, 11 percent of Ukrainians changed their opinion of NATO for the better, 9 percent for the worse (compared in the same time span with 21 percent and 3 percent concerning the appeal of EU membership). The majority (61.9 percent), however, continued to oppose Ukrainian membership in NATO.

18. Kissinger quoted in "Unconventional Wisdom," *International Herald Tribune*, July 1, 2008.

19. President of Russia, "The Foreign Policy Concept of the Russian Federation" (http://eng.kremlin.ru/text/docs/2008/07/204750.shtml [September 2009]).

20. John Kriendler, "Ukrainian Membership in NATO: Benefits, Costs and Challenges," Occasional Paper 12 (Garmisch-Partenkirchen, Germany: George C. Marshall European Center for Security Studies, July 2007), pp. 6–10.

21. Consolidated autocracies are often based on strong presidential systems or one-party systems, with the opposition political parties having only weak power. In these regimes economic power is also derived from political patronage. Usually the economic sphere is controlled by high-ranking officials (the president and his inner circle) leaving no space for a true opposition to develop (www.freedomhouse.org/inc/content/pubs/fiw/inc_country_detail.cfm?year=2008&country=7351&pf [August 2008]).

22. On April 2, 1996, the Treaty Establishing the Commonwealth of Russia and Belarus was signed. Following this, the decision was made to institute a parliamentary assembly—the representative organ of the Commonwealth—in which both Russia and Belarus would be equally represented. The commonwealth was a more consolidated interstate structure than the CIS, and it should have developed into a United States of Russia and Belarus. At the moment this union remains a political project that depends primarily on the personal relationship between the respective presidents.

23. On Russia's foreign policy orientation see Sergey Lavrov, "Munich: World Politics at the Crossroads," *Moskovskiye Novosti*, March 23, 2007 (www.russianembassy.org).

24. According to Aleksander Milinkievich, head of the democratic opposition force in Belarus, the entire population needs to undertake a process of "de-sovietization" and "de-communitization." See interview, "Quelle situation en Biélorussie?" (Fondation Robert Schuman, May 13, 2008), p. 1.

25. Belarus supplies Venezuela with modern weapons, including medium-range air defense systems. In return, Venezuela provides Belarusian companies access to its oil. Belarus and Venezuela also signed an agreement on visa-free travel.

26. For an analysis of survey data on Russia, Belarus, and Ukraine toward Europe, the EU, and EU membership, see Stephen White, Julia Korosteleva, and Ian McAllister, "A Wider Europe? The View from Russia, Belarus and Ukraine," *Journal of Common Market Studies* 46, no. 2 (March 2008): 219–41.

27. Gazprom agreed to pay $2.5 billion for half ownership of Beltransgaz.

28. Russia currently exports about 80 percent of its oil products through ports in the Baltic states. The building of a seaport at Ust-Luga in the Gulf of Finland outside St. Petersburg should ensure steady transit of oil and gas from both Russia's oil-rich regions and Kazakhstan to Europe via the Baltic Pipeline System-2 (BPS-2), stretching from western Russia's Bryansk region to the Leningrad region. The Ust-Luga port is expected to reach an annual transit capacity of 100–130 million tons of oil and oil derivatives by 2015. BPS-2 is the second stage of the Baltic Pipeline System, which was commissioned in 2001 and has a current capacity of 75 million tons.

29. On this see Rainer Lindner, "Friendship Blockaded," *SWP Comments* 2 (January 2007).

30. As Gvosdev puts it, "Why should it be Russia's problem whether citizens in Tbilisi, Tashkent or Kiev have sufficient power and heat during the winter, or an effective health-care and educational system?" Nikolas K. Gvosdev, "The Sources of Russian Conduct," *National Interest* (Spring 2004).

31. Natural gas consumption per capita in Ukraine and Belarus is among the highest in the world. See Grzegorz Gromadzki and Wojciech Konończuk, "Energy Game, Ukraine, Moldova and Belarus between the EU and Russia" (Warsaw: Batory Foundation, August 2007).

32. For instance, the Turkish mobile telephone firm Turkcell announced in the summer of 2008 the acquisition of an 80 percent stake in the state-owned Belarusian Telecommunication Network (BeST). In October 2007 a controlling stake in the second-largest mobile operator, MDC, was sold to Telekom Austria for US$1 billion. A stake in Belinvestbank was sold to Germany's Commerzbank in 2008.

LUCA GORI

9 The Balkans and the European Union

The consternation and sense of horror caused by the crises that overwhelmed the former Yugoslavia for so long in the early 1990s are still vivid in Europe's collective memory. Those events have by no means been forgotten, nor have the impotence and the lack of preparation with which the European Union addressed them between June 1991 and October 1995.

It was not until the negotiation of the Dayton peace accords, between February 1996 and April 1997, that the EU began to draw up a wide-ranging strategy, opening up "a European perspective" for all the countries in the area. The EU initiative has gradually changed the underlying political "datum" of the Balkans and the history of the whole region. The "European perspective" triggered a new way of thinking that it is hoped will direct them toward the future.

What assessment is to be made of the outcome of European policy in the region at the end of ten years (1996–2006)?[1] What lessons have we learned? Could the EU have done more and better?

The commitment of the European Union, particularly since 1996, has certainly had a very positive, and in many respects decisive, impact on the Balkans, especially with regard to the political stabilization of the area. Results have been equally noteworthy on European "integration" and the "transformation" of those countries. However, it cannot be denied that greater and more rapid progress might have been possible, both considering the vast amount of resources invested in the region by the international community over these years and by virtue of the parallelism of the timing and, above all, the methods followed by eastern Europe in its rapprochement with Brussels. Gauged in terms of these two criteria, any judgment about EU policy toward the region, while strongly positive, must necessarily be nuanced and take the form of a glass both half empty and half full.

The glass is half full when one thinks of Croatia and the former Yugoslav Republic of Macedonia. These two countries were in a state of war and on the brink of internal implosion until very recently, but are now candidates for EU membership. The glass is full if we gauge the progress made by the countries in the region in their relations with each other: after being embroiled in savage fighting, they have now established what are essentially good neighborly relations and important forms of regional cooperation, such as the free trade area and the South Eastern Europe Regional Energy Market. The glass is also full if we consider that security and stability on the other side of the Adriatic do not appear to be seriously threatened, and the economies in those countries have been evolving and growing.

The glass is empty, on the other hand, when one recalls that after so many years the issues of statehood have still not yet been definitively resolved, that Serbia has not yet concluded a contractual agreement with the EU, that Bosnia and Herzegovina still have a very fragile institutional structure, that radical nationalism has not yet been reined in, that the problems of "hard" security are being replaced by "soft" security problems, and that GDP growth does not necessarily bring about widespread well-being.

As for the explanations for this important but partial success, it should be remembered that it is always extremely complicated to operate in the Balkans. A "happy ending" is something that does not seem to belong to the history or culture of those troubled lands. Explanations must therefore be sought in the aftermath of the civil wars in the 1990s, including the policies of the local governments. Their political, economic, and administrative weaknesses, insufficient human and financial resources, and the prevailing ethnic and nationalistic interests and rationales made them unable and unwilling to carry out the reforms needed.

To discover whether and where the European Union could have done more, it is worth focusing on how the two key instruments of the EU's Balkan strategy, the "European perspective" and "conditionality," have been used. Experience has shown that in order to facilitate progress on reform in the countries in the region, a fair balance must be maintained between the quantity and the quality of the incentives offered, on the one hand, and the type and severity of the conditions with which the countries must comply in order to obtain them, on the other. Put another way, a balance between a clear and tangible "European perspective" and a strong and equitable "conditionality" must be obtained. EU policy toward the region has only intermittently achieved this "virtuous" combination.

The "European perspective" on the western Balkans, set forth with the adoption of the Regional Approach between February 1996 and April 1997, was the result of Europe's political failure in the early 1990s, its failed attempt to prevent, and subsequently to stop, the wars in the former Yugoslavia, its historical awareness of the link between security in the Balkans and security in western

Europe, and a state of necessity, exploiting the Dayton peace accords to recover the political initiative it had previously lost.

However, this perspective embodied a timid political commitment that was much more concerned with responding to the past than with paving the way for the future. That commitment was "dragged along" by events, and its power of attraction in the region was inevitably limited. It was a strategy with strong elements of conditionality, but contained no prospect for future membership in the Union. At most, it held out the possibility of a privileged relationship between the EU and the countries in the region. In essence, this was merely the same kind of cooperation and financial assistance agreement that had existed between Brussels and Belgrade since 1970.

Having said that, it has to be recognized that the persistence of a post-conflict climate and of authoritarian governments in the area, with values and technical standards far removed from the "European family," made it objectively difficult to envisage a more explicit and advanced integration project during those years. Until 1999 the Regional Approach remained, with all its limitations, the EU benchmark strategy.

It was only with the emotional backlash of the Kosovo crisis that, in the spring of 1999, the European Union seemed to opt for a clear EU "accession perspective" for all the countries on the other side of the Adriatic. This decision was further heightened in 2000 by the death of Croatian president Franjo Tudjman and by Yugoslav president Slobodan Milosevic's political demise. This is how, in June 1999, the Stability Pact for South Eastern Europe was launched, which spoke for the first time of possible EU "accession" and of the "Stabilization and Association Process" (SAP, launching the Stabilization and Association Agreements). One year later, in June 2000, the European Council in Feira declared the Balkan countries to be "potential candidates," and in November of that year the first summit was held in Zagreb between the EU heads of state and government and the Balkan states. This development on the side of the "European perspective" was matched by an enhancement of "conditionality." The EU began to incorporate the Copenhagen criteria that had been laid down in 1993 for the eastern European candidate countries into the benchmark principles for the integration of the Balkan countries.

At the end of 2000, the European Union had managed to establish a more balanced relationship between supply and demand, between the "carrot and the stick," laying the foundation for the strategy to become more effective and to produce the hoped-for results. With specific conditions, it had put forward what was certainly a more attractive political proposal representing a significant conceptual development. It had, however, two weak points. First, it was only partially accompanied by substantive measures, though in 2000 the CARDS (Community

Assistance for Reconstruction, Development and Stabilization) financial assistance instrument was approved, and autonomous preferential commercial measures granted. Second, it appeared to have been dictated by the contingent crisis in Kosovo and not inspired by any properly deliberated political choice.

In the wake of the Kosovo experience, the Union also made progress on crisis prevention and management, demonstrating that it was able to act more promptly and effectively on at least two occasions: in 2001, when the EU prevented the civil war in the former Yugoslav Republic of Macedonia from threatening the very survival of the country; and in 2002, when it defused the constitutional dispute in Serbia and Montenegro between Belgrade and Podgorica.

Unlike before, the EU was able to rely on a more mature strategy for the region that was more broadly endorsed by the member states (the Stability Pact, the Stabilization and Association Process), and more effective Common Foreign and Security Policy (CFSP) instruments (the Maastricht and Amsterdam Treaties). Above all, it succeeded in exploiting the greater balance that had been struck between the "European perspective" and "conditionality" to help reach an agreement. In the case of the former Yugoslav Republic of Macedonia, which was in a state of all-out crisis, Brussels signed the Stabilization and Association Agreement with Skopje on the condition that the parties adopt more constructive positions. With regard to the dispute between Podgorica and Belgrade, the CFSP High Representative, Javier Solana, sent a clear message: by remaining together, the two republics would make faster progress in the European integration process.

In June 2003, with the approval of the Salonika Agenda, the EU policy toward the region improved substantially. The summit of heads of state and government under the Greek Presidency approved the document. It sent out a clear message that dispelled any doubt that the promise of EU accession made to the Balkans in 1999 was merely a contingent choice dictated by the Kosovo crisis. The agenda gave concrete substance to their promise, extending to the countries in the region the same working methodology and advantages that had previously been granted to the candidate countries of eastern Europe, with the exception of pre-accession funds. And it was at Salonika that the Union also completed the conditionality framework, placing particular emphasis on cooperation with the Hague tribunal and the mechanisms for ascertaining compliance.

In essence, in the summer of 2003 the EU was able to claim that, for the first time, it had a consistent and well-articulated Balkan policy covering every aspect. This strategy rested on two robust pillars, now conceptually and operationally well structured: a clear European perspective and a powerful conditionality.

Between June 2003 and the spring of 2005, that policy produced major results in the Balkans, epitomized in June 2004 by the recognition of Croatia as a candidate country. There was then a very strong feeling that the "transforming power" of the Union was working, despite the difficulties in making the carrot sufficiently appetizing and the "stick" sufficiently credible to cause the countries of the former Yugoslavia to emulate the behaviors of the former USSR satellite countries. Those were the years in which a maximum consensus was established between the member states regarding the Union's policy toward the region. The European Council discussed how and to what extent to apply the conditions that would enable the countries concerned to make progress toward European integration, but there was no doubt about the soundness of the process they had embarked upon.

This consensus collapsed in the spring of 2005, and in 2006 it was openly challenged. After the failure of the French and Dutch referendums on the European constitution, the decision to begin negotiations with Turkey and "enlargement fatigue" led the EU to adopt a more severe approach to conditionality for both accession and pre-accession. Simultaneously, a number of mental reservations reemerged among certain member states regarding the European perspective for the western Balkans. This perspective became more fragile and uncertain. The balance between the two driving forces of the EU policy toward the region, so painstakingly and slowly elaborated, broke down.

In formal terms, the Union did not appear to pull back from its commitments, however. Indeed, in December 2005 the Union recognized the former Yugoslav Republic of Macedonia as a candidate country. But the decision to begin a debate on the future of enlargement and the introduction of concepts according to which, when deciding on new enlargements, account would in the future have to be taken of the Union's "absorption capacity" and of the public's views, inevitably made the European future of the Balkans look increasingly uncertain. The decision in Salzburg in March 2006, under the Austrian Presidency, to relaunch the Salonika commitments clashed with this new situation and had to address it. The EU policy toward the region once again became timid and ambiguous. While the results of the debate on the future of enlargement in December 2006 reiterated, in principle, the "European perspective" for the Balkans, they also formalized the awareness that the path to Brussels had been lengthened and made more difficult, to the point of making the finishing line opaque.

It was only between 2000 and 2004 that the EU managed to strike a balance between the incentives offered and the conditions with which countries needed to comply, producing concrete and welcome results. For the rest, it is difficult not to note that, beyond all the rhetoric, the "European perspective" often appeared even weaker than the "conditionality" accompanying it. That had been the case between 1996 and 1999, and once again between 2005 and 2006. In both periods the promise of a place in Europe often seemed to be vaguely defined in form and substance and accompanied by too many caveats.

There was a feeling that the European perspective for the Balkans had been, and had once again become, too vague and too distant to act as a stimulus to comply with the greater conditionality required. The reward was no longer considered so appetizing, as demonstrated by the slowing of the reforms throughout the region beginning in 2006.

This slowdown was obviously also due to internal factors, but for the EU institutions it must have sounded like a warning bell signaling Europe's reduced capacity to have any effect on the governments' policies in the area. Despite all the attempts to make the European perspective more concrete and tangible, they have proved unsuccessful and inadequate to convince the citizens of the Balkans of the benefits they would derive from it. For they have continued to feel that this was a political commitment addressed primarily to the governments and the institutions, and that Europe, in the ultimate analysis, would only have a marginal effect on their personal, economic, and social condition. It has to be admitted that in many respects this perception was accurate.

The future of the European perspective for the Balkans will depend on the outcome of the enlargement debate in Brussels in 2010 and on its significance and implications. While reiterating that "the future of the Western Balkans is in the EU," the European Council in December 2006 confirmed a substantial imbalance between the incentives of the European perspective for those countries and the conditions with which they had to comply in order to benefit from it. On the basis of this, the crucial political issue the Union has been faced with since then is keeping the Balkan governments committed to the Community agenda, considering that they cannot realistically expect accession to the EU to take place in the short or medium term. Will it be possible to regenerate the momentum of the process transforming the Balkans? How can a long phase of stagnation be avoided as the region moves along the path toward Europe?

There is no shortage of ideas on the subject. Some observers propose a customs union between those countries and the EU along the lines of what was done in the past with Turkey. Others would like to set a "target date" for accession as a short- or medium-term incentive or stimulus. Still others are demanding more active use of "visa liberalization," as well as giving countries pre-accession funds, drafting a more aggressive strategy for agriculture and economic and social development, putting in place a regional mechanism to foster direct investment, and focusing on educating and providing vocational training for the younger generations and for people-to-people contacts.

These are interesting proposals, all of which offer pros and cons that have to be examined with care. Whatever steps are taken, it must be noted that between 2005 and 2006 the accession process became lengthier and more complex, and an incisive and bold political initiative is needed to reactivate a virtuous process in relations between Brussels and the countries in the area. The high road to be taken is therefore managing the pre-accession phase in a less rigid manner. And if all of us are interested in ensuring that the Balkan countries become EU members only when they are ready to do so, it would benefit no one if cooperation between the Union and the region ran aground and stagnated. This would be pernicious immobility. Brussels would continue with its stale rhetoric about the "European perspective" pretending to want to integrate the region into the Community structures, while the Balkan governments would persist in pretending to adopt and carry through the reforms requested of them. The effects of such a scenario would likely be doubly negative: first, the stability of the area would have to be guaranteed by keeping costly military and policing missions there and forms of international protectorates for many years to come; second, a "black hole" that would generate soft insecurity—illegal trafficking, organized crime, and migration problems—would have to be dealt with.

To avoid this eventuality and at the same time give a powerful incentive to these countries to comply with the European standards, Europe should play the candidate status card more actively. In other words, under certain conditions the EU could recognize the Balkans' status as candidate countries without embarking on accession negotiations as such. Such a move would have no institutional impact on the EU, because its only effect in practice would be to qualify the candidate countries for pre-accession funding. And this kind of funding has played a key part in helping the eastern European countries move in the direction of Brussels.

If the western Balkan countries still see accession as a long-term prospect, the Union must grant them candidate status as a short-term objective. In so doing, the EU would be opting for an active strategy, rather than a wait-and-see or reactive strategy. It would provide tangible incentives that lie within these countries' grasp, which could drive the governments to energetically relaunch the reform processes and more rapidly get in line with European standards. Choosing an approach of this kind would nevertheless require political courage and strategic farsightedness on the part of the member states and the Community institutions. These are qualities that the EU today is lacking, and not only in its policy toward the Balkans.

Note

1. This chapter analyzes the origin and development of the "European perspective" for the western Balkans from 1996 (when it took shape with the Regional Approach policy) to December 2006 (when the European Council held a major debate on the future of EU enlargement). It does not deal specifically with the question of the final status of Kosovo, which would have required more space and a different approach.

JOSEPH S. JOSEPH

10

EU Enlargement: The Challenge and Promise of Turkey

The geographic expansion of the European Union, known as "widening," brings challenges and opportunities to the EU, its member states and the candidate countries. It also affects the "deepening" of the Union and its efforts for institutional reform. This is a challenging task, as shown by the failure of the Constitutional Treaty and the difficulties faced by the Lisbon Treaty. At present there are three candidate countries: Turkey and Croatia, which started accession negotiations in 2005, and the former Yugoslav Republic of Macedonia (FYROM), which has not yet started the accession negotiations. There are also five potential candidate countries: Albania, Bosnia-Herzegovina, Montenegro, Serbia, and Kosovo under UN Security Council Resolution 1244. These countries have been promised the prospect of EU membership as and when they are ready.

Of these countries Turkey is the most interesting case. It signed an Association Agreement in 1963 and applied for full membership in 1987. This chapter explores EU-Turkish relations and provides an overview of the challenges and opportunities that Turkey presents to the EU, and vice versa. The chapter addresses issues and aspects of EU-Turkish relations in the past, Turkey's present and future Western orientation, and the EU's future expansion in southeastern Europe.

The history of contemporary Turkey is characterized by change. The main causes have been external stimuli and incentives, particularly the drive for transformation from an oriental Islamic empire to a secular national state. This transformation, known as Westernization, has been slow and occasionally painful. It has been aptly called "the Turkish revolution," and, as Bernard Lewis pointed out, it could be defined not only "in terms of economy or society or government, but of civilization."[1] It gained momentum with the establishment of the Turkish Republic in 1923 and the ascent of Kemalism, when "everything had to be rebuilt, above all a new identity."[2] Its main goal was to transform Turkey from a medieval Islamic theocracy to a modern capitalist Western democracy. At the center of the Kemalist ideology and its state- and nation-building efforts was the consolidation of the Turkish Republic. It was based on a political system whose core principles were "heavily tainted by a historically developed authoritarian understanding of the unitary state and its functioning as well as an organic and homogenous understanding of the nation."[3]

The scope of Westernization was eventually broadened to include economic, social, and cultural changes. In the wake of the dismantling of the Ottoman Empire and in the process of reformation and sociopolitical reorientation, "the replacement of old, Islamic conceptions of identity, authority, and loyalty by new conceptions of European origin was of fundamental importance. In the theocratically conceived polity of Islam, God was to be twice replaced: as the source of sovereignty, by the people; as the object of worship, by the nation."[4] As a result of these changes, which have taken decades to consolidate, Turkey has become a secular democracy, although the politicization of Islam and the political role of the military are still striking features of the Turkish political landscape.

The success or failure of these protracted reforms has been the topic of an ongoing debate. Turks are "still struggling to digest the heavy burden of Ataturk's legacy" while the prospect of accession to the EU is posing new challenges.[5] In 2005, French president Jacques Chirac commented on Turkey's European aspirations, suggesting that it will have to undergo a "major cultural revolution" to realize its dream of joining the EU.[6] It can be argued, however, that during the past few decades Turkey's changes and achievements have been remarkable and irreversible in many areas of public life.

Today the challenge of Westernization is taking the form of Europeanization, a reform of domestic structures, institutions, and policies to meet the requirements of the systemic logic, political dynamics, and administrative mechanisms of European integration. The role of Turkey in this process can be catalytic, as it will become the EU's first Islamic member state. Indeed, the challenge and promise for both Islamic Turkey and Christian Europe is about seizing the moment and moving beyond the clash of civilizations as the modus operandi of history and the modus vivendi of governments and peoples.

A Long Road of Ups and Downs

Following a protracted period of ups and downs in EU-Turkish relations, accession negotiations started in October 2005. The decision to begin accession negotiations was made by the Brussels European Council in December 2004 "on the basis of a report and recommendation from the Commission, that Turkey fulfills the Copenhagen political criteria."[7]

Although accession negotiations and preparations will last for many years and accession is unlikely to take place even within the next decade, in political terms Turkey is at the threshold of the EU.[8] Pessimists note that although the objective of the negotiations is accession, there can be no automatic guarantee that they will be successfully completed. However, on both sides there is positive predisposition and political will for successful conclusion of the negotiations and full membership for Turkey.

The commencement of the accession negotiations was the culmination of a long relationship that goes back to the EU's early years. Turkey expressed an interest in institutionalizing its relations and becoming an associate member of the European Community in the late 1950s. In 1959 it applied for associate membership, and in 1963 it signed an Association Agreement that was intended to pave the way for full membership. The Association Agreement, known as the Ankara agreement, went into effect in 1964 and provided that when the relations of Turkey with the EC have "advanced far enough to justify envisaging full acceptance by Turkey of the obligations of the [EC] Treaty, [the EC] shall examine the possibility of the accession of Turkey to the European Community."[9]

In 1971 an additional protocol was signed between Turkey and the EC aimed at further strengthening and broadening their economic and political relations. The Association Agreement did not achieve its objective and failed to prepare Turkey for membership. It has been argued that the EU looked at it as a "framework for its containment policy rather than a pre-accession strategy, because it had serious reservations about Turkey's prospects for EU membership on political and economic grounds."[10] Despite its failure, however, the Association Agreement provided a useful link with the European integration process and bolstered Turkey's Westernization policy.

Following the two Mediterranean enlargements of the EU in the 1980s, Turkey applied for full membership in April 1987. The response of the EU was not positive and cited various reasons why "it would be inappropriate for the Community . . . to become involved in new accession negotiations [and] it would not be useful to open accession negotiations with Turkey."[11] After the collapse of the Soviet Union and the end of the cold war, the deepening and widening accelerated. In 1997 the European Council in Luxemburg decided to commence accession negotiations with six countries (the Czech Republic, Cyprus, Estonia, Hungary, Poland, and Slovenia), while excluding Turkey on economic and political grounds. A turning point came two years later at the Helsinki European Council where it was decided that "Turkey is a candidate State destined to join the Union on the basis of the same criteria as applied to the other candidate states."[12] At

Helsinki, a decision was also made to establish an accession partnership with Turkey that would serve as a roadmap to accession. The accession partnership was adopted in 2001 and defined the principles, priorities, conditions, and short- and medium-term objectives for Turkey's integration with the EU.

Another milestone in Turkey's European course was the publication in October 2004 of the positive "Recommendation of the European Commission on Turkey's Progress towards Accession." The recommendation concluded "that Turkey sufficiently fulfills the political criteria and recommends that accession negotiations be opened."[13] This was the first time an EU institution firmly and clearly recommended the opening of accession negotiations. The *Washington Post* said that "Turkey seemed to shift geographically westward."[14] The Commission, however, pointed out that accession negotiations would be an open-ended process, with no automatic final accession. It also warned that the negotiations could be suspended if Turkey violated the principles of democracy, human rights, and the rule of law.

Two months later, in December 2004, the Brussels European Council adopted the recommendation of the Commission and decided to open accession negotiations on October 3, 2005. The message from Brussels was clear: "Turkey has taken its European destiny in its own hands."[15] The decision came at a time when the majority of the European public did not favor Turkey's accession to the EU.[16] The president of the European Commission noted that the challenge for Turkey was "to win the hearts and minds of those European citizens who are open to, but not convinced of, Turkey's European destiny."[17]

At this writing four years after the launching of accession negotiations, not much has been achieved. Only one chapter (Chapter 25, Science and Research) has been opened for negotiations, and it was provisionally closed in June 2006. Following a recommendation by the Commission and a decision by the Council of Ministers in December 2006, which was endorsed by the European Council in December 2006, no other chapter will be provisionally closed (although several chapters have opened) "until the Commission verifies that Turkey has fulfilled its commitments related to the Additional Protocol."[18] The Council of Ministers also decided that eight chapters "covering policy areas relevant to Turkey's restrictions as regards the Republic of Cyprus" will not open.[19] Fulfillment of commitments under the additional protocol has become a benchmark for opening negotiations on eight chapters. Commenting on the decision to partially suspend negotiations on several chapters of the *acquis communautaire* (the total body of EU law), the president of the European Commission stressed "that a breach of legal obligations cannot be accepted. At the same time, continuing this negotiation process clearly lies in our own strategic interest. We need both sides to play by the rules. It is now up to the Turkish side to show its willingness to fulfill its obligations."[20]

Efforts have been made in Brussels, however, to sustain the momentum and political will for Turkey's European course, with the opening of new chapters for accession. As the European commissioner for enlargement put it, "Despite the stalemate on issues related to Cyprus, there has been no train crash. The journey continues steadily, even if at a somewhat slower speed."[21]

The Negotiating Framework and the Principles Governing the Accession Negotiations

Accession negotiations opened because Turkey had met the Copenhagen political criteria.[22] With full regard for all the Copenhagen criteria, including the absorption capacity of the Union, if Turkey is not in a position to assume in full all the obligations of membership then it must be assured that she is fully anchored in the European structures through the strongest possible bond.[23]

Turkey is expected to sustain the process of reform and to work toward further improvements with regard to the principles of liberty, democracy, the rule of law, and respect for human rights and fundamental freedoms, including relevant European case law; to consolidate and broaden legislation and implementation measures specifically in relation to the zero tolerance policy in the fight against torture and ill treatment and the implementation of provisions relating to freedom of expression, freedom of religion, women's rights, ILO standards including trade union rights, and minority rights.

In the case of a serious and persistent breach in Turkey of the principles of liberty, democracy, respect for human rights and fundamental freedoms and the rule of law on which the Union is founded, the European Commission will, on its own initiative or at the request of one-third of the member states, recommend the suspension of negotiations and propose the conditions for eventual resumption. The Council of Ministers would decide by qualified majority on such a recommendation, after having heard Turkey, whether to suspend the negotiations and on the conditions for their resumption.

The advancement of the negotiations is guided by Turkey's progress in preparing for accession within an economic and social framework. This progress is measured in particular against four sets of requirements. The first set is the Copenhagen criteria. The second is Turkey's unequivocal commitment to good neighborly relations and efforts to resolve any border disputes in conformity with the principles of the United Nations Charter, including, if necessary, the jurisdiction of the International Court of Justice. The third is Turkey's continued support for efforts to achieve a comprehensive settlement of the Cyprus problem within the UN framework of and in line with EU principles, and progress in the normalization of bilateral relations between Turkey and all the EU member states, including the Republic of Cyprus. The fourth is the fulfillment of Turkey's obligations under the Association Agreement and its additional protocol pertaining to the EU-Turkey customs union and the implementation of the accession partnership, as regularly revised.

Parallel to the accession negotiations, the European Union is engaged with Turkey in an intensive dialogue on political and civil issues. The aim of this dialogue is to enhance mutual understanding in order to ensure the support of European citizens for the accession process.

Accession implies the acceptance of the rights and obligations derived from the *acquis communautaire*, such as (a) the content, principles, and political objectives of the treaties on which the Union is founded; (b) legislation and decisions adopted pursuant to the treaties, and the case law of the Court of Justice; (c) other acts, legally binding or not, adopted within the Union framework, such as interinstitutional agreements, resolutions, statements, recommendations, and guidelines; (d) joint actions, common positions, declarations, conclusions, and other acts within the framework of the Common Foreign and Security Policy; (e) joint actions, joint positions, conventions signed, resolutions, statements, and other acts agreed within the framework of Justice and Home Affairs; (f) international agreements concluded by the European Community, the Community jointly with the member states, the Union, and those concluded by the member states among themselves with regard to Union activities.

Turkey's acceptance of the rights and obligations arising from the *acquis* may necessitate specific adaptations to the *acquis* and may, exceptionally, give rise to transitional measures that must be defined during the accession negotiations.

The financial aspects of Turkey's accession must be set in the applicable financial framework. Since Turkey's accession could have substantial financial consequences, the negotiations can be concluded only after the establishment of the financial framework for the period from 2014 together with possible consequential financial reforms.

In all areas of the *acquis*, Turkey must bring its institutions, management capacity, and administrative and judicial systems up to EU standards, both at the national and the regional level. This is needed in order to implement the *acquis* effectively or, as the case may be, to implement it effectively in good time before accession. At the general level, this requires a well-functioning and stable public administration built on an efficient and impartial civil service and an independent and efficient judicial system.

The EU will lay down benchmarks for the provisional closure and, where appropriate, for the opening of each chapter.[24] Turkey will be requested to indicate its position on the *acquis* and to report on its progress in meeting the benchmarks. Turkey's correct transposition and implementation of the *acquis*, including effective and efficient application through appropriate administrative and judicial structures, will determine the pace of negotiations.

Issues, Prospects, and Challenges

The accession negotiations and the eventual Turkish accession present challenges to both Turkey and the EU. It is widely accepted that "Turkey's accession would be different from previous enlargements because of the combined impact of Turkey's population, size, geographical location, economic, security and military potential."[25] The negotiations are taking place in the framework of an intergovernmental conference, and decisions must be reached with the unanimous agreement of all member states. Keeping in mind that by the time of Turkish accession the EU will include at least twenty-seven members, the issue of unanimity becomes a critical and complicated one. The case of Turkey will be different and more challenging from previous accessions for a number of reasons, some of which are presented below.[26]

Turkey is a country with a large population and geographic area. With a population of 71 million today, it is projected that it could be the largest member state at the time of accession. To compare, the 2004 EU enlargement included ten countries with a total population of 75 million, while the 2007 enlargement included two countries (Bulgaria and Romania) with a total population of 30 million.

As a secular Muslim country, Turkey will also add a new demographic and religious dimension to the EU. The presence of a large number of Turkish immigrants in European countries raises the issue of possible additional migration. A natural consequence of accession, it may affect the labor market and demography of small member states. The social repercussions of such a development raise sensitivities and pose challenges with political ramifications.

In an effort to address cultural and religious differences at the grass-roots level, the EU is promoting political and cultural dialogue between the people of Turkey and the EU member states. This dialogue addresses concerns and perceptions on issues such as "difference of cultures, religion, issues relating to migration," and "concerns on minority rights and terrorism."[27] The view from Brussels is that although "the negotiation process will be essential in guiding further reforms in Turkey . . . the civil society should play the most important role in this dialogue."[28] This is an interesting and innovative strategy designed to upgrade the role of civil society. Strengthening civil society in Turkey is a major objective of the EU pre-accession strategy.

The Kurdish question is a multifaceted challenge that is becoming more and more an accepted reality and an item on the agenda of EU-Turkish relations. As a "major fault line within Turkish democracy" and a problem without "a solution on the horizon," it is a source of concern at home and in the EU.[29] The EU assessment is that "progress has been slow and uneven. In some cases, it has even deteriorated."[30] The position of the EU is that "a comprehensive strategy should be pursued, to achieve the socio-economic development of the region [the eastern and southeastern part of Turkey] and the establishment of conditions for the Kurdish population to enjoy full rights and freedoms."[31] The Kurdish issue also has ramifications in some EU member states where Kurdish immigrants live and have established active political and cultural organizations. Another transnational aspect of the Kurdish issue is the fact that developments in the neighboring countries of Iraq, Iran, and Syria can easily have an impact on Turkey. As Andrew Mango put it, "Kurdish nationalism is a many-headed hydra, and it will survive somewhere, if not everywhere."[32]

The strategic location of Turkey presents a unique challenge to the EU's external role and policies as "it lies at the epicenter of a series of conflicts, real and potential"[33] in the region. Turkish accession will bring closer to the EU the instability and tensions of a strategically vital region with strong conflicting energy-related interests. As a major power in the region, "Turkey could be drawn into conflicts that work against European, Central Asian, and Middle Eastern integration and peace."[34] In conjunction with this point, the addition of new long external borders will present a major challenge to the EU because it will involve critical policies and issues such as migration, asylum, and drug smuggling.

Turkey's participation in the European Common Foreign and Security Policy could also be controversial. Its role in NATO is a central one, and so far it "has not witnessed a strong 'Europeanization' of its foreign policy."[35] Its large military force will make it a major military power in the EU with the largest number of military personnel. Turkey, like other member states, has already shown that on issues of vital national interest it is not willing to compromise and align its foreign and security policy with the positions of other states. The willingness and ability of Turkey to meet European expectations on issues of security and defense are also largely determined by domestic factors such as civil-military relations and secular-religious dichotomies.

The discussion over external policy and orientation points to the fact that "modern Turkey has functioned as part of several systems—European, Middle Eastern, Eurasian—while remaining on the cultural and political periphery of each."[36] It cannot go unnoticed that Turkey has uneasy bilateral relations with some of its neighbors and has been characterized as a "reluctant neighbor."[37] For example, relations with Syria have been bad in recent decades for various reasons, including water resources and Kurdish connections. Iran's Islamic political orientation and nuclear ambitions are sources of concern for Turkey. Turkey's policy of expanding its influence in the Turkic states of the Caucasus and Central Asia have alarmed Russia, while Armenia has no diplomatic relations with Turkey and the border between the two countries has been closed (an accord for the establishment of diplomatic relations was signed in October 2009).

Turkey has unresolved issues and unstable relations or no relations at all with some EU member states. Greece and Cyprus are cases in point. In recent years, Greek-Turkish relations have improved considerably, and Greece favors Turkish accession, but the political barometer is not steady. The fact that Turkey does not recognize the Republic of Cyprus, a full member of the EU since May 2004, has been a source of legal controversies and political complications. In that regard, there is still an open question: how can a candidate country conduct accession negotiations and sign an international treaty (such as the accession treaty) with a country it does not recognize? The dispute over the implementation of the additional protocol and the European Council's suspension of negotiations on eight chapters in December 2006 as well as the decision not to provisionally close any additional chapter are indicative of the serious problems that can arise.

Turkey has a level of economic development well below the EU average, and its accession will have a considerable budgetary impact on the EU. Among the economic consequences Turkish accession will have for the EU is the creation of a regional economic disparity and financial burden for other member states. According to current regulations and practices, Turkey would receive considerable support from the cohesion and structural funds at the expense of other member states that may no longer be eligible for these funds. The prospect of such a development presents another challenge with political and economic ramifications. Along these lines, Turkey's huge agricultural sector also receives special attention.

The participation of Turkey in the EU institutions will dramatically affect the allocation of power and influence on decisionmaking, policy formulation, and the dynamics of the broader European political arena. As a large member state, Turkey will have a powerful voice in the European Parliament and the Council of Ministers, where most decisions must be approved by a qualified majority. This shift of power from the western Christian capitals to the eastern Islamic frontier is already causing skepticism and reactions in some countries.

There are also issues and aspects inherent in the EU itself and its ability to absorb a new member state like Turkey. Already in 1993, the Copenhagen European Council, besides defining the political and economic criteria, raised the issue of the EU's capacity to grow without undermining the integration process. As stated by the heads of state and government, "the Union's capacity to absorb new members, while maintaining the momentum of European integration, is also an important consideration in the general interest of both the Union and the candidate countries."[38] Structural, political, and economic developments in the EU over the next decade may affect the deepening and widening of the EU in a way that can have an effect on further enlargement, including the accession of Turkey. As it was reconfirmed by the European Council in December 2006, to "sustain the integration capacity of the EU the acceding counties must be ready and able to fully assume the obligations of the Union membership and the Union must be able to function effectively and to develop."[39]

Conclusion: Oriental Past versus Western Future

While accession talks and preparations are under way, the debate over Turkey's European prospects is heating up and a variety of perspectives, positions, opinions, and arguments are being put forward. The former president of the European Commission, Romano Prodi, while arguing for the commencement of accession negotiations, asked Turkey to show "determination in pursuing further reforms and wisely conducting an accession process which, like all the others, will display both periods of progress and moments of tension and unavoidable difficulties." He also appealed to the member states and the European public to demonstrate equal perseverance, as "Europe has nothing to fear from Turkey's accession."[40]

Europe's confusion and ambivalence about Turkey is not a new phenomenon, although it has become more visible. For example, in March 2007, Turkey's government was not invited to the Berlin summit, which marked the fiftieth anniversary of the Treaties of Rome, causing disappointment in Ankara. A few years earlier, the fears of many Europeans about Turkish accession were expressed and stirred up by the former French president and head of the European constitutional convention, Valéry Giscard d'Estaing. In a blunt and provocative manner he declared that Turkey was "not a European country" and that its inclusion in the EU "would be the end of Europe."[41] In a similar vein echoing Turco-skepticism, a European commissioner brought back memories of the Ottoman siege of Vienna by stating that "the liberation of 1683 would have been in vain" if Turkey were to join the EU.

On the other hand, there are strong voices arguing that Turkey can play the role of "a cultural and physical bridge between the East and West. . . . [and]

become one of Europe's most prized additions."[42] Across the Atlantic, the United States has a clear pro-Turkish position that cannot be ignored. In June 2004, during the NATO summit in Istanbul, the American president George W. Bush underlined that position and called on Europe to prove that it "is not the exclusive club of a single religion" and that "as a European power, Turkey belongs in the EU."[43]

The polarized discussion over Turkey's position and role in Europe will continue for years to come at various levels. The debate may even outlast the protracted period of accession negotiations during which not only negotiations on the *acquis* chapters will be conducted, but also a lot of diplomatic maneuvering and political twisting will take place. Throughout this period, the Christian and Islamic worlds will have to show that they can accommodate each other and prove false Samuel Huntington's argument that "the clash of civilizations" will lead to the reconfiguration of the political world "along cultural lines."[44] Both Europe and Turkey will find out what they expect from each other and whether they can share a common future that will reconcile their different pasts. The real question will be whether the internal sociopolitical dynamics and external orientations of Turkey can be compatible with the changing dynamics of the European integration, which aims at deepening the solidarity among peoples "while respecting their history, their culture and their traditions," and creating "firm bases for the construction of the future Europe."[45]

In the long run and in a broader sense, the challenge for the EU will be to develop a forward-looking worldview based on a multicultural civilization that has ample room for different religions, including Islam. In a shrinking world of increasing interdependence this may no longer be a political option, but an urgent imperative for European integration, which is a process of building unity through diversity.

Notes

1. Bernard Lewis, *The Emergence of Modern Turkey*, 2nd ed. (Oxford University Press, 1968), p. 486.

2. N. Pope and H. Pope, *Turkey Unveiled: A History of Modern Turkey*, 2nd ed. (Woodstock: N.Y.: Overlook Press, 2000), p. 59.

3. H. Kramer, *A Changing Turkey: The Challenge to Europe and the United States* (Brookings, 2000), p. 9.

4. Lewis, *The Emergence of Modern Turkey*, p. 486.

5. Pope and Pope, *Turkey Unveiled*, p. 67.

6. Jacques Chirac talking at a press conference on October 4 (the day after accession talks with the EU were launched); see *Guardian Unlimited*, October 5, 2005.

7. Brussels European Council, December 16–17, 2004, "Presidency Conclusions," para. 17 (http://ec.europa.eu/enlargement/pdf/turkey/presidency_conclusions16_17_12 _04_en.pdf [February 2009]).

8. The European Commission recommended that "the EU will need to define its financial perspectives for the period from 2014 before negotiations [with Turkey] can be concluded." See European Commission, Communication from the Commission to the Council and the Parliament, "Recommendation of the European Commission on Turkey's Progress towards Accession," October 6, 2004, p. 5. The recommendation was issued together with the 2004 "Regular Report on Turkey's Progress towards Accession."

9. Agreement Establishing an Association Agreement between the European Economic Community and Turkey, art. 28. The Association Agreement (known as the Ankara agreement) was signed on September 12, 1963, and went into effect on December 1, 1964.

10. H. Arikan, *Turkey and the EU: An Awkward Candidate for EU Membership?* (Burlington, Vt.: Ashgate, 2003), p. 74.

11. Commission of the European Communities, "Commission Opinion on Turkey's Request for Accession to the Community," December 18, 1989, paras. 10 and 11.

12. Helsinki European Council, December 10–11, 1999, "Presidency Conclusions," para. 12 (www.europarl.europa.eu/summits/hel1_en.htm [February 2009]).

13. European Commission, Communication from the Commission to the Council and the Parliament, "Recommendation of the European Commission on Turkey's Progress towards Accession," October 6, 2004, p. 8.

14. *Washington Post*, "Turkey's Continental Drift," October 10, 2004.

15. José Manuel Barroso, president of the European Commission, statement at a press conference, December 17, 2004.

16. The results of a poll carried out in October–November 2005 showed that 55 percent of the Europeans were against Turkish accession, 31 percent in favor, and 14 percent undecided. Standard Eurobarometer 64, published by the European Commission in December 2005. These results are consistent with similar findings of polls carried out before and after 2005.

17. Barroso, press conference, December 16, 2004.

18. Council Conclusions, 2,770th Council Meeting, December 11, 2006.

19. The eight chapters are: 1. Free movement of goods; 3. Right of establishment and freedom to provide services; 9. Financial services; 11. Agriculture and rural development; 13. Fisheries; 14. Transport policy; 29. Customs union; 30. External relations.

20. José Manuel Barroso, president of the European Commission, speech before the European Parliament, December 23, 2006.

21. Olli Rehn, commissioner for enlargement, "Enlargement: The EU Keeps Its Doors Open for South Eastern Europe," speech before the European Economic and Social Committee, January 17, 2007.

22. The "Copenhagen criteria" were decided by the Copenhagen European Council, June 21–22, 1993, and spelled out in the "Presidency Conclusions" as follows: "Membership requires that the candidate country has achieved stability of institutions

guaranteeing democracy, the rule of law, human rights and respect for the protection of minorities, the existence of a functioning market economy as well as the capacity to cope with competitive pressure and market forces within the Union. Membership presupposes the candidate's ability to take on the obligations of membership including adherence to the aims of the political, economic and monetary union."

23. This section of the chapter is a compilation of the main points in the 2005 EU paper "Negotiating Framework for Turkey: Principles Governing the Negotiations" (www.euh. gov.hu/negotiating_framework_turkey.pdf [September 2009]). It also draws on the 2005 "EU Opening Statement for the Accession Conference with Turkey" (www.consilium. europa.eu/uedocs/cmsUpload/Opening_statement_Turkey.pdf [September 2009]).

24. For the purposes of the accession negotiations, the *acquis* has been divided into the following chapters: 1. Free movement of goods; 2. Freedom of movement for workers; 3. Right of establishment and freedom to provide services; 4. Free movement of capital; 5. Public procurement; 6. Company law; 7. Intellectual property law; 8. Competition policy; 9. Financial services; 10. Information society and media; 11. Agriculture and rural development; 12. Food safety, veterinary and phytosanitary policy; 13. Fisheries; 14. Transport policy; 15. Energy; 16. Taxation; 17. Economic and monetary policy; 18. Statistics; 19. Social policy and employment (including antidiscrimination and equal opportunities for women and men); 20. Enterprise and industrial policy; 21. Trans-European networks; 22. Regional policy and coordination of structural instruments; 23. Judiciary and fundamental rights; 24. Justice, freedom, and security; 25. Science and research; 26. Education and culture; 27. Environment; 28. Consumer and health protection; 29. Customs union; 30. External relations; 31. Foreign, security, and defense policy; 32. Financial control; 33. Financial and budgetary provisions; 34. Institutions; 35. Other issues.

25. European Commission, "Recommendation of the European Commission on Turkey's Progress towards Accession," October 6, 2004, p. 3 (www.ena.lu/recommendation_commission_turkeys_progress_accession_october_2004-020005677.html [September 2009]).

26. An elaborate presentation of the issues and challenges arising from the prospect of Turkish accession is included in the European Commission's staff working document "Issues Arising from Turkey's Membership Perspective," SEC (2004) 1202 (http://ec.europa.eu/enlargement/archives/pdf/key_documents/2004/issues_paper_en.pdf [September 2009]).

27. European Commission, "Recommendation," p. 7.

28. Ibid., p. 9.

29. Kramer, *A Changing Turkey*, p. 52.

30. European Commission, "Turkey: 2005 Progress Report," November 9, 2005, p. 38 (www.unhcr.org/refworld/publisher, EUCOMMISSION,,TUR,43956b6d4,0.html [September 2009]).

31. Ibid., p. 22.

32. A. Mango, *The Turks Today* (London: Murray, 2004), p. 211.

33. J. W. Mountcastle, "Foreword," in *Turkey's Strategic Position at the Crossroads of World Affairs*, edited by S. Blank, S. Pelletiere, and W. Johnsen (Honolulu: University Press of the Pacific, 2002 [reprinted from the 1993 edition]), p. 5.

34. Blank, Pelletiere, and Johnsen, *Turkey's Strategic Position*, p. 2.

35. F. S. Larrabee and I. O. Lesser, *Turkish Foreign Policy in an Age of Uncertainty* (Santa Monica, Calif.: RAND, 2003), p. 65.

36. Larrabee and Lesser, *Turkish Foreign Policy*, p. 189.

37. H. J. Barkey, ed., *Reluctant Neighbor: Turkey's Role in the Middle East* (Washington: U.S. Institute of Peace, 1997).

38. Copenhagen European Council, "Presidency Conclusions," June 21–22, 1993, para. 7 (A) iii (www.europarl.europa.eu/enlargement_new/europeancouncil/pdf/cop_en.pdf [September 2009]).

39. Brussels European Council, "Presidency Conclusions," December 14–15, 2006, para. 6 (www.consilium.europa.eu/ueDocs/cms_Data/docs/pressData/en/ec/92202.pdf [September 2009]).

40. Romano Prodi, "The Commission's Report and Recommendation on Turkey's Application," presentation to the European Parliament, October 6, 2004.

41. Valéry Giscard d'Estaing, "Pour ou contre l'adhésion de la Turquie à l'Union Européenne," interview with *Le Monde*, November 9, 2002.

42. Frits Bolkestein, European commissioner for internal market and services, speech at the University of Leiden, September 6, 2004. In his speech, Bolkestein cited the eminent historian and Islamic expert Bernard Lewis.

43. Remarks at Galatasaray University in Istanbul by President George W. Bush, June 29, 2004 (www.gpo.gov/fdsys/pkg/WCPD-2004-07-05/pdf/WCPD-2004-07-05-Pg1177.pdf).

44. Samuel Huntingon, *The Clash of Civilizations and the Remaking of World Order* (New York: Simon and Schuster, 1996), p. 20.

45. Treaty on the European Union (consolidated version), Preamble.

ALFRED TOVIAS

11

The EU and the Mediterranean Nonmember States

The European Neighborhood Policy (ENP), established in 2004, deals with trade, aid, and migration flows between a European Union of twenty-seven member states and a series of countries on its immediate external periphery. Not all of them are new neighboring countries, nor are all of the new or old neighbors dealt with by the new policy.

It is interesting to note that the enlarged EU has found it useful to combine several external economic policy instruments to deal specifically with developing countries on its periphery to reach certain policy objectives. This chapter focuses on a subset of countries in the EU's neighborhood, namely the nine partner countries currently treated under the framework of the so-called Euro-Mediterranean Partnership. Apart from Israel, they are all middle-income Arab countries in North Africa and the Near East and part of the MENA (Middle East and North Africa) group: three Maghreb countries (Morocco, Algeria, and Tunisia) and five Mashreq countries (Egypt, Jordan, the Palestinian Authority, Lebanon, and Syria). How coherent is the new policy directed to these eight countries? How well are the different components being combined? Is the new policy well conceived? This chapter offers preliminary answers to these questions.

The chapter first deals with the new policy's rationale. It then deals with substantive issues: what the EU is offering to or asking from its neighbors in terms of trade (new preferential market access for goods and services), aid (grants and loans), and migration (visa requirements, readmission arrangements, and temporary migration). Next it presents the EU methods and instruments for achieving the declared goals, as well as the institutional, legal, and financial arrangements. The chapter ends with a critical assessment of the internal coherence of the EU's ENP.

The Rationale for the ENP

The international environment had enormously changed by early 2004. The ENP was conceived barely eight years after the adoption of the Euro-Mediterranean Partnership and the so-called Barcelona Process in November 1995. At the time of the ENP elaboration, certain considerations had to be kept in mind. The EU was going to grow from fifteen to twenty member states, increasing the Union's territory by 23 percent, its population by 19 percent, and its GDP by 5 percent; two candidate countries were going to leave their Mediterranean status in the EMP and become full member states (Malta and Cyprus); Turkey had already been declared a candidate state in 1999, and two more countries, Romania and Bulgaria, were negotiating accession to become members no later than 2008; the Oslo Process had failed; the role of the United States in the eastern Mediterranean and the Middle East had grown enormously; the Multi-Fiber Arrangement (MFA) was to be phased out, eroding completely the value of the preferences given on textile products to Mediterranean neighbors in the mid-1970s; uncontrolled migration originating in the southern and eastern neighborhoods of the EU had increased by leaps and bounds; and the weight of Asia in world economic affairs was skyrocketing, leading to enormous pressure on oil and gas prices.

Regarding the last parametric change, there is an important implication: the EU's energy dependence on its neighbors is set to grow substantially in the coming years. Europe's dependence on oil imports should grow from 53 percent in 2006 to 85 percent in 2030, on gas imports from 3 percent in 2006 to 63 percent in 2030. Forty percent of its oil is currently imported from the Persian Gulf, 4 percent comes from Russia and North Africa; 96 percent of natural gas comes from one source, Russia. With the rise of China and India, Europe will be more dependent on the immediate neighborhood for energy supplies in coming decades.

Regarding uncontrolled migration, the Seville European Council of 2002 symptomatically declared that any future EU-signed Association Agreement should include a clause on joint management of migration flows and on compulsory readmission in the event of irregular immigration.[1] The European Commission was explicitly authorized to negotiate readmission agreements with Tunisia and Morocco.[2] It was decided then, well before the adoption of the ENP, to give incentives to neighbors that cooperate in readmission. These incentives were in the form of assistance in implementation, greater market access, and a larger number of temporary migrants admitted to the EU. The EU was even prepared to give assistance to those neighbors wishing to negotiate a readmission agreement with a third country.[3]

Since the conclusion of the Amsterdam Treaty in 1997, the EU member states have moved toward adopting a common migration policy. Thirty-nine measures were agreed on in the five-year period between 1999 and 2004. They deal mainly with coercive aspects of migration policy: irregular migration, trafficking, smuggling, and border controls. A special EU budget of €250 million, called AENEAS, was devoted to helping countries negotiate readmission agreements with the EU during the period 2004–08.

It is in this context that the idea of launching a new neighborhood policy toward the EU's Mediterranean partner countries crystallized in 2003. On the one hand, the success of enlargement seemed undeniable. It was perceived as successful reform. On the other hand, with the future accession of Cyprus, Malta, and Turkey to the EU, the number of Mediterranean partners to the EMP would diminish from twelve to nine, of which eight are middle-income Arab economies. Moreover, the optimism prevailing in EU circles regarding the conflict in the Middle East in the mid-1990s had been replaced by profound pessimism and fear that the Euro-Mediterranean Partnership would stagnate. Furthermore, after September 11, 2001, personal security and the fight against terrorism rose on the ladder of EU priorities and were conflated with migration and asylum issues.

A possible EU answer to all this could have been to erect a fence around the enlarged Union (raising the old specter of "Fortress Europe"). Apart from the fact that there is a clear distaste for such a solution in the EU, such an exclusion strategy is clearly infeasible, given the member states' limited military, technological, administrative, legal, and security assets. The only alternative was engagement, trying to integrate economically those less volatile neighbors, which would then function as a buffer between the EU and failed states to its south and east. In other words, as in the time of Charlemagne in the ninth century, when Catalonia functioned as the "Marca Hispanica," now some Arab Mediterranean countries were envisioned as a "Marca Europea."

The ENP also reflects the EU's unofficial conviction that any EU enlargement tends to have destabilizing consequences for excluded countries via trade, investment, and aid diversion.[4] Countries particularly concerned are those whose export patterns to the EU overlap with those of the new members. Most of the concerned countries are in the (new) neighborhood. Therefore the ENP can also be taken as reflecting the intention of the EU to reverse these unwanted effects of the 2004 and 2007 enlargements. We see much of the same in previous EU enlargements.[5]

Of course, at the official level the justification is to share the benefits of the EU's 2004 enlargement with neighboring countries and to establish around the EU a ring of well-governed countries sharing EU values. In ENP jargon, this is "a ring of friends."

The method used to obtain these goals is "deep integration." To move those neighbors from shallow to deep economic and regulatory integration, the

European Commission has suggested offering them benefits "previously associated only with membership." Among the cited benefits, the following ones deserve particular attention: "a stake in the internal market" (see below); progressive and/or partial integration (at least as observers) into certain EU policies, programs, agencies, and networks that promote cultural, transport, educational, environmental, technical, and scientific links (the European Environmental Agency or standardization bodies such as the European Committee of Standardization [CEN] or the European Committee for Electro-technical Standardization [CENELEC]); and new forms of assistance to help partners meet EU norms and standards: technical support to revamp the regulatory framework and institution building and sharing best practices made available as part of the TAIEX (Technical Assistance and Information Exchange) mechanism, which has been very successful in the context of the EU accession process. EU and member states' civil servants will be made available to give seminars on implementation of the *acquis* and approximation of laws; "cross-border cooperation," a new form of cooperation with neighbors, will take place in clearly defined subregional regions located along the EU borders that include regions along land borders and on sea crossings of significant importance or around common sea basins. The program will normally be managed by a region in a member state; the Commission monitors the implementation of the program in all aspects.

All of this is built on the existing Association Agreement (AA) signed in the context of the Euro-Mediterranean Partnership (EMP). A regular review process already provided for in the AA will monitor implementation of the Action Plans, distinguishing between short-term and medium-term priorities. The EU Commission states that after three to five years the possibility of drawing a new contractual link between the neighbor and the EU will be studied (in the form of so-called Neighborhood Agreements).

The European Commission insists that the ENP is its newest foreign policy tool and is nowadays the main external relations priority of the EU, putting economic reform in its neighborhood in the center. At the same time, in the case of Mediterranean neighbors, the ENP is to be taken as a supplement to the EMP, not as a substitute, as it simply adds incentives framed in a context of positive conditionality and reflects a more active engagement of the EU.

"A Stake in the Internal Market"

The EU Commission uses the slogan "a stake in the internal market" ad nauseam in all relevant documents of the ENP, though curiously, the term "stake" has not been clearly defined in any official text. It is apparently understood as a substantial reduction of barriers by partners to trade agreements, a progressive but selective integration into aspects of the internal market (IM). In the eyes of the Commission it is a step-by-step approach.

This approach has been somewhat marginalized in the ENP package since 2003 when it was popularized by the president of the Commission at the time, Romano Prodi, in favor of other items, such as people-to-people contacts. One of the reasons for this is, according to an EU Commission official, the difficulty in persuading the relevant commissioners and directorates besides those dealing with the external relations that opening the IM to the Mediterranean partners is desirable for the EU. Another official said in an unofficial interview that "a stake in the internal market" is a long-term objective that bears the question of how long the long term is. The Commission has said that most actions are to be expected in the domain of goods, but less so in services and freedom of establishment. Labor movements are practically left out.

The EU says that it wants to negotiate bilaterally with the Mediterranean neighbors' trade liberalization in services. However, it mentions almost exclusively financial services, in which Mediterranean countries do not seem to have much comparative advantage. In terms of the General Agreement on Trade and Services (GATS) supply modes, the Mediterranean partners seem to have a comparative advantage in Mode 2 (consumption abroad) and Mode 4 (movement of natural persons), a feature typical of middle-income developing countries. The distribution of supply modes in the world trade in services is actually skewed against these two modes. Shares in world trade are as follows: Mode 1, 25 percent; Mode 2, 15 percent; Mode 3, 60 percent; Mode 4, 2 percent.

The EU Commission's ENP website states that integration in the internal market will have to take into account the capacity and interests of both sides. It is already stated explicitly that the "free movement of persons is not in the agenda for the foreseeable future."[6] However, it does not explicitly exclude the "temporary movement of people" within Mode 4 of GATS. If the EU offer at the Doha Round serves as an indication, Mediterranean neighbors should be optimistic that Mode 2–related concessions will be obtained from the EU. They should be less optimistic regarding Mode 4, but the Mediterranean countries will have more opportunities if they negotiate with individual member states.

What is important for the Mediterranean partners and the EU member states alike is to realize that the advantage of eliminating non-trade barriers (NTBs) on a preferential basis rather than tariffs in mutual trade is that trade diversion against third countries is not welfare-reducing and that NTBs are not revenue-raising but cost-increasing.[7] Therefore, the offer of the EU can only be welfare-enhancing for both partners, if we discount the short-term costs of adjustment.

To take care of the latter, Mediterranean partners should ask the EU to reduce NTBs on their exports to the EU and apply strict reciprocity only in the medium and long run.

Agricultural Trade Liberalization

As is well known, the EMP agreements postulating the creation of free-trade areas between the EU and Mediterranean countries exclude all agriculture from the free-trade rule. This happens at a time when (a) most of these countries have a significant revealed comparative advantage in fruits, vegetables, and other typical Mediterranean products; (b) the average EU agricultural tariff is still 30 percent; and (c) tariff quotas still dominate in trade relations between the two partners.

As indicated above, the EU says it will shortly engage in discussions toward trade liberalization in agricultural products. Meanwhile it is simply proposing the alignment of the Mediterranean neighbors with the EU sanitary and phytosanitary standards. In the Action Plan for Morocco, agriculture is mentioned only as part of environmental policy. In the one of Tunisia, agriculture is totally excluded. Only the Action Plans for Jordan and the Palestinian Authority mention agriculture explicitly. It seems therefore that the more importance ENP documents give to agriculture, the less the partner concerned has a comparative advantage in it. Finally, one Commission official stated that the EU is likely to ask for protection of geographic indications and for meeting specific standards of quality.

Methodology

The ENP methodology and terminology is inspired by the accession process applied in the last enlargement: Action Plans, monitoring, country reports, "promise of upgrading," benchmarks, positive conditionality, TAIEX, twinning.[8] The list of chapters in the Action Plans is similar to the one used in the accession process.[9] There is no visible inspiration drawn from the European Economic Agreement (EEA) negotiations in the Action Plans submitted. This is not surprising. Many of the Commission officials who had worked in the Directorate-General (DG) for Enlargement were transferred between 2002 and 2004 to the DGs dealing with the new ENP. But since the original "Wider Europe" communication, the language of conditionality and benchmarks has been toned down, probably because the staff from the DG for External Relations (RELEX) has taken over.[10] Now more use is made of the word "incentive." This is a pity because the EU Commission has proven to be very effective in the follow-up and implementation by future member countries of economic and administrative reforms. The problem is that in the specific case of the ENP there cannot be a mechanical link between EU commitments and the neighbors' commitments.

Conditionality has a central role in the ENP, but the one built in is of a very specific type. The EU traditionally refrains from imposing economic and political sanctions (that is, negative conditionality), because they require unanimity in the Council of Ministers. Here the commercial and strategic interests of some member states prevail. This is why even in the case of EU enlargement it was decided early on to prefer positive conditionality. The latter relies on the willingness of the partner to implement reforms successfully. It does not require any effort per se from the member states themselves. For the EU, positive conditionality would seem to be less expensive than negative conditionality. Although the EU must provide some incentive, it need not be in the form of aid. If it takes the form of trade liberalization it will also be good for the EU. And even if the incentive is in the form of aid, the amount devoted to it might be less than the corresponding losses made if sanctions are imposed (and let us note here that the EU has a surplus in its trade balance with its Mediterranean neighbors).

In the case of the last enlargement, conditionality was geared to economic development and capacity building and not to political objectives such as democratization. There is a consensus among experts that the central and eastern European countries (CEECs) did that on their own, without much EU intervention. This situation bears many similarities with what the EU aims to do in the context of the ENP. The ENP approach is a chapter-by-chapter microeconomic and administrative approach, with not much intervention by the relevant legislatures (from the European Parliament or the local parliament of the target country). It is, however, important to note here that conditionality was a way of reassuring member states that the new members would not become a burden after accession. But neighbors are not candidates for accession. Therefore, in some sense, there is no need to reassure and less justification in favor of conditionality. What is needed is reciprocity.

Institutional Provisions and Financial Arrangements

The ENP does not provide for the establishment of new institutions to monitor the ENP and the new neighborhood agreements. There is no apparent intention to strengthen dispute settlement mechanisms. Even minor institutional developments such as those found in the context of the EEA or the creation of an ENP Secretariat are not contemplated. Furthermore, new neighborhood agreements would continue to be intergovernmental with no supra-national dimension.

EEA-type participation of the Mediterranean neighbors in decision-shaping, let alone decisionmaking, is excluded. However, the obligation of information by the EU Commission on future directives related to the internal market would become part of the new Neighborhood Agreements with its Mediterranean neighbors.

The central piece of the financial arrangements is the so-called European Neighborhood and Partnership Instrument (ENPI), based on an EU regulation already approved and ratified that replaces a series of previous instruments, such as MEDA (to assist Mediterranean countries) and TACIS (to assist the Commonwealth of Independent States, CIS). The EU aid policy has been streamlined for the 2007–13 period. Only six aid instruments survived, three general and three functional. The first three are: pre-accession assistance (for example, in the case of Turkey); the ENPI (covering all the ENP countries, including the three southern Caucasus countries, but also Russia); and development cooperation. The second three are: a stability instrument (for emergency cases); a macro-financial assistance instrument; and an instrument for humanitarian aid. According to the new regulation, there is a basic amount for each Mediterranean neighbor based on objective criteria. A pool of funds is allocated to well-performing countries. The ENPI uses a structural funds approach based on multi-year programming, partnership, and cofinancing. The cross-border cooperation component of the ENPI is cofinanced by the European Regional and Development Fund (ERDF).

The Commission, which had allocated €8.5 billion in aid to TACIS and MEDA for the period 2000–06, proposed an amount of €14.9 billion in the new financial perspectives for 2007–13, an increase of 60 percent. It is worth noting that the ENP covers more countries than MEDA and TACIS. The annual allocation would increase progressively, doubling between 2006 and 2013. The ENPI represents 15 to 17 percent of EU spending on external action (while 49 percent will still go to development policy), which in itself accounts for 10 percent of EU's total spending.

Another financial component of the ENP is the loans granted by the European Investment Bank (EIB), which is now a more important factor in supporting Mediterranean countries' reforms than the World Bank. The EIB established the Facility for Euro-Mediterranean Investment and Partnership (FEMIP) in October 2002, before the endorsement of the ENP by the EU. It was created to help the countries of the region meet the challenges of economic and social modernization, similar to the way the European Bank for Reconstruction and Development (EBRD) helped eastern Europe. FEMIP's main activities include supporting infrastructure projects and creating an appropriate environment for the development of private enterprise. The partnership finances private sector

Figure 11-1. *Facility for Euro-Mediterranean Investment and Partnership (FEMIP) Lending by Sector, 2004*

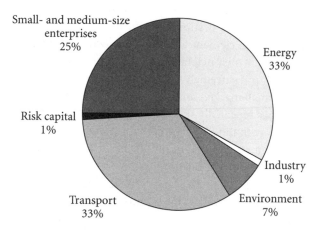

Small- and medium-size enterprises 25%

Energy 33%

Risk capital 1%

Industry 1%

Transport 33%

Environment 7%

Source: European Investment Bank, 2005.

ventures, whether local initiatives or foreign direct investment, through loans, investment capital, and grants.

For several years FEMIP has helped finance important infrastructure projects to improve transport in Egypt and Tunisia and power generation and gas transmission in Jordan, Morocco, and Syria (figure 11-1).

FEMIP is now lending at a rate of over €2 billion per year. In 2004, FEMIP lent a record €2.2 billion. Grants under its technical assistance support program reached €13.8 billion, up from €1.8 billion in 2002.

The trend toward increased financing of private sector operations continued when 30 percent of the funds went to support foreign direct investment (FDI) initiatives. Since the ENP was adopted, FEMIP also strengthened its local presence in some countries, opening offices in Tunisia, Egypt, and Morocco. Learning from the eastern European experience, local offices of FEMIP play an important role in the eyes of foreign investors, giving them a greater sense of security and an address to turn to in certain cases.

Is Approximation of Laws and Economic Reform What Arab Mediterranean Countries Need? A Critical Assessment

With successive EU enlargements, the EU's presence in the economic life of non-member Mediterranean countries has become overwhelming. Fewer and fewer options are open to them: trade, aid, market, migration, technology, monetary, and service (tourism) dependence is increasing. Ever better economic relations with the EU's economic block are a must. Of course, oil producers (such as Algeria, Egypt, and Syria) can escape this predicament for longer than others (such as Morocco, Jordan, the Palestinian Authority).

An aggravating common element to all of the North African countries analyzed is that most of their own neighboring countries to the south are largely arid, loosely populated, and extremely poor. Beyond the Sahara Desert there are more neighbors with small markets and few resources. Not surprisingly, a country such as Morocco has repeatedly stated that it wants "more than association, less than membership" with the EU. Together with Jordan and Tunisia, Morocco has demonstrated on more than one occasion that it has no patience with the stagnating, simple free trade area relations imposed by the EMP in 1995. Nor does Morocco want to wait until other laggard Arab countries start implementing their FTA Association Agreement (for example, Syria). Jordan is pressing for implementation of pan-European accumulation and/or Qualified Industrial Zone (QIZ)-type agreements allowing for goods produced by joint ventures with Israel's manufacturers to enter duty-free in the EU-27. The United States conceded a similar treatment to these two partners (and, more recently, also to joint ventures between Egypt and Israel).

Mediterranean nonmember countries have asked a series of questions about the adequacy and design of the ENP in their specific case. Several years into the ENP, many wonder whether the requirement of "approximation of laws" and "adoption of the *acquis*" is legal colonialism. Adopting the EU legal norms sometimes means adjusting to a different legal culture, a paternalistic approach aggravated by the fact that future EU membership is not in the cards. Furthermore, adoption of some EU laws but not others can lead to legal incoherence between systems. In addition, the cost of the approximation of laws could impose substantial costs on the Mediterranean countries, mainly of an institutional nature, as domestic authorities would have to be as effective as the EU authorities of control.

More generally, the approximation of laws is suitable depending on whether the law to be adapted corresponds to the objective needs of the Mediterranean neighbor in terms of size of market, standard of living, environmental and labor standards, and development level. The ENP might require too much from Arab middle-income developing countries, according to well-known figures in the development community. Dani Rodrik has claimed that the extended Washington Consensus, which includes institutional reform, is too ambitious to be accomplished by many developing countries even in the medium term, and that it did not set clear priorities.[11]

An important issue specifically affecting some eastern Mediterranean countries, such as Jordan, Egypt and Israel, but that could also affect Morocco and Tunisia in the future, is the large share of manufactured exports that goes to the United States, whose standards differ from those of the EU. Wide differences exist in the markets for goods and services, on which Mediterranean neighbors are highly trade-dependent. A good example is the hotly debated case of genetically modified organisms (GMOs). Although the Arab countries under focus (except Jordan) are much more trade-dependent on the EU than on the United States, this could change after the progressive implementation of the FTA agreements between the United States and several Arab countries (e.g. Morocco, Tunisia), which also cover agricultural and food products.

Experts at the World Bank and other international economic institutions also say that the focus on the need for economic reform in the Mediterranean neighbors is not always justified. The ENP website insists that the reduction of artificial trade and investment barriers of Mediterranean countries is beneficial, particularly because, as middle-income economies, governance issues are particularly relevant to them. There is also the assumption that FDI will flow into the EU's southern neighbors the moment that they deal with their red tape. But the difficulty that most southern Mediterranean countries have in attracting FDI does not come from administrative inefficiencies, but from the lack of human capital and knowhow.

This becomes obvious by making a comparison with India, for example. Why does India attract FDI in high-tech industry and services while MENA countries have not done so? After all, FDI flows to MENA when OECD countries need something from there (e.g. crude oil/gas), and nobody seems to be bothered by red tape. And why has Turkey not attracted FDI after all the reforms (including elimination of administrative hassles) it has undertaken over the years? Scholars should look thoroughly into the correlation by countries and sectors between implemented reforms and subsequent FDI flows. It seems that the empirical link is much more tenuous than what is always assumed and that the problem is more one of lack of professional competence and know-how than of red tape.

This chapter argues that the ENP suffers from asymmetries because it does not contemplate setting up an Action Plan for the EU. The ENP assumes that only the neighbors should undertake economic reforms to benefit from the extension of the internal market. The EU's only role is to offer incentives and monitor the implementation of the Action Plans—that is, the economic reforms of the neighbors. This is a totally different approach from that of the EEA, where everybody is supposed to adjust equally. It is also different from the OECD system of peer review, where every member can apply peer pressure. There is also a moral dimension here, something so important to many Europeans nowadays. Anchoring economic reform in neighboring countries is an activity that consists in demonstrating and not in preaching. The EU should set an example not by telling Mediterranean neighbors what to do, but by adjusting. This could be called the "we-are-in-the-same-boat" effect, reflecting that the EU and its Mediterranean neighbors are indeed involved in a real partnership, something frequently questioned by Arab countries, particularly after 9/11.

Conclusion: An Impression of Déjà Vu

In a way, insisting on the need for economic reforms by its Mediterranean neighbors is a way for the EU to shift the spotlight from the EU's lack of offering preferential market access concessions to them since the mid-1970s. This is awkward, because over time the relative positioning of Mediterranean countries in the hierarchy of EU preferences has eroded. The liberalization of most-favored-nation (MFN) trade (Tokyo Round, Uruguay Round) must be factored in as well. To illustrate, consider that the Tunisia-EU Action Plan does not contain any significant item addressing agriculture and labor movements. Instead it deals with tariff legislation, labeling, veterinary and phyto-sanitary rules, state aid, and competition policy and government procurement.

The specific incentives offered to most Mediterranean countries in the context of the ENP are not sufficiently appealing for them to accept Europeanization. It is clear that the Action Plans already in place fall short of expectations in most Mediterranean countries. They initially thought they would be admitted to all EU programs and that the four freedoms (freedom of movement of goods, capital, services, and persons) would soon be extended to them. Now it appears that, contrary to what the former Commission president Romano Prodi said at the time, they would not have "everything but the institutions," but rather "something, but not the institutions." Official documents speak of "a measure of economic integration" rather than "a stake in the internal market." According to Schumacher and Del Sarto, given the reluctance of southern European EU member states to speak about the four freedoms, the Commission had to withdraw references to them from speeches early on.[12] In fact, there are no direct references to the four freedoms after the publication of the 2004 EU Strategy Paper, while they were still mentioned in the 2003 "Wider Europe" Communication from the European Commission.[13]

With respect to services, the EU would like to start with financial services, information technology, transport, and energy. Probably with the exception of energy, these are sectors in which the Mediterranean neighbors do not have a comparative advantage. In financial services, the EU has rejected the possibility of conferring an ENP passport for financial services providers in the Euro-Med area since it would imply accepting the principle of mutual recognition. With regard to temporary migration, the jury is still out under Mode 4.

In the meantime, trade liberalization in agricultural products has once again been left behind. This occurs at a time when agricultural lobbies in southern Europe are in fact much weaker than they were ten or twenty years ago, when Spain and Portugal entered the EU, and even weaker than when the EMP was adopted. The Commission's apprehensions seem unwarranted. If *délocalisation* is accepted for textiles, why not accept it also for flowers, fruits, and vegetables? Is it also not easier to convince European governments that it is better to "delo-calize" to the neighborhood than to China? There are also profound political economy reasons to strengthen agriculture in the Arab world.

In recent years, the Commission has stressed that negotiations with the MENA countries on further agricultural trade liberalization were dependent on progress in negotiations at the multilateral level in the Doha Round of trade talks. But now the talks are off and the Commission has no more excuses. An important point here must be made about the internal market in agricultural products: for the relocation of Mediterranean agriculture to North Africa to succeed, Arab countries must eliminate restrictions on buying land there. This restriction now already applies to new member states, to the dismay of some political parties in Poland.

Notes

1. A. Geddes, "Europe's Border Relationships and International Migration Relations," *Journal of Common Market Studies* 43, no. 4 (2005): 787–806.

2. L. Hugelin, "L'incidence d'une nouvelle politique communautaire de l'immigration sur le partenariat euro-méditerranéen," in *Euro-Med Integration and the "Ring of Friends,"* edited by P. Xuereb (Malta: European Documentation and Research Centre, 2003), pp. 201–32.

3. Ibid., p. 219.

4. A. Tovias, "Normative and Economic Implications for Mediterranean Countries of the 2004 European Union Enlargement," *Journal of World Trade* 39, no. 6 (2005): 1135–59.

5. A. Tovias, *Foreign Economic Relations of the European Community: The Impact of Spain and Portugal* (Boulder, Colo.: Lynne Rienner, 1990).

6. See European Commission, European Neighbourhood Policy website (http://ec.europa.eu/world/enp/index_en.htm [October 2008]).

7. An exception to this rule is contingent protection. In this respect it must be recalled that the EU has frequently applied anti-dumping duties on imports originating in Egypt.

8. TAIEX is legal advice and technical assistance offered by experts from EU member states to help public authorities in the target countries. Twinning is similar to TAIEX, but the advice is given by officials of the member states' civil service, who are dispatched to the target country for a given period.

9. M. Leigh, "The EU's Neighbourhood Policy," in *The Strategic Implications of European Union Enlargement,* edited by E. Brimmer and S. Frohlich (Washington: Center for Transatlantic Relations, Johns Hopkins University, 2005), pp. 101–27.

10. See Commission of the European Communities, "Communication from the Commission to the Council and the European Parliament," March 3, 2003 (http://ec.europa.eu/world/enp/pdf/com03_104_en.pdf [October 2008]).

11. D. Rodrik, "What Do We Learn from Country Narratives?" in *In Search of Prosperity: Analytic Narratives on Economic Growth,* edited by D. Rodrik (Princeton University Press, 2003).

12. R. Del Sarto and T. Schumacher, "From EMP to ENP: What's at Stake with the European Neighbourhood Policy towards the Southern Mediterranean?" *European Foreign Affairs Review* 10 (2005): 17–38.

13. See Commission of the European Communities, "Communication from the Commission to the Council and the European Parliament," March 3, 2003 (http://ec.europa.eu/world/enp/pdf/com03_104_en.pdf [October 2009]).

STEFANIA PANEBIANCO

12 | *The EU and the Middle East*

The European Union has traditionally considered the Mediterranean third countries (MTCs) as strategic partners. However, several political, economic, and institutional constraints have rendered the adoption of a clear EU Mediterranean policy a difficult endeavor. The Euro-Mediterranean Partnership (EMP) and the European Neighborhood Policy (ENP) are depicted by the European institutions as two complementary wings of the EMP. Yet they use specific concepts that reflect different approaches to Euro-Mediterranean relations: "partnership" lies in fact at the basis of the EMP, while "neighborhood" is the basis of the ENP. This is not just a terminological phenomenon. It rather reflects a change in the content and approach of EU policy. Over time, different priorities, goals, and instruments have been identified in the EU's relations with the MTCs.

This chapter makes an assessment of the EU Mediterranean policy, and more generally of European foreign policy, by exploring current trends in EU relations with the MTCs.[1] First, it is difficult to see the Med policy as one coherent policy because it contains two distinct cooperation frameworks. Second, the EU's international action in the Mediterranean is currently focused more on security interests and needs than on ideas, principles, and values. While in the 1990s the EU seemed to be developing an ethical approach to foreign policy, at the turn of the century European foreign policy seems to have become more interest-oriented than principle- and value-driven. Still, in 2001 the European Commission depicted the EU as an international actor with "political and moral weight" that needs to shoulder its responsibilities in the governance of globalization.[2]

The ethical dimension of EU external action has recently been replaced by a more pragmatic vision of the EU's global role. As the ENP indicates, securing the EU borders has become a more prominent EU interest than human rights and democracy promotion. Moreover, the EU fears that democratizing the Mediterranean countries' regimes too quickly might have local and regional destabilizing effects. For this reason, the EU now prefers to depict itself as a "soft power" that pursues its own interests and is able to extend norms and values to third countries only as long as those countries are willing to adopt them.[3] The European Commission precisely defines the concept of "soft power of persuasion" as "support for transformation which is not about imposing specific models from the outside."[4] Thus the EU's power of attraction depends more on the MTCs' interest in cooperation than on the EU's power to export norms.

In the Mediterranean, the EU has chosen to play the role of regional stabilizer via economic integration and cooperation. As the ENP documents imply, the EU assumes that the MTCs' integration into the EU internal market will produce a spillover effect of radical structural reforms (legislative, administrative, and institutional) that will be conducive to greater political and democratic change. The EU is acting as a soft power whose international action follows the "logic of utility": interests provide the push for EU political action in the Mediterranean, and energy security, terrorism, and migration are the current EU priorities.

The EU Med Policy: A Policy with Two Different Cooperation Frameworks

Since the late 1950s the EU, at that time still the European Community (EC), stipulated association and trade agreements with Greece, Portugal, Spain, Cyprus, Malta, Israel, Egypt, Lebanon, Morocco, Tunisia, Turkey, and Yugoslavia. The EC was linked to many of these MTCs by colonial legacy, and bilateral cooperation was perceived as the best way to guarantee a special relationship. However, this was not a sufficient condition to develop a true Mediterranean policy. With the adoption of the Global Mediterranean Policy (1972–91) and the Renewed Mediterranean Policy (1991–95), the EC/EU attempted to launch a multilateral cooperation framework. The Global Mediterranean Policy was a bilateral policy based on trade and financial and technical cooperation. The Renewed Mediterranean Policy adopted in 1991 was new in some respects: it created new financial instruments and specified new fields of cooperation such as the environment; assistance programs such as MedCampus, MedInvest, and MedUrbs provided technological transfer; and the innovative "horizontal financial cooperation" was adopted for regional environmental and financial improvement. Despite these innovations, the Renewed Mediterranean Policy failed, particularly in integrating the MTCs with the internal market.

In this policy context, the signing of the Barcelona Declaration in November 1995 appeared to be a breakthrough in EU relations with the MTCs. The EMP aimed to launch a true innovative region-building process, but the regional dimension disappeared when the EU adopted the ENP in 2003.

The EMP and the Region-Building Process in the Mediterranean

The EMP provided a multi-dimensional framework of cooperation for the EU countries and the twelve Mediterranean partners: Morocco, Algeria, Tunisia, Egypt, Malta, Cyprus, Israel, Jordan, Lebanon, Syria, Turkey, and the Palestinian Authority. The Med partners acquired a stronger Arab component over time: Libya has obtained observer status since the Stuttgart Conference in 1999; in May 2004 Malta and Cyprus entered the EU and thus lost their MTC status; in October 2005 Turkey started the accession process and became an EU candidate; in November 2007 the ministers of foreign affairs welcomed Mauritania and Albania to the EMP.

As indicated in the Barcelona Declaration, the EMP aimed to create an area of dialogue, exchange, and cooperation that would guarantee peace, stability, and prosperity in the Mediterranean. The EMP consisted of a political and security partnership, an economic and financial partnership, and a social, cultural, and human partnership. It reflected the three-basket structure of the CSCE/OSCE (Commission on Security and Cooperation in Europe/Organization for Cooperation and Security in Europe), which considers human security extremely important.[5] The EMP regional cooperation framework coexisted with the bilateral cooperation established with the Euro-Mediterranean Agreements that the EU has now stipulated with all the MTCs.[6]

The EMP had institutionalized Euro-Mediterranean relations through a "light" institutional structure.[7] The EMP institutional architecture did not involve international treaties or formal agreements but was established through political documents and substantial agreements. The EMP institutions ranged from meetings of government representatives (ministers of foreign affairs and sectoral ministers, senior officials, young diplomats) to civil society networks; the EMP also had a parliamentary dimension.[8] The nongovernmental dimension of cooperation was considered an important advantage of the EMP, and the EU also supported it financially. In this respect, it should be noted that since 1996 EuroMeSCo has acted as a concrete example of partnership-building measures by bringing together researchers debating security-related issues. In December 2003 the EuroMed Parliamentary Forum was transformed into the Euro-Mediterranean Parliamentary Assembly. In April 2005 the Euro-Mediterranean Anna Lindh Foundation was established in Alexandria to foster cross-cultural dialogue.

As far as Euro-Mediterranean cooperation areas are concerned, the Barcelona Declaration listed a large number of issues to be tackled by the EMP. The declaration reflected the political and academic discourse that in the early 1990s pointed out that security is no longer shaped by the military. In this view, the multi-dimensional definition of security describes much better the situation of the post–cold war era. In particular, in view of wider challenges to state and societal security, scholars belonging to the so-called Copenhagen school stressed the need to adopt a "broad" concept of security that moves beyond the military dimension and takes into account the societal aspects of security.[9] If the *new* security challenges imply mainly societal threats, then security cooperation strategies have to deal with political, economic, social, and environmental factors more than with the traditional military dimension.[10] Moreover, these new threats to security require cooperation among both traditional state actors and nonstate actors in civil society, such as local authorities, academic institutions, think tanks, and NGOs. This is the type of security cooperation envisaged by the EMP, reflecting a systematic EU rhetoric on human security as one of the key EU goals in regional cooperation frameworks launched in the 1990s.

However, after more than ten years of cooperation within the EMP, the main goal set in the Barcelona Declaration in 1995—that is, the creation of an area of peace, stability, and prosperity in the Mediterranean—has remained mostly unachieved. This is primarily due to the dramatic change of the systemic context in which the EMP actors are embedded. The scenario that has emerged for the EU at the beginning of the twenty-first century is rather different from the one in the mid-1990s. First, after 9/11 the concept of security was redefined again. Second, the recrudescence of the Middle Eastern conflict and the stalemate in the Middle East peace process have blocked any regional political cooperation. Third, the enlarged EU is opting for a more pragmatic Med policy that is less shaped by ideas, values, and principles and more fact-oriented. As will be argued later, this reflects more generally a realist turn in European foreign policy.[11]

At the beginning of the twenty-first century, the ambitious regional cooperation framework set out in Barcelona had been redefined and complemented by the ENP, a EU policy that provides the EU's "ring of friends" (including the MTCs) with a framework for cooperation that is essentially bilateral. The EU claims that the ENP has not replaced the EMP and that the former supports and strengthens the latter. Although the ENP and the EMP are formally two distinct cooperation frameworks, EU official documents depict them as "two legs," two complementary components of the EU Med policy that will need to be more coordinated in the years ahead.[12] However, the ENP is not specifically devoted to the MTCs, since it also includes the eastern neighbors. Thus the ENP is necessarily much less "Mediterranean"-oriented than the EMP. The EMP's long-term goal—to build a Euro-Mediterranean region—seems to be fading slightly.

The Bilateral Shift of the ENP

The idea of launching a policy addressed to the EU neighbors was first expressed by Romano Prodi, the former president of the European Commission, in a speech delivered in 2002. The ENP was then outlined by the European Commission in March 2003 in the communication entitled "Wider Europe-Neighborhood: A New Framework for Relations with Our Eastern and Southern Neighbors," which was later endorsed by the European Council in Thessaloniki in December 2003. Finally, in May 2004 the European Commission adopted the strategy outlined in the "European Neighborhood Policy Strategy Paper."[13]

The ENP aimed to redefine the EU's relations with its southern Mediterranean neighbors (Morocco, Algeria, Tunisia, Libya, Egypt, Israel, Lebanon, Jordan, Syria, and the Palestinian Authority) and eastern post-Soviet neighbors (Belarus, Moldavia, and Ukraine, plus three southern Caucasus republics: Armenia, Azerbaijan, and Georgia). Since the enlargement of May 1, 2004, the EU has completely new eastern borders, while little has changed on the southern border, where two Mediterranean islands, Cyprus and Malta, joined the EU. The ENP cooperation areas are political dialogue and reform, trade exchange, participation in the internal market, and human security. In particular, a clear priority is attached to economic development support for the "ring of friends," with the long-term goal of the neighbors' integration in the internal market. At first reading, this might appear similar to the EMP's long-term goal of creating an "area of peace, stability, and prosperity in the Mediterranean," in line with the 1995 Barcelona Declaration. A closer look at the ENP documents and institutional structure shows that the EU is more concerned than ever about its security and stability. These are the most important interests to be defended with the ENP: the EU seeks to secure its borders and to promote stability in the neighboring countries through bilateral cooperation. Although political and democratic reforms are mentioned among common goals, the operative instruments remain weakly identified, as if the EU wanted to avoid any destabilizing effects provoked by political and democratic reforms.

Despite the declared similarities and complementarities, the EMP and the ENP are different in many respects. First, the EMP and the ENP have a different approach to Euro-Mediterranean relations. The EMP envisages a region-building process, while the ENP relies on a bilateral tailor-made and targeted approach. The MTCs often criticized the EU for not involving the partners in the definition of cooperation. In fact, in their view Euro-Mediterranean cooperation within the EMP was unilaterally planned and managed. In order to avoid this criticism, cooperation within the ENP framework has been based on the "Action Plan" instrument, which is elaborated and regularly updated with the participation of the MTCs.[14] Both the principle of differentiation (which relies on a country-specific approach) and the principle of joint ownership (which implies the involvement of the MTCs on the elaboration and implementation of the Action Plans) have been included in the ENP to take into account the MTCs' needs and interests. The neighbors welcomed these principles, since they hope that individual merits of each country can be recognized. However, the implementation of the differentiation principle de facto is freezing region-building processes in the Mediterranean.[15]

In this manner, the EU Med policy has been partially redefined, and the liberal regionalism has been replaced by a more realist bilateralism. Moving away from the EMP's optimistic regional approach, the ENP marked a clear shift toward a more pragmatic definition of Euro-Mediterranean cooperation. The regional dimension that was the basis for the EMP has disappeared in the ENP, which relies instead on bilateral Action Plans. The ENP includes clear reference to EU values such as human rights and democracy, good governance, and rule of law, but the ENP Action Plans do not specify deadlines for reforms to be adopted. Although these principles are officially stated, no operative instruments are adopted. Following the differentiation principle, the EU leaves the partners free to set their own calendar for political change. According to the EU institutions, the ENP has an intrinsic added value: as a tailor-made targeted approach and not a "one-size-fits-all" policy, it benefits both the EU and MTCs, and it is preferable to the EMP "in the neighbors' interests."

Moreover, the EMP (through the Euro-Mediterranean Association Agreements) refers to "negative conditionality" to foster political change, while the ENP offers "more for more"—that is, it adopts positive conditionality using benchmarking of human rights and democratic development. The conceptual issues underlying these two processes are also quite different: "partnership" for the EMP and "neighborhood" for the ENP.

In certain respects, the ENP has replaced the EMP, suggesting new instruments and approaches for overcoming the difficulties encountered by the EMP in its more than ten years of existence. However, with the full support of the ENP, the EU de facto rejects the regional EMP framework. The European Commission has recently stated that "the bilateral frameworks of the ENP are better suited to promoting internal reforms."[16] Being in favor of a closer coordination between the two processes, and in *extrema ratio* allowing for a sort of merging of the two processes, the EU has almost abandoned the EMP, which remains symbolically important, but not operatively.[17]

Mediterranean Third Countries: EU Partners or (Stable) Neighbors?

After the illustration of the EU Med policy and its two complementary (as officially defined) cooperation frameworks (the EMP and the ENP), some assessment of the *quality* of EU relations with the MTCs can be suggested. "Quality" here refers to the essence of the EU relationship with the MTCs as the EU defines it. What does "partnership" mean? And what is the meaning of "neighborhood" in geopolitical terms? One of the most frequent criticisms of the EMP concerns the definition of partnership itself, because it did not establish relations based on an equal contractual basis. What has changed with the passing from the EMP to the ENP? Is there any substantial change in the way the EU treats MTCs? Also, the nature of the neighborhood relationship depends on the EU's definition of "neighbor," which does not reflect a geographic location. Instead, it has a strong geopolitical connotation.[18]

Exploring the "Partnership" Concept That Underlies the EMP

In European foreign policy the word "partnership" is associated with the kind of legal or political framework of cooperation with third countries. Since the early 1990s, the partnership agreement has been an instrument of EU foreign policy that reflects the multi-dimensional concept of security. It does not reflect the equality of the parties involved. This meaning was clear when in the year 2000 the Cotonou Agreement replaced the Lomé Convention and the EU signed new "partnership" agreements with the ACP (African, Caribbean, and Pacific) countries. The Cotonou Agreement envisages a comprehensive cooperation framework based on five interdependent pillars, with the underlying objective of fighting poverty: an enhanced political dimension, greater participation, a more strategic approach to cooperation focusing on poverty reduction, new economic and trade partnerships, and improved financial cooperation.

EU-Russia relations also provide a meaningful example of the kind of partnerships the EU stipulates with third countries to cooperate on a multi-dimensional basis. Russia was originally invited to take part in the ENP, but it declined, preferring instead to foster bilateral relations with the EU via a strategic partnership. In 1994 the EU signed a Partnership and Cooperation Agreement (PCA) with Russia that was inspired by a comprehensive concept of security. Economic instruments, which were conceived to replace the state-planned economy with a market economy, were to be accompanied by political cooperation to manage domestic political crises and support democratic reforms. At the Cologne European Council in June 1999, the EU adopted a common strategy to initiate a strategic partnership with Russia. At the St. Petersburg summit in May 2003 "four common spaces" were identified as the main goal of EU-Russia relations. A formal council was established. According to this strategic partnership, the EU will seek to reduce Russian political and economic instability and to anchor Russia to the European political and economic system without full accession. However, despite the multi-dimensional aspect of the EU-Russia partnership, EU interests prevail over political and democratic reforms. The EU has important strategic and economic interests in Russia's economic development, mainly due to its dependence on energy supplies. These interests have prevented the EU from taking a tough stand toward Russia, in particular in the Chechen case.[19]

Since the mid-1990s almost all of the new independent states have signed PCAs with the EU. All PCAs have a similar structure: economic cooperation is accompanied by political cooperation, which usually includes political dialogue on democratic and institutional reforms and support for human rights. To strengthen (at least in principle) this multi-dimensional approach, the EU has included the conditionality clause in all PCAs since then.

Many scholars have pointed out the limitations of the EU multi-dimensional approach to external relations, which should take into account the partners' democratic development. The EU's relations with Russia and China, for instance, prove that the EU's strategic interests prevail over the defense of principles and values such as human rights and democracy. It is thus debatable whether the EU is able to act as a normative power when dealing with strategic countries. In these cases, security or economic interests prevail over the narrative of the EU as a worldwide "force for good" (as stated in the European security strategy elaborated by Javier Solana in 2003). Moreover, the "conditionality clause" (the main instrument adopted since the 1990s to foster human rights and democracy) is rarely applied when powerful partners violate human rights. The EU tends instead to apply negative conditionality only to poor and strategically insignificant countries.[20]

The European Parliament is very critical of the EU's inconsistency and periodically urges the EU to apply the clause of conditionality to sanction violations of human rights and democracy. In the "Resolution on the European Neighborhood Policy" adopted in January 2006, the European Parliament emphasized "the need to establish an effective monitoring mechanism and a readiness to restrict or suspend aid and even to cancel agreements with countries which violate international and European standards of respect for human rights and democracy, and calls on the Commission to operate a vigorous policy of support for democratic forces in those neighboring states, in particular by ensuring access to independent media and information."[21]

An analysis of these EU partnerships illustrates that the concept of "partnership" does not imply a balanced relationship between two or more actors with the same political and economic weight, as the MTCs desire. On the other hand, when applied to multilateral or regional forums, the term "partnership" does not necessarily imply parity or equality. It cannot apply to group actors with the same international or regional influence, because in global politics actors play different roles. State actors, for instance, are all sovereign states, but sovereignty does not indicate their political or economic weight or the role they play in global politics. In a similar manner, in Euro-Mediterranean relations the EU retains the most influential role: it has a leading role within the Euro-Mediterranean institutional architecture and has a central role in the financial dimension as the primary donor. These are the structural conditions that shape uneven relations between the EU and the MTCs: the EU offers economic aid to Med partner countries and sets up an institutional consolidated framework for cooperation. This fact impedes the establishment of a balanced partnership.[22] For this reason, many in the region would characterize this asymmetric partnership as a form of "soft imperialism."[23]

What Is the role of the EU in the Mediterranean? The Ongoing Debate

This critical analysis of EU Med policy and its two main components (the EMP and the ENP) is more generally related to the theoretical debate on the EU as an actor in global politics. The adoption of European foreign policy (including the EU Med policy) has traditionally been influenced by the EU's understanding of its global role as a regional power, which extends through its external relations its own model of political and economic development. But the implementation of the normative ethical dimension of EU international action (principles and values such as human rights and development, good governance, and the rule of law) that was stressed in the 1990s has had to come to terms with reality.[24]

For many years European foreign policy has been influenced by the assumption that the evolutionary model of political and economic development the EC/EU has elaborated in more than fifty years of integration can be usefully extended to third countries. In this respect, enlargement is often regarded as the most successful and effective instrument of European foreign policy. The EU has in fact acted as a normative power extending the totality of its *acquis communautaire* to applicant countries. When dealing with the EU neighborhood, it is more problematic to talk about "normative regional development." In order to extend EU norms through regional cooperation, the will of the partners to accept and implement them is essential. Otherwise, this regionalist attitude might be considered "Eurocentric" by third parties. Moreover, it would be naive to believe that what has proved successful within the EU can be applied in third countries. So far the MTCs have been slow to reach EU norms, in particular on the political dimension and the so-called human dimension of security. More generally, the regionalist approach is losing ground in EU relations with the MTCs. The time is not yet here for close regional political and economic cooperation, and with the ENP the EU opted for a more concrete and pragmatic bilateral approach to Euro-Mediterranean relations. Or to put it differently, the economic normative process has prevailed over the political/democratic normative one. The EU itself acknowledges that the ENP is driven by security needs more than by a need to achieve regional norms.

The way the EU conceives the MTCs, either as potential regional partners or as neighbors integrated with the internal market, is an important projection of two different conceptions of EU Med policy. An EU Med policy conceived to tackle specific issues (such as the ENP) is much different from a policy conceived to implement a democratic political design (such as the EMP). Via the ENP, contingent security needs and strategic interests influence and shape the EU Med policy more than values and principles. The EMP is nominally more inclined to call the MTCs "partners," since partnership implies a multi-dimensional regional cooperation process. Through the ENP, instead, the EU fosters primarily economic cooperation with neighbors, which are warned that they are not prospective EU candidates. The risk of the ENP approach is that it might result in a never-ending bilateral cooperation project, since the Action Plans do not identify clear strategies, procedures, or timetables for accomplishing the political reforms necessary to build democratic domestic institutions.

The semantic shift from the EU Med policy to the ENP clearly reflects a change in approach. In order to pursue stability and security in its neighborhood, the EU is currently more inclined to play a stabilizing role in the promotion of economic development in the Mediterranean. If the ENP is focused more on economic interests than on political cooperation, does it reflect a broader shift in EU foreign policy? A more fact-oriented EU foreign policy and framework of cooperation may be the result of the enlargement to twenty-seven EU member states. It may indicate a weakening of the EU's political role, or more simply a "rationalization" of EU international action according to the logic of utility. Over the past decade the EU's potential to act as a normative power even beyond the enlargement process was probably overestimated. The EU's normative power is a politically limited concept that depends on the partners' interest in adopting the EU's norms. This interest is basically linked to the long-term objective of EU cooperation: full integration with the EU or just close economic cooperation.

The 1990s were marked by widespread interest among international relations scholars in ethics and ethical behavior in foreign policy. The fall of the Berlin Wall opened a Pandora's box and raised doubts about the dominant realist approach to foreign policy studies. Since the 1990s the debate over civilian power in Europe, the notion originally espoused by François Duchêne in 1972, has experienced a sort of renaissance.[25] Karen Smith and Margot Light, for example, have explored features of the EU's ethical foreign policy; Ian Manners has elaborated the often quoted "normative power Europe" concept; and Thomas Diez and Michelle Pace, and Esther Barbé and Elisabeth Johansson-Nogués, have addressed the issue of the EU as a "force for good" striving to make the world a "better place."[26] Central to the argument of an ethical European foreign policy is the assumption that international actors have the capability for moral action. The new normative power Europe literature tends to stress the EU's will to act internationally as a normative power–that is, to "extend its norms into the international system"—without paying much attention to the instruments the EU adopts to achieve these normative objectives.[27]

It would be a mistake to assume that since the EU has promoted democracy and other values in the central and eastern European countries, the EU has elaborated a value-driven foreign policy that can be widely implemented in its external relations. Policy processes beyond enlargement are driven by interests in addition to values and principles. Or more precisely, the political discourse regularly refers to the EU's ethical commitment, but political action is not stringent. Unless the EU's partners are willing to "go for democracy," to defend human rights and implement the required institutional reforms, the EU does not want to "die for democracy and human rights" since political reforms in Arab countries might have destabilizing effects and thus threaten security and stability in the Mediterranean.

In the Mediterranean the EU is not implementing an ethical foreign policy, for it doesn't have the ability to act normatively against the partners' will. In this respect the EU is similar to the "soft power" conceived by Joseph Nye Jr.: "A country may obtain the outcomes it wants in world politics because other countries—admiring its values, emulating its example, aspiring to its level of prosperity and openness—want to follow it."[28] This notion reflects exactly the power of attraction, distinct from coercive force, that the EU refers to in documents that distinguish between *push* for change and *pull* for change. The latter is the current EU strategy.

In less than ten years the official language of the EU has changed; the EU is no longer depicted as a proactive normative power. It is rather the partners' duty to accept EU support to reform. In a speech delivered at the first European Neighborhood Policy Conference in 2007, the president of the European Commission emphasized the importance of the neighbors' commitment to political reform: "The closer you want to be to the EU, and the greater your commitment to reform, the more we will offer you in terms of both assistance to reach those goals, and opportunities to expand and deepen our relations."[29]

If we recall the distinction between "possession" goals (goals related to the EU states) and "milieu" goals (goals dependent on change in the international system), it is clear that European foreign policy is currently pursuing the former more strongly than the latter. The ENP reflects this approach. It was in fact adopted as an instrument of border management to deal with specific EU security concerns. Through cooperation with neighboring countries the EU aims to combat illegal migration and offer more opportunities for legal migration, to reinforce energy security in the neighborhood, and to safeguard EU citizens from terrorist acts. The Barcelona Process is also becoming more interest-oriented, with an increase in energy-related initiatives. All this proves that it is wrong to assume that the EU's distinctiveness as an international actor derives from the preeminence of an ideational dynamic in its external action. Faced with the choice between "interests" and "values," the EU defends the former.

Notes

1. This chapter was originally presented at the XIII International Summer School, "The Mediterranean as the New Centre for Europe: On the Waterfront of European Policies," University of Trieste, Gorizia, September 3, 2007. This was before the adoption of the joint declaration "The Barcelona Process: Union for the Mediterranean" on July 13, 2008, which restructured the Barcelona Process. The main objective of this chapter is to evaluate the patterns of change in EU security priorities and strategy toward the Mediterranean since 1995, the institutional change brought about by the "Union for the Mediterranean."

2. European Commission, COM (2003) 104 final, "The European Union's Role in Promoting Human Rights and Democratization in Third World Countries," Communication from the Commission to the Council and the European Parliament, May 8, 2001.

3. The notion of "soft power" was first elaborated by Joseph Nye and applied to U.S. foreign policy; see J. Nye, "Soft Power," *Foreign Policy* 80 (1990): 153–71.

4. B. Ferrero-Waldner, "The EU, the Mediterranean and the Middle East: A Partnership for Reform," speech/06/341 delivered at the German World Bank Forum, "Middle East and Germany: Change and Opportunities," Hamburg, June 2, 2006.

5. For a comparison between the EMP and OSCE, see D. Xenakis, "The Barcelona Process: Some Lessons from Helsinki," Jean Monnet Working Papers in Comparative and International Politics, JMWP 17/98, University of Catania (www.fscpo.unict.it/Euro Med/jmwp17.htm [May 2009]).

6. The agreement with Syria has been negotiated but not yet signed.

7. F. Attinà, "Conclusions: Partnership-Building," in *The Barcelona Process and Euro-Mediterranean Issues from Stuttgart to Marseille*, edited by F. Attinà and S. Stravridis (Milan: Giuffrè, 2001), p. 273.

8. For a detailed analysis of the EMP institutional structure, see S. Panebianco, "Introduction. The Euro-Mediterranean Partnership in Perspective: The Political and Institutional Context," in *A New Euro-Mediterranean Cultural Identity*, edited by S. Panebianco (London: Frank Cass, 2003), pp. 1–20.

9. See, for instance, B. Buzan, *People, States and Fear* (Boulder, Colo.: Lynne Rienner, 1991); and B. Buzan and others, *Security: A New Framework for Analysis* (Boulder, Colo.: Lynne Rienner, 1998).

10. H. Sjursen, "Security and Defence," in *Contemporary European Foreign Policy*, edited by W. Carlsnaes, H. Sjursen, and B. White (London: Sage, 2004), p. 61.

11. Adrian Hyde-Price adopts a realist perspective to analyze "ethical power Europe" and illustrates the weakness of an ethical EU foreign policy. For its conduct, the EU is "open to the charge of hypocrisy when it proclaims its ethical intentions but then pursues policies that favor European economic, strategic or political interests"; see A. Hyde-Price, "A 'Tragic Actor'? A Realist Perspective on 'Ethical Power Europe,'" *International Affairs* 84, no. 1 (2008): 43.

12. Their complementarity is being reinforced with some coordination at the institutional level, as described in more detail later in the chapter.

13. During the EU policymaking process that led to the adoption of the ENP, the European Commission acted as a "policy entrepreneur." For an analysis of the European Commission's proposals and ideas as the engine behind European integration, see S. Panebianco, "La Commissione europea nell'Unione a 25: tra influenza nazionale e autonomia sopranazionale," in *Quale Europa? L'Unione Europea oltre la crisi*, edited by G. Baldini (Soveria Mannelli: Rubbettino, 2005), pp. 85–109.

14. By December 2007 the EU had stipulated action plans with twelve of the sixteen ENP partners. Plans for Algeria, Syria, Libya, and Belarus did not yet exist.

15. Some critics point out that the principle of differentiation might be an elegant EU strategy to launch intense cooperation with eastern post-Soviet countries while slowing down cooperation with Mediterranean countries. On the other hand, some eastern post-Soviet countries such as Georgia and Ukraine are experiencing liberalization processes that might be conducive to democracy, while in the Mediterranean third countries old authoritarian elites are still in power.

16. European Commission, COM (2007) 774 final, "A Strong European Neighborhood Policy," Communication from the Commission, December 5, 2007.

17. The new institutional setting envisaged by the Paris Joint Declaration that set up the Union for the Mediterranean confirms that the EMP needed a profound restructuring.

18. It has to be stressed that many neighbors (in particular eastern neighbors) do not share the EU's geopolitical definition of "neighbor."

19. S. Panebianco, "Promoting Human Rights and Democracy in European Union Relations with Russia and China," in *Values and Principles in European Union Foreign Policy,* edited by S. Lucarelli and I. Manners (London: Routledge, 2006), p. 136.

20. An empirical survey conducted by Karen Smith denounced the EU for enforcing the conditionality clause only to countries with a marginal international role; see K. Smith, "The Use of Political Conditionality in the EU's Relations with Third Countries: How Effective?" *European Foreign Affairs Review* 3, no. 2 (1998): 253–74. On the EU's inconsistency, see K. Smith, "Beyond the Civilian Power Debate," *Politique Européenne* 17, no. 1 (2005): 63–82 (http://eprints.lse.ac.uk/812 [February 2008]).

21. European Parliament, "Resolution on the European Neighborhood Policy," P6 TA(2006)0028, January 19, 2006, p. 2.

22. On the other hand, the Mediterranean is at the center of two historical cleavages in international politics: the North-South and the center-periphery cleavages, both of which are reflected in the EU's relations with the MTCs.

23. B. Hettne and F. Söderbaum, "Civilian Power or Soft Imperialism? The EU as a Global Actor and the Role of Interregionalism," *European Foreign Affairs* 10, no. 4 (2005): 535–52.

24. See, for example, Lucarelli and Manners, eds., *Values and Principles in European Union Foreign Policy.*

25. For an illustration of the current debate over civilian power drawing on Duchêne's definition, see Smith, "Beyond the Civilian Power Debate."

26. K. Smith and M. Light, eds., *Ethics and Foreign Policy* (Cambridge University Press, 2001); Ian Manners, "Normative Power Europe: A Contradiction in Terms?" *Journal of Common Market Studies* 40, no. 2 (2002): 235–58; T. Diez and M. Pace, "Normative Power Europe and Conflict Transformation," paper presented at the EUSA Conference, Montreal, May 17–19, 2007; E. Barbé and E. Johansson-Nogués, "The EU as a Modest 'Force for Good': The European Neighborhood Policy," *International Affairs* 84, no. 1 (2008): 81–96.

27. Manners, "Normative Power Europe," p. 252.

28. Joseph Nye Jr., *Soft Power: The Means to Success in World Politics* (New York: Public Affairs, 2004), p. 5.

29. J. M. Barroso, "Shared Challenges, Shared Futures: Taking the Neighborhood Policy Forward," speech 07/502 delivered at the European Neighborhood Policy Conference, Brussels, September 3, 2007.

KHALID EMARA

13

Is Sarkozy's Union for the Mediterranean Going to Work?

Attempts to develop North-South cooperation among countries around the Mediterranean can be traced back to the early 1970s. Cooperation agreements were then offered by the European Community (EC) to southern Mediterranean countries, and in 1975 the Euro-Arab dialogue was launched with two objectives. It was an attempt to find both a permanent solution to the Arab-Israeli conflict and a platform for Europe to handle the consequences of the first global oil crisis.[1]

In the early 1980s a Euro-Mediterranean policy started to emerge. During this period, one could detect a growing interest both in the North and the South in developing forms of political, economic, and cultural dialogue and cooperation schemes around the Mediterranean. Then in the early 1990s an intense dialogue among Egypt, France, and Italy paved the way for the creation of the "Mediterranean Forum." The forum was meant to provide a platform for governments around the Mediterranean basin to brainstorm on the prospect of Euro-Mediterranean cooperation. Participation included Mediterranean members of the EU and southern Mediterranean countries from Lebanon to Morocco. The free discussions that characterized the forum contributed positively to the launch and adoption of the Barcelona Declaration in 1995.

Meanwhile, other platforms for Mediterranean cooperation were being explored. An important one was the "5+5" initiative between the Maghreb Union countries and the EU Mediterranean member states. The early 1990s also witnessed the convening of the Madrid Conference for Peace in the Middle East, in which the United States played a key role. Despite Europe's active political and economic participation in the Madrid process, its role was clearly secondary to that of the United States. Consequently, Europe felt the need to engage its southern neighbors in a wider cooperation project. As such, the Barcelona Process was launched with its three baskets (political, economic, and sociocultural), formulated along the model of the OSCE-Helsinki Process.

The Mediterranean region is an area of vital strategic importance to the EU in political, economic, and cultural terms. The Barcelona Process has been the central instrument for Euro-Mediterranean relations since 1995. Representing a partnership of thirty-nine governments and about 750 million people, it provides a framework for continued engagement and cooperation. The Barcelona Process is the only forum in which all Euro-Mediterranean partners exchange views and engage in political dialogue. Today it is considered one of the important tools contributing to regional stability and cooperation. Moreover, it creates a shared view of the need to pursue a path of political and socioeconomic reform and modernization. However, the persistence of the conflict in the Middle East has challenged and stretched the partnership to the limit of its abilities to preserve the channels of dialogue among all partners.

In recent years, the EU launched the European Neighborhood Policy to complement the Barcelona Process and as an instrument to accompany needed reforms for the modernization of societies in the southern Mediterranean. On July 13, 2008, forty-three heads of state and government met in Paris. They launched the Union for the Mediterranean (also known as the Mediterranean Union or MU), an idea advanced by the new French president, Nicolas Sarkozy, during his presidential campaign. It is worth noting that the European Council on March 13–14, 2008, approved the principle of a Union for the Mediterranean and invited the European Commission to present proposals defining its scope. After consulting with member states and partner countries, the Commission presented its proposals for priorities and for how best to channel a new political and practical impetus into the Euro-Med process.

The Union for the Mediterranean and Changing Geopolitical Realities

Despite the growing European interest in the Mediterranean since the early 1970s, and the different projects launched to advance peace, stability, and cooperation around this vital sea, the Mediterranean region remains submerged in conflict, its security and stability threatened, its economic development lagging, and its sociocultural heritage questioned.

Sarkozy's Mediterranean vision is undoubtedly shaped by his personal experience as the interior minister of France. He perceives the Mediterranean from a security lens. Looking at the Mediterranean region from Europe, he sees major security challenges, including cross-border terrorism, illegal immigration, growing movements of people, and the integration of migrant communities. This is a defensive posture that Europe should avoid adopting in its relations with its southern neighbors.

The major challenges facing the EU and France in conjunction with the Mediterranean can only be confronted in cooperation with non-EU Mediterranean countries. The agenda is much wider than security. It includes peace and stability for future generations, disarmament and confidence building, sustainable economic development, environmental management, and water resources.

As Europe attempts to redefine its role in the Mediterranean through a renewed commitment to the newly launched Mediterranean Union, it should consider the changing geopolitical situation around the Mediterranean region, particularly the U.S. direct military presence in Afghanistan, Iraq, and the Arabian Gulf. Moreover, the significance of the newly created American military command in Africa should be closely considered.

Another input in the changing geopolitical equation is the growing Iranian role in the Mediterranean through its privileged relations with Syria, Lebanon, and the Palestinian Authority. The Turkish role is also important in the Mediterranean and in the wider geopolitical context. Finally, traditional Russian interests in the region are being revived and should be evaluated.

What Can Europe/France Do?

In order for Europe to capitalize on its potential as a leader in international affairs, it should exercise its "soft power," as advanced by Joseph Nye Jr.[2] Europe has a vested interest in building an area of peace, cooperation, and prosperity around the Mediterranean. This should strengthen Europe's position on the world stage and provide an alternative to America's growing militarism. What the countries of the Mediterranean region need most is a sort of "Marshall Plan" to rebuild conflict-torn societies, to modernize the socioeconomic fabric of Mediterranean societies, and to integrate them into the global marketplace. The Mediterranean Union should provide the needed momentum to initiate such a plan.

What Is Different about the Mediterranean Union?

It is important to note the Mediterranean Union's added value in terms of institutional arrangements. Its members have chosen a system of rotating co-presidency, held at this writing in 2009 by Egypt and France. It will be endowed with an independent secretariat, whose location is to be decided. Its members will hold regular summits, besides the regular meetings of a Council of Foreign Ministers. From its conception, the Union claims a growing role of southern countries in its work in order to underline their co-ownership of the process.

Moreover, the MU founders underline its project-driven disposition. Among the areas of interest, the Mediterranean environment is central. Environmental projects include plans to clean up the Mediterranean by 2020 and to establish a

Mediterranean water agency and a marine environment protection agency. In the energy field, projects include creating a common energy market and advancing the renewable energy program (MEDREP). Culturally, initiatives incorporate encouraging sustainable tourism, the founding of a Euro-Mediterranean university, promoting cultural and civilization dialogue through the work of the Anna Lindh Foundation based in Alexandria, and the intensification of student exchange programs.

Economic cooperation is crucial for the future of the Mediterranean Union, particularly in order to bridge the growing gap between the rich North and the developing South. Several ideas are being considered: strengthening investment networks, providing funding for small and medium-size enterprises, financing trans-Euro-Mediterranean transport networks, enhancing vocational training programs, the mutual recognition of diplomas, and assessing the benefits of establishing a development bank for the Mediterranean.

In the area of security, priorities include maritime security, civil protection, combating illegal immigration and managing migratory flows, promoting human rights, combating terrorism, and cooperation in counter-narcotics.

Challenges and Impediments Facing the MU

Major challenges continue to confront Europe and its Mediterranean partners. The most significant is how to create shared values and institutions. In addition, the persistence of several conflicts, chief among them the Arab-Israeli one with the Palestinian tragedy at its center, creates a growing sense of despair and injustice. Reconciliation based on international laws and agreed principles is essential for creating the basis for the coexistence of Arabs and Israelis. For the EU, the question of how to deal with Israel without reverting to double standards represents a serious challenge. Furthermore, the question of what to do with Turkey remains open.

Another open question is how to set a common agenda for the MU. Current priorities mostly reflect a European vision rather than a shared one. The priorities of the southern Mediterranean countries should be high on the agenda. They include resolving the major conflicts, providing the basis for people to move legally, freely, and in an orderly fashion within the Euro-Med area, technology transfers from North to South, and securing financial resources with national developmental objectives in mind.

Notes

1. The content of this essay strictly represents the personal views of the author.
2. Joseph Nye Jr., *Soft Power: The Means to Success in World Politics* (New York: Public Affairs, 2004).

*Relations between the EU
and Other Countries*

ANDREW MORAVCSIK

14

U.S.-EU Relations: Putting the Bush Years in Perspective

In taking a big picture view, this chapter challenges the conventional wisdom about the transatlantic relationship during the George Bush Jr. years, which is that transatlantic relations were in bad shape or disarray. That claim, which is 100 percent incorrect, has three parts to it.

First, it is often said that in the "good old days" of the cold war transatlantic relations were good, that Europe and America had a common purpose, and that they showed great unity because there was a common threat. After the end of the cold war in 1989, Europe and the United States did not have the same common purpose. The best piece of evidence for this is the war in Iraq, which most portray as a typical and severe crisis in the Western alliance. A well-known Washington-based analyst, Simon Serfaty, has said that without a doubt America and the states of Europe faced one of the most difficult and demanding crises over the United States' effort to use force in Iraq. Almost every analysis of the transatlantic relationship started with and dwelled on the crisis in Iraq and what that meant for transatlantic relations.

Second, according to the conventional wisdom, the crisis in transatlantic relations and the war in Iraq represented a clash of opposing principles of international order: multilateralism and unilateralism. Many people view foreign policy in terms of competing visions. One just needs to pick up a French paper, or a book by Robert Kagan, to find evidence for this. Analysts and journalists often start their articles by citing one or the other. One insightful analyst, David Calleo, said that transatlantic differences spring from contrary readings of recent historical trends: American political elites see the Soviet collapse opening the way to their own global hegemony, while Europeans reject this view. During a year in China, in 2007–08, I often heard the Chinese speak about the need to oppose American unilateralism, making this a global view.

Third, according to conventional wisdom, one important reason why transatlantic relations were in disarray and the United States asserted itself unilaterally was because the European pillar of the transatlantic alliance lacked unity and common purpose. The best evidence, according to the conventional view, is the lack of a serious European security and defense identity. If it existed, according to this view, then there would be stronger opposition to the United States or at least some coherent alternative. Europe might, for example, make common cause with the Chinese. David Shambaugh, one of Washington's leading China watchers, has written eloquently about a possible Euro-Chinese axis. The underlying idea here is that some sort of geopolitical realignment or some sort of counterweight to the United States in the world is needed, and that the place to start is with a more robust European defense. The failure of the Constitution means the Europeans cannot deliver.

My view is that all three of these claims (that is, that transatlantic relations were in crisis, that there were two opposing principles, and that it all came back to European disunity) are demonstrably false. The truth is almost exactly the contrary: first, transatlantic relations were already measurably better than they were during the cold war on almost every dimension. When we look at issues and concrete disputes rather than visions, U.S. and European policy was quite convergent, much more convergent than the policies of Europe and, say, China. And Europe's current policy of pursuing civilian power rather than military power speaks to its comparative advantage and gives it the most weight that it is likely to have in the world. The rest of this chapter develops these ideas.

First, was the transatlantic relationship more or less harmonious now than it was during the cold war? Anyone who thinks that the cold war was a period of Western harmony really needs to go back and reread history. What about the epic battles between the United States and Europe over policy toward Russia, over détente and Ostpolitik, over trade policy in the 1960s and 1970s? What about the brutal way that Americans pulled the rug out from European efforts to maintain their colonial possessions: the battleships deal during Suez, Algeria, etc.? How about the way in which U.S. dollar policy overturned European governments one after the other (for example, leading to Helmut Schmidt's fall from power)? What about Europeans ignoring the American blockade of Cuba in area after area? There was also Charles de Gaulle's decision to pull France out of NATO's military command. The West was in total disarray in the face of the energy crisis. Millions of Europeans were on the streets demonstrating every week against American decisions to deploy missiles in Europe throughout the late 1970s and early 1980s. When the United States bombed Libya in 1986, only one country in Europe, Britain, allowed American F-111 jets to take off. They supposedly flew through the Straits of Gibraltar because no one would give the United States flyover rights (the French secretly did, but could not admit it). Pollsters asked the British the next day whether they thought the American military presence in the United Kingdom increased their security: 4 percent thought it did. That is how bad the situation was. All this was *incomparably* worse than it is now, or was even at the height of the Iraq crisis.

The toughest case to make in favor of my argument is "out of area" military intervention. I believe the United States and Europe have never been in as much agreement about intervention in third countries as they were in the past years. Since the end of the cold war there's been a lot of Western intervention. The United States has intervened in Panama, Somalia, Haiti, Macedonia, Bosnia, Kosovo, Afghanistan, and Iraq several times. Europe has intervened in Mozambique, Rwanda, Bosnia, Kosovo, Sierra Leone, Macedonia, and Côte d'Ivoire. Of all those interventions, there is only *one* place where the United States and Europe disagreed. That place is Iraq. And in fact they disagreed on this only in 1998 and 2003, not in 1989–90. Iraq is entirely exceptional. Moreover, it is an exception that proves the rule. The United States now recognizes, just as most Europeans do, that that intervention was an unsustainable mistake, not something that the United States would be inclined to do again. It was so costly that it could not be repeated more than once a generation. Thus, in the post–cold war period there is a record of almost total agreement between the United States and Europe on the use of military force out of area.

Compare that to the period of the cold war after the end of the Korean War. There were Suez, Vietnam, Latin America under Reagan, where the Europeans were funding the opposition to U.S. covert interventions, and the case of Libya just discussed. Indeed, one is hard pressed to find a single U.S. military or European operation "out of area" on which there was Western agreement. I can think of only a couple: the Congo in 1960 and Lebanon in 1958.

The truth is that in almost every respect the cold war was a much *more* contentious period than the current one. We live in a more friendly and cooperative period of transatlantic relations than at any time in the past fifty years. The foundation of the conventional wisdom is incorrect.

Let us turn to the second premise of that conventional wisdom, that there was a clash of principles between America and Europe: unilateralism vs. multilateralism. It is true that the United States has, for deep-set constitutional reasons, a greater disinclination than most Western countries to engage in multilateral legal engagements. But this mode of analysis is a bit legalistic. The United States and Europe find flexible ways to pursue their interests despite the lack of formal legal agreement on how that should be done.

It is particularly odd to read the opinion that Europe might have more business to do with a country like China because it agrees *in principle* with a multilateral legal worldview rather than a unipolar legal worldview, without taking into account the underlying substantive convergence of interest. There is something very abstract about this position: a tendency to privilege abstract legal principles over concrete national interests.

Consider the positions of the United States and Europe toward East Asia. It is true that the United States is more engaged in East Asia, that it has a military presence with different priorities in certain respects. But the two positions are quite similar. Both the United States and Europe have roughly the same conception of stability in East Asia, roughly the same position on the Taiwan issue. Within the context of deterring any forceful effort to change the regional status quo, both the United States and Europe share a basic strategic goal of engaging China economically, politically, and diplomatically. Europe backs six-power efforts with regard to North Korea. On the economy, Europe and the United States have taken the same position toward China on currency, trades, and energy issues. Both favor a stronger Chinese currency. Both are concerned about China's trade surge. Both are concerned about intellectual property matters. As U.S. policy shifts, both are likely to take a similar stance on environmental issues. Both have taken very similar positions on democracy and human rights, as well as Tibet. China, unlike the United States and Europe, continues to oppose in principle diminutions in sovereignty to address issues of human rights and genocide, as in Darfur, or nuclear proliferation, as in Iran.

So, if China and Europe sat down and agreed on the need for a multipolar world, *what would they talk about then*? What would the substance of those negotiations be? The truth of the matter is that the claim that Europe and China agree on multipolarity is purely abstract. It has no concrete meaning. When one starts talking issues, real concrete issues that diplomats have to deal with day to day, the United States and Europe have almost precisely the same positions toward East Asia. So I believe it would be a mistake to treat visions of foreign policy as if they are more important than concrete issue positions. So much for the second leg of the conventional wisdom, namely that the United States and Europe differ in principle on multilateralism.

Finally, there is the third piece of the conventional wisdom: the main reason Europe gets less respect around the world, and that the United States can promote unilateral policies, is because Europe is not unified. This is something heard a lot in the United States and in China as well. During my year in China, I often heard the claim that the Chinese do not have to pay any attention to Europeans (except maybe on some trade issues) because they aren't unified. If they ever get their act together and have a common foreign policy, then China will have to pay attention. It is very difficult to contest this position because this is what Europeans tell the world (and themselves) all the time. The European debates about Europe are dominated by people who believe in a particular ideal which demands that things like foreign policy be centralized. Thus one is always being told that Europe will not have an effective foreign policy until it is centralized. No wonder foreigners tend to believe it.

I think this view greatly understates the current effectiveness of European foreign policy. In Asia, in the United States, and even in Europe it is said that in the twenty-first century there will be two great superpowers, or maybe three: the United States, China, and possibly India. One often reads in the newspapers that the most important geopolitical relationship of the twenty-first century will be the U.S.-China relationship. That may well be the case, but my guess is it will be a while before that happens.

Today there are two superpowers in the world. One is the United States and the other is Europe. Europe is the *quiet superpower,* specializing in forms of power other than military: civilian, "soft," and military short of all-out war. Even though it is not unified in the classic sense, Europe is more effective at projecting power globally and getting things done than anyone else, including the Chinese. The Chinese today are a middle-rank regional power, with a power projection capacity about 500 or 1,000 miles outside their borders, at most.

Let us catalog what Europe is. Nobody denies, including the strongest critics, that China is a global superpower in trade and investment. Europe and the United States continue to dominate the World Trade Organization (WTO). Nothing happens without the Europeans wanting it to happen. Europe trades more with China than with the United States, and its trade balance is more favorable. It is the largest trading partner of every country in the Middle East (except Jordan, which trades with Israel). As SAIS professor Dan Hamilton reminds us every year, predictions about the economic rise of Asia based on trade statistics are vastly misleading. Measured by investment, intrafirm trade, and R&D, the transatlantic zone remains far more robust and more important than the transpacific relationship. It accounts for well over half of the world's economic activity. Europe dispenses 70 percent of the world's foreign aid, and it is much better at dispensing it than the United States or anybody else.

Europe's most effective power projection instruments are civilian in nature, but Europe is an appreciable military power as well. At any given time there are 75,000 to 100,000 European troops stationed abroad. Since the 1990s, European-led diplomacy or intervention has helped stabilize governments in Sierra Leone, Libya, Morocco, Lebanon, Ukraine, Congo, Macedonia, Côte d'Ivoire, and Chad. Until recently, Europeans were the only Western diplomats talking to Iran. Europe welcomes more foreign students than the United States. It is the major worldwide supporter of international law and institutions. Global polling suggests that the European social model is more attractive worldwide than the libertarian American model.

None of this even mentions the single most powerful tool Europe possesses: the enlargement of the European Union. The EU enlargement is the single most cost-effective tool that Western powers have deployed to spread peace and democracy since the end of the cold war. Fifteen countries have already joined the European Union since the end of the cold war. Half a dozen more are queued up to do so. The majority of those countries, to a greater or lesser degree, have been assisted in the transition to democracy and capitalism. Compare that to the U.S. efforts in Iraq and you can see how cost-effective and prudent that strategy is at spreading peace and democracy.

Some complain that Europe is decentralized and nonmilitary, and thus that all its power is for naught. This has been Robert Kagan's critique all along: decentralized civilian power is nice, but when you want something done, you need to call in the marines. Yet Europe is much stronger than it seems, and part of that strength is a function of the decentralized way in which it operates, as well as its focus on nonmilitary means. The successes of European enlargement and neighborhood diplomacy over the past two decades belie this critique. If large amounts of political capital were expended or diverted today to build up a European military force, this would simply deplete Europe's power projection capability. I pose the following challenge to Europeans. Suppose Europe had had a centralized army of 100,000 crack troops under the personal command of Javier Solana, deployable at twenty-four-hours' notice anywhere in the world, what difference would it have made over the past fifteen years? Is there any moment at which Europe could have intervened effectively to change outcomes? And would it have made as much difference as enlargement of the European Union to ten countries in central and eastern Europe? My answer to that question is no. The only case about which one would really want to argue is Afghanistan, and the reason there is that the United States bogged down its troops in Iraq.

In any case, in the real world of political trade-offs, governments make choices, and they are constrained by the choices their predecessors made. Europe has splendid civilian power and low-level military tools; the United States has splendid military tools. We live in a world in which Europe and America are good at different things, a world in which Europe is specialized in one kind of power and the United States is specialized in another kind of power. We have to work within those constraints. These differences, like any comparative advantages, can work for us. None of this is to imply, however, that transatlantic relations were in decline. To the contrary, U.S.-European relations are immeasurably friendlier, less affected by conflict than they were twenty, thirty, forty, or fifty years ago. This fact fundamentally contradicts the conventional wisdom underlying most analyses that we read today. With that said, we can now start solving all those detailed problems that remain.

MARTA DASSÙ *and* ROBERTO MENOTTI

15

Economics and Security:
A Reversed Alliance

A "rebound" in the Euro-American dialogue has come sooner than expected, but brings with it a paradoxical risk in transatlantic relations. In a sense, the post–George W. Bush era began without waiting for his successor. Europe, however, may not be ready to seize the opportunity and exploit the more promising climate: the European Union seems to be—again—in an introverted mood following the rather frustrating post-Lisbon "pause for reflection" and a deep economic recession. Americans, for their part, are gripped by their own economic crisis and their attempt to sort out (and get out of) two complicated wars. In this context, Barack Obama is the ideal U.S. president for Europeans, but support for the man does not translate into concrete support for his policies.

Our central thesis is that the main problems for the transatlantic relationship will be of an economic rather than a security nature. We do not deny that security issues remain crucial (starting with Afghanistan) and can abruptly take center stage, but economic decisions will have long-lasting consequences and will possibly shape a new set of international deals.

Although there are precedents in post–World War II history, such as the end of the gold standard and the oil shocks of the 1970s, there is a fundamental difference between then and now: the Western economies are more tightly intertwined with emerging economies and are relatively weaker overall. More specifically, the rising (or re-emerging) powers of the early twenty-first century have the means to bargain with the West from a position of significant influence. Their relative weight has grown substantially thanks to a mix of internal reforms generating rapid growth, globalized markets, and vast imbalances in most of the Western economies (especially in the key sectors of finance and energy). This combination creates conditions of unusually high interdependence, which raise the probability of a contagion effect from economic competition to diplomatic and security frictions. At the same time, the United States remains the major economic hub on a global scale, and competitors suffering in the current crisis and Europe's choices must take this reality fully into account.

From the central thesis we see two likely consequences: first, there will be a tendency by the United States to view the Europeans as important allies among other important allies, but no longer as unique. This trend has been evident since the end of the cold war, was reinforced by the effects of 9/11, and could now become a long-term strategic reality. After losing its position as the main strategic theater of the cold war, Europe may well become secondary to American-led efforts to tackle security problems globally, all the more so if the economic relationship should deteriorate or simply become less crucial to American interests.

Second, there are growing risks of a geo-economic, and geopolitical, divergence between the United States and Europe with regard to two crucial global actors: China and Russia. To put it simply, while the United States is becoming increasingly dependent on China in key economic sectors, Europe is becoming increasingly dependent on Russia—perhaps excessively if we look at Russia's limited market potential. Such a divergence cannot fail to have strategic ramifications.

If the analysis we present here is sound, we can derive a few coherent recommendations for cultivating transatlantic relations and avoiding unrealistic expectations early in the term of the new U.S. administration.

Structural Reversal and Growing Asymmetry

Let us begin with the core argument that transatlantic economic ties are becoming more problematic for structural reasons. On the European side, after the short-lived hopes that the European economic model could prove more resilient or somehow insulate itself from the global turmoil, there has been a recurring temptation to blame only Wall Street and its regulators for the whole "state of the world." Too many leaders and observers seem to forget that Europe's anemic growth is not a recent problem. In the background, the saga of the Constitutional/Lisbon Treaty has certainly not bolstered confidence in the long-term future of a tightly knit EU.

Even though Europe's aggregate economic outlook is more balanced than America's, any self-congratulation on Europe's part would be badly misplaced. The last thing we need in the midst of an economic crisis is the ugly combination of fear and hubris.

The depth and duration of the recession of 2008–09 on the U.S. side is uncertain, but we argue that, in any event, it should be evaluated in the context of a new international set of relationships—potentially a whole new pecking order, which hardly benefits Europe.

Regarding Euro-American relations, until very recently, most transatlantic debates reflected serious concerns about security but tended to find reassurance in the solid economic foundations of the alliance. Indeed, it has been rightly noted that during the worst phase of Euro-American (and inter-European) disagreement over Iraq, economic ties actually boomed. In short, security may often divide the Atlantic, but the economy unites it, regardless or even in spite of government choices. The web of "deep interdependence" linking Europe and America provides a precious safety net, and a crucial task for policymakers was to preserve this state of affairs, ensuring that there was no spillover of security/diplomatic frictions onto the economic/business sector. The likely direction of negative contagion was almost taken for granted: it would travel from security to the economy.

It is not easy to separate short-term analyses and long-term trends. For instance, a standard analysis in the first few weeks of the financial crisis was that economic growth is being led by Asia and a few emerging economies in other areas, while Europe muddles through and the United States is in trouble. Now there is a growing sense of worry about the U.S. economy, with the political economy of the transatlantic relationship called into question.

One remarkable effect is that the risk of contagion in transatlantic relations now flows in the opposite direction than in the past: from the economy to security and diplomacy. Should the U.S. role as the leading world economy be quickly eroded (accelerating a secular trend and reaching the tipping point where confidence collapses), the political leadership of the United States would also suffer, despite the "Obama effect."

American policymakers have always drawn a great amount of political legitimacy and even a form of moral authority from the objective strength of the American growth engine. The alliance will be reshaped in unpredictable ways in the event of a deep and protracted economic crisis originating essentially from America itself. A paradox for Bush's successor might be the following: even if the U.S. administration takes all the right steps to burnish America's image abroad through "public diplomacy," the economy's slowdown may inflict serious damage on U.S. leadership.

In the meantime, a contradictory feeling is gripping European policymakers, businesspeople, and pundits alike: after having feared a security "decoupling" from the United States for decades and then having tried to achieve a modicum of "autonomy" at least on crisis management, they now begin to ponder the costs and benefits of a partial economic decoupling, though not the simplistic type that seemed possible at the start of the subprime mortgage drama. The case of Germany is very telling in this respect: the German argument against deficit spending is rhetorically linked to strong criticism of "cheap money" and the

American model. The reality is that Germany is not ready to share more of the burden of a European recovery plan.

With all of this in mind, the real decoupling may be the result of different energy strategies and geopolitical considerations. There are strong objective forces pushing toward a close Europe-Russia relationship. Europe's dependence on Russian oil and gas (or Russian-controlled sources in any case) has become a structural feature of the continent's political economy, affecting not only immediate choices in the energy sector but also the more general interest in developing the Russian economy as a whole and forging closer links, which in turn is seen as a way to improve "energy security." Russia is for Europe an indispensable partner, as well as a neighbor.

Instead, when Washington looks at Russia, it sees an optional partner at best, and a relatively marginal economic actor, despite the serious effort to "reset" the bilateral relationship. What is more important, the very different degree of interdependence produces different strategic attitudes and priorities, so that the United States can afford to be tougher (at least rhetorically) toward Moscow, while the essential opposition in the major continental capitals (Paris, Berlin, Rome) to NATO's enlargement to include Ukraine reflects a Russia-first view. President Obama may face a rather united pro-Russia European front, comprising members of both "old" and "new" Europe.

The situation is almost exactly reversed if we look at the United States and its deepening Asia-Pacific connections. There, growing commercial integration has served as the key component of an entire system of massive imbalances: the economic models of the United States and China over the past two decades have come to need each other, to the point that there now exists a sort of symbiotic relationship. It is no accident that Asian sovereign wealth funds are not heavily invested in Europe. As an effect of this transpacific interdependence, Washington is understandably inclined to tackle issues such as climate change by pursuing arrangements directly with China, India, and Japan.

In contrast, most Europeans just have too much at stake in and around Europe itself to forgo opportunities in the Mediterranean, but also the Balkans and the Caucasus. East Asia is a great economic magnet, but it is distant. No one can deny the huge importance of China and the Far East, but Europe's destiny is inextricably tied to other regions closer to home. Heavy investments in eastern Europe—including Russia—also make sense from a security perspective, to the point that in some cases the profit margin may prove less important than the overall political investment.

If Europe continues to gravitate toward Russia and the United States toward China and the Pacific, the already significant transatlantic differences in strategic outlook will be magnified and might even solidify as a fundamental geopolitical fracture. The largest question mark in this context is probably the future of the euro as a reserve currency, since it could give the euro-zone a truly global clout, but also further widen the Atlantic by contributing to the weakening of the dollar, and presumably of America's world leadership.

The precise evolution of transpacific and Eurasian relations is not wholly predetermined, of course, but the general trend in economics and security is toward growing asymmetry.

All of these considerations took a new twist with the bursting of the financial bubble in 2008 and the full-blown economic crisis. With a protectionist impulse palpable across public opinion on both sides of the Atlantic, the asymmetry could widen: the United States, in a phase of economic retrenchment, may actually continue to expand its security outreach; Europe, now much less confident in the viability of America's economic role, will have to take on more responsibilities in its neighborhood even as Washington looks for more worldwide contributions, beginning in Afghanistan. Again, NATO is a litmus test, as most EU countries are trying to persuade Washington that the alliance is badly overstretched and that a further widening might kill it. Instead, some of Obama's advisers seem to have an "expansionist" view of NATO, arguing that it is (and should remain) the main multilateral security forum to which Washington is steadfastly committed, an argument the Europeans find hard to reject. Though a global NATO (as the hub of a potentially global web of democratic partnerships) is less bad than a "league of democracies" from a European viewpoint, the relative European weight would still be diminished by a further widening of the alliance's portfolio. Of course, there are also concerns that the Euro-American alliance would be perceived ever more as a self-legitimizing world policeman.

The terrorist attacks on Mumbai at the end of November 2008 dramatically vindicated a more specific policy trend (common to the Bush administration and the Obama campaign): devoting increasing attention to India's role as a key regional actor while seeing the Afghanistan issue as part and parcel of the much wider complex that comprises India and Pakistan.

However delicate this may be, the economic side of the equation is probably even more troublesome. Here, a strong focus on domestic priorities might easily produce, sometimes unintentionally, a penchant for international confrontation on trade issues. If coupled with the diverging perceptions of the geographical global center of gravity, the urgent need for a "positive economic shock" will produce rather different priorities.

Having TEA Together

Not all these factors are a source of friction, however; there are opportunities as well. Here are some of them, in brief. It should be clear, by now, that the notion of de-linking Europe's economic trends from America's is factually illusory and politically costly; thus the ultimate solution—one that safeguards both common economic and political interests—lies in getting out of the crisis together by restarting the transatlantic engine. If the roots of Euro-American frictions are now in the economy, it is the right time for the Europeans to take a wide-ranging policy initiative in the economic sphere, while it is more important than ever that we cultivate our security ties.

The initiative we advocate is to accelerate discussions about a transatlantic economic area (TEA), which should be presented as exactly the kind of "safety net" we may now be losing under the pressure of economic change/crisis. The project would help boost the existing level of interdependence across the Atlantic, extending it to areas that so far have been poorly integrated and reducing tensions in hard times. The concept of a TEA seemed to be in search of specific content for a while: the time is now ripe for completing the opening up of transatlantic exchanges by focusing as a matter of urgency on the regulatory framework—but not stopping there.

If we needed any confirmation, it has now become all too evident that finance is at the heart of globalization. What follows is that there will be no true transatlantic market until financial transactions are subject to the same rules. These rules—once adopted in an area inhabited by nearly 800 million rather affluent people—would set an essential standard on a world scale. As such, they would clearly be central to further discussions in the G-7 and G-20 formats.

Interestingly, one leader who has been openly supportive of the TEA concept is German chancellor Angela Merkel, who has also made headlines by declaring to the *Financial Times* that the "Anglo-Saxon model" of financial deals is to blame for the ongoing crisis. In fact, Chancellor Merkel's remarks would be useful when interpreted as a call for more transatlantic harmonization in sectors that have become increasingly central to the global economic system. Here, the EU should resist its temptation to overregulate, while the United States should overcome its allergy to regulation.

For the Obama administration, the TEA would be a tool to concentrate minds (especially in Congress) on the continuing practical benefits of open exchanges with Europe. We all have a lot to gain by taking the controversy on a whole wave of regulations out of the purely domestic context, if only because the nature of financial transactions is definitely cross-border. Given the obvious need for creative and unconventional thinking on how to "relaunch and reform" finance, there is space for European proposals to become an integral part of the American debate.

Over time, the policy mix we advocate would really amount to laying the transatlantic foundations of a new open, but rule-based, international order. A strong transatlantic consensus is needed, first of all, to seriously reform the

International Monetary Fund (IMF), enhancing its surveillance role. The EU would prove its seriousness if it could agree on a "consolidation" strategy of the national quotas in the IMF.

Moreover, the TEA should not be conceived as an alternative to current multilateral trade negotiations such as the Doha Round, but as a trigger for a wider consensus. The political significance of such moves should not be underestimated, as they would send a powerful signal of cohesion between the two largest economic areas of the world at a time of growing doubts about the resilience of the international structures they have created since around the middle of the twentieth century.

In a nutshell, the West still has some time before it is too late to propose an overhaul of global rules—an overhaul, that is, partly on the West's own terms.

Europe's Security Burden

A reformed and updated Western alliance will not come about if the Europeans remain mired in their EU institutional paralysis: once Lisbon is adopted, progress must be achieved, first and foremost, in the field of coordinated policies. And while good policies can certainly be made easier to coordinate in the presence of effective EU institutions, they do not depend mainly on the institutional machinery. The key areas where scarce resources should be concentrated are European defense and energy policy.

It is thus good news that France is finally ready to overcome its self-imposed constraints on working within NATO, because a rock-solid NATO-EU link is crucial to European cohesion: poor NATO-EU operational cooperation has often provided a big excuse and a useful alibi. It is time to move on.

In this perspective, only a few EU members actually provide the bulk of the EU's overall defense capabilities and have the ingrained habit to deploy them. As a consequence, a "core group" on European defense, comprising France, the United Kingdom, Germany, Italy, Spain, and Poland, can lead the EU on the path to a greater international role. From a specifically Italian viewpoint, a core of six is a much preferable alternative to the "Big Three," for the obvious reason that the proposed formula places Italy itself inside the leading group. But more generally, the six-country grouping is rather diverse in its military traditions and geopolitical priorities, so its very composition would ensure a fairly good representation of the range of opinions in the EU. Indeed, this arrangement can inject needed political dynamism into an EU security and defense policy as well as provide the resources to make it real.

Of course, problems would remain even if such an arrangement were fully agreed to in principle. Foremost among them is the lack of public support for inherently risky combat missions of uncertain duration, especially when no clear prospect of political "success" is in sight.

No new "mission statement" or strategic concept will ever solve the problem of insufficient public support among European publics for close coordination with the United States on key potential missions that NATO is already pursuing (Afghanistan) or might undertake in the near future. Instead, better performance is the key.

Against this background, the only basis needed for sharing political and military burdens is sharing financial burdens. The reasoning applies to the EU as much as it applies to NATO, since they share the same problem when it comes to solidarity. Its logical implication is that the current mechanism of "costs lie where they fall" is counterproductive and should be abandoned in favor of a sizable "common funding" for stabilization and peacekeeping missions. A legitimate objection may be that having some countries pay for dangerous missions that others would undertake is like hiring a mercenary force. The current arrangement is somehow even worse, overburdening those who do more and leaving the others free to abstain and criticize. In fact, a common funding mechanism provides an incentive for active participation since all members of the group are paying upfront in any case.

The EU and NATO will sink or swim together in the field of international security, though not always in perfect harmony. We should avoid unrealistic expectations: the EU-NATO relationship most likely will not operate like clockwork, but it should not be dysfunctional either.

In order to improve practical cooperation, a great opportunity is now offered by the more relaxed U.S. attitude toward an EU role in defense as a complement to NATO. Probably for the first time, European defense is seen by significant sectors of the U.S. security community as a value added, not just a polite concession to be made.

Henry Kissinger has written about "the transformation of the traditional state system of Europe. . . . With the nation no longer defining itself by a distinct future and with the cohesion of the European Union as yet untested, the capacity of most European governments to ask their people for sacrifices has diminished dramatically." Kissinger captures a central dilemma for all EU members in their relations with each other as well as with the United States: while their own collective ambition and international expectations of a strong EU role grow, their ability to act accordingly is severely limited. At the same time, Europe no longer enjoys the luxury of staying aloof from the problems of the rest of the world, precisely because of the other two revolutions cited by Kissinger: "the radical Islamist challenge to historic notions of sovereignty; and the drift of the center of gravity of international affairs from the Atlantic to the Pacific and

Indian Oceans."[1] From a European perspective, these tectonic shifts are just too big to be left to the United States alone.

We can conclude that the EU is almost condemned to act. To avoid the risk of permanent insolvency (a mismatch between ends and means), it must raise the stakes: only more public awareness of the EU's true interests in the world will produce more willingness to spend time and resources on world affairs. A "global Europe" will only emerge as part of a renewed transatlantic link. It will be a pragmatic and cautious process, based on performance rather than on empty ambitions. And it will not posit autonomy (from the United States) as a goal in itself.

The EU as a whole should be regarded (and first regard itself) as a contributor to wider efforts by the transatlantic community or even more diverse groupings: it should thus adopt the same standard that individual countries are increasingly committed to—that is, influence tied to direct (and mostly measurable) contributions to collective tasks. In short, the onus is on Europe to demonstrate its usefulness as a major security partner.

Developing a coordinated energy policy worth the name is the other, and equally important, policy requirement for Europe. The need for such a step is self-evident precisely because all European leaders realize the degree of dependence on Russian and Middle Eastern supplies, and more generally on energy imports from outside the continent.

Energy dependence is a headache per se (as the United States knows well), but Europe's distinctive bargaining problem is that, absent a common position, outside counterparts can easily play some EU members against the others and systematically close better deals. Europe will never be a credible partner of the United States unless it can speak with a single voice on all the central security issues of the twenty-first century.

Anticipating Crises and Seizing Opportunities

Even under the best of circumstances, a number of crises are very likely in the near future, and all of them related to countries that are particularly important to the world's political economy. Two seem paramount.

Number one is Iran, which is probably just the first of several challengers of the established "regional order." Certain aspects of the challenge posed by Tehran are unique, as regards the legacy of 1979 with the United States and the Shia-Sunni divide in the Muslim world. However, on other counts today's Iran is a harbinger of things to come: it has a hybrid political regime (theocratic and repressive, but not totally closed to outside influences), and a hybrid economic system (underdeveloped and facing huge demographic pressure, but with great potential); it is highly nationalistic and feels frustrated by Western attitudes. The reality is that other countries in the European neighborhood (both to the east and to the south) may well display some of these features in the next decades.

It is thus crucial to walk a narrow diplomatic path by combining stronger pressures on the Tehran regime—especially after the postelection drama—and keeping open the option of EU sanctions in parallel to the UN Security Council sanctions. That would raise the costs of Iran's nuclear program while laying the groundwork for engagement on a wider set of issues. This should include a search for innovative solutions to the problem of nuclear proliferation, such as a consortium for the provision of fissile materials. In any case, each further step should be based on a strong Euro-American agreement: direct American involvement is indispensable and additional European sanctions remain a precious potential asset in preventing Washington from going it alone.

The number two "crisis epicenter" is China, not so much as a classic security threat but as a factor in U.S. politics and, consequently, in transatlantic relations. Avoiding major frictions with Beijing was one of the untold success stories of the George W. Bush years. We got a taste of how explosive the China factor can become on the occasion of the transatlantic spat over the possible end of the EU arms embargo. That episode (which reached its most acute phase to date in 2004–05) brought to the surface the fundamental asymmetry in geopolitical outlook toward China and Asia that separates the United States from Europe. But the most striking discovery was that each side of the Atlantic badly misjudged the importance of China for the other side, almost as if Beijing was just a marginal international concern. What is absolutely necessary is a sustained transatlantic dialogue on China, designed to tackle behind closed doors a host of interrelated issues well before—not after—they become acute crises.

As in other sectors, in tackling the China issue it will be essential to understand the evolving balance between security and economic considerations: the United States seems somewhat more at ease than most Europeans with a Chinese economic superpower, while the Europeans do not regard China as the potential military threat that Washington is quietly working to contain. Their perceptions are thus almost exactly opposite. A regular dialogue unhindered by the need to publicly display unity can do a lot to smooth some of the differences and avoid unpleasant surprises.

There may be a third large epicenter of crisis, Russia, which continues to hang in the balance between providing hopeful signs of moderation (even large-scale cooperation) and being the source of permanent tension. This is more than a topic of transatlantic disagreement because Russia, as we argued earlier, directly affects the nature of the Euro-American relationship: it is the country that can redefine the meaning of Europe's borders, for better or for worse. The big question mark is whether conditions are ripe for a grand bargain in which Europe would also play a major role. In the meantime, two extreme scenarios seem plausible but are equally exaggerated: one is a new cold war set in motion by a Russian attempt at "rollback" in parts of central and eastern Europe, dragging the EU into a disastrous battle of attrition; the second is a Washington-Moscow deal bypassing Europe, perhaps based on America's desire to focus on the greater Middle East and China and on forms of technical cooperation on missile defense.

Europe's weaknesses are well known, and few concessions will be obtained from Russia without Europe's getting its own act together, first and foremost on energy issues. Diversification of energy sources is prudent in any case. The issue of Ukraine and Georgia will not easily go away from the NATO agenda, but procrastination cannot become a strategy.

In the face of these daunting challenges, the fact remains that the coming to power in Washington of a new administration—and to some extent a new generation—is a rare opportunity. The transatlantic relationship should be viewed in the wider context of an almost worldwide, but brief, window of opportunity for the United States. Instead of just relying on the Obama effect, Europe must quickly offer something tangible of its own not to waste the opportunity.

Precisely because of the common concern regarding a large-scale economic crisis, all members of the transatlantic club may have finally realized the sheer magnitude of the forces that will shape the international system in the next decades; when seen through these systemic lenses, traditional internally squabbles look much smaller and manageable.

Note

1. Henry A. Kissinger, "The Three Revolutions," *Washington Post*, April 7, 2008.

JOAQUÍN ROY

16

Relations between the EU and Latin America and the Caribbean: Competition or Cooperation with the United States?

Modern Latin America and the Caribbean trace their roots, history, political culture, languages, and predominant religion to the "Old Continent." Consequently, there should not be a more fertile spot for the installation of the model of regional integration developed by the European Union during the past half a century.[1] Latin America and the Caribbean would be ideal candidates to receive the greatest attention from Europe and its institutions, resulting in solid integration systems mirroring the European Union.[2] However, the reality is that this would be an uneven political marriage. Their commercial exchanges are comparatively limited, while regional integration in Latin America and the Caribbean seems to be lagging in commitment and results.[3]

The collective profile is impressive. The combined bloc composed of the European member states and the Latin American and Caribbean countries includes sixty sovereign states with a population of over 1 billion people that create over a quarter of the world's GDP. For the most part the dominance of the EU bloc is overwhelming, although for positive reasons. Europe is the leading donor in the Latin American region. It has become the biggest foreign investor, and it is the second most important trade partner.[4] In addition to the subregional programs (as described below), the EU offers a series of horizontal programs: AL-INVEST (to help small and medium-size companies), ALFA (to promote cooperation in higher education), URB-AL (to foster links between European and Latin American cities), ALBAN (to reinforce cooperation in higher education), @LIS (to support information technologies), and EUSOCIAL (to promote social policies, health, education, the administration of justice, employment, and taxation policies).

This unequal relationship is shaped through a plan known as the Strategic Partnership. The EU's aim in its policies toward the region is to strengthen the political dialogue to better address new global challenges.[5] The EU's relations with Latin American countries have developed through a number of specialized "dialogues" with specific subregions and two individual countries (Mexico and Chile).

This relationship is based on three pillars: economic cooperation, institutionalized political dialogue, and trade relations. The aim of the EU is to support regional integration, to increase the competitiveness of Latin American enterprises in international markets, and to facilitate the transfer of European know-how.

The recognition of Latin America and the Caribbean in the institutional framework of the European Union is a late phenomenon. This peculiarity is in part explained by some complementary dimensions. First, the original membership and aims of the European Community in the 1950s must be taken into account. In its early years, the EC concentrated its efforts on developing its common commercial policy. The European Political Cooperation (EPC), the predecessor of the EU's Common Foreign and Security Policy (CFSP), was very modest in its reach.

Second, Latin America was not even mentioned in the Schuman Declaration, which propelled the formation of the original European Coal and Steel Community (ECSC). Only Africa was named as an additional beneficiary of the aims and purposes of European integration. This apparent discrimination was due to the large role played by France, the only European Community state power that at the time had colonies, with the exception of Belgium's colonial control over Congo. The Caribbean was not seriously considered by the EU until the accession of the United Kingdom to the European Community.

Because of the French and German interests, European institutions began to pay attention to this region. Latin America at last received the favors of Brussels when Portugal and especially Spain became members in 1986. The rest of the 1980s and the decade of the 1990s were the golden era of EU–Latin American/Caribbean relations, in part because of the European interest in contributing to the pacification of conflict zones, such as Central America. The impetus given to the exportation of the European model of integration was the other decisive factor for EU involvement in the region.

Institutional Framework and Subregions

The structure of EU–Latin American relations is based on periodic summits at the highest level of government on both continents. Every two years, the heads of state and government of the European Union, Latin America, and the Caribbean meet, alternating between Europe and Latin America.[6] The May 2008 meeting was held in Lima, Peru.[7] Earlier gatherings have taken place in Rio de

Janeiro (1999), Madrid (2002),[8] Guadalajara (2004),[9] and Vienna (2006).[10] This bilateral relationship has been reinforced by the Rio Group, a forum created by Latin America and the Caribbean, designed more for political consultation.[11] At the level of ministers of foreign affairs, the officers of the EU and the Latin American/Caribbean region discuss overall political matters. Biannually, the meeting site alternates between the two continents. Having met for the last time in 2007 in Santo Domingo, Prague is the host in 2009.

Respectful of the Latin American/Caribbean subregions, the EU has organized its framework of activities with individual trading blocs and subregional integration schemes, including the Andean Community, Mercosur, Central America, and the Caribbean. The fact that Mexico and Chile do not belong to any of these subregional Latin American schemes has led the EU to make individual agreements with those countries. In fact, those agreements have so far produced the closest economic relations. The Dominican Republic and Haiti have been added to the Africa, Caribbean, Pacific (ACP) grouping, qualifying them to receive EU aid. Cuba became a member, pending its application for the Cotonou (successor of the Lomé Convention) Agreement.

The Andean Community

The Andean Community was founded in 1969, with the Andean Pact.[12] Theoretically, its institutional framework mirrors the model of the EU. Today it comprises only four countries of the Andean region (Bolivia, Colombia, Ecuador, and Peru). Chile left early. Original member Venezuela changed affiliations in 2005, becoming a member of Mercosur (although this is still subject to confirmation by each of the members). The EU political dialogue with the Andean Community began in 1996 with the drafting of the Declaration of Rome (1996). Still pending ratification, the Political Dialogue and Cooperation Agreement of 2003 will rule European-Andean relations. The EU's actions follow the guidelines outlined in the regional strategy paper for 2007–13. Among other things, this document stipulates that the EU is the leading donor of official development aid to the region. Although progress has been slow, in June 2007 negotiations began on a new Association Agreement with the aim of reinforcing links and facilitating bi-regional trade and investment. The first two rounds of negotiations were held in Bogota and Brussels in September and December 2007, and the third took place in Quito in April 2008.[13]

Central America

The small region composed of the Central American countries (structured as the Central American Integration System, successor to the Central American Common Market) has enjoyed special attention from the EU over the past two decades.[14] Costa Rica, El Salvador, Guatemala, Honduras, Nicaragua, and Panama have received a notable level of development aid and political support from Brussels. This fruitful relationship was originally founded in the San José Dialogue, inaugurated in 1984. Its initial goals were primarily political—to contribute to finding practical solutions for armed conflicts and to facilitate a framework of negotiations. Toward this end, the EU has offered visible contributions to peace, the democratization process, and the socioeconomic development of the region. Data show that the EU is the leading donor of official development aid to Central America and its countries.[15] A draft agreement of cooperation was signed in 2003 and in 2007. Elaborate negotiations began on an Association Agreement, covering a wide number of issues, including trade and investments.

Mercosur

The Common Market of the South (Mercosur) has received the most attention from the EU in recent decades since its conception in the late 1980s and its founding in 1991 by the Treaty of Asunción.[16] Since then, the EU has expressed its hopes for institutional development with the aim of supporting a workable customs union. This subregional bloc comprises four original countries (Argentina, Brazil, Paraguay, and Uruguay). Venezuela has also applied for membership. The European Union has favored the strengthening of Mercosur and has endorsed its initiatives, notably through an interinstitutional agreement to provide technical and institutional support for its newly created structures. In 1995 the EU and Mercosur signed an Interregional Framework Cooperation Agreement, which entered into force in 1999. A joint declaration annexed to the agreement provides the basis for political dialogue between the parties, which takes place regularly with meetings of senior officials from the two regions. The latest political dialogue was held in Buenos Aires on April 25, 2008.

In 2000, both parties opened negotiations for the signing of an Association Agreement based on three pillars: political dialogue, cooperation aid, and a free trade area. While negotiations on the political and cooperation chapters have been virtually concluded, the trade chapter remains unfinished at this writing, owing to obstacles presented mostly by the agricultural products that the Mercosur countries would like to place in Europe. The slow implementation of integration stages in the subregion has presented an additional problem. On December 17, 2007, the European Commission and Mercosur issued a joint communiqué confirming the political will to relaunch and then conclude the pending Association Agreement. This intention was confirmed by the leaders of the two regions, meeting in Lima in May 2008 as part of the EU–Latin America summit. At the same meeting it was decided to explore opportunities to launch joint projects in the areas of renewable energy, infrastructure, and science and

technology. The EU provides assistance to Mercosur through a regional program scheduled for 2007–13 that was adopted in August 2007 in the framework
of the regional strategy for Mercosur. This program provides support for projects in three priority areas: institutional strengthening, preparing for the implementation of the Association Agreement, and the participation of civil society
in the integration process. The EU is by far the largest supplier of development
assistance to the region.[17]

The Caribbean

The relations of the EU with the Caribbean Community (CARICOM) are managed by a 2007 strategy communication dealing with political, economic, and
developmental issues, geared to the subregional implementation of the ACP-
wide Lomé/Cotonou Agreements.[18] Institutional support has been a priority,
supporting the establishment of entities following the EU model. Brussels is
aware that the challenges facing the subregion can be transformed into opportunities. The EU has based its strategy on the existence of shared values and
helping the Caribbean countries to attain sustainable development. This should
be administered with a sense of mutual responsibility in the form of an enriched
EU-Caribbean partnership, which is quite a challenge in comparison with the
former unconditional aid concept. The new approach is couched in the need
for effective governance, the needed consolidation of democracy, and attention to the urgent political issues of the region, in addition to the constant EU
preference for effective regional integration. In the economic field, the EU will
support integration efforts to increase competitiveness, diversify exports, and
establish regional markets. The EU also pays close attention to trade-related
assistance, the support of small and medium-size enterprises, poverty reduction, and health.[19]

Comparative Analysis

The EU has experienced great economic difficulties and political defeats in the
course of its deepening (constitutional experiments) and widening (enlargement) processes. European integration still faces further challenges regarding
Turkey, the Balkans, and the eventual expansion toward the borders of Russia.
However, the EU is still the most successful and ambitious accomplishment of
voluntary integration and cooperation among sovereign states. In addition to
its imprint in Latin America, the EU as a point of reference is felt in the Mediterranean, Africa, and Asia.[20]

    One reason for this success is that Europe enjoys comparatively dense cul-
tural, historical, and social cohesion that coexists with the diverse profile of its

nations. Although this specific European identity may have been accomplished by eliminating peoples of other origins, the fact is that there is something unique that makes citizens feel European. In addition, the progress that led to the formation of the EU has been dominated by a pragmatic political consensus. The EU leadership detected early the benefits of integration, especially the completion of the stages of deepening that imply the sharing of sovereignty in important sectors.

Chances are that in the long run the current obstacles that affect the EU will be overcome, as has happened in previous chapters of the EU experiment. However, the truth is that the indecision produced by the failure to get a constitution approved has been interpreted as the tip of the iceberg of the imperfections of the system and of its innate peculiarity. This "collateral damage" has already had a negative impact on the integration processes of the rest of the world, especially in Latin America.

Latin American sectors that are skeptical about the deepening schemes for economic cooperation feel strengthened by what they perceive as a mixed European example and express some distaste for what is erroneously interpreted as "loss of sovereignty" or "cession of national prerogatives." "Pooling" is an alien expression in Latin America. This view claims that the European citizens are uneasy about too much integration beyond economic issues, and that they do not understand the centrality concepts such as supranationality and shared sovereignty. The European model, in essence, fails in its effective projection all over the Americas.

As a consequence, the Western hemisphere experiments have been modest until now, limited primarily to free trade. One obstacle is the taboo represented by national sovereignty that does take into account the political complications of a leadership in transition. The other is the economic and cultural gap between different subregions, especially between the United States and the rest of the continent. Observers wonder if there is a basis for dividing the hemisphere into two versions of a Free Trade Area of the Americas (FTAA).[21] One would be northern, linked to Washington. The other would be a numerically reinforced Mercosur, but weaker in practical terms.

Nonetheless, on a comparative basis, it would appear that in recent years the process of Latin American integration has been proceeding at a faster pace than the European one, which stalled after the leap taken by the enlargement and the crashing of the constitutional project. Optimism was the order of the day in Mercosur after its own peculiar and shocking enlargement with the membership of Venezuela. A resurrected Andean Community was dressed up after the reincorporation of Chile as an associate, to make up for the Venezuelan desertion. Moreover, the plans of both schemes to be conflated in a more ample one, as envisioned by a South American union, inspired high hopes. For its part, the EU has pressured the Central American Integration System to implement a solid customs framework. This will lead the region to receive the benefits of free trade, coming out of a weak position to take a leadership role. As a whole, this panorama would integrate the Latin American nations quite quickly. Given the apparent inertia of the European process, an era of greater Latin American advancement seems likely.

Appearances, however, may lead to wrong conclusions. Although the European process has been slow, it may in the long run outpace Latin America, whose path has been contradictory and frustrating. The EU pattern of behavior shows a legacy of prudence and steady movement, in the tradition of functionalism and spillover effects. Only when circumstances dictate otherwise have bold decisions (usually taken by elites) been executed, but always after considerable homework. In retrospect, the disaster encountered with the constitutional project and its sequel, the Treaty of Lisbon, can be explained by a relative lack of preparation of public opinion, which has taken center stage when leadership goes into hiding. But the EU record also shows that it usually learns from its mistakes. "Utopian" in its true sense can be applied to the European balance sheet in the fifty years since the founding of the European Economic Community, which was meant to remedy the failure of the European Defense Community and the apparently limited mandate of the Schuman Declaration of May 9, 1950.

In contrast, the Latin American process of integration has been characterized more by spectacular announcements about the founding of new entities. The latest addition is the Bolivarian Alternative of the Americas (ALBA) founded by Venezuela to compete with the U.S.-dominated Free Trade Area of the Americas (FTAA-ALCA). At the same time, there is formidable resistance to the consolidation of independent institutions. Claiming that previous entities lacked budgets and authority and were the victims of past failures, Latin American leaders have been consumed by a fever for summitry. The result has frequently been a string of media declarations that grab headlines and leave no time between one announcement and the next.

Balance

The results of a dozen Western hemisphere elections held since 2006 have left observers with a mixed view of the prospects for regional integration. The electoral balance in Mexico, the United States, and Canada only pointed to a moderate strengthening of the basic tenets of NAFTA.[22] In addition, the contradictory declarations of the Democratic U.S. presidential candidates in the primary process of 2008, questioning the validity of NAFTA, left more confusion in the

air. The victory of the reformed Sandinista party in Nicaragua added a counterweight to the internal debate between the deepening of the feeble integration scheme and the option presented by the free trade pacts with the United
States through the Central American Free Trade Agreement (CAFTA). Where
the tenuous group will go all depends on the political will of the diverse leadership of the Andean countries. Some countries seem to be more inclined to opt
for a free trade pact with Washington, questioning the validity of deepening
indigenous blocs. Threats that Bolivia might follow the path of Venezuela are
alarming. The radicalization and nationalization process exercised by Venezuela's Hugo Chávez adds more questions than answers for the reinvigoration of
Mercosur. Facing the disintegration of the Andean Community and the instability of Mercosur, Brussels seems to have exhausted its energies for pushing
veritable integration. It is not surprising then that the EU has crafted a strategic
partnership with Brazil.

Other obstacles make the EU–Latin America front difficult. On the one hand,
the EU resists reforming the Common Agricultural Policy (CAP) that would
open up the market to Latin American products, still subject to quotas and
quality limitations. Europe has now irritated Latin American governments and
societies by restricting immigration. On the other hand, most Latin American
countries refuse to liberalize their economies and have not met the request of
the EU to form effective customs unions. However, the most daunting obstacles
for progress and regional integration are poverty and inequality, the worst in
the world. Social exclusion and discrimination fuel criminality in all sectors of
the societies, which in turn leads to the establishment of authoritarian regimes.
The alternative is the rise of populist regimes, usually not inclined toward
market-oriented regional integration experiments. This situation determined
the appearance of the ALBA.

In sum, the European Union faces its own challenges and will be forced to
choose between two alternatives. One is the complete abandonment of the
ambitious process as envisioned in the constitutional experiments. That will
ultimately lead to a freezing of the entity, an incomplete common market, with
only half of its members adopting the common currency and no joint foreign
policy. This would in turn send the wrong message around the world, especially to Latin America. How then could Brussels deepen the different stages
of regional integration with a model that apparently has exhausted its capacity
and has lost the support of the Europeans? The second alternative is the pursuit of a solution acceptable to the most important leaders of the EU to enable
them to sell it to electorates. The EU must confront the difficulties presented
by the Lisbon Treaty in order to send the message worldwide that the EU is not
renouncing its principles, that it is flexible, and that again it has learned from

its mistakes and will ultimately prevail. Only time will be able to issue the final verdict.

Notes

1. This chapter relies heavily on two kinds of references. One is the official description and assessment given by the European Commission documents (europa.eu [October 2008]). The second reflects a series of research publications produced by the European Union Center/Jean Monnet Chair of the University of Miami. See Joaquín Roy and Roberto Domínguez, eds., *The European Union and Regional Integration: A Comparative Perspective and Lessons for the Americas* (Miami: European Union Center/Jean Monnet Chair, 2005) (www6.miami.edu/eucenter/books/The%20EU-Regiional-text+cover-final.pdf [October 2008]); Joaquín Roy and Roberto Domínguez, eds., *After Vienna: Dimensions of the Relationship between the European Union and the Latin American-Caribbean Region* (Miami: European Union Center/Jean Monnet Chair, 2007) (www6.miami.edu/eucenter/books/After%20Vienna-text+cover.pdf [October 2008]); Joaquín Roy and Roberto Domínguez, eds., *Regional Integration Fifty Years after the Treaty of Rome (March 25, 1957): The EU Model in the Americas, Asia and Africa* (Miami: European Union Center/Jean Monnet Chair, 2008) (www6.miami.edu/eucenter/books/Fifty%20years-text+cover.pdf [October 2008]).

2. For a general consideration of the prospects and limitations of regional integration, see Gaspare M. Genna, "Power Preponderance, Institutional Homogeneity, and the Likelihood of Regional Integration," in *Regional Integration*, edited by Roy and Domínguez, pp. 19–34; Laura Gómez-Mera, "Obstacles to Regional Integration in Latin America and the Caribbean," in *Regional Integration*, edited by Roy and Domínguez, pp. 11–132.

3. On the relationship between the European Union and Latin America and for a comparative analysis of the corresponding regional integration networks, see Angel Casas, ed., *Integración en Europa y América* (Mexico: Instituto Tecnológico de Monterrey, 2007); Eric Tremolada Alvarez, ed., *Crisis y perspectiva comparada de los procesos de integración* (Universidad del Externado de Colombia, 2008); José María Beneyto and Patricia Argerey, eds., *Europa y América Latina: el otro Diálogo Transatlántico* (Madrid: Biblioteca Nueva/Instituto Universitario de Estudios Europeos, Universidad CEI, 2008).

4. For a general description and figures, see data provided by the European Commission (http://ec.europa.eu/trade/issues/bilateral/regions/lac/index_en.htm [October 2008]).

5. European Commission, Regional Programming Paper (http://ec.europa.eu/external_relations/la/rsp/07_13_en.pdf [October 2008]); European Commission, Latin America (http://ec.europa.eu/external_relations/la/index_en.htm [October 2008]).

6. For analytical essays on the summits, see Alejandro Chanona, "An Assessment of the Summits," in *After Vienna*, edited by Roy and Domínguez, pp. 35–49; Thomas Cieslik, "The Future of the Strategic Association," in *After Vienna*, edited by Roy and Domínguez, pp. 51–62.

7. European Commission, EU-LAC Summit, Lima 2008 (http://ec.europa.eu/external_relations/lac/index_en.htm [October 2008]).

8. European Commission, EU-LAC Summit, Madrid 2002 (http://ec.europa.eu/external_relations/lac/madrid/dec_02_en.pdf [October 2008]).

9. European Commission, EU-LAC Summit, Guadalajara 2004 (http://ec.europa.eu/external_relations/lac/guadalajara/decl_polit_final_en.pdf [October 2008]).

10. European Commission, EU-LAC Summit, Vienna 2006 (ec.europa.eu/external_relations/lac/vienna/index_en.htm [October 2008]); For an evaluation, see Roberto Domínguez, "Between Vienna and Lima," in *After Vienna,* edited by Roy and Domínguez, pp. 23–32.

11. European Commission, "The EU and the Rio Group" (http://ec.europa.eu/external_relations/la/riogroup_en.htm [October 2008]).

12. European Commission, Relations with the Andean Community (http://ec.europa.eu/external_relations/andean/index_en.htm [October 2008]).

13. For evaluations of the EU-Andean relationship, see Angel Casas-Gragea, "Lessons from the Andean Community," in *After Vienna,* edited by Roy and Domínguez, pp. 131–45; Erneko Adiwasito, Philippe de Lombaerde, and Ramón Torrent, eds., *The Future of Andean Integration and the Relations with the EU* (Brussels: Studia Diplomatica, 2006).

14. European Commission, Relations with Central America (http://ec.europa.eu/external_relations/ca/index_en.htm [October 2008]).

15. Fernando Rueda-Junquera, "Perspectives of Central American Integration," in *After Vienna,* edited by Roy and Domínguez, pp. 95–116.

16. European Commission, Relations with Mercosur (http://ec.europa.eu/external_relations/mercosur/index_en.htm [October 2008]).

17. Aimee Kanner, "Prospects for New Governance in South American Insights from Europe," in *The European Union,* edited by Roy and Domínguez, pp. 165–76.

18. European Commission, Relations with the Caribbean (http://ec.europa.eu/development/geographical/regionscountries/eucaribbean_en.cfm?CFID=1306536&CFTOKEN=53102587&jsessionid=2430648ae4ad105f444d [October 2008]).

19. Wendy Grenade, "CARICOM: Coming of Age?" in *Regional Integration,* edited by Roy and Domínguez, pp.145–64.

20. Olufemi Babarinde, "The African Union: Finally in the Path of the EU?" in *Regional Integration,* edited by Roy and Domínguez, pp. 53–72; Katja Weber, "European Security Integration: Lessons for East Asia?" in *Regional Integration,* edited by Roy and Domínguez, pp. 73–100; Astrid Boening, "The Euro-Med Partnership and Regional Integration," in *Regional Integration,* edited by Roy and Domínguez, pp. 101–09.

21. Ambler H. Moss, "Reflections on the Development and Prospects of the FTAA: Does It Relate to the European Experience?" in *The European Union,* edited by Roy and Domínguez, pp. 271–80.

22. Roberto Domínguez, "North America after NAFTA," in *Regional Integration,* edited by Roy and Domínguez, pp. 133–44.

FINN LAURSEN

17

EU-Canada Relations:
A Case of Mutual Neglect?

This chapter deals with the relationship between the European Union and Canada, both bilaterally and in a wider context, providing a brief historical overview of the development of the relationship and a discussion of various tensions, or "irritants," as they are called.[1] Based on trade shares, the relationship is asymmetrical, with Canada having a relatively greater interest in developing freer trade and more cooperation than the EU. The United States is the most important third party affecting the relationship because of its importance for both Canada and the EU.[2]

The Context of EU-Canada Relations

The EU-Canadian relationship is a bilateral one that is also embedded in wider international regimes. If one focuses on the economic relationship, in particular trade, then the international regime is the General Agreement on Tariffs and Trade (GATT)/World Trade Organization (WTO). Trade relations between the EU and Canada are based on the GATT rules, including most-favored-nation (MFN) treatment. This puts Canada at the bottom of the so-called trade hierarchy that the EU has built up. In this respect Canada is part of the group of industrialized countries, together with the United States, Australia, Japan, and a few other countries to whom no preferential treatment is offered. Free trade has been on the agenda continuously, especially on the Canadian side. The EU side has not been so interested in a free trade agreement (FTA), mostly because it would raise the question of what to do with the United States.

If we look at the security part of the relationship, the international regime, apart from the United Nations (UN), we have the North Atlantic Treaty Organization (NATO) and to a lesser degree the Organization for Security and Cooperation in Europe (OSCE), which Canada is also party to. The EU's Common

Foreign and Security Policy (CFSP) remains intergovernmental in nature, and it is only since 1999 that the EU has become more serious about developing a European Security and Defense Policy (ESDP). There is a political dialogue on these matters with Canada going back to the 1980s.[3] It is probably fair to say that these relations are less important than the economic relations, even if the two sides share many political values and attitudes, including support for multilateralism.

The next thing that should be emphasized about the bilateral relationship is that there is an important third party involved, the United States. One cannot study EU-Canada relations without considering the importance of the United States, both for Canada and for the EU. Canadian trade and EU trade relations with the United States are much more important than trade between the EU and Canada.

Trade and Investments

Today Canada is the EU's tenth-largest trading partner; 1.8 percent of total EU trade is with Canada, compared to 16.6 percent with the United States. Seen from Brussels, the United States is much more important than Canada. But seen from Ottawa, the EU is Canada's second-largest trading partner. According to 2007 estimates, the EU accounts for 9.8 percent of total Canadian trade, and the United States for 67.3 percent.[4] These figures have changed over time. There has been a relative decline of Canadian trade with the EU and an increase in trade with the United States.

If one looks at the composition of trade, machinery is at the top of both imports to and exports from the EU, and raw materials is second on the list. In these major categories of trade it is notable that in many areas trade is reciprocal. This is typical for trade relations between industrialized countries. The main exception is in nonagricultural raw materials, where the EU imports a lot from Canada, but does not export much. Canada is rich in resources, including oil and minerals.[5]

It should also be mentioned that foreign direct investment (FDI) between Canada and the EU has become important since the 1980s. Roughly one quarter of FDI in Canada comes from the EU, approximately €127.4 billion in 2006; roughly a quarter of Canadian FDI abroad has gone to the EU, approximately €83.8 billion in the same year.[6]

The size of the two markets varies greatly. Canada has about 33 million inhabitants, the EU-27 close to 500 million. These figures mean that economic relations between the EU and Canada are asymmetrical, giving Canada a greater interest in their development than the EU.

Historical Overview

The early period of European-Canadian relations, at the start of the European integration process, is sometimes called the period of indifference. European integration in the 1950s created some unease in Canada due to the Canadian preference for North Atlantic free trade.[7] Article 2 of the North Atlantic Treaty deals with economic cooperation, but it has never been implemented. Canada played an important role in getting it into the treaty.[8] The fact that Canada's most important trading partner in Europe, the United Kingdom, did not take part in the European Community at the beginning eased the Canadian situation. Although the United Kingdom first applied for membership in the European Economic Community (EEC) in 1961, the bid for membership was vetoed by General de Gaulle in 1963 and 1967. UK negotiations had the Canadian government of Prime Minister John Diefenbaker very worried. What would happen to the commonwealth's preferences?

The United Kingdom finally joined in 1973. Before then another event was to influence Canadian thinking, the so-called Nixon shocks in 1971, when the U.S. government put a 10 percent surcharge on imports and made no exemption for Canada. Canadian politicians began considering how to diversify trade in order to become less dependent on the United States. Three options were discussed in 1972.[9] The first option was to do nothing and resign to "continentalism," the term used for developing relations first of all with the United States. The second option considered was to embrace continentalism and seek more integration with the United States. The third option was to diversify trade using the EC as counterweight and was supported by the government of Pierre Trudeau during the 1970s.

By 1973, after the British accession, the EC's trade policy was taking shape. The customs union was in place, as well as the Common Agricultural Policy (CAP). There were negotiations for compensatory measures under GATT article XXIV, and an agreement was reached in 1975.[10] Those that lose because of trade diversion in connection with the creation of a customs union can ask for compensation. The Kennedy Round of GATT trade talks led to a further lowering of industrial tariffs.

Since 1972, when the EC enlargement was confirmed, there have been high-level bilateral consultations between the EC and Canada. Since 1973 Canada has had an ambassador to the EC, and since 1974 parliamentarians have met regularly. Since 1976, Canada has had a Framework Agreement for Commercial and Economic Cooperation with the EC.[11] It created what was called a contractual link. It confirmed the MFN treatment and spoke in general terms about commercial and economic cooperation. Institutionally it created a joint cooperation committee (JCC) to "promote and keep under review the various commercial and economic co-operation activities envisaged." The JCC would normally meet at least once a year. (Interestingly, the United States did not have a similar contractual link with the EC at the time.) But the outcome was modest.[12] According to Andrew F. Cooper, "instead of being readily and rapidly translated into a wide number of specific programs of co-operation, the contractual link withered away through mutual neglect."[13]

Given the meager results of the third option, the second option, continentalism, increased in importance. In the 1980s the government of Brian Mulroney promoted the Canada–U.S. Free Trade Agreement (1988), and then, in 1993, it also included Mexico in the North American Free Trade Area (NAFTA). These developments, of course, further increased Canada's trade dependence on its southern neighbors.

In the late 1980s and the 1990s, the internal market plan in Europe affected EU-Canada relations as the creation of the customs union had done at the beginning. But it actually affected FDI flows more than trade. A number of Canadian companies, especially the bigger ones, invested quite a bit in Europe at this point. The same thing happened with American and Japanese companies, because of the fear of a "Fortress Europe."

At the end of the cold war, the idea of free trade was again being promoted by some Canadian politicians, and the Americans also became interested in developing relations with the EC. In both cases the new interest led to the Declaration on Transatlantic Relations (or Transatlantic Declaration, TAD), which introduced increased policy consultation and coordination and further developed the institutional framework. It began by adding summit meetings between the prime minister of Canada on one side and the president of the European Council and the president of the European Commission on the other. However, the TAD was vague on specifics.

Later in 1996 a joint political declaration and an Action Plan were adopted. The objective was to strengthen bilateral relations and to enhance economic and security cooperation. Although the Action Plan dealt with a number of issues, including new trade policy issues, such as the environment, investment, competition, labor standards, and intellectual property rights, commitments were not very specific.

More recent developments include an EU-Canada partnership agenda in 2004, agreed at the summit that year in Ottawa. The economic section mentions the negotiation of a trade and investment enhancement agreement and the development of a voluntary framework for regulatory cooperation.

In June 2007 an EU-Canada summit in Berlin brought the leaders together face-to-face for the first time since 2005. Specific priorities for enhanced cooperation were put together, one of them being to increase the involvement of civil society in transatlantic policy discussions. The focus is now on following up the June 2007 EU-Canada summit with discussions on bilateral economic partnership, foreign policy cooperation, and global challenges, including especially climate change.

Tensions and Irritants

Tensions have varied over time. The CAP has been a constant problem. Of course, other countries have the same problem with the CAP because it leads to the dumping of surplus products on the world market and makes access to the EU market more difficult. And certainly Canadian wheat exports to Europe have been affected by the CAP. The reforms forced on the EU in connection with the Uruguay Round of trade talks should gradually reduce the external impact of the CAP, but the CAP is still an issue in international trade diplomacy.

Hormone-treated beef has created tensions because of the EU ban on imports going back to the 1980s. Here Canada has the same problem as the United States.[14] Seal hunting has also been an issue. Some environmentalists, including the International Fund for Animal Welfare, claim that slaughter methods are inhumane. The import of fur products made from the pelts of seal pups has been banned by the EU for more than twenty years, and the import of other seal products has been banned by some EU countries. Canada banned harvesting of harp seal pups in 1987. There is probably some poaching going on.[15]

Furs, other than those made from seals, have been an issue because of the way the animals traditionally have been trapped with the leg-hold traps. Objections by environmental groups in Europe to these killing and trapping methods have led to bans on the import of furs from Canada. The EU has worked to phase out leg-hold traps and signed an agreement with Canada in December 1997 to do so.[16]

Fisheries have also been a source of tension. Canada has a wide continental shelf in the Atlantic, which means that it goes farther out than the 200-mile exclusive economic zone. There are stocks of fish that straddle the border of the economic zone. In the economic zone, it is clear that Canada has a sovereign right to set quotas and reserve these stocks for Canadian fishermen. The rules are less clear outside the 200-mile zone. The Northwest Atlantic Fisheries Organization (NAFO) sets quotas for the stocks that straddle the border. Despite NAFO's efforts, stocks of halibut, capelin, redfish, and cod have declined severely in recent years.[17] Canada has accused some European fishermen, especially those from Spain and Portugal, of not respecting these quotas and not using legal fishing gear, so there have been a number of incidents. In 1995 the

Spanish fishing vessel *Estai* was boarded by the Canadians outside the 200-mile economic zone. In May 2004 there were similar incidents with Portuguese vessels. The 1995 conflict, known in Canada as the turbot war, seriously affected EU-Canadian relations for several months.[18]

Phyto-sanitary standards for forestry products have also caused problems. The pinewood nematode (PWN) is a worm transmitted from one tree to another by a beetle. It is quite common in North American forests, but does little damage because it needs temperatures of –20 degrees Celsius to develop. When Canada exports untreated, so-called "green" lumber, there is the risk of exporting PWNs to Europe. When PWNs were found in shipments in Europe in the 1980s some European countries started requiring the lumber to be treated to kill the PWNs. This led to a significant decline in Canadian lumber exports to Europe.[19]

There is also a series of current irritants.[20] In 2006, Canada introduced wine and beer excise duty exemptions for certain domestic producers, which resulted in differential treatment of domestic and foreign products. According to the European Commission, this is a WTO violation and a question of substantial economic interest for the EU. At stake is the GATT principle of "national treatment." About 50 percent of Canadian wine imports originate from the EU. An earlier conflict in the wine area had been the names of wines and spirits. In 2003 an agreement was reached according to which names like Champagne, Chianti, and Bordeaux, associated with specific wine-producing regions in Europe, will have to be phased out within a decade.[21]

Another irritant is a compositional standard for cheese, which imposes a de facto domestic content requirement. It was introduced in December 2007. When fully implemented, the regulation will effectively reduce imports to Canada of both cheese and related products, according to the Commission. This would also break WTO rules that prohibit countries from creating unnecessary obstacles to trade. Thirty-nine percent of all dairy products entering Canada come from the EU.[22]

Also an irritant is the question of how quickly Canada abolishes visa requirements for the new member states after the enlargements in 2004 and 2007. Citizens of Romania and Bulgaria are still required to get visas to visit Canada. Canada, however, has been faster than some other countries, including the United States, to abolish visa requirements for the other new EU member states in central and eastern Europe.

Global challenges, including climate change, are on the bilateral agenda too. For many years, Canada remained one of the EU's closest partners and allies in addressing global environmental challenges. However, since February 2006, when Stephen Harper became prime minister of Canada, there have been concerns about the direction of climate change policy in Canada.[23] The EU continues to encourage Canada to participate actively in the international climate arena. Canada is seen as an important ally in establishing the successor to the Kyoto Protocol on the environment. A high-level dialogue on the environment is taking place where the issues of climate change, emission trading, Arctic environment, and other issues of common interest are being discussed.

Concluding Remarks

The various proposals for a Canada-EU FTA have not produced results for far. Canada used to be more interested than the EU. However, things have slowly changed in recent years. In January 2007 Premier Jean Charest of Quebec spoke out in favor of an FTA with the EU. At the time the EU member states were divided. But a joint study by the European Commission and the government of Canada, which was published before the EU-Canada summit in Quebec City in October 2008, suggested important gains for both sides by addressing tariff barriers and nontariff barriers, including discriminatory regulation and standards, as well as liberalizing trade in services.[24] The summit meeting therefore agreed to explore the idea of a "stronger, ambitious and balanced economic partnership."[25]

The following EU-Canada summit in Prague, on May 6, 2009, then decided to launch negotiations toward a "comprehensive economic partnership agreement."[26] It is too early to predict whether those negotiations will be successful.

This chapter has outlined a number of trade irritants and conflicts between Canada and the EU over the years: the CAP; various nontariff barriers (NTBs) to trade, including phyto-sanitary standards; and fisheries. Owing to the reduction of tariffs through successive GATT deals, tariffs are, with a few exceptions, no longer important. Apart from fisheries, a typical zero-sum resource conflict, most conflicts are inside-the-border conflicts because of national regulations and standards. This makes regulatory cooperation important.

Canada, as a member of NATO and a participant in foreign policy dialogues, is also engaged with the EU on matters of wider global interest. Afghanistan is considered especially important, since Canadian soldiers have been involved in one of the more dangerous regions there. Canada's request for more European and NATO troop participation has produced tensions as well.

If the ongoing negotiations about a comprehensive economic partnership should fail, there is not only the danger that Canada will become more and more dependent on trade within NAFTA, but that it will increasingly turn its attention to East Asia and other emerging economies. As a former Canadian ambassador to the Netherlands and Germany wrote in 2006: "Canada's old obsession with the United States and new obsession with emerging markets leave little room for Europe."[27]

Immigrants from non-European parts of the world make Canada an increasingly multicultural society. It would require a lot of political attention on both sides of the Atlantic to move toward freer trade across the Atlantic. In the end it is a question of political will and leadership. Economists say that free trade would have economic advantages for both sides. Why it has not been implemented between the EU and Canada is one of those puzzles of political economy. What is economically rational does not always happen because of vested interests and entrenched practices.

Notes

1. For a more detailed overview, see Evan Potter, *Trans-Atlantic Partners: Canadian Approaches to the European Union* (McGill–Queen's University Press, 1999).

2. EU-Canada relations have not received much attention from academics. The best and most recent book-size treatment is Potter's *Trans-Atlantic Partners*. A useful article is Osvaldo Croci and Livianna Tossutti, "That Elusive Object of Desire: Canadian Perceptions of the European Union," *European Foreign Affairs Review* 12, no. 3 (2007): 287–310.

3. Charles Pentland, "Canada and Britain in Europe," in Centre for Foreign Policy Studies, *Canada and the United Kingdom: The Dalhousie Colloquium* (Dalhousie University, 1984), p. 36.

4. According to the Directorate-General for Trade of the European Commission; see http://trade.ec.europa.eu/doclib/docs/2006/september/tradoc_122529.pdf and http://trade.ec.europa.eu/doclib/docs/2006/september/tradoc_113363.pdf [May 2009].

5. Some trade statistics are available on the website of the European Commission: trade.ec.europa.eu/doclib/docs/2006/september/tradoc_113363.pdf [October 2008].

6. Eric Hayes, "The EU and Canada: Partners That Matter," speech at a joint meeting of the Empire Club and the European Chamber of Trade and Commerce, Toronto, April 10, 2003.

7. For details on the Canadian reaction to the formation of the EEC, see B. W. Muirhead, *The Development of Postwar Canadian Trade Policy: The Failure of the Anglo-European Option* (McGill–Queen's University Press, 1992), chap. 6.

8. Robert Bothwell, "'The Canadian Connection': Canada and Europe," in *Foremost Nation: Canadian Foreign Policy in a Changing World*, edited by Norman Hillmer and Garth Stevenson (Toronto: McClelland and Stewart, 1977), pp. 24–36.

9. See Potter, *Trans-Atlantic Partners*, pp. 35–36.

10. Peter C. Dobell, *Canada in World Affairs*, vol. 17 (Oxford University Press, 1971–73), p. 138.

11. The text, and other official documents, can be located on the website of the EU Commission Delegation in Ottawa (www.delcan.ec.europa.eu/en/ [October 2008]).

12. On this, see also Roy Rempel, *Counterweights: The Failure of Canada's German and European Policy 1955–1995* (McGill–Queen's University Press, 1996), chap. 5.

13. Andrew F. Cooper, *Canadian Foreign Policy: Old Habits and New Directions* (Scarborough, Ontario: Prentice Hall Allyn and Bacon Canada, 1997), p. 253.

14. See, for instance, Nicholas V. Gianaris, *The North American Free Trade Agreement and the European Union* (Westport, Conn.: Praeger, 1998), pp. 139–40.

15. *Agence Europe*, various issues, incl. March 3, 2006, and April 27, 2006.

16. Ibid., December 16, 1997.

17. John C. Crosbie, "Bleak, but There Is Still Hope for the Cod," *European Voice*, September 20, 2007.

18. David Long, "Canada-EU Relations in the 1990s," in *Canada among Nations 1998: Leadership and Dialogue*, edited by Fen Osler Hampson and Maureen Appel Molot (Oxford University Press, 1998), pp. 193–210.

19. The story is told in Potter, *Trans-Atlantic Partners*, pp. 151–55.

20. Yasmina Sioud, lecture at Dalhousie University, Halifax, N.S., Canada, February 20, 2008.

21. "'Cheers!' at EU Wine Deal," *European Voice*, September 18, 2003.

22. Neil Merrett, "EU Exporters Face Canadian Cheese Change" (www.dairyreporter. com/Safety-Hygiene/EU-exporters-face-Canadian-cheese-change [October 2008]).

23. Sioud, lecture at Dalhousie University.

24. Canada and European Union, *Assessing the Costs and Benefits of a Closer EU-Canada Economic Partnership. A Joint Study by the European Commission and the Government of Canada* (www.international.gc.ca/trade-agreements-accords-commerciaux/ assets/pdfs/EU-Canada_Joint_Study-Introduction_Executive_Summary.pdf [September 2009]).

25. Council of the European Union, EU-Canada Summit, Quebec, October 17, 2008 (www.consilium.europa.eu/ueDocs/cms_Data/docs/pressData/en/er/103466.pdf [September 2009]).

26. Council of the European Union, EU-Canada Summit Declaration, Prague, May 6, 2009 (www.consilium.europa.eu/uedocs/cms_data/docs/pressdata/en/er/107542.pdf [September 2009]).

27. Marie Bernard-Meunier, "Did You Say Europe? How Canada Ignores Europe and Why That Is Wrong," in *Canada among Nations 2006: Minorities and Priorities*, edited by Andrew F. Cooper and Dana Rowlands (McGill–Queen's University Press, 2006), p. 109.

MAURIZIO CARBONE

18

The EU in Africa: Increasing Coherence, Decreasing Partnership

The relationship between the European Union and Africa has undergone major changes since the beginning of the twenty-first century. First, the Cotonou Agreement, adopted in June 2000, brought transformations to the long-standing relationship between the EU and the African, Caribbean, and Pacific (ACP) group of countries, particularly in the areas of foreign aid and trade. These transformations not only ended a system of preferential treatment, but also put a strain on the traditional partnership that had characterized the Lomé Convention. Second, the EU-Africa summit held in Cairo in April 2000 marked the EU's intention to pursue a continent-wide approach and to politicize its relations with Africa. The 2005 EU's Africa strategy and the 2007 joint Africa-EU strategy aimed to integrate trade, foreign aid, and political affairs in order to create a coherent EU foreign policy and give new emphasis to the idea of partnership. In reality, the second EU-Africa summit held in Lisbon in December 2007 showed that the two parties were pursuing different goals.

Against this background, this chapter is divided into two broad sections. The first section looks at EU-Africa relations in the context of the various EU-ACP conventions, with a focus on the Cotonou Agreement. Three areas of particular relevance are analyzed: the introduction and implementation of multi-year programming; the involvement of nonstate actors (NSAs) in the development process; and the negotiation of new economic partnership agreements (EPAs). The second section examines the evolution of EU-Africa relations since the Cairo summit. The conventional argument is that the partnership and the extended privileges that had distinguished the EU's approach to Africa from the 1960s through the 1990s have been replaced by a more normal relationship. However, although the new relationship puts an apparent emphasis on African ownership and responsibility, it often hides the pursuit of European interests. An important component of this chapter is to understand the type of role that the European Union plays or wants to play in this process.

EU-ACP Relations between Rome and Cotonou

The EU's policy toward Africa has its origin in the Treaty of Rome and has evolved through a number of agreements. Initially influenced by France, it was limited to francophone Africa and then, following the first EU enlargement in the early 1970s, was extended to cover the African members of the British Commonwealth, as well as other former colonies in the Caribbean and the Pacific. The Yaoundé Convention (1963–75) maintained the system introduced by the Treaty of Rome: an aid allocation for five years, channeled through the European Development Fund (EDF), and a trade regime based on reciprocal preferences.

The ensuing Lomé Convention (1975–2000), negotiated at five-year intervals (Lomé II in 1980, Lomé III in 1985, Lomé IV in 1990, and Lomé IV-bis in 1995), was initially considered the most comprehensive, innovative, and ambitious agreement for North-South cooperation. First, it was conceived as a partnership: decisions were not imposed by the EU, but discussed and agreed with the ACP governments. A set of joint institutions was also established to ensure a permanent dialogue between the parties.[1] Second, it was based on a "contractual right to aid": resources were committed to the ACP countries for a five-year period, irrespective of performance. Third, it reversed the previous trade regime to allow nonreciprocal preferences: almost all ACP goods entered the EU free of tariff or quota restrictions.[2]

Nevertheless, the development record of the Lomé Convention was disappointing. Although a small number of ACP countries managed to improve their level of development, the conditions of the majority worsened. The progressive inclusion of economic and political conditionalities meant that by the mid-1990s the Lomé Convention was "no longer the model of development cooperation to which other agreements could aspire" and that "the unique features of the Convention have been so diluted and undermined as to become almost indistinguishable from other development aid programs."[3]

Following a long period of consultation and negotiations, the Cotonou Agreement was signed in June 2000. It built on the Lomé *acquis*, but in several respects it represented a fundamental departure from it.[4] The major changes were as follows: aid allocation would be made conditional not only on needs but also on performance through a system of rolling programming; new free trade agreements, the so-called economic partnership agreements, to be negotiated and agreed on a regional basis before January 2008, would replace the previous preferential trade regime; nonstate actors (for example, civil society, social groups, business associations) would be involved in all phases of the development process; the political dimension, which included issues that had previously fallen outside the field of development cooperation (peace and security, arms trade, migration, drugs, corruption) would be reinforced.[5]

These changes had profound implications. Adopting a neo-Gramscian perspective, Stephen Hurt argued that the nature of the relationships between the EU and the ACP shifted from "cooperation" to "coercion."[6] The new trade arrangements and the need to comply with the principles and rules of the WTO were a reflection of the hegemonic dominance of neoliberalism. Kunibert Raffer argued that in the new Cotonou Agreement the idea of real partnership is largely absent: "The present 'partnership' is an Orwellian relation where one partner has no rights at all, the other perfect arbitrariness. It is a horse and rider relation, as the rider also depends on the horse as a means of transport while ACP countries appear to be a historical burden the EU might not be unhappy to get rid of."[7]

Less than two years after it had come into force (because of the protracted process of ratification), the Cotonou Agreement was revised in February 2005. The overall structure was not altered, but the changes largely reflected the EU's priorities. Security became a central concern, and the new provisions in this area—such as combating terrorism, countering the proliferation of weapons of mass destruction (WMD), preventing mercenary activities, and committing to the International Criminal Court (ICC)—were strongly criticized by African countries. The EU's proposal to introduce further flexibility into the EDF allocations so that funds could be made available to meet exceptional needs in the event of crises was also opposed by African countries out of fear that funds would be diverted from socioeconomic development to security-oriented programs. Nevertheless, a larger reserve was instituted, with the possibility to alter the amounts allocated for each country or region in light of special needs or exceptional performance or to cover international initiatives benefiting the whole ACP group.[8]

Foreign Aid

One of the most important components of the Cotonou Agreement is the reform of aid management. Resources are disbursed using a three-step process. First, a draft country strategy paper (CSP) and an accompanying national indicative program (NIP) are prepared by the EU delegation in collaboration with local governments and nonstate actors, the EU's member states, and other international donors. The CSP offers an analysis of a country's situation and outlines the development strategy based on the EU's comparative advantage, while the NIP provides a detailed account of how resources must be spent.[9]

Second, the draft documents are scrutinized by an interservice Quality Support Group (iQSG) and then by the EU member states in the EDF committee. Third, the CSP and NIP are adopted by the College of Commissioners. The CSP and the NIP can be adjusted in the course of the mid-term review (MTR) process, which is meant to assess how recipients have performed in the implementation of the development strategy.

The assessment of the first-generation CSPs produced mixed results. A report published by the European Commission in November 2002 emphasized the successful efforts to ensure coordination and complementarity between the EU and the member states and to involve NSAs in the programming process. Little analysis was devoted to how the money was used or how the EU aid contributed to poverty eradication.[10] A less optimistic view came from a number of assessments supported by European nonstate actors. The most important point concerns the contribution of the CSPs to poverty eradication. Budget support, which prioritizes human development, had indeed increased. But despite the fact that sub-Saharan Africa is the region that is the furthest from achieving the Millennium Development Goals (MDGs), only a very small number of CSPs identified education and health as focal sectors. Moreover, the failure to mainstream gender implied that the EU's contribution to the fight against HIV/AIDS and child mortality was not optimal. Support to the transport sector, by contrast, appeared in a larger number of CSPs. While the European Commission often emphasizes that transport benefits poverty eradication, in a large number of cases the EU supported the building of international roads, which, unlike rural roads, are usually not driven by pro-poor interests.[11]

Similarly, during the mid-term reviews conducted in 2004, limited changes were made to the existing development strategies.[12] At the same time, new emphasis was given to political issues, such as the fight against terrorism, the protection of human rights, the promotion of democracy, and the prevention of migration.[13] Even the European Commission acknowledged this time that "there is obviously a tension between new policy commitments defined unilaterally by the EU and the principle of country ownership of national development strategies and donor support to them."[14]

The preparation of the second-generation CSPs for Africa started in early 2006. Although the revised Cotonou Agreement included the achievement of the MDGs as the key objective of the EU's development policy for Africa, initial evidence seemed to show that there was "a very distinct de-prioritization of the MDGs" and that the priorities set by the EU still dominated the various strategies. It should also be noted that the CSPs are developed worldwide at the same time and do not respect the economic and business cycles of the country in question. The involvement of local governments was in most cases limited to the trade and transport ministries, whereas the social ministries were rarely consulted.[15] The EU delegations often imposed their priorities; in some instances the ACP officials even saw the programming process as a serious challenge to their sovereignty.[16]

Participation

The new provisions on the participation of nonstate actors in the development process are another major innovation of the Cotonou Agreement. NSAs, which include business associations, social partners, and civil society, must be involved in all phases of the programming process, including the elaboration of the CSPs and the NIPs, the mid-term reviews, and the final evaluation.[17] They must also be provided with financial resources, to be agreed on during the programming process; up to a maximum of 15 percent of the initial NIP allocation could be directly allocated to nonstate actors. These provisions, according to Jean Bossuyt, were important because they contributed to strengthening the role of NSAs in countries where a participatory culture was largely absent and to enhancing their visibility and the credibility of civil society in relation to governments.[18]

By contrast, Stephen Hurt argues that the EU's new emphasis on civil society should be understood as part of the neoliberal nature of its relations with developing countries, which supports the retrenchment of the state, the promotion of the private sector, and the greater integration of developing countries into the global economy.[19] Claims to partnership and participation are thus designed to give legitimacy to the Western model of democracy and to create conditions that are conducive to the operation of a liberal market democracy. For these reasons, Hurt argues, participation is often limited to those actors that support the EU approach.

The first opportunity to assess the practice of participation was in the context of the ninth EDF programming process. According to the European Commission, in almost all countries some form of consultation took place. In half of the cases, the draft CSP was changed, though nothing is said about whether the changes were due to the involvement of the NSAs. In the remaining cases, no changes were introduced because of a coincidence of intents between the NSAs and the recipient governments, a lack of capacity by the NSAs to participate in the programming process, and significant delays in the consultation process. This trend was broadly confirmed in the case of the mid-term reviews, when similar problems were faced. A number of reports funded by European NGOs offered a more critical view. Several limitations were shown: a too-short period set aside for consultation and invitations on short notice; ad hoc instead of institutionalized dialogue; a limited range of NSAs involved, with urban NGOs and private sector groups privileged; limited information provided before the meeting and insufficient reporting back to NSAs on the results of the consultations; government-led discussions.[20]

This situation did not change significantly in the context of the tenth EDF programming exercise. Again, the European Commission claimed that "effective consultation" occurred in about half of the countries, whereas in the remaining cases dialogue was ad hoc and consultation took the form of information sessions at a late stage in the process.[21] A number of case studies written by African NGOs maintained that the programming exercise failed to adequately involve nonstate actors. While some forms of consultation occurred, the exercise was neither inclusive nor comprehensive. In most instances, there was a lack of transparency in the selection of participants, inadequate provision of preparatory documents, and little feedback on the results.[22]

Trade

The most controversial innovation of the Cotonou Agreement is in the area of trade. The European Commission argued that the existing preferential regime had to be replaced by regional free trade agreements, compatible with the WTO rules. The aim of these new trade arrangements was to accelerate the integration of the ACP countries into the global economy by enhancing production and the capacity to attract investment, while taking into account different development levels. During the negotiations in the Council of Ministers, various options were on the table, such as preserving the status quo by asking the World Trade Organization (WTO) for a waiver or integrating the whole ACP group into the EU's Generalized System of Preferences (GSP).[23]

In the end, the European Commission presented the establishment of regional economic partnership agreements as the most feasible option. The preferences of the member states broadly reflected their approach and traditions in international development. On one side, France wanted to preserve the integrity of the ACP group and the existing trade regime; it also wanted to avoid trade liberalization as a way to protect its agricultural sector. On the opposite side, Germany wanted to "normalize" relations between the EU and the developing world and therefore suggested regrouping the ACP states into three regions. Trade liberalization and regional integration would complement this project. In the middle, the United Kingdom and the Nordic states shared concerns about the potential marginalization of the least-developed countries (LDCs) caused by the proposed free trade agreements. The final compromise softened the initial proposal by granting an extended interim period before the EPAs entered into force in January 2008, and by maintaining trade privileges for "essentially all products" coming from the LDCs.[24]

Using a two-level game theory, Genevra Forwood argues that the EU's margin to maneuver in the negotiations with the ACP was restricted by its negotiating mandate, which had been the result of a compromise that could not easily be changed.[25] On the contrary, the ACP group, rather than playing a proactive part in the negotiations, often reacted against the EU mandate. The weakness of the ACP group can be explained by the lack of a coherent and firm position, which followed the rule "the more, the better." It should be added, however, that the ACP group is a more informal entity than the EU; it also lacks a strong supranational institution. The ACP Secretariat had no formal role in the negotiations, whereas the European Commission played a key role.

The EU's mandate and subsequent negotiation strategy, therefore, were heavily influenced by the achieved compromise. The European Commission, with the Directorate-General for Trade in the lead, drafted a "vague" negotiation mandate that left little room for changes during the Council discussions. Some member states (Denmark, Sweden, the United Kingdom) were still critical of the mandate and expressed their doubts in the official minutes of the meeting, a highly unusual practice in EU trade politics. The negotiation mandate was agreed to unanimously in June 2002 because all the member states wanted to present a united front to the outside world. Negotiations with six regional groups—four for Africa, one for the Caribbean, and one for the Pacific—started in September 2002, but for a few years there was little publicity and only marginal involvement by the member states.

The negotiations conducted by the Directorate-General for Trade emphasized the trade aspect of the EPAs to the detriment of the development side. Still, it was surprising that in March 2005 the United Kingdom issued a statement in which it urged the EU to stop its "mercantilist approach and offensive interests." This statement was followed by some "non-papers" (informal discussion documents) underlying the social and development aspects of the EPAs sent to the Council committee in charge of monitoring the negotiations.[26] The majority of African countries acted passively since they perceived the European Commission to be ignoring the concerns of the developing world.

As time passed and the ACP countries and NGOs became more dissatisfied, additional member states publicly criticized the Commission's approach. In March 2005 the U.K. trade and development secretaries issued a very critical statement that was immediately censured by the European Commission. This statement was not coordinated with the "friends of EPAs," a group that included Denmark, the Netherlands, Sweden, and sometimes Ireland, Belgium, and France. They became more vocal in the Council group that monitored the EPA negotiations, emphasizing the development and social dimension of the EPAs. This behavior started to have its effects, and the European Commission was forced to take into account these heterodox views.[27] By the autumn of 2007, it was clear that no full EPA would be signed with African countries. This meant that the LDCs would be subject to the provisions of the "everything but arms" (EBA) regulation and non-LDCs were subject to the Generalized System of Preferences. Some alternatives to the EPAs were requested, such as the extension of the previous preferential regime through the prolongation of the WTO waiver and the granting of GSP+ (duty-free access to European goods in addition to the preferences extended by the standard GSP) to all ACP countries. The European Commission stated that there were no alternatives to the EPAs. Many African countries continued to denounce the pressure exercised by the European Commission, which was contrary to the partnership principle. It was not surprising that, by the agreed deadline, no full EPA had been signed with any African region.

EU-Africa Relations between Cairo and Lisbon

With the adoption of the Treaty of Maastricht and the institutionalization of the Common Foreign and Security Policy (CFSP), it became clear that the European Union wanted to play a significant role in international politics. The Treaty of Maastricht also introduced the principle of coherence, which referred to the fact that all EU external policies must work in synergy. Africa became the natural place to exercise these ambitions. Traditional EU policy toward Africa had to broaden its original goals from foreign aid and trade preferences to include more political issues, such as democracy, human rights, and conflict prevention and management.[28]

Moreover, the adoption of the European Consensus on Development in December 2005 committed member states and the European Community to a common view on the promotion of international development. The Africa strategy became the first opportunity to operationalize the European Consensus on Development.[29] The evolution of EU-Africa relations was also strongly influenced by events in Africa. The adoption of the New Partnership for Africa's Development (NEPAD) and the setting up of the African Union (AU) reassured the international community that African leaders wanted to take ownership in their future.[30]

This context contributes to understanding why, since the beginning of the 2000s, the European Union has attempted to pursue a unitary policy toward the entire African continent, under the slogan "one Europe, one Africa." This task was not easy. In addition to relations with the members of the ACP group, the EU had developed formal relationships with North Africa through the Euro-Mediterranean Partnership (EMP) and European Neighborhood Policy (ENP), and with South Africa through the Trade and Development Cooperation Agreement (TDCA). Moreover, the EU member states had different development priorities that were not easy to reconcile.

The first EU-Africa summit in 2000 was an initial attempt to address these issues. One of the unofficial messages of the summit was that Europe cared about Africa, but not enough to commit new resources.[31] European representatives placed more emphasis on political issues, notably democracy and peace and security, while African representatives concentrated on economic aspects, notably trade and aid.[32] The ensuing Cairo plan of action laid out the main aims of the new Africa-EU dialogue: to strengthen political, economic, and sociocultural relations between the EU and Africa; to eradicate poverty and attain the MDGs; and to promote human rights, democracy, and the rule of law.[33]

New plans were made for a second meeting in Lisbon in April 2003, but the summit was postponed owing to lack of agreement over the presence of Robert Mugabe and other Zimbabwean leaders. The EU member states did not want to allow President Mugabe to enter the EU area and urged African leaders to take a stronger stance against his poor record on human rights and democratic practices. African leaders, however, argued that it was not possible to hold a meeting without representation from all the African states.[34] In the absence of a more formalized dialogue at the highest political level, the European Commission tried to pursue an alternative strategy, such as holding regular meetings between senior officials.

Meanwhile, Africa had taken a central place on the global as well as the European agenda, as confirmed by a number of important initiatives and commitments. Following the report of the Commission for Africa, the United Kingdom was instrumental in the adoption of the Gleneagles commitments on foreign aid and debt relief. At the European level, under the leadership of the European Commission, in April 2005 the EU decided to boost its volume of aid, including doubling development assistance to Africa by 2010. In the same context, a new ambitious agenda was agreed to on policy coherence for development.[35]

A number of decisions and initiatives confirmed that the European Union saw its involvement in conflict prevention and management as necessary to become a significant player in Africa. In June 2003 the Council of Ministers adopted a resolution authorizing the presence of EU military forces in the Democratic Republic of the Congo. According to some this was meant to show that, following the failures in the context of the war in Iraq, the EU member states were still willing and able to work together. In March 2004 a decision to establish the Africa Peace Facility concluded a long discussion on the importance of tackling conflict prevention as a precondition to development.[36]

The EU's Africa Strategy

Following up on the April 2005 initiatives and a specific request of the June 2005 European Council, the European Commission published a communication in which the central concern was the achievement of the MDGs. Peace, security, and good governance were also seen as preconditions to development. These views were emphasized even more in a paper written by the High Representative for the CFSP, Javier Solana, in which he argued that peace and security were not only central to the new EU's strategy for Africa but also to the CFSP.[37]

In December 2005, the European Council adopted a rather short document entitled "The EU and Africa: Towards a Strategic Partnership." This new EU Africa strategy, which set up a single framework for all EU players (that is, the European Commission, its member states, and nonstate actors), rested on three elements: (1) peace, security, and good governance as preconditions to development; (2) a central role for regional integration and trade in fostering economic growth; and (3) the need for better access to social services (such as health and education) and environmental sustainability in order to achieve the MDGs by 2015.[38]

The EU Africa strategy did not, however, result in any new commitment by Europe to support Africa's efforts to develop. For instance, it was decided that the strategy would be implemented with existing financial resources, while major emphasis was placed on non-aid policies through the ambitious agenda on policy coherence for development.[39] Integration into the world trading system would be ensured through the new EPAs. Finally, the EU's Africa strategy did not mention the issue of political conditionality, but the EU spelled out its support of the African peer-review mechanism (APRM), an instrument for assessing governments' progress toward democracy and the protection of human rights.[40]

But the EU's Africa strategy was criticized not only for its lack of ambitions, but also because it was agreed without adequate consultation of all stakeholders. On the European side, the drafting process was led by the European Commission and the British Presidency, with the remaining member states and nonstate actors playing a marginal role, if any. On the African side, there was limited consultation outside the AU Commission.[41] In light of this criticism, at the EU-AU ministerial meeting in Bamako in December 2005 it was agreed to develop a new joint EU-Africa strategy—"a partnership *with* Africa, rather than a strategy *for* Africa."[42] This time the drafting process was more participatory. Negotiations started in February 2007 and an earlier draft was approved in May 2007. The final version was presented at the second EU-Africa summit in December 2007.

The joint Africa-EU strategy was a much longer and comprehensive document than its predecessor. The starting point was the idea of a "new strategic partnership" based on a "Euro-African consensus on values, common interests and common strategic objectives." Four main objectives were included: (a) to address issues of common concern, in particular peace and security, migration and development, and a clean environment; (b) to strengthen and promote peace and security, democratic governance and human rights, and sustainable development, and to ensure that all African countries meet the MDGs by 2015; (c) to jointly promote and sustain a system of effective multilateralism, making sure that the system of global governance is more representative, and to tackle global challenges together; (d) to promote people-centered development, including a better involvement of nonstate actors.

To meet these objectives, a very detailed action plan for the 2008–10 period was adopted, including eight EU-Africa partnerships: peace and security; democratic governance and human rights; trade and regional integration (including the implementation of the EU-Africa Partnership for Infrastructure, launched in 2006); Millennium Development Goals; energy; climate change; migration, mobility, and employment; and science, information society, and space. In sum, as Siegmar Schmidt has cogently argued, there was hardly any field where EU and Africa were not meant to cooperate.[43]

Unavoidably, the EU's renewed interest in Africa cannot be separated from the threats coming from China's heavy involvement in Africa as well as the new strategic interest of the United States. Moreover, although the joint Africa-EU strategy was a comprehensive document, the result of an extensive dialogue between European and African actors, the EU's motivations and views were still dominant. The Lisbon summit was overshadowed once again by the debate over the presence of Mugabe, which several EU member states opposed. Although the British prime minister did not attend the summit, the African leaders did not publicly condemn Mugabe's behavior. But the differences ran deeper, and it seemed clear that leaders on the two continents still had different agendas: for the EU, the priorities were security and migration; for Africa, they were more and better aid and improved trade deals.

Conclusion

Following the end of the cold war, it seemed that the EU was losing interest in Africa. The post-Lomé debate and the adoption of the Cotonou Agreement showed that the relationship with the ACP group had become almost "normal." Changes in the areas of foreign aid, trade, and political dialogue sent a clear signal: the preferential treatment given to post-colonial Africa had come to an end. The process toward a comprehensive strategy for Africa, beyond the division of northern and sub-Saharan Africa, which started in Cairo in April 2000 and culminated in the joint Africa-EU strategy adopted in Lisbon in December

2007, meant that the EU was trying to play a leading role in international politics and development.

Africa therefore became central not only to the EU's development policy, but to all of its external relations. The cases of trade and aid, however, show that the rhetoric of partnership does not match the reality. On the one hand, the EU seems too preoccupied with improving its development record and image; on the other hand, it has failed to take into account the voice of the developing countries. Another element that has characterized the EU's approach to Africa since the turn of the century is the attempt to pursue a coherent external policy. To some, however, this attempt has purposely concealed the real concerns of the EU: security and migration. This may or may not be true, but the search for coherence has once again bypassed the traditional partnership that had typified the EU's approach when the Lomé Convention was signed in the 1970s. The 2007 joint Africa-EU strategy seems to go in the right direction, but its implementation will be central to understanding whether a new chapter in the EU's external relations has begun.

Notes

1. These institutions include the Council of Ministers, which comprises the members of the Council of the European Union (or EU Council) and one government representative from each ACP country and has the authority to make changes to the EU-ACP Partnership Agreements; the Committee of Ambassadors, which prepares and monitors the work of the EU Council; and the Joint Parliamentary Assembly, which is composed of members of the European Parliament and parliamentarians from the ACP countries and is a forum for dialogue.

2. See Enzo Grilli, *The European Community and the Developing Countries* (Cambridge University Press, 1993); Marjorie Lister, *The European Union and the South: Relations with Developing Countries* (London: Routledge, 1997); William Brown, *The European Union and Africa: the Restructuring of North-South Relations* (London: IB Taurus, 2002).

3. Gordon Crawford, "Whither Lomé? The Mid-Term Review and the Decline of Partnership," *Journal of Modern African Studies* 34, no. 3 (1996): 516.

4. Martin Holland, *The European Union and the Third World* (New York: Palgrave, 2002).

5. Two issues were discussed at length: good governance and migration. The EU wanted good governance to be included as an "essential element" of the partnership, whose violation could lead to suspension of aid, but after extensive discussions it was included only as a "fundamental element": only serious cases of corruption constitute grounds for suspension of aid. As for the migration issue, while the right to fair treatment of the ACP workers in the European Union was reaffirmed (through legal migration), the issue of illegal migration was very controversial: the ACP group agreed to accept the readmission of people illegally present on the territory of an EU member state at that member state's request and without any further formalities.

6. Stephen Hurt, "Civil Society and European Union Development Policy," in *New Pathways in International Development: Gender and Civil Society in EU Policy*, edited by Marjorie Lister and Maurizio Carbone (Aldershot, UK: Ashgate, 2006), pp. 109–22.

7. Kunibert Raffer, "Slowly Undoing Lomé's Concept of Partnership," European Development Policy Study Group Discussion Paper 10 (Manchester: EDPSG, 2001).

8. Charlotte Bretherton and John Vogler, *The European Union as a Global Actor*, 2nd ed. (London: Routledge, 2006); Amelia Hadfield, "Janus Advances? An Analysis of the EC Development Policy and the 2005 Amended Cotonou Partnership Agreement," *European Foreign Affairs Review* 12, no. 1 (2007): 39–66; Maurizio Carbone, *The European Union and International Development: The Politics of Foreign Aid* (London: Routledge, 2007).

9. Following the adoption of the EU development policy statement in November 2000, it was decided to concentrate aid in two sectors (three in some exceptional cases).

10. Maurizio Carbone, "Better Aid, Less Ownership: Multi-annual Programming and the EU's Development Strategies in Africa," *Journal of International Development* 20, no. 2 (2008): 118–229.

11. Mirjam Van Reisen, *2015-Watch: The EU's Contribution to the Millennium Development Goals. Halfway to 2015: Mid-term Review* (Copenhagen: Alliance 2015, 2007); Walter Eberlei and Denise Auclair, *The EU's Footprint in the South: Does European Community Development Cooperation Make a Difference for the Poor?* (Brussels: CIDSE, 2007); Carbone, "Better Aid, Less Ownership."

12. For details, see Carbone, "Better Aid, Less Ownership"; and Maurizio Carbone, "Theory and Practice of Participation: Civil Society and EU Development Policy," *Perspectives on European Politics and Society* 9, no. 2 (2008): 241–55.

13. Eberlei and Auclair, *The EU's Footprint in the South.*

14. Cited in Carbone, "Better Aid, Less Ownership," p. 227.

15. Reisen, *2015-Watch.*

16. Florent Sebban, *We Decide, You "Own"! An Assessment of the Programming of European Community Aid to the ACP Countries under the 10th EDF European Development Fund (EDF)* (Brussels: Eurostep, 2006); Carbone, "Better Aid, Less Ownership."

17. The Cotonou Agreement established that NSAs should be also involved not only in the aid pillar of the Cotonou Agreement, but also in the political and trade pillars. But little progress has been made. For additional analysis, see Jean Bossuyt, "Mainstreaming Civil Society in ACP-EU Development Cooperation," in *New Pathways*, edited by Lister and Carbone, pp. 123–38.

18. Bossuyt, "Mainstreaming Civil Society."

19. Stephen Hurt, "Co-operation and Coercion? The Cotonou Agreement between the European Union and ACP States and the End of the Lomé Convention," *Third World Quarterly* 24, no.1 (2006): 161–76.

20. Carbone, "Theory and Practice of Participation."

21. Ibid.

22. Sebban, *We Decide, You "Own"!*

23. The GSP gives tariff preferences to developing countries, with the aim of providing an incentive to traders to import products from developing countries. The EBA regulation gives the fifty poorest countries in the world (least-developed countries)

duty-free access to the EU for all products except arms and ammunition, including rice and sugar, for which duty-free quotas are established until full liberalization is achieved in September 2009 (for rice) and October 2009 (for sugar).

24. Genevra Forwood, "The Road to Cotonou: Negotiating a Successor to Lomé," *Journal of Common Market Studies* 39, no. 3 (2001): 423–42; Olufemi Babarinde and Gerrit Faber, eds., *The European Union and Developing Countries: The Cotonou Agreement* (Leiden: Brill, 2005).

25. Forwood, "The Road to Cotonou."

26. Ole Elgström and Jes Pilegaard, "Imposed Coherence: Negotiating Economic Partnership," *Journal of European Integration* 30, no. 3 (2008): 363–80.

27. Elgström and Pilegaard, "Imposed Coherence."

28. Gorm Rye Olsen, "Challenges to Traditional Policy Options, Opportunities for New Choices: The Africa Policy of the EU," *The Round Table* 93, no. 375 (2004): 425–36; Mary Farrell, "A Triumph of Realism over Idealism? Cooperation between the European Union and Africa," *Journal of European Integration* 27, no. 3 (2005): 263–83.

29. Carbone, "Better Aid, Less Ownership."

30. House of Lords, *The EU and Africa: Towards a Strategic Partnership* (London, 2006).

31. Olsen, "Challenges to Traditional Policy Options."

32. European Centre for Development Policy Management (ECDPM), *The EU and Africa: Towards a Strategic Partnership* (Maastricht, 2006.).

33. House of Lords, *The EU and Africa.*

34. Ibid.

35. Carbone, *The European Union and International Development.*

36. Gorm Rye Olsen, "Coherence, Consistency and Political Will in Foreign Policy: The European Union's Policy towards Africa," *Perspectives on European Politics and Society* 9 no. 2 (2008): 157–71.

37. Carbone, "Better Aid, Less Ownership."

38. See Council of the European Union, "The EU and Africa: Towards a Strategic Partnership" (http://ue.eu.int/ueDocs/cms_Data/docs/pressData/en/er/87673.pdf [October 2008]).

39. In 2006 and 2007 the European Union began implementing some of the actions outlined in the EU Africa strategy. The EU launched the EU-Africa Infrastructure Partnership and the EU Governance Initiative, increased funding for an AU-led peace support operation (such as the AMIS mission in Darfur) under the African Peace Facility (APF), and provided support for the AU's Neyere program for student exchanges and opened up the European Erasmus Mundus program for African universities, professors, and graduate students.

40. Siegmar Schmidt, "Towards a New EU-African Relationship—A Grand Strategy for Africa?" *Foreign Policy in Dialogue* 8, no. 24 (2008): 8–18.

41. ECDPM, *The EU and Africa.*

42. House of Lords, *The EU and Africa.*

43. Schmidt, "Towards a New EU-African Relationship."

PHILOMENA MURRAY

19

Regionalism, Interregionalism, and Bilateralism: The EU and the Asia-Pacific

The European Union attempts to project itself as an effective regional interlocutor with East Asia, and it actively encourages interregionalism. It projects itself as a regional actor with the Association of Southeast Asian Nations (ASEAN) and as a bilateral actor in relations with individual Asian nations. There is increasingly common ground between the EU and the East Asian countries, in an engagement that is becoming more multidimensional, comprising trade, investment, development, market access, and various aspects of foreign policy. Many shared values and global goals reinforce and extend the relationships, but only up to a point, owing to problems related to the EU's attempt to project itself as a coherent international actor in the region. This chapter draws on scholarly analysis, official documents, and interviews conducted by the author with European Commission officials in 2006 and 2007 regarding the EU's engagement with Asia. The interviews constitute an attempt to redress the lack of data on elite perceptions in the EU regarding EU–East Asia relations.[1]

Regionalism: The Development of the EU's Engagement with East Asia

The historical context for the relationship between Europe and East Asia has been largely forged by past colonial links between some EU member states and East Asian nations, in a state-to-state bilateralism. The postcolonial "special relationships" have also been characterized by special interests in Asia, on the part of the United Kingdom, France, and the Netherlands in particular. Yet despite the past colonial link these member states have not promoted a coherent or cohesive EU approach to relations with East Asia. This is in considerable contrast with Spain's efforts to promote closer links with South America.

The EU–East Asia engagement is based on strategic evaluations of both national and regional interests. The EU's primary objective is to seek better trade relations through greater access to East Asia's burgeoning markets, thereby also seeking to offset the considerable EU trade deficit with East Asia.[2] Redressing the trade deficit is a priority of the EU's "global Europe strategy" of 2006, as follows: "European exports are strong in countries where demand is static but they are less well placed than Japan and the U.S. in rapidly growing markets, particularly in Asia."[3]

Economic engagement encompasses the EU's efforts to promote and protect its interests and norms in a more open Asian market in the areas of investment, protection of intellectual property rights, services, government procurement, and sustainable development. This is in keeping with its global Europe strategy.[4] For their part, East Asian governments are interested in seeking economic engagement too, as well as European influence to counterbalance the United States.[5]

Little attention had been paid by the EU to either EU bilateral or interregional relations with Asia in the past. Until the EU's first Asia strategy in 1994 the continent of Europe was internally preoccupied, with little interest in Asia.[6] The Asia strategy was a reaction to the new economic dynamism of the East Asian region and was motivated by the European trade deficit with the region. The key elements were trade and political and security cooperation, and the key objectives were to strengthen the EU's economic presence; to contribute to stability through expanding economic and political relations; to encourage economic growth, especially in poorer countries; and finally, to develop and consolidate democracy and respect for human rights.[7] The EU therefore sought to engage as a regional entity with a new and dynamic region and later, in its 2001 document, to develop the 1994 approach.[8]

Interregionalism

The beginning of interregionalism is evident in the commencement in 1978 of the European biennial meeting between EU and ASEAN foreign ministers. ASEAN, which currently consists of ten nations, was formed in 1967 with the objectives of accelerating economic growth, social progress, and cultural development in the region.[9] Unlike the EU, this regional body is characterized by an intergovernmental format and a policy of noninterference in each other's affairs. The formal ASEAN-EU relationship commenced with the 1980 cooperation agreement and the development of political dialogue in the form of regular ministerial meetings.

The desire for a more regularized yet informal interregional format became evident at the time of the 1994 EU Asia strategy, with the initiative of Singapore in that year, which led to the creation of the Asia-Europe Meeting (ASEM).[10] This new forum for cooperation aimed to strengthen dialogue and interaction between the EU and ASEAN-plus-three (Japan, South Korea, and China). The first ASEM summit of heads of government was held in 1996, and summits have been held since then at two-year intervals. The participants in the ASEM summit in October 2008 in Beijing were the twenty-seven EU members, thirteen ASEAN-plus-three plus India, Pakistan, and Mongolia (following a decision at the 2006 ASEM summit in Helsinki), and the European Commission. This interregional summit and associated meetings constitute a process that is based on informal dialogue, framed around three pillars of cooperation: political, economic, and cultural. The ASEM structure encompasses an Asia-Europe business forum; a university program for student exchange; a meeting of economic ministers; Asia–Europe Foundation meetings, a "vision group"; and an action plan to promote trade and investment.[11]

In interviews conducted by the author with Commission officials, there is in evidence a commitment to developing the relationship with ASEAN across the various directorates-general of the Commission. This coherence of views does not extend to the evaluation of the success of ASEM. When asked how important ASEM is, an official expressed a position of extreme skepticism: "I think that at the end of the day, what really matters is our relationship with ASEAN, our relationship with China, and . . . our bilateral relationships. In most cases, the issues you discuss [in ASEM] are interesting, but you discuss them much more deeply and in a much more productive manner when you are meeting with ASEAN or when you are meeting and discussing certain issues bilaterally." This view is shared by an official who considers that the EU "should try to work with ASEAN a little bit more, at the political level . . . because it's more focused, more doable," while "ASEM is fine for exchanging views . . . but I have some doubts about it." Another official was of the opinion that ASEM is an internal, rather than an external, visibility tool for the EU, with "confidence-building measures." A more enthusiastic Commission official view is that the EU is attempting to "demonstrate that the Asia-Europe meeting is the prime point of convergence between Europe and Asia, as far as our relationship is concerned, at the multilateral level."

The value of dialogue, socialization, and mutual understanding—such as that fostered within ASEM—cannot be underestimated, as evidenced by the Commission's recognition in its 2001 document, "Europe and Asia: A Strategic Framework for Enhanced Partnerships," that there is a measure of mutual ignorance: "One element which does not seem to have evolved greatly is the degree of mutual awareness between our two regions, with stereotypes on both sides still casting Europe as introspective and old-fashioned, and Asia as a distant and exotic continent, presenting more challenges than opportunities."[12]

Interregional relations can be advanced if there is a recognition of common experiences and shared interests. The fact that East Asia does not constitute a region in the way that the EU does means that engagement must encompass a comprehension of differences and of the lack of comparability of some experiences. Although Europe is not without its diversity, the defining features of East Asia include a remarkable heterogeneity of race, ethnicity, religion, and historical experiences. Democracy, authoritarianism, and communism are all present in the region.[13] These contrasts mean that the relationship based on regionalism and interregionalism currently operates under considerable constraints.

Conflicting Agendas?

The EU's increased visibility in international affairs and its desire to take a more active role in international governance and multilateralism have led to expectations that the EU will be a more active international actor, moving from external relations to foreign policy. Karol De Gucht argues that European citizens expect the EU to use its substantial international influence to protect and promote their interests and that the rest of the world expects the EU to develop a greater weight in international affairs.[14] Yet the effectiveness of the EU's strategy in East Asia needs to be questioned. It can appear to be characterized more by promissory rhetoric than action, in the way that it attempts to be an effective regional interlocutor with East Asia and to project its soft power. The evidence to date suggests that where the EU is visible or recognized as an actor, it is predominantly in trade and not in soft power or promotion of governance or regional integration.[15] Further, it is not always clear what outcomes the Commission wishes to achieve. According to the EU's most recent policy guidelines toward East Asia, released in December 2007:

> The attitude of the major East Asian players is also increasingly important to the EU's wider global agenda. The EU needs, and seeks to promote, multilateral solutions to global challenges. The EU is promoting an open and fair trading system and further liberalization under the WTO [World Trade Organization] and in its bilateral and regional agreements, including those currently being negotiated with ASEAN and the Republic of Korea.[16]

Yet there is an uneasy coexistence of the desire to promote multilateralism in the WTO and to conclude bilateral free trade agreements (FTAs) with ASEAN and Korea. The "global Europe" strategy applies two major criteria for new FTA partners: market potential (economic size and growth) and the level of protection against EU export interests (tariffs and nontariff barriers).[17] The document also sees the need to evaluate "potential partner" negotiations with EU competitors, their likely impact on EU markets and economies, and the risk that current partners' preferential access to the EU markets may be eroded. Using these criteria, the EU has made ASEAN and Korea priorities.

In addition, while regionalism is actively promoted by the EU in ASEAN, as seen in Commission officials' meetings with ASEAN's Eminent Persons Group, the EU is also hopeful that its own experience of integration will "position it well to play an important role in helping to bolster regional security" based on the EU's "economic presence in the region, and its unique experience of post-war reconciliation and political and economic integration."[18] One Commission official interviewed referred to the EU as consisting of "countries which really have a stake in the future of Asia and in the security of Asia."

This issue of security is exercising the minds of the EU and especially the Commission, as seen in the recent East Asia guidelines and in perceptions of officials that the EU can be perceived as neutral, giving Asian partners the impression that "the EU can be used in a neutral fashion without necessarily infringing on their own interests." Officials view security as an emerging field for the EU but say "we have to see our limits very clearly" because the EU is more a soft power, which is "what we also want to be, for the moment."

A Promoter of Regional Integration

The EU's experience is admired by many Asian leaders.[19] There is admiration for the EU's success in creating a unified entity, with a significant internal market and institutional reforms, and a regional peace settlement.[20] However, there is equally a perception that the Asian experience is distinctive and requires a different approach. The promotion of the European integration experience as an example or template is not an approach that all Commission officials agree with. The official EU perspective is that it promotes regional integration, as seen in the June 2008 transatlantic summit declaration, which states: "We also encourage greater regional integration as a means for promoting prosperity and stability in East Asia."[21] Commission president José Manuel Barroso has stated: "While we acknowledge that every situation has its own specificities, we feel proud when so many of our partners and friends in Asia consider the European experience as a source of inspiration for their own cooperation and integration efforts."[22] And Commission officials have stated, "We think that the better ASEAN integrates, or East Asia integrates, the better it is for the rest of the world."

Regional Actor

The EU is not perceived as an effective regional actor by many interlocutors in the region, but as a multi-actor entity with many voices and ongoing problems of policy inconsistency and incoherence.[23] Interviews reveal that there is Commission recognition that the EU's internal and external policies need to be more closely linked and that there is a need for more Council-Commission cooperation on a strategy for East Asia.

Yet the EU continues to project itself as a form of soft power internationally and in East Asia. Commission officials perceive the EU as "very definitely a value-driven global actor" and the EU's international ambitions as "value-driven." They refer to the EU's "global ambitions in terms of dousing civil wars wherever possible."

Commission officials understand that the EU needs more visibility, expertise, and capacity, as well as negotiating clout with third countries. They are also aware that the EU is not easy to understand. One Commission official stated: "It is a big task to require interlocutors to understand the EU and member states' competences." The EU's complexity is also a challenge to its institutional coherence and to its "attempts to bring together disparate policies of the EU" toward East Asia. There is recognition of the need for institutional consolidation in the region. East Asia is now firmly on the EU radar screen because of its economic competitiveness, the awareness of common global agendas, the desire by the EU to be a more active political and security actor in the region, and the desire to concurrently exercise its soft power capabilities.[24] Dialogue on economic, political, and sociocultural issues is also a means to advance the EU's norms and agendas.

In addition, the emergence of China as a powerful economic player and interlocutor is central to all EU policies with regard to Asia (see Mara Caira's chapter in this volume). There is also a perception among some Commission officials that the EU is a soft power competitor, with the United States as a regional hegemon, although this view has been actively disputed within Asia itself as well as in Europe. The 2007 East Asia Policy Guidelines put the issue in the following context:

> The U.S.'s security commitments to Japan, the Republic of Korea and Taiwan and the associated presence of U.S. forces in the region give the U.S. a distinctive perspective on the region's security challenges. It is important that the EU is sensitive to this. Given the great importance of transatlantic relations, the EU has a strong interest in partnership and cooperation with the U.S. on the Foreign and Security policy challenges arising from East Asia.[25]

The guidelines set an agenda for future engagement. They state that the EU should develop its cooperation with all regional partners on many global issues, expanding dialogue and cooperation in areas such as development assistance, environmental sustainability, climate change, non-proliferation of WMD, conflict prevention, and peace support. They seek engagement for the promotion and protection of human rights and fundamental freedoms in East Asia, and this includes encouraging Asian partners to adhere to and comply with UN human rights instruments and mechanisms. The guidelines see this as potentially narrowing existing gaps in values that hamper efforts to find common policy ground. Further, they suggest that the EU should promote the development and consolidation of democracy and the rule of law, and that it should continue to promote cultural and civil society exchanges as a cornerstone of mutual understanding.

The EU's roles of integration exporter and multilateralism supporter are evident in the statement that the EU should "encourage and support regional integration as a means for promoting prosperity and stability" and "encourage and support the integration of countries in the region into existing multilateral non-proliferation and disarmament instruments and assist them in the full implementation of these instruments as well as in the establishment of effective export controls."[26]

Bilateralism

The EU continues to advance an EU-to-state bilateralism, such as that between the EU and South Korea. Another common form of bilateralism is that of individual EU member states negotiating with individual Asian states. The desire for the EU member states to pursue individual policies with Asian nations is in part the legacy of the colonial heritage. It is also due to the reluctance to regard the European Union, and especially the Commission, as the key negotiator on Asia policy. De Gucht perceives what he calls vertical inconsistency within the EU, defined as "the inadequate support from national diplomacies for EU foreign policy," as regrettable because it reveals a perception of EU foreign policy as zero-sum game, involving loss of national influence and prestige, as in the case of China.[27]

Bilateralism can be regarded as the most pragmatic approach to making progress on regional coherence within Asia itself. The fact that neither ASEAN nor ASEAN-plus-three is a regional actor with embedded institutions means that bilateral relations with individual Asian nations will be a hallmark of the EU's policy toward East Asia. A Commission official has admitted that "our Asia strategy has been a bit a function of the integration pace in Asia, which is quite slow and . . . that explains why we go for bilateral relations . . . we individualize the countries and we deal with them individually."

Concluding Observations

The EU is developing an approach that seeks to act as a cohesive actor in East Asia and to support the development of regionalism in East Asia. It remains largely committed to engagement in interregional dialogue. Until recently, there has been little concern about the need to understand the EU's impact on its interlocutors and to move beyond the essentially self-reflexive nature of the EU's pronouncements. The EU and the countries of East Asia have differing experiences and understandings of regionalism. This means that the EU needs to be cautious in advancing its experience of integration because it is not always clear what kind of regional paradigm the EU is promoting and how that might be perceived.

The EU is reviewing the effectiveness of its approach to East Asia. The time appears to be right to review the EU's policy leverage, its instruments, and its requirements for a coherent strategy in this regard. It can appear that, as the EU attempts to spread its more established policies, such as trade and development aid, and establish or broaden its more recent approaches based on security, humanitarian assistance, "norm entrepreneurship," and governance promotion, the EU is spreading itself quite thinly across a number of policies and an enormous region. It is certainly the case that the EU has adopted a multidimensional approach to East Asia. The EU will need to continue to monitor developments in the region, such as the implementation of closer regional cooperation. It will monitor the roles of China and Japan, as well as the difficult relationship between those two interlocutors. It will also be obliged to redress what is perceived as a lack of recognition by the Commission "of just how rapidly the entire Asian landscape is changing."[28] There are many challenges, but also opportunities. It is clear that the EU is, and will continue to be, engaged in a multidimensional relationship of regionalism, interregionalism, and bilateralism as it continues to develop its role as a regional interlocutor with East Asia.

Notes

1. The author conducted a series of interviews with European Commission officials in Brussels in September 2006 and July 2007, which are quoted in this chapter. The respondents preferred to remain anonymous.

2. Philomena Murray, "Introduction: Europe and Asia, Two Regions in Flux?" in *Europe and Asia: Regions in Flux*, edited by Philomena Murray (Basingstoke, UK: Palgrave, 2008).

3. European Commission, COM (2006) 567 final, "Communication from the Commission to the Council, the European Parliament, the European Economic and Social Committee and the Committee of the Regions," *Global Europe: Competing in the World: A Contribution to the EU's Growth and Jobs Strategy*, Brussels, October 4, 2006,

p. 4 (www.lex.unict.it/eurolabor/en/documentation/com/2006/com(2006)-567en.pdf [October 2008]).

4. Ibid., p. 6, states: "We will require a sharper focus on market opening and stronger rules in new trade areas of economic importance to us, notably intellectual property (IPR), services, investment, public procurement and competition."

5. Murray, "Introduction: Europe and Asia," in *Europe and Asia*, edited by Murray.

6. Commission of the European Community, Com (94) 314 final, "Towards a New Asia Strategy," Communication of the Commission to the Council, Brussels, July 13, 1994.

7. Commission of the European Community, Com (94) 314 final; Philomena Murray, "Contemporary European Perspectives on East Asia and EU-Asia Relations," in *Europe and Asia*, edited by Murray.

8. European Commission, Communication from the Commission COM (2001) 469 final, "Europe and Asia: A Strategic Framework for Enhanced Partnerships," Brussels, September 4, 2001 (http://ec.europa.eu/external_relations/asia/doc/com01_469_en.pdf [October 2001]).

9. The five original members were Indonesia, Malaysia, Singapore, Philippines, and Thailand. Today's ten members are Brunei Darussalam, Indonesia, Malaysia, Philippines, Singapore, Thailand, Vietnam, Laos, Burma (Myanmar), and Cambodia.

10. Yeo Lay Hwee, "The Origins and Development of ASEM and EU–East Asia Relations," in *Europe and Asia,* edited by Murray.

11. Bertrand Fort, "Can Asia and Europe Cooperate?" paper presented to the International Conference on EU-Asia Relations: A Critical Review, at the Contemporary Europe Research Centre, University of Melbourne, March 27–28, 2008.

12. European Commission, "Europe and Asia," p. 14.

13. Murray, "Introduction: Europe and Asia."

14. Karol De Gucht, "Shifting EU Foreign Policy into Higher Gear," EU Diplomacy Papers, 1/2006 (Bruges: College of Europe, 2006).

15. Natalia Chaban and Martin Holland, eds., "The EU through the Eyes of the Asia-Pacific," NCRE Research Series no. 4 (University of Canterbury, 2007).

16. Council of the European Union, "East Asia Policy Guidelines," 16460/07, Brussels, December 14, 2007, p. 3.

17. European Commission, *Global Europe*, p. 9.

18. Council of the European Union, "East Asia Policy Guidelines," p. 4.

19. Toshiro Tanaka, "Asian Perspectives on European Integration," in *Europe and Asia*, edited by Murray.

20. François Godemont, "Europe-Asia: The Historical Limits of a Soft Relationship," in *Europe-Asia Relations: Building Multilateralisms*, edited by Richard Balme and Brian Bridges (Basingstoke, UK: Palgrave, 2008).

21. Council of the European Union, 10562/08 (Presse 168), "2008 EU-US Summit Declaration," Brdo, Slovenia, June 10, 2008.

22. José Manuel Barroso, speech at the opening ceremony of the Asia-Europe Meeting, September 10, 2006 (www.asem6.fi/news_and_documents/en_GB/1157887132984/ [October 2008]).

23. Philomena Murray, Adam Berryman, and Margherita Matera, "Coherence, Effectiveness and Recognition in EU-East Asia Relations," paper presented at EU-Asia Relations: A Policy Review Workshop, jointly hosted by the Contemporary Europe Research Centre, the University of Melbourne, and the European Institute of Asian Studies, Brussels, July 10, 2008.

24. Council of the European Union, "East Asia Policy Guidelines," 16460/07, Brussels, December 14, 2007.

25. Ibid., p. 4.

26. Ibid., p. 5.

27. De Gucht, "Shifting EU Foreign Policy."

28. Malcolm Subhan, "Europe and Asia: A Common Future?" in *L'Europe et l'Asie*, edited by Dumoulin Michel, Actes de la IXe Chaire Glaverbel d'études européennes (Brussels: PIE-Peter Lang, 2004), p. 104.

MARA CAIRA

20

The EU-China Relationship: From Cooperation to Strategic Partnership

The relationship between the European Union and China has developed in depth and extent over the past thirty years. Many points of disagreement as well as many important achievements have punctuated its evolution. The relationship was triggered in the 1970s by the Chinese interest in the birth and development of the new political entity represented by an integrated Europe. It grew in the 1990s, as the European Commission became concerned with protecting and consolidating European interests in an evolving East Asia. The idea was to have them materialize through "an action-oriented, not a merely declaratory" policy aimed at what was becoming the most important regional power.[1] This relationship grew into a cherished strategic partnership. Since roughly 2006, relations seem to have stalled or taken a step backward. This relationship has been said to have entered the mature "marriage" phase after a "honeymoon" period.[2]

An Overview

The establishment of official relations between the EU and China goes back to 1975, when Sir Christopher Soames, vice president of the Commission of the European Community in charge of external relations, made a trip to China on the invitation of the Chinese Institute of International Studies.[3] China had been showing sustained, though not continuous, interest in European integration for at least ten years.[4] In the Chinese analysis, developed within the framework of the "three world" theory, an integrated Europe would eventually play a significant role on the international stage. Since 1964 Western Europe had been situated in the "second intermediate zone," distinguished from the other two camps, the socialist and the imperialist.[5] As a consequence, like other countries belonging to the "intermediate zones," Western Europe was a potential ally in reducing China's isolation.

There were of course economic reasons for building closer relations with Europe, since China needed technology and equipment for its modernization. But it seems that the Chinese motive was essentially political, as was also reflected in the opinion of the European Community (EC) leaders. From the European perspective, China was offering the EC member states the opportunity to acquire a new market. The prospect of consolidating China's separation from the socialist bloc was perceived as a valuable political outcome.

The trip of the vice president of the Commission resulted in an agreement to have the European Community recognized by the People's Republic of China (PRC), and to have the Chinese ambassador in Belgium accredited as ambassador to the EC as well. China was, therefore, the first country of the socialist camp to recognize integrated Europe as a political entity. The EC commissioner was not empowered to make declarations concerning Taiwan, but Sir Christopher Soames stated at a press conference that the EC had neither an official relationship nor agreements with Taiwan, and that all the EC member states recognized the government of the PRC as the sole legal government of China. However, a European delegation office was opened in Beijing only in 1988.

Until the end of the 1980s, the initial phase of the EU's relationship was characterized by cooperation arrangements designed to assist China's development in many areas, such as science, rural economy, and training, and by the signing of economic and trade agreements. The first trade agreement was signed in 1978, followed by a new agreement on trade and economic cooperation between the European Economic Community and the People's Republic of China in 1985. Even though the emphasis at that time was on the economic opportunity offered by the development of China and the resulting opening of vast markets for European goods and services, political dialogue also existed. It was initiated in 1984, although it remained confined to meetings between the presidency of the European Council and the Chinese ambassador to that country.

A real political relationship took shape in the mid-1990s, when the first communication addressed to China by the Commission was published, COM (1995) 279, "A Long Term Policy for China-Europe Relations." That first communication activated a wider and more institutionalized political dialogue. It had been established in 1994 through an exchange of letters, in order to include all issues of common interest and global significance. Meetings were introduced between the foreign ministers, between the Chinese foreign minister and the EU ambassador in Beijing, and between the Chinese ambassador in the country holding the EU Presidency and the foreign minister of that country. Their intention was to create a network of regular consultations, with the aim of engaging China progressively in full-fledged political cooperation and gradually developing a more mature relationship.

The next communication, COM (1998) 181, "Building a Comprehensive Partnership with China," went further. It established the annual EU-China summit at the heads of state and government level, the first of which took place in April 1998 in London. Altogether, and apart from the first communication, the Commission issued several documents concerning European policy toward China: COM (1998) 181, "Building a Comprehensive Partnership with China"; COM (2001) 265, "EU Strategy towards China: Implementation of the 1998 Communication and Future Steps for a More Effective EU Policy"; COM (2003) 533 "A Maturing Partnership: Shared Interests and Challenges in EU-China Relations"; and COM (2006) 631 "EU-China: Closer Partners, Growing Responsibilities," accompanied by the working paper "Competition and Partnership," COM (2006) 632.[6]

A few key words sum up the European Union's China policy: engagement, cooperation, and partnership. Engagement reflects the idea that, due to its rise as an economic power and as a global actor, China is "both part of the problem and of the solution to all major issues of international and regional concern."[7] Therefore it is essential for the Europeans to develop a common understanding on all issues of concern and to involve China in global governance. The best way to reach this goal is to develop a policy of engagement through cooperation with the PRC. Engagement implies opposing containment, especially in the mind of the Chinese leaders, and it underlines the different European and U.S. approaches to China's rising role in the world.

Cooperation between the EU and China occurs through a wide range of projects (including the Galileo satellite navigation system, biological technology, aviation, good governance, training of officials, and others) and through sectoral dialogues ranging from political analysis to environmental and trade issues.[8] Sector dialogues are one of the most interesting features of Sino-European relations. Each one involves officials and experts from both sides in a broad discussion. As a whole, they are conceived as a means to closely examine issues and to make progress in analysis through discussion and confrontation of the parties' respective points of view. The idea is to reach convergence and solutions and to avoid misunderstandings and different interpretations of the letter of the agreements. The very existence of institutionalized frameworks of discussion, under the general structure of the political dialogue, makes the Chinese side ready to engage frankly and openly on even difficult issues, which would very probably be impossible in a different context. Political and civil freedom and human rights are the object of a separate specific dialogue.

Political dialogue, sector dialogues, and cooperation projects are of course linked. The interaction among them strengthens political dialogue and cooperation, with the sector dialogues being a kind of conveyor belt. The whole system ensures that the EU's priorities are pursued in concrete and practical ways when projects are implemented. The system and the structuring of the relationship are specific and have been effective.[9]

Through this peer approach to issues, cooperation was upgraded to partnership. Cooperation and partnership have developed into a comprehensive strategic partnership since 2003, as formulated in COM (2003) 533 and in "China's EU Policy Paper" issued by the Chinese government in October 2003, the first document of its kind ever issued by the PRC. In the opinion of many analysts, the sense of comprehensive strategic partnership still needs to be defined in a clear way by both sides.[10] On the Chinese side, the concept of a comprehensive strategic partnership was elucidated by Prime Minister Wen Jiabao in May 2004:

> By "*comprehensive*," it means that the cooperation should be all-dimensional, wide-ranging and multi-layered. It covers economic, scientific, technological, political and cultural fields, contains both bilateral and multilateral levels, and is conducted by both governments and non-governmental groups. By "*strategic*," it means that the cooperation should be long-term and stable, bearing on the larger picture of China-EU relations. It transcends the differences in ideology and social systems, and is not subjected to the impact of individual events that occur from time to time. By "*partnership*," it means that the cooperation should be equal-footed, mutually beneficial and win-win. The two sides should base themselves on mutual respect and mutual trust, endeavor to expand converging interests and seek common ground on the major issues while shelving differences on the minor ones.[11]

From the European Union's point of view, as reflected in the first two communications by the Commission, strategic partnership is a relationship in which the two parties reciprocally recognize the strategic relevance of the partner on issues concerning both bilateral relations and global governance.

The partnership should address both sides' interests, and the EU and China need to work together as they assume more active and responsible international roles, supporting and contributing to a strong and effective multilateral system. The final goal is for China and the EU to use their respective strengths to offer joint solutions to global problems.[12] Strategic partnership is still under construction. It should be the driving force for the Partnership and Cooperation Agreement currently under discussion and should be embodied in it.

Negotiations over a Partnership and Cooperation Agreement began in January 2007, after the two partners agreed in 2005 that a new framework for the EU-China relationship was necessary because the former legal tool, the Trade and Economic Agreement (1985), was out of date. The new agreement is expected to be comprehensive, and it should embody both the political and economic dimensions of the partnership, covering a wide range of fields of cooperation and including existing small separate agreements. It should also reflect the complexity, breadth, and depth of the relationship, its strategic relevance, and enhanced cooperation in political matters.

Over time, the relationship has become more complex than initially expected. Political and strategic issues (human rights and the arms embargo) proved more difficult to handle, economic and trade interests became more conflicting, and member states took different positions on themes to which China is sensitive (Tibet, protection of human rights, the arms embargo). From China's perspective, these are not separate issues because they all concern the respect for Chinese sovereignty and international status.

Convergence and Frictions

The first convergence lies in the lack of conflicts of interest between the two partners: no territorial conflict or dispute exists between them, and Europe does not represent a security challenge to China. A convergence of interests between the EU and China has been evident in many circumstances. The aim of the Commission at the time of the first communication in 1995 was to facilitate China's accession to international institutions, in that case the World Trade Organization (WTO). With this commitment, the EU was responding to the Chinese effort to assert itself as a peer nation on the global stage. The EU was a strong supporter of China's accession to the WTO, arguing that a WTO without China was not truly universal in scope. For China, formal accession to the WTO in December 2001 symbolized an important step of its integration into the global order and community. The commitments made by China in the context of WTO accession secured greater access for EU firms to China's market. Thus the economic interests of the EU were met. China appreciated the support given by Europe, in contrast with the ambivalence of the United States, at a time when joining international institutions was a paramount goal of Chinese foreign policy.

A false convergence exists in the international role that China credits to the EU. This can be defined as a kind of wishful thinking or "cognitive dissonance," in the sense that China supports an international role that the EU only partially accomplishes.[13] This role consists in a stance for the democratization of international organizations and for the construction of a multi-polar world, the international order China would like to achieve. The Chinese view elaborates on the EU's advocacy of a multi-polar order in which superpowers are conditioned by supranational institutions, peaceful conflict resolution through international multilateral organizations, an enhanced role for the United Nations, promotion of a political space open to all actors, and opposition to the superpower politics that would impose a unilateral view of the international order.

Not long after the mutual endorsement of engagement in a strategic partnership, both sides put forward requests and expectations. Since 2003 the Chinese side has required the strategic partnership to fulfill a list of conditions. First, it requires proper handling of the Taiwan issue. China hopes that the EU will continue to respect China's major concerns, keeping exchanges with Taiwan strictly on an unofficial and nongovernmental basis, and that it will avoid selling weapons to Taiwan. Second, the EU should lift its ban on arms sale to China "at an early date so as to remove barriers to greater bilateral co-operation on defense industry and technologies."[14] Third, the EU should not have any contact with the "Tibetan government in exile."

Taiwan in itself does not represent a real problem in EU-China relations because the EU and its member states are committed to the one-China principle. But the arms embargo and the Taiwan issues came to be connected after the so-called anti-secession law, passed by the National People's Assembly in March 2005, which touches on two questions: China's sovereignty and its international status. Against this background, the strategic partnership conflicts with those two crucial issues of Chinese domestic and international politics. As a consequence, China claims that the EU is not treating it as a strategic partner.

Another source of misunderstanding lies in the peculiar characteristic of European external relations, which is defined by three actors: the European Commission, the European Council, and the Parliament. The Commission develops the general lines of the common European action to be pursued toward China; the Council expresses and protects member states' individual interests; and the Parliament's resolutions criticize China on human rights and political freedom issues, often more harshly than the two other institutions. Moreover, the Parliament has recently exerted greater influence on the Council than in the past. Because the three actors' positions are not homogeneous, China must deal with what it perceives as an unbalanced and inconsistent attitude. Besides that, each member state, or at least the major ones (Great Britain, France, and Germany), has its own "China policy," which in turn makes it difficult for China to evaluate the "European" stance.

Also, in light of the war in Iraq and the arms embargo, China has become more aware of the weight of transatlantic relations, of the connections between the China-EU relationship and the EU-U.S. relationship. It has become aware that the relationship is in fact triangular.[15]

From the European point of view, the strategic partnership also means that China should assume more responsibility on global issues (the environment, nuclear non-proliferation, relations with African countries) and in bilateral relations (property rights protection; opening the Chinese market to European economic actors, especially in the financial sectors; reducing the trade imbalance). Increasing criticism has been expressed by experts and by the economic and business milieu.[16] This was reflected in the COM (2006) and the accompanying document on trade. All of these frictions keep the EU-China relationship at a suboptimal level. But at same time, the articulation of the different instruments and mechanisms has built up a solid flow of information, know-how, aid, and transfer of knowledge concerning Western institutions, which has helped mold the Chinese bureaucracy, political culture, and legal conceptions. Those influences are not always evident, but are nonetheless metabolized in the "Chinese way."[17]

Another reason why the relationship is deepening is of course the economic interdependence or complementarity of the two parties.[18] The relevance of economic ties is reflected in the ever increasing number of new "mechanisms." For example, the high-level economic and trade mechanism, launched in Beijing in April 2008, will deal with the already mentioned issues of crucial importance to the EU-China relationship (trade relations and economic cooperation, investments, market access and intellectual property rights protection). Trade, investments, economic interests, and political engagement should be, as noted before, integrated in a new agreement (PCA), which the two partners are still negotiating.

It has to be noted that the relationship's most interesting feature is the support given to China's internal reform process. It comes as a challenge to the EU, but it engages both sides in a more and more mature cooperation.

Notes

1. COM (1995) 279, "A Long Term Policy for China-Europe Relations," p. 3 (www. delchn.ec.europa.eu/download/com95_279en.pdf [October 2008]).

2. David Shambaugh, Eberhard Sandschneider, and Zhou Hong, eds., *China-Europe Relations. Perceptions, Policies and Prospects* (London: Routledge, 2008), pp. 303–17.

3. The trip was then upgraded to a high-level visit.

4. See Mara Caira, *Europa e il Drago. Le relazioni fra Unione Europea e Cina dal 1975 ad oggi* (forthcoming); and Harish Kapur, *China and the EEC: The New Connection* (Dordrecht: Martinus Nijhoff, 1986). Evidence can be found in the Chinese press and in the Archives Historiques de la Commission, Brussels.

5. *Renmin ribao* (People's Daily) editorial, January 21, 1964.

6. European Commission, External Relations, "China" (www.ec.europa.eu/external_relations/china [October 2008]).

7. COM (2001) 265, "EU Strategy towards China: Implementation of the 1998 Communication and Future Steps for a More Effective EU Foreign Policy," p. 7 (www. delchn.ec.europa.eu/download/com01_265.pdf [October 2008]).

8. European Commission, External Relations, "An Overview of the Sectoral Dialogues between China and the EU" (http://ec.europa.eu/external_relations/china/sectoral dialogue_en.htm [October 2008]).

9. European Commission, "Evaluation of the European Commission's Co-operation and Partnership with the People's Republic of China, Country Level Evaluation, Final Synthesis Report," April 2007, p. 16.

10. See, for example, Zhang Tiejun, "EU, China and Global Governance," presented at "Current Situation and Future Prospects of Asia-Europe Security Cooperation," Fifth Shanghai Workshop in Global Governance, Shanghai Institute for International Studies and Friedrich-Ebert-Stiftung, January 23–24, 2007 (library.fes.de/pdf-files/bueros/china/04642.pdf [October 2008]).

11. Wen Jiabao, "Vigorously Promoting Comprehensive Strategic Partnership between China and the European Union," speech at the China-EU Investment and Trade Forum, Brussels, May 6, 2004.

12. COM (2006) 631, "EU-China: Closer Partners, Growing Responsibilities" (www.delchn.ec.europa.eu/download/communication-paper-ENG_070622.pdf [October 2008]).

13. Shambaugh, Sandschneider, and Zhou, *China-Europe Relations*, p. 128.

14. "China's EU Policy Paper," 2003 (www.mfa.gov.cn/eng/topics/ceupp/t27708.htm [October 2008]).

15. Jean-Pierre Cabestan, "European Union–China Relations and the United States," *Asian Perspective* 30, no. 4 (2006): 11–38; and Bates Gill, "The United States and the China-Europe Relationship," in *China-Europe Relations*, edited by Shambaugh, Sandschneider, and Zhou, p. 128.

16. Katinka Barysch, Charles Grant, and Mark Leonard, *Embracing the Dragon: The EU's Partnership with China* (London: Centre for European Reform, 2006) (http://www.cer.org.uk/pdf/p_610_dragon_partnership.pdf [October 2008]).

17. Zhou Hong, "EU Social Policy Studies in China," *Asia Europe Journal* 2, no. 3 (2004): 425–27.

18. Bernadette Andreosso-O'Callaghan and Françoise Nicolas, "Complementarity and Rivalry in EU-China Economic Relations in the Twenty-First Century," *European Foreign Affairs Review* 12, no. 1 (2007): 13–28.

*Promoting Values
and Models Abroad*

BERNARD YVARS

21

EU Integration and Other Integration Models

Comparing the process of regional integration in the world and in history is a complex matter. Attempts at regional economic integration precede the Second World War. They existed in the nineteenth century, particularly in Europe, and were concerned with the birth and consolidation of nation-states (Germany, Italy) and the realization of monetary unions designed to facilitate trade without any economic integration (Latin monetary union, Scandinavian monetary union). These experiences, mainly monetary, are instructive for contemporary process integrators. They have developed simultaneously in the General Agreement on Tariffs and Trade (GATT) and the World Trade Organization (WTO) and in harmony with them. The largest process in the world is the creation of free trade areas (the European Free Trade Association, EFTA; the North American Free Trade Agreement, NAFTA; or the Association of Southeast Asian Nations, ASEAN), which is nothing other than a transitional move toward globalization by putting in place WTO rules. Some associations, such as the Community of Independent States (CIS), do not seek regional integration; and some do not have a record of blocking its installation, such as the Union of the Arab Maghreb (UAM).

The deepest regional integration by far has been achieved by the European Union. Its complex and specific process can serve as a model for other integration efforts (the Common Market of the South, Mercosur; the Caribbean Community, Caricom) or to establish monetary union (the Western Africa Economic and Monetary Union, Waemu; the East Caribbean Currency Union, Eccu).

A Partially Transferable European Model of Regional Integration

The second half of the twentieth century was without doubt an era of regional integration. The process of commercial, economic, and institutional rapprochement had two phases. The first, which roughly coincided with the 1960s, saw the birth of the European Economic Community (EEC). The second was rooted in the U.S.-Canadian free trade agreement, which was later extended to Mexico to form NAFTA. It extended over the 1990s and 2000s and has achieved only limited integration.

The European Union, an Original Model of Regional Economic Integration

Among the many regional entities that have emerged during the 1960s, the EU occupies a unique place. From its beginning, the European common market has been a source of inspiration for developing countries. Actions taken by the Union of States of East Africa, the Central American Common Market, the East African Community, Caricom, the Andean Pact, and Mercosur have tried to reproduce the European Community experience of rapprochement between neighbors and economically equal countries. On the economic dimension, one can see parallel progress in the theoretical analysis and practical experience of European integration.[1] Two decisive steps taken by the European Community over the past ten years illustrate.

The first relates to the realization of the "single market" of goods, services, and factors of production. Since the mid-1980s, this experience has stimulated reflections on the effects of intense competition or market size on trade between partner countries. Pioneering work such as that of Paul Krugman on "new theories" of international trade based on the prevalence of imperfect forms of competition with the deepening of the single European market led to a genuine renewal of the theory of economic integration.[2] A second well-known illustration of European integration is the theory of optimum currency areas, which emerged in the early 1960s.[3] Growing discussion of monetary unification in Europe in the late 1980s gave new relevance to the theory of optimum currency areas. In particular, the terms of cost-benefit analysis of monetary unions have been profoundly deepened and enriched, at the same time that the problems of transitioning to an exchange rate regime were unavoidable.

The European Union also offered a legal and institutional apparatus that has no equivalent in the world. The theoretical corpus encompassed by the Community's legislation illustrates this singularity. The integration process was influenced by several theoretical analyses, including federalism, a confederal approach, and a middle ground between the two. The thorny issue of supranationality remains: should we rely on cooperation between agencies, with final decisions made by an intergovernmental body, on bodies independent of member states, or on intergovernmental structures making decisions based on a simple or qualified majority?

The status gradually acquired by the European Union is also due to the fact that, under various names, the EU rose through the first levels of regional integration in less than fifty years. First a free trade area and then a customs union with a common trade policy, the former European Economic Community (EEC) has sought to build a truly unified internal market for goods, services, and factors of production. Having achieved that at the turn of the 1990s, it then marked the last decade of the twentieth century with its monetary unification project. The EU now addresses openly the future stages of its construction and whether they should be federal. The developing countries have found many reasons to follow the European regional integration "model" in their effort to form solid and consistent regional blocs. It has become commonplace to say that the effective globalization of markets, of production processes, and even of social norms calls for regional rapprochement.

A STRONG SPECIFICITY OF THE EUROPEAN PROCESS OF THOROUGH INTEGRATION. A look at European integration since the mid-twentieth century reveals that there has been a willingness to develop economic cooperation between states faster than the GATT agreements could do so. The consideration of whether the European model of regional integration is exportable raises two main issues: (1) identifying the transferable elements, and (2) developing the capacity of the receiving area to adopt them. Because of its complex combination of different degrees of integration, the EU is not an unambiguous model.

The European Union promotes economic development in a framework that respects democracy and human rights. This model is a priori more institutional and political than economic. The EU's essential institutional and regulatory framework is characterized by real decisionmaking powers granted to joint bodies. There is direct European legislation through regulation. The European Court of Justice (ECJ) is a common legal body that reduces the risk that the EU integration process can be reversed. Community economic development has two components: an old and transferable component corresponding to the phase of the customs union or single European market, and a more recent but nontransferable component corresponding to the monetary union—that is, to the regional integration process in Europe.

Difficulties can occur in the first stage of integration (the free movement of products) especially if member states' exchange rate regimes differ. This first phase occurred when European states were affected by significant national economic disparities—that is, shocks that affected individual nations rather than regions. The economic gain of integration is based primarily on the development of trade that removes visible obstacles to trade (relatively high tariffs and quotas). It was also at this time that the implementation of the most significant common policy began: the Common Agricultural Policy (CAP). The CAP benefited from an agreement with the United States that provisionally accepted some European agricultural protectionism. European construction was based from the beginning on the general policy of a market moderated by the prerogatives of centralized economic policies, like the CAP.

A MAJOR ELEMENT OF PORTABILITY: THE MARKET LOGIC OF THE EUROPEAN CUSTOMS UNION. We know that the theory of customs unions establishes that one of the conditions for net positive welfare of a customs union (when trade creation outweighs trade deviations) is that member economies must be effectively competitive before the customs union is established and potentially complementary once the customs union has been achieved. The creation of trade initially requires protected production, and because of reciprocal customs protection the production structures of the economies must be almost identical before the formation of the customs union: they must be competing effectively.

However, each member must also be the most efficient producer of goods that are protected and produced inefficiently by its partner. This requirement ensures that there will be exchanges of differentiated products between nations of the union and trade creation rather than diversion. It is more likely that a customs union will lead to mutual gains for its member states than would be the case if their economies were at similar levels of development. The growth of intra-industrial trade reflects the degree of closeness of the member states' productive structures. The changing regulatory framework achieved in this phase of the European customs union was completed on January 1, 1968. At that time there was a customs union for industrial products and a single market for agricultural products. A drastic change of rules governing trade was bearable only by developed economies to the extent that tax revenues from trade contribute only weakly to the budgetary resources.

This is less true for developing countries, where the gradual liberalization of trade is without doubt the most appropriate solution (unilateral trade liberalization, lists of product derogations, safeguard clauses, and so forth). Today, as the main common policy, the CAP cannot be a model for other regional groupings because, first, the original CAP was dismantled by the European reform of 1992 and by the agreements of the Uruguay Round of trade talks. The next phase negotiated in the WTO was achieved with a European agricultural market guided by international prices. Second, direct aid, which in Agenda 2000 partially compensates for the decline in support prices, saw its fate sealed: as in the American agricultural model, it will be decoupled from the quantities produced.

Another common policy, competition policy, requires minimal integration of the internal market (the elimination of intra-zone tariffs and quotas). Many regional experiences do not aim to build a highly integrated area with common policies, but to develop intra-zone trade and foreign direct investment (FDI). This is the logic of NAFTA and ASEAN. A priori, the realization of monetary union would seem to be a process that cannot be developed elsewhere in the world. This construction, which is also not consolidated in Europe, has a high specificity that limits its transferability.

THE EUROPEAN MONETARY UNION, A PROCESS QUITE SPECIFIC AND UNTRANSFERABLE. Over a long period of time, production conditions have favored regions in the northern and central parts of the EU, including low transport costs and a strong expense ratio for industrial goods. Any policy of regional integration aimed at reducing transport costs, and more generally the costs of interaction in trade of industrial goods, led to a relationship between central and peripheral regions that has favored the more developed central European region. The achievement of the monetary union seems likely to increase regional divergence by strengthening the economic advantage of the richest areas. The European productivity gaps between rich and poor regions will solidify the concentration of resources by the developed areas of the monetary union. Infrastructure networks (sometimes with the assistance of EU funds) can open up relatively less favored areas. Today, there is also the possibility of operating outside the monetary union, which creates differences in the relative costs of factors, determining the emergence of a vertical division of regional labor.

Integration and economic diversification reduce the vulnerability of a monetary union to asymmetric shocks. The Organization for Economic Cooperation and Development (OECD) identifies three major vectors of economic integration: trade interdependence, intensity of cross-border trade, and the convergence of revenues. Over the past twenty years, these three factors have contributed to a greater synchronization of cycles in the European economy. Obtaining nominal convergence with the Maastricht criteria has also contributed to a macroeconomic rapprochement for the countries in the euro zone. Krugman has argued that the deepening of integration could lead to greater specialization and make regions of the monetary union more sensitive to asymmetric shocks.[4] The existence of increasing returns can explain the emergence of dynamic regional divergence causing an agglomeration of economic activities. The exploitation of economies of scale brought about by the opening of markets leads firms to concentrate their production. Trade integration, by reducing transaction costs between regions, facilitates that process.

At the EU level, the completion of the internal market has resulted in concentration. However, the existence of growing intra-industrial trade between the countries of the monetary union shows that the realization of the single market has led to productive quality differentials, which are the source of asymmetric shocks (and costly social adjustments).[5] The analysis of trade, which showed

Europe as a whole made up of states with diverse industrial structures, must be nuanced. European countries have diversified production structures that use different specialized technological scales. The consequence is that European regions are more specialized than individual nations, increasingly so with the deepening of European integration. Even if specialization of member states did not increase, regional differences would be exacerbated inside states, causing a divergence that the market mechanisms of monetary union would not reverse. We also know that the variability of inflation has always been more important than the variability of output growth in most European countries. With a common monetary policy the variability of inflation between regions is expected to decline while output fluctuations between regions could rise owing to the loss of the instrument of change as a measure of economic adjustment. Such a scenario would create difficulties for member states with vulnerable economies. The variability of production in labor markets that are not sufficiently flexible (European peripheral regions) can cause even more significant production losses. The spatial differentiation of monetary union seems to deepen, resulting in an operating cost to the monetary union (a cost that does not, however, threaten the viability of monetary union).

The successive enlargements of the European Union, the questions of cooperation in the East with the new neighboring countries, relations with Russia, and a new impetus to cooperate with the Mediterranean countries have complicated the EU's external relations, especially with its natural trade zone. Globalization appears to create an opportunity for growth and higher living standards at the international level. Gains are, however, uneven across countries and economic agents. In this globalized economy, competition seems to cover all the costs of production, including the social aspects of these costs. What is questionable is the production for export when the absorption capacity of a country's domestic market is smaller than that of countries with stronger social norms and higher costs of production. Asian competition, especially from China, falls under this scenario. The exchange becomes even more unbalanced in a global economy, where no longer the comparative advantages but the absolute advantages are the determinants of international trade.[6]

Today the European Union faces a double challenge: a necessary and pragmatic deepening and better integration of the international and regional division of labor. Reinforcing this sort of cooperation seems necessary to achieve these objectives, including developing innovative relations with neighboring third countries.

THE CONSTRAINTS OF GLOBALIZATION ON CURRENT DEVELOPMENTS IN THE EUROPEAN UNION. The main lessons of the theory of international trade are based on the assumption that factors of production are immobile. Countries hiding behind tariff and nontariff barriers no longer represent the framework for production and trade by developed countries. One consequence is that the Ricardian model of comparative costs is largely inadequate to reflect the international reality.

The conditions of trade between nations have evolved and contributed to the polarization of activities and employment in the zones with the lowest taxes. The social responsibility of firms is a major issue, in particular in the new economic context of production and international trade. In this connection, two points deserve to be further clarified. First, Ricardian comparative costs as a foundation for international specialization and the superiority of free trade over any form of organized trade are not relevant. Second, an international exchange arranged hierarchically would continue to create winners among both developed and developing countries. The differentiation of similar products should theoretically lead to an unlimited trade capacity. This argument is largely academic. Intra-industry exchanges anywhere in the world, including among the most-developed countries of the European Union, are mainly intra-industrial vertical trade, not intra-industrial horizontal trade. One is confronted with a problem of economic adjustment costs because the inter-industrial vertical trade leads to specialization and to asymmetric shocks caused by loss of activity. Three situations should be considered.

—*Comparative advantages versus absolute advantages.* Although the world economy is not yet completely liberalized, the trend is toward greater trade liberalization through: (1) more multilateral negotiations under the GATT/WTO and (2) more regionalism, with the frequent creation of free trade areas and, more rarely, customs unions.

Free trade is usually the best solution in the neoclassical analysis that posits the greatest welfare gains for nations that engage in trade. "Suitable" participation in international trade then is based on specialization according to comparative advantages in an institutional framework of completely open trade.[7]

Such a productivity gain for countries is possible simply because of the international diffusion of innovation and research and development (R&D) and the absorption capacity of an increasingly educated, skilled, and mobile workforce throughout the world. Even if R&D progresses mainly in the more developed countries, in the future recovery will reduce the gaps between nations. New processes, inventions, and innovations still come mainly from the United States, Japan, and the European Union and will be increasingly used in countries with lower social costs of production. The temptation of protectionism may be strong in developed countries, but it is stigmatized because there exist advantages brought by free trade.[8] Indeed, developed countries that exploit the cheaper supplies and lower labor costs of developing countries would promote their productive processes and increase their range of goods produced, but would perpetuate a model of international cooperation where the most advanced countries would always be at a comparatively advanced technological stage. This pattern of economic development cannot meet the socially necessary employment requirements of the developed countries.

—*The final barrier to product differentiation.* Jagdish Bhagwati recommends that the developed countries with relatively more expensive labor produce a wider range of products to maintain their trade advantage.[9] The mechanical diagram of a permanent increase in the range of production by the developed countries while the production of lower value-added products is delocalized in the developing countries with lower social costs of production is a model that would work only in the short term. In addition, trade based on product differentiation would grow less robustly because of the speed of technology transfer, which would contribute to the production of similar product lines and to the number of firms with monopolistic or oligopolistic market strategies. Ultimately, these products would compete with each other because of the narrowness of differentiation, which would disrupt the development of production and trade.

Today the European Union is facing a process of deterritorialization of activities toward the eastern European countries and the Asian zone (India and especially China). To some extent, the workers in those countries (countries with a high level of social protection) are being injured, with profits being divided between labor abroad and capital.[10] This division is also uneven as holders of real and monetary capital recover a large portion of the profits in emerging countries. This type of trade can lead to the emergence of external diseconomies (such as congested sea lanes, rising energy costs, and pollution).

At the same time, a new geography of economies of scale is set up. It can appear on two levels: transitorily at the European level and gradually at the Asian level. The activities to increasing returns have been developed in the European "pentagon" (London, Paris, Milan, Berlin, and Hamburg). The rest of the European Union constitutes a productive space of second choice, a lesser level of development where incomes and skilled employment are lower. The eastern European countries constitute a space of delocalization of activities for firms in search of less expensive skilled labor, with more advantageous social and fiscal conditions of production. This situation can be only transitory because the eastern European countries will quickly offer fewer competitive advantages than the Asian countries. The Asian markets of production and consumption are the best examples of the exploitation of remote economies of scale. A change in the geography of industrial specialization is under way.

—*The European Union in the current context of globalization.* At the international level, the EU is trying to strengthen its competitiveness by raising its

Figure 21-1. *The Evolution of Export Products by Geographic Area,*
1990 and 2002

Percentage of world total

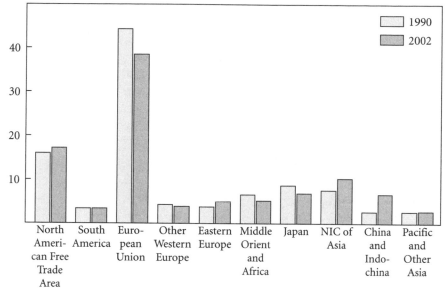

Source: Database Chelem, Cepii.

performance in research, development, and quality of work. While still the larg-est trading region in the world, the EU can expect to see its relative position eroded in world exports (see figure 21-1).

The European Union seeks to promote a model of the rules and policies negotiated at the multilateral level around market forces. The EU strategy of sustainable development attempts to reconcile economic growth, social cohe-sion, and environmental protection. Its most recent free trade agreements relate to emergent or developing zones (of Latin America, the Mediterranean, and eastern Europe). Latin America, and in particular Mercosur, represents a commercial stake that NAFTA and the EU are well aware of. The progressive opening of the markets in Latin America can generate an expansion of com-mercial exchanges and an intensification of direct foreign investment. In recent years the EU became the principal partner of Mercosur for foreign trade and the establishments of foreign subsidiary companies and is thus inclined to con-tinue its cooperation with this imperfect customs union. In the absence of a similar agreement with the EU, a free trade area of the Americas would lead to a significant decline in European exports (around 20 percent) in this region, particularly at the sectoral level.[11] Beyond its borders, the EU is trying to promote cooperation and regional and subregional integration, all of which are preconditions for political stability, economic development, and the reduction of poverty and social divisions.

The enlargement of the European Union has changed the geopolitical context in Europe. A population of more than 450 million and a GDP of approximately 10,000 billion euros give it considerable political, geographic, and economic weight. The zone of political and institutional influence of the European Union has increased. On an economic level, the allocation of resources (factors of production, the production and exchange of goods and services) has changed substantially. And beyond the borders, enlargement affects the EU's political, economic, and social relations with other parts of the world, including in its area of natural exchanges with neighboring countries. However, this enlargement has increased the economic and social disparities within the European Union. How has the European integration process influenced the rest of the world?

Mercosur, an Example of Regional Integration along the EU Path

Regional groups such as Mercosur, WAEMU, and SADC (the Southern African Development Community) seem to have been modeled after the institutional and legal institutions of Europe. In fact, the similarities are very basic, with little deepening of economic interdependence. Moreover, the economic process of integration is very specific, since it relates to developing economies with a strong tradition of protectionism. Difficulties in the first stage of integration (involving the free movement of products) are reinforced by the heterogeneity or incompatibility of member states' exchange rate regimes.

The development of regionalism during the contemporary period seems guided by the two models of the EU and NAFTA. The EMU, the last stage of European regional economic integration, requires a federal framework of operation to be fully effective. NAFTA seems to provide a minimalist process of integration rather close in spirit to the bilateral agreements of the nineteenth century: it preceded multilateralism, which was brought about through the WTO. In other words, NAFTA is the vector for the globalization of activities. The creation of regional integration zones inspired by this model will fulfill one objective of exchanges by removing the tariff and nontariff obstacles to trade; this logic of free trade, which is also that of the WTO, must lead to an open economic space. The countries of Mercosur and Caricom, which seem to want to build a process of economic integration similar to the European Community, share a strong conflict between the regional and the global, which is embodied in the American hemispheric zone of free trade. Compared to the European Community,

Mercosur presents both convergences (relatively low) and differences (mostly basic). It is an experiment strongly influenced by European integration.

Mercosur was created on March 26, 1991. The first article of the Treaty of Asunción provides that the new unit will rest on freedom of movement of goods, on a common external tariff, and on the adoption of a common market policy with respect to third countries. The coordination of macroeconomic and sectoral policies is also considered. The transitional period was accelerated so that the opening of the interior market occurred on January 1, 1995. In December 1994, with the conference of Ouro Preto, Mercosur acquired its current fundamental features with characteristics resembling those of the EU.

Institutional Convergence: Democratic Principles and the Rule of Unanimity

Mercosur member states have opted for an intergovernmental model, common positions therefore remaining dependent on the willingness of each nation. Because of their constitutions, Brazil and Uruguay cannot participate in supranational bodies, unlike Paraguay and Argentina, which reformed their constitutions in this respect in 1992 and 1994 respectively. From a legal point of view, Mercosur operates according to the classical rules of international law. Comparisons with the creation and legal construction of the EEC and the EU can only be approximated.[12] Decisions are reached by consensus and in the presence of all member states. The institutions of Mercosur are similar to those of the EU but do not have any supranational role, and there is no equivalent of the ECJ. The clearest institutional deficiency is undoubtedly the absence of a mechanism for the resolution of conflicts among member states. Without institutions with specific prerogatives or controlled community legislation, and with the presence of a unanimity rule, the integration process cannot deepen.

In the construction of Mercosur, member states play a dual and contradictory role. They install the institutional mechanisms and establish their contours. But decisions by the trade commission can be vetoed by any of the governments. Mercosur's Economic and Social Forum, which is composed of the representatives of consumers, civil society, and trade unions, can only make recommendations in an advisory capacity. In addition, in the liberal architecture of Mercosur, public intervention is excluded, contrary to the experiment of the European Community. Unlike the EU, Mercosur does not have a budget. What follows is a lack of assistance for restructuring activities and a high cost of specialization at the expense of private economic agents. The absence of devices that can attenuate the inequalities of distribution allows variations in development between rich and poor areas. Only the market imposes order on economic adjustments within the customs union. However, trade union organizations of member states support this regional integration project, calling for simple adjustments and effective participation. They want to work for a social Mercosur and demand higher wages, recognition of social rights, and freedom of movement for workers. Resistance to this project is evident in some agricultural sectors in Brazil and Paraguay.

Mercosur has made progress on cooperation at other levels. In spite of a thorough administrative centralization, provincial governors and even city mayors have concluded official agreements with their counterparts in other member states that are difficult to characterize according to traditional public international law.[13] Their economic impact is low, but progress has been made in some areas, such as judicial cooperation. The resulting changes also affect the "small countries" of Mercosur: Paraguay and Uruguay were forced to abandon their traditional strategy of balance between the two regional giants, Argentina and Brazil. After a coup attempt failed to topple General Oviedo in Paraguay in April 1996, Mercosur adopted a democratic clause envisaging the suspension of a member whose government ignored the rule of law. In this case, Argentina and Brazil, supported by the United States, openly interfered in the internal affairs of Paraguay and contributed to the failure of the operation. The prevention of such interference is an appropriate political role for an intergovernmental organization such as Mercosur.

Forced to work with the unanimity rule, the intergovernmental organization can only be a hindrance to the deepening of economic integration: the European experience demonstrates that unambiguously. Overall, monetary union may be desirable to facilitate the deepening of trade integration, but the exchange rate regimes of Brazil (flexible anchoring of the real to the dollar) and of Argentina (with a currency board), accompanied by a strong debt in dollars among Argentinian firms, did not facilitate the installation of such a union. With the Argentinian crisis in 2000 (that led to the abandonment of the currency board and the "pesification" of the economy), Mercosur has been seriously threatened with disintegration. The existence of productive structures gradually converging in a "blue banana" (that is to say, a more economically developed region) may, however, eventually facilitate the transition to monetary union. It must then establish a mechanism for dealing with asymmetric shocks. There are also factors of economic divergence within Mercosur that are likely to hinder the deepening of the integration process.

Important Macroeconomic Factors of Divergence

General factors of divergence can be highlighted in the current experiment of Mercosur. This is a relatively narrow market insofar as, on the one hand, it represents an insufficient outlet for Brazilian production, the principal regional economic power, and on the other hand, its development is blocked by relatively significant internal and external protection. Mercosur is also characterized by the Brazilian paradox: with a standard of living half that of Argentina, Brazil has twice the productive capacity of its Argentinian neighbor. Last, the existence of the American project of a hemispheric zone of free trade is likely to represent an alternative to the internal difficulties of Mercosur integration despite the political hostility of Brazil.

In summary, we can consider two main factors of economic divergence: the first is an aversion to relations with the outside world that leads to a low degree of openness to international trade and strong national protectionism; the second is the relatively small size of the Mercosur market, which makes the hemispheric project of a free trade zone attractive, a phenomenon that is likely to slow the deepening of regional integration.

ECONOMIES MARKED BY AN AVERSION TO TRADE. The countries of Mercosur are characterized by a low level of opening to international exchange and by a high degree of intra- and extra-community protection. The two main countries of Mercosur, Argentina and Brazil, are relatively closed to international exchange. Mercosur's protectionism toward third countries and between member states is significant. Several tariff and nontariff measures intervene to regulate trade. First, in relation to third countries, it may be noted that since January 1, 1995, a common external tariff has been in effect. It was adopted gradually, respecting exceptions for each country's "sensitive" products. Those exceptions, initially scheduled to expire in July 2001, were extended to December 31, 2002. With regard to intra-zone relations, Mercosur is an imperfect internal market. Some nontariff trade barriers affect the dynamism of trade (antidumping sanctions, intra-Mercosur export subsidies, safety and environmental protection standards, sanitary and phyto-sanitary requirements) even if there is a slow process of harmonization.

MERCOSUR: A NARROW INTERNAL MARKET. The increase in the number of exchanges within Mercosur is subordinated to intra-zone trade to prevent imbalances and the unilateral adoption of protection measures. As during the European phase of the customs union, during which intra-community exchanges increased, the (incomplete) liberalization of intra-Mercosur trade, which reduced customs tariffs and increased cross-country investments, generated a very strong increase in exchanges between the member states. All export sectors have benefited from these tariff advantages, especially agriculture. But intra-zone commercial relations respond badly to foreign exchange rate crises, which produce considerable competitive shocks on economies already little adapted to international opening. Over the period 1996–99, exports among member states dropped by almost 32 percent because of the Brazilian and Asian crises. The monetary difficulties of Argentina led to a reduction in the share of intra-Mercosur trade, which reached a little more than 10 percent of total trade within the zone in 2001 (this share reached 25 percent in 1998).[14]

Despite the growth in intra-zone exchanges, free movement is still not completely in place: approximately 80 percent of the exchanged goods are part of Mercosur internal free trade and identical customs tariffs with respect to third countries. The existence of an Argentinian dollar standard until December 2001 and the devaluation of the Brazilian real raised questions about the construction of the Mercosur monetary system.

Mercosur will not be able to continue its commercial integration without a mechanism for foreign exchange rate stabilization. From this point of view, Europe's experience with the creation of the European Monetary System (EMS) following the failure of the "currency snake" in the 1970s is instructive. The EMS has made it possible to safeguard European commercial integration in spite of some distortions.

MERCOSUR MEMBERSHIP IN THE NAFTA EXCHANGE ZONE? Although Chile and Bolivia were initially not part of Mercosur, they signed a framework agreement with Mercosur in January 1995 and December 1996 respectively. It included a progressive liberalization of trade, the granting of tariff preferences, and investment regulations. In addition, Mercosur signed a framework agreement with the European Union in December 1995. These two areas are determined to cooperate formally, which concerns the United States. The observation that trade within Mercosur has progressed much faster than trade with the rest of the world has led to criticism by the United States and the World Bank. A. Yeats has pointed out important deviations from trading rules, or noncompliance with the rules of the World Trade Organization.[15] Indeed, the intra-Mercosur exchanges do not exploit the comparative advantages of countries within the zone (in agricultural and food products, textiles, wood and paper, the iron and steel industry) but seem to exploit comparative disadvantages behind a shelter of protectionist barriers (for the mechanical engineering industries, the transport sector, electric and electronic activities, and others). The opposition of the United States is based on political rather than commercial considerations. It had wanted to establish a hemispheric free trade zone before 2005, the deadline for the creation of a Free Trade Area of the Americas (FTAA). Today this project is still not in place. The United States has not abandoned it, but has had difficulty gaining approval by countries in South America (Brazil, Venezuela, and Bolivia, among others), which fear negative social consequences. This project would involve the elimination of tariffs protecting the productive sectors of Latin America. Brazil, whose industry is young and still fragile, has a large domestic market. Integration with the FTAA would likely lead to competition that could not be supported by vast sectors of the national economy. Brazilian decisionmakers seem interested in a regional unit that is relatively closed in the short run, such as Mercosur. Thus their national interests would be preserved better in Mercosur, where the weight of their economy (in terms of GDP) accounts for approximately 70 percent of the bloc, whereas in the FTAA it would not exceed 10 percent. However, in spite of the strong progress in establishing intra-zone commercial trade, Mercosur represents a small share of trade in Brazil. This appears to be a new manifestation of the Brazilian paradox: although posing as its biggest defender, Brazil is the country least dependent on Mercosur!

A traditional ally of the United States since the middle of the nineteenth century, Brazil expresses a desire for economic independence that is little appreciated by the United States, which has proposed to Argentina the exceptional status of ally outside NATO. The negative reactions of Brazil and Chile, with which Argentina has a border dispute in the Andes, show that Mercosur is politically a fragile regional unit. Furthermore, the weakness of interstate institutions is not likely to neutralize destabilization attempts. Finally, the commercial position of the United States in Mercosur reveals increasingly open competition between the United States and the EU. The EU is more strongly established in the Mercosur marketplace, while the opposite is true for direct investment. Indeed, Latin America (and Brazil in particular) is a privileged site for the North American capital. Taking into account the interregional cooperative projects of the EU and NAFTA, it is possible to envision a large single market comprising the FTAA and the EU. Such a result would lead to the establishment of the American model of regional integration (a free trade zone) that is much less constraining than the European model. J. Pelkmans says that the stability of regional integration will lie in the capacity to establish three dynamic bases with the Community: a reinforcement of the Community's capacities; a deepening of the level of integration; and an increase in the number of regional participants.[16] The European Community has always been devoted to the pursuit of one or two of these objectives but never all three simultaneously. It is possible that simultaneous action in the three directions exceeds the capacity of any regional integration agreement.

In the case of Mercosur, the question of the reinforcement of Community capacities is not now on the table because such a regional unit would require intergovernmental agreement. The construction of a customs union raises many difficulties, in particular the suppression of protection for significant activities and the frightening anticommercial effects resulting from unstable foreign exchange rates. In the short term, a stabilization mechanism for the exchange rate seems indispensable to the pursuit of the Mercosur experience. Otherwise, the hemispheric project of a free trade zone could constitute a credible alternative with the help of safeguard clauses provided by the dominant economic

Table 21-1. *Features of the Main Current Experiments
in Regional Economic Integration*

Areas of regional integration	Degree of economic ntegration planned	Economic integration achieved	Consolidation of integration by a supra-national court (tribunal or court of justice)	Dilution of the area of globalization according to WTO rules
Europe				
European Union	Economic and monetary union	Partial	Yes	Yes
EFTA	Free trade area	Yes	No	Yes
CIS	None	Yes	No	...
Africa				
UAM	Customs union	No	No	Yes
Waemu	Economic and monetary union	No	No	Yes
SADC	Free trade area	Yes	No	Yes
Americas				
NAFTA	Free trade area	Yes	No	Yes
Mercosur	Customs union	Partial	No	Yes
Caricom	Free trade area	Yes	No	Yes
Asia				
ASEAN	Free trade area	Yes	No	Yes

Source: Author.

power (the United States). Recent developments seem to favor such a scenario. Indeed, the Declaration of Cuzco on December 8, 2004, envisaged the progressive integration of Mercosur and the Andean Community in a political and economic union of all of South America into a "South American Community of Nations" (SACN). Chile, Guyana, and Suriname would join. On December 17, 2004, three new members were incorporated into Mercosur: Ecuador, Colombia, and Venezuela. Panama, Mexico, Bolivia, and Ecuador also announced their intention to integrate fully into Mercosur. It seems that, from now on, expansion will prevail over integration (as it does in the EU today) and create better prospects for an FTAA, which proposes an elementary level of integration. These successive expansions of the various communities would seem likely to make the economic project more of a political project.

Table 21-1 indicates that the objectives of economic integration are more frequently reached when the level of integration is elementary. From the moment the integration process deepens, the objectives of integration are partially obtained, as they have been for the European Union. Only the EU has sufficient capacity (through the ECJ) to create true community legislation and guarantee the performance and continuation of the zone of integration. Last, insofar as the zones of economic integration were conceived (and accepted) as a transition toward a future of generalized free trade, the globalization of activities in compliance with the rules of the WTO is the ultimate objective. For the member states of the regional zones of integration, which are unequally vulnerable to generalized free trade, that implies the maintenance of sufficient national prerogatives in setting economic policy.

Notes

1. J. Viner, *The Customs Union Issue* (London: Stevens and Sons, 1950).

2. P. R. Krugman, "Lessons from Massachusetts for EMU," in *Adjustment and Growth in the European Economic Union*, edited by F. Torres and F. Giavazzi (Cambridge University Press, 1993).

3. The founding contributions were made by R. A. Mundell, "A Theory of Optimum Currency Areas," *American Economic Review* 51 (1961): 657–65; R. I. McKinnon, "Optimum Currency Areas," *American Economic Review* 53 (1963): 717–25; C. Kindleberger, "International Public Goods without International Government," *American Economic Review* 76 (1986): 1–13; P. Kenen, "The Theory of Optimal Currency Areas: An Eclectic View," in *Monetary Problems of the International Economy*, edited by R. A. Mundell and A. K. Swoboda (University of Chicago Press, 1969), pp. 41–60.

4. Krugman, "Lessons from Massachusetts."

5. L. Fontagné and others, "Intra-industry Trade and the Single Market: Quality Matters," CEPR Discussion Paper 1959 (1998).

6. P. A. Samuelson, "Where Ricardo and Mill Rebut and Confirm Arguments of Mainstream Economist Supporting Globalization," *Journal of Economic Perspectives* 18, no. 3 (Summer 2004): 135–46.

7. Ibid.

8. J. Bhagwati, *Lectures on International Trade* (Oxford University Press, 2003).

9. Ibid.

10. H. Bourguinat, "Le libre-échange: un paradigme en situation d'inconfort," *Revue d'Economie politique* 5 (2005): 531–43.

11. H. Bchir and others, "Mercosur: Free Trade Area with the EU or with the Americas? Some Lessons from the Model MIRAGE," *Economie internationale* 3 (2003): 77–108.

12. R. Seitenfus, "Acquis et dilemmes du Mercosur," *Cahiers des Amériques latines* 27 (1998): 100–13.

13. Seitenfus, "Aquis et dilemmes."

14. P. Paiva and R. Gazel, "Mercosur: Past, Present, and Future," *Nova Economia* 13, no. 2 (2003): 115–36.

15. A. Yeats, "Does Mercosur's Trade Performance Raise Concerns about the Effects of Regional Trade Arrangements?" *World Bank Economic Review* 12, no. 1 (1998): 1–28.

16. J. Pelkmans, *Comparando las integraciones economicas: prerequisitos, opciones e implicaciones*, Centro de Formacion para la Integracion Regional (Montevideo: CEFIR, 1993).

LAURA C. FERREIRA-PEREIRA

22

Human Rights, Peace, and Democracy: Is "Model Power Europe" a Contradiction in Terms?

The principles of human rights, peace, and democracy have been deeply embedded in the European integration experiment since its inception. The triad reflects the intrinsic core values of the European project's ontology and teleology. As the process of integration crystallized, the respect for human rights as well as the promotion of democracy and peace became concrete goals guiding the European Union's foreign policy actions and tools. More recently, since European reunification, with the return of the central and eastern European states to the coveted ideational fold of liberal democracy, this trend was consolidated with the European Union's move from a continental to a global foreign policy agenda and its endeavors to assert itself as a global peace-builder and norm-setter.

The quest for peace and the pursuit of democracy and respect for human rights, among other coveted values, have justified the depiction of the EU as a "force for good" in line with the perspective of a "normative power Europe" (NPE).[1] A similar approach was taken by the proponents of an "ethical power Europe."[2] Such contemporary designations, inspired in the tradition of the conception of a "civilian power Europe" (CPE) forged by François Duchene in the 1970s, have fueled a topical academic debate between those holding a realist view and those advocating a more idealist-liberal understanding of the role of the EU in contemporary international relations.[3]

Moreover, the development of the Common Foreign and Security Policy (CFSP), which in 1999 came to incorporate the European Security and Defense Policy (ESDP), led to contrasting interpretations of the emergence of a "military power Europe" (MPE), similar to that envisaged by Hedley Bull in 1982.[4] Some saw evidence of the militarization of the EU in the capacity-building efforts based on the Helsinki Headline Goal (HHG) established in 1999 and the subsequent launching of ESDP operations in various parts of the world.

This was a development with the potential to undermine the Union's normative exceptionality.[5]

This academic debate largely echoes the diverging national perspectives of the EU member states regarding the role of the Union in the world and, ultimately, the teleological objective of the European venture. Such differing views surfaced in October 2007 with renewed vigor under the political impetus of French president Nicolas Sarkozy toward a greater European military integration conducive to the emergence of a genuine "Europe of defense." In the context of an anticipatory announcement about the future priorities of the EU's French Presidency (July–December 2008), Sarkozy declared that his country intended to seize its presidential term in office to boost the ESDP to the point where the Union would gain more military autonomy.[6]

The emphasis placed by Sarkozy on an enhanced military élan for the ESDP matching a vision of an MPE was opposed by the British foreign secretary, David Miliband, in his celebrated speech at the College of Europe in November 2007. In what was described as "the first great political speech on Europe at a crucial moment for Europe,"[7] Miliband countered Sarkozy's push for greater military integration with the statement that the EU "is not going to become a superstate. But neither is it destined to become a superpower."[8] Hinting at a 2030 time horizon, the vehemence and recurrence with which Miliband underlined this idea backed up the reading that the EU is still far from becoming a state actor endowed with significant military power.[9]

The head of British diplomacy depicted the EU as a "model power" derived from a "role model that others follow."[10] Drawing on this and taking into consideration the increasing identification of the EU as a model, a key truism in the discourse of the EU's global role, this chapter raises the theoretical and empirical question of a "model power Europe" (MoPE). This means that it engages in a polyphonic debate on the international role and identity of the Union. In this chapter, the concepts of *model* and *modeling* are used in accordance with the classical and mainstream work of the renowned psychologist Albert Bandura. In particular, this chapter uses his social learning theory, which introduced the social learning paradigm to the domain of psychology.[11] This application of Bandura's theoretical framework to critically assess the power of influence exerted by the EU is based on the assumption that it can provide a measure of explanatory power that has never been applied to EU studies or to the Union's foreign policy.

The learning process framework offers a good way to describe the idiosyncratic interplay between the Union and other actors (states and organizations alike) and how the former is both perceived by and affects the latter. It has the potential to help reconceptualize the manner in which the EU can exert influence and be a role model in the world both as a peace-builder and as a promoter of well-established, ethically informed principles. As was noted, the task of exporting norms viewed as universally valid and beneficial is a daunting one because of the limited demand among major players such as China and Russia.[12] The concept of MoPE can therefore open new avenues of reflection on how the EU can improve its ability to disseminate its principles and values in the world and thereby enhance its global power. The effective modeling of third states' behavior has the potential to mitigate the difficulties of sharing a normative agenda with key international actors in the areas of human rights and democracy. Indeed, reflection on and appraisal of the Union's power of modeling will facilitate understanding of its future successes and failures in diffusing norms and values or in enhancing its normative appeal in different regions of the world.

We will not invoke here all the theoretical complexity of Bandura's social learning paradigm, but rather a set of major tenets or core notions considered relevant to the main argument developed in this chapter. This means that we will concentrate on the concept of *model* and *modeling*. Social learning theory certainly does not explain all the intricacies and nuances related to the assertion of the EU's role, identity, and influence on the international scene. However, it is a sound analytical tool that can help explain the power of influence that the EU exerts in the contemporary international system.

The Concepts of "Model" and "Modeling": A Review of Bandura's Social Learning Theory

> From the outside it looks like a loose *"European model"* exists, both as a way of organizing our societies and in approaching international affairs. Others around the world are *paying close attention*. The African Union, Mercosur, Asean—these are all examples of strengthening regional regimes. They are explicitly taking their inspiration from the EU experience. There can be no simple export of whatever we think the *European model* is, but the EU is seen as a source of inspiration. And of course, *imitation* and adaptation are easier than invention.[13]

Although the affirmation that the "EU is a model" has become a widely repeated truism cherished by political leaders, diplomats, and Eurocrats, as the passage quoted above illustrates, it is possible to identify objectively characteristics typical of a model in the nature of the EU. Here I do this in light of Albert Bandura's paradigm of social learning, which posits that the learning process is based on imitation through the observation of a given model's behavior. The learning process or modeling that follows from the observation of the model's pattern of behavior is consolidated when the observer readily discerns the positive consequences of the modeled behavior.

Social learning theory points out three aspects of a model that are key to the present discussion and to which we will return later in connection with the European Union's external action. The first feature typical of a model is *salience,* which can be equated with distinctiveness or uniqueness. For Bandura, the more distinctive the characteristics of a given model, the higher the likelihood that the model will draw the attention of others and eventually generate modeled behaviors. The second aspect is *prevalence,* which relates to the endurance of the model over time and generates attention by observers. The third characteristic aspect relates to the *power of attraction* of the model, the ability of the model to appeal to and attract followers.[14]

All of these aspects are critical in defining a model, and consequently in triggering the so-called cognitive modeling that shows when a learning process takes place. According to Bandura, there is no learning process without attention, which means that the capacity to attract attention and sustain it over a period of time is central to Bandura's conceptualization of both the model and modeling. Attention on the part of the observer is therefore the starting point of any modeling dynamic. This is so since a model can simply be ignored by the observer. Moreover, the mere exposure of an observer to a modeled behavior is not enough for the observer to learn a rule or behavior. Hence Bandura insists that modelling should not be squarely equated with automatic behavioral imitation. Rather, it suggests a cognitive imitation involving the reproduction of a behavioral repertoire that is accompanied by the internalization of a rule or a discourse that can be generalized and used in multiple applications.

In light of this social learning theory, the efficacy of the modeling process is largely dependent on motivational processes that stand between the initial observation of a specific behavior and its motor reproduction (that is, imitation). These processes involve direct reinforcement or, as originally designated by Bandura, "vicarious reinforcement." Direct reinforcement occurs when a modeled or replicated behavior receives an immediate reward that can take a material or verbal form. Such prompt reinforcement of the modeling stimuli makes the observer inclined to continue to perform imitative responses for their inherent reward value.[15] As Bandura stressed, the "observation of a model performing responses for which he is positively reinforced may be expected to produce disinhibition, and positive incentive learning in the observer, thus facilitating the occurrence of imitative behavior."[16] From this it follows that the more immediate external reinforcement, the stronger the likelihood of the behavior exhibited by a model's being replicated or imitated by the observer. When an individual is punished for a certain modeled behavior the likelihood increases that the individual will stop imitating the behavior. Bandura has also demonstrated that "vicarious reinforcement" increases the likelihood that an individual will reproduce a given behavior. In other words, the observation of others being reinforced with approval for matching the model's behavior increases the likelihood of an imitative response by the observer for its intrinsic reward value. Therefore, attention and modeling stimuli are significantly conditioned by the perceived functional value inherent in the imitative behavior for the readily discernible positive consequences resulting from it.

Bandura has established that an individual can learn vicariously through "observing the behavior of others and its response consequences without the observer's performing any overt responses himself or receiving any direct reinforcement during the acquisition" of a certain behavior.[17] The modeling dynamic is decisive for the acquisition of a certain behavioral pattern, while the practice, through continued imitation, accompanied by frequent reinforcement is crucial for reproducing motor responses by one model.[18]

Within the social learning framework, Bandura underscored the importance of incentives that draw the observer's attention toward a given a pattern of behavior or activity while hinting at the likely benefits resulting from the duplication of the model's actions. Anticipated consequences play an "influential role. . . in regulating imitative behavior."[19] Punishment tends to redirect the observer's attention to an alternative model, different from the one that was being "wrongly" imitated, and to cause a change in behavior. It has the potential to foster a process of counter-modeling or "counter-conditioning," as Bandura called it.[20] The anticipation of attractive incentives and punishment may increase the likelihood of response duplication; and the nexus of response and consequences, either to the model or to the observer, may influence the performance of imitatively learned responses.[21]

Other factors such as similarity (notably, cultural) between the observer and the model, as well as the model's perceived prestige and competence, facilitate the observation, attention processes, and the subsequent learning dynamics. Finally, if the model's responses are highly consistent and sufficiently distinctive, this ultimately ensures observation and imitative learning.[22]

The European Union on the International Scene: A Model for Emulation and a Modeling Agent

It is by now recognized that the EU has been increasingly emerging as a model in the eyes of other international actors, states, and organizations in distinct situations. Since the mid-1990s, academic controversy has grown about not only the universal validity and appropriateness of that model, but also its consistency and coherence as mirrored in the Union's collective external action. However, few studies, if any, have endeavored to unpack the conception of "model" as applied to the Union's international performance and to assess the imitative learning process resulting from the continued exposure of third states to the Union's modeling behavior.

Based on the application of the learning theory framework to the EU's international role, it can be asserted objectively that the Union is a model. This is so, first, for the salience founded on differentiated characteristics that it exhibits. This stems from the politico-institutional exceptionality of the Union, which is neither a state nor a typical international organization, but rather a "coagulating hybrid."[23] It encompasses what Manners called the EU's "normative difference," which ascribes to it a normative appeal.[24] Second, the EU can be considered a model for emulation because of its endurance as a peace and economic project for more than fifty years. Its success was achieved by means of a reiterated modus vivendi and modus faciendi that created conditions for the continued existence of a democratic norm, the constant promotion of a more equitable distribution of wealth, and the sustained avoidance of the use of military force to resolve interstate conflicts.

The fact that the Union came to present itself as both a prosperous regional community and a powerful international economic actor helps explain its power of attraction, another typical feature of a model. Moreover, the magnetic force exerted by the EU as a peace project resulted from the power of both ideas and deeds, which culminated in the absence of war in western Europe for more than a half century. The Union's power of attraction is reflected in the successive enlargement rounds completed from 1973 to 2007 and, at present, in the number of candidate countries (Turkey, Croatia, the former Yugoslav Republic of Macedonia) and potential candidate states (Albania, Bosnia-Herzegovina, Montenegro, Serbia, and Kosovo) that are queuing up for admission to the EU. This is not to mention those that have been forced to abandon their ambition to join the club of prosperous Western democracies primarily because of the geographic *diktat* (for example, Morocco and Cape Verde).

As the consolidation of the European experiment exposed other actors to the multiple activities of the Union, the EU's behavioral repertoire attracted their attention and eventually became a source of a (vicarious or imitative) learning process. Third countries incrementally duplicated the repertoire, having witnessed its positive consequences both for the founding countries of the European Community and for the states formally seeking accession. The observation of the model being reinforced thus constitutes "positive incentive learning" for other countries. Furthermore, it is important to note that the anticipated (positive) consequences associated with the prospect of membership played a critical role in stimulating a modeling dynamic—that is, an imitative behavior conducive to the full acceptance of the *acquis communautaire*. The *acquis*, among other regulatory items, incorporated a normative or ethical agenda embedded in the defense of democracy, the rule of law, and respect for human rights that all states willing to join the European club were supposed to adopt unconditionally.

Indeed, the disposition of other states to engage in imitative behavior has traditionally been reinforced through a broad spectrum of expedients ranging from economic and trade incentives to (formal and informal) diplomatic praise. The establishment of free trade agreements, Association Agreements, and the newly conceived Stabilization and Association Agreements are examples of direct (positive) reinforcement for their perceived inherent reward value to the recipient countries. The same can be said about granting a country "candidate" and "potential candidate" status.

The modeling dynamic fostered by the EU, however, has not confined itself to the enlargement policy. It has transcended that to cover a multilevel relationship and partnership with various regions of the world. The fact that provisions regarding respect for human rights and democratic principles have acquired substantial weight in the conditionality engineering designed by Brussels (in the framework of development policy and bilateral and multilateral trade agreements) is symptomatic of the transverse nature of the modeling stimuli engendered by the Union in its international relations. The same can be said about coercive features involving sanctions and embargoes through which the Union has on various occasions punished states that failed to incorporate into their own repertoire the European principled way to behave.

The application of "sticks" to punish those exhibiting an "imitative deficit" (those failing to produce imitative behavior) and of "carrots" to reward those disposed to perform imitative behavior, on the basis of a vast array of economic and bureaucratic instruments, has led some to depict the Union as a sui generis empire. Jan Zielonka noted that the Union, acting as an imperial collective entity, "tries to make other actors accept its norms and standards by applying economic incentives and punishments."[25] On the other side of the coin, the recognized success and competence exhibited by the Union, particularly in economics, finance, and trade, which have traditionally enabled it to control and distribute both rewarding and punishing resources, provide an important basis of attraction.

According to this line of reasoning, the Union can be considered a model for "what it is" *tout court*. Yet it can only cause the reproduction of behavior among third actors on the basis of "what it does" and achieves in different modeling situations. And this is seen in terms of positive consequences that are closely observed by third parties (that is, states and organizations). In other words, it can only encourage modeled behavior through its own actions and activities, which eventually reinforce other actors who are exposed to the attractive European model. As an example, other countries' identification with the value system of the Union can only take place when the normative rhetoric forged in Brussels results in actions whose effects are discerned as being intrinsically positive. More generally speaking, it is only by showing others that the European standards and norms are practical and effective and that they can bring about tangible benefits that the EU is then able to act as a modeling agent and exert influence on the international scene.

To be sure, the Union's modeling dynamic underlying its efforts to be an example of the appropriate way to behave in different functional fields is both globally oriented and intentional. There is consensus that by promoting democracy, human rights, and sustainable peace and development as universal values in the wider world, the EU shapes its milieu and consequently reduces the likelihood of external shocks.[26] Furthermore, the modeling stimuli generated by the Union have been mainly a function of economic power. This is so to the extent that the EU's economic leverage enables it to control and selectively distribute a vast array of incentives and punishments (diplomatic, legal and administrative, and economic) as part of diverse strategies designed to produce behavioral change. In the framework of the accession process, besides economic incentives, the possibility for third states to gain access to the Union's decisionmaking process has also played an important role.

"Model Power Europe": A Conceptual Tool to Assess the European Union's Influence in the World

The concepts of model and modeling offered by Bandura's social learning paradigm have inspired a new assessment of the type of power the Union displays in its interaction with other actors: model power Europe (MoPE). This conception should not be regarded as a substitute for those already offered in the literature, notably, CPE, NPE, and EPE, which coexist and also overlap. It rather points to an additional prism through which it is possible to further understand the Union's power projection and, subsequently, the growing influence that it exercises in various parts of the world. The reasons for this are fourfold.

To begin with, unlike the notion of NPE, the concept of MoPE embraces both civilian and military power, as well as economic power. As such, it reflects the evolution that has taken place since the formal launching of ESDP in 1999. It further matches the self-perception of the EU's proactive responsibility as a global crisis peace-builder and democracy-promoter, as underlined by Miliband in his speech at the College of Europe: The EU "must be able to deploy soft and hard power to promote democracy and tackle conflict beyond its borders."[27] In the realm of the ESDP, the EU has been acquiring a broad spectrum of civilian and military capacities that have been utilized in the context of collective missions directed at the promotion of democracy, rule of law, and respect for human rights. Some have argued that the new military dimension strengthened the Union's ability to enforce respect for the democratic credo and, ultimately, move it to pursue a more ambitious policy of democratic enforcement.[28] The Union's operational capabilities also have a sustainable peace rationale since they are aimed at promoting peacekeeping, conflict prevention, and the strengthening of international security.[29] While adding a military dimension to its traditional civilian ethos, the EU has been viewed by some authors as conducting its external strategy in a "smart" manner. Accordingly, it can be said that underlying the notion of MoPE is the view of the EU as a "smart power."[30]

Second, the concept of MoPE helps transcend the discussion of the limits of the concept of NPE, which have been manifest in economic and trade relations with both Russia and China. It also goes beyond the discussion about the failures of the CPE in the Balkans and moves away from the dilemma over ethical choices confronting the EU when resorting to its broad range of civilian or military capabilities. Indeed, the conception of MoPE is not concerned with the deontological debate centered on ethics, or with the dichotomy CPE/NPE versus MPE. Nevertheless, the concept of MoPE recognizes not only the significance of ethical considerations as intrinsic to the Union's identity, but also the fact that, featuring itself as a model, the EU tends to act in accordance with a set of ethically informed principles, of which it is a long-standing repository.[31]

Third, the MoPE approach encourages one to look at the role played by individual major member states in the assertion of the Union as a consistent model to be imitated. More often than not, the postures adopted by some key states on the basis of national preferences and to safeguard specific interests undermine the EU's modeling stimuli and dynamics. As an example, the lack of consistency and coherence regarding human rights policy sends mixed signals to other actors. This can eventually interfere with third states' behavioral changes through the imitative learning process.

Finally, and above all, the notion of MoPE centers on the Union's exercise of influence through its behavior or action in modeling situations across functional fields. This conceptual tool shares with the notion of EPE an analytical shift from what the EU *is* to what the EU *does*[32] in order not only to move third countries to play by its rules and establish global standards, but also to secure its own success, competence, and leadership on the international scene.[33] The success of the model's behavior (and the consequences this entails) is central since it tends to determine the degree to which a pattern of behavior will be reproduced by observers.

Conclusion

This chapter advances a conceptual approach that encourages one to think of the EU as a "model power" when considering its behavioral impact on the contemporary international scene. The concept of model power Europe is articulated in light of Bandura's notions of "model" and "modeling," and sheds further light on the EU's global power while opening up new avenues for reflection on how the Union can improve its tangible contribution to international peace and security.

According to the MoPE approach, it is not enough for the EU to espouse the values of peace, democracy, and respect for human rights and to promote them in world politics. It needs to *be* a "model power" that others emulate in a consistent way, at the international level. This is of enormous relevance since it is through what the Union does, especially through the perception of the positive consequences that follow from its behavior and from its interaction with other actors, that the EU is able to stimulate observation and imitative learning. The result will be the reproduction of its principled pattern of behavior, with all this implies for shaping the international milieu in which it operates. This reading of the EU's role as a global actor informed by the MoPE concept does not overlook the fact that the modeling stimuli are intentionally engendered by the EU to secure and promote European interests, although they can ultimately contribute to a "better world." Incidentally, the title chosen for the 2003 European Security Strategy, "A Secure Europe in a Better World," seems to convey this prioritization of concerns.

Much of the success that the EU can achieve in spreading peace, democracy, and human rights in the context of its international relationships, notably within the CFSP/ESDP realm, depends on its ability to stimulate imitative or vicarious learning. In other words, the power of influence exercised by the EU derives not purely from its being a model per se, but particularly from its ability to capture others' attention and foster behavioral changes according to its own standards, rules, principles, and values. For this power to be preserved the EU needs to invest time and energy in improving at least four situations.

First, it should keep up its *differentia specifica* when compared to other actors. This requires, among other things, preserving its normative agenda and the modes to promote it in various parts of the world. It should maintain its shared normative agenda with the United States but not necessarily the strategies of the latter to export or spread it across the world. The Union should adhere to its preference for "system change" rather than "regime change," as Javier Solana put it.[34] Second, there is a need to enhance the EU's attractiveness by extending its economic success to other areas, such as the CFSP/ESDP, where shortfalls remain substantial. The issue of success is of some importance because observers tend to choose a successful actor as their model, regardless of the form of behavior. In this regard, the perceived economic and social success of China in Africa in the absence of a normative agenda represents a challenge for the EU to promote the duplication of its own value system in the region. Third, it is critical for the EU to improve the coherence and consistency of its own behavior. This means living by its own standards beyond its borders. This is so because unrelated and disunited actions in a formal political setting have the potential to cause mixed feelings among peripheral states and, subsequently, to impede the learning process. Fourth, it is important that the EU sustain systematically the exposure of third states and organizations to its modus operandi as well as the perception of its functional value by means of explicit reinforcement of imitative responses, be it in the context of the ESDP operations, in the framework of cooperative arrangements such as the Barcelona Process and the European Neighborhood Policy, or under the aegis of institutionalized strategic partnerships (with Africa, Russia, Brazil, China, and others).

Indeed, only by being able to promote and reinforce modeling stimuli for their inherent reward value to other actors, while keeping up a distinctive behavioral pattern characterized by consistency, success, and competence in diverse functional fields, can the EU be considered a genuine "model power." And only then will the MoPE conception gain concrete rather than merely rhetorical significance.

Notes

1. Ian Manners, "Normative Power Europe: A Contradiction in Terms?" *Journal of Common Market Studies* 40, no. 4 (2002): 235–58.

2. Lisbeth Aggestam, "Introduction: Ethical Power Europe," *International Affairs* 84, no. 3 (2008): 1–11.

3. For the realist view, see Adrian Hyde-Price, "'Normative' Power Europe: A Realist Critique," *Journal of European Public Policy* 13, no. 2 (March 2006): 217–34. For the idealist-liberalist understanding, see Ian Manners, "Normative Power Europe Reconsidered: Beyond the Crossroads," in *Civilian or Military Power? European Foreign Policy in Perspective*, edited by Helen Sjursen (London: Routledge, 2007), pp. 14–31; Ian Manners, "The Normative Ethics of the European Union," *International Affairs* 84, no. 1 (2008): 45–60.

4. Hedley Bull, "Civilian Power Europe: A Contradiction in Terms?" *Journal of Common Market Studies* 21, no. 2 (1982): 149–64.

5. Manners, "Normative Power Europe Reconsidered."

6. Laurent Zecchini, "La France veut profiter sa présidence de l'UE pour relancer la défense européenne," *Le Monde*, October 17, 2007.

7. Jean Luc Dehaene as cited by Ian Traynor, "Britain Scorns France's Plans for EU Defence," *The Guardian*, November 16, 2007, p. 26.

8. David Miliband, "Europe 2030: Model Power Not Superpower," speech to College of Europe, November 15, 2007.

9. This links to Sarkozy's proposal to create a Groupe des Sages to reflect and envisage the EU of 2030.

10. Miliband, "Europe 2030," p. 3.

11. This new paradigm came to oppose the classical assumption that the learning process was based exclusively on direct experience and its consequences; and to demonstrate on the basis of intense investigation that for a person to learn it is not necessary that he or she engage in a trial-and-error process (that is, it is not necessary to fail in order to learn a given behavior).

12. Jan Zielonka, "Europe as a Global Actor: Empire by Example," *International Affairs* 84, no. 3 (2008): 472.

13. Javier Solana, "Shaping an Effective EU Foreign Policy," speech by the High Representative for the Common Foreign and Security Policy at the Konrad Adenauer Foundation, Brussels, January 24, 2005. Emphasis added.

14. Óscar Gonçalves, *Introdução às Psicoterapias Comportamentais* (Coimbra: Quarteto 1999), p. 91.

15. Albert Bandura and Peter Barab, "Conditions Governing Nonreinforced Imitation," *Developmental Psychology* 5, no. 2 (1971): 244.

16. Albert Bandura, Dorothea Ross, and Sheila Ross, "Vicarious Reinforcement and Imitative Learning," *Journal of Abnormal and Social Psychology* 67, no. 6 (1963): 601.

17. Ibid.

18. Gonçalves, *Introdução às Psicoterapias Comportamentais*, p. 87.

19. Bandura and Barab, "Conditions Governing Nonreinforcement Imitation," p. 254.

20. Albert Bandura, "Psychotherapy as a Learning Process," *Psychological Bulletin* 58, no. 2 (1961): 143–59.

21. Albert Bandura distinguished between learning and performance. While learning implies the acquisition of the cognitive equivalents of the model's behavior, performance involves the translation of this learning into the corresponding motor responses. Bandura, Ross, and Ross, "Vicarious Reinforcement," pp. 606–07.

22. Ibid., p. 281.

23. Laura C. Ferreira-Pereira and A. J. R. Groom, "Solidarity in the European Union's Security and Defence Policy," paper presented at the Second Global International Studies Conference, Ljubljana, July 25, 2008.

24. Manners, "Normative Power Europe Reconsidered," p. 240.

25. Zielonka, "Europe as a Global Actor," p. 475.

26. Ibid., p. 481; Hyde-Price, "'Normative' Power Europe," pp. 222, 231.

27. Miliband, "Europe 2030," p. 1.

28. Sten Rynning, "Providing Relief or Promoting Democracy? The European Union and Crisis Management," *Security Dialogue* 32, no. 1 (2001): 89, 91–92.

29. Manners, "Normative Ethics," p. 49.

30. Olli Rehn, "Europe's Smart Power in Its Region and the World," speech at the European Studies Centre, St. Antony's College, University of Oxford, May 1, 2008.

31. Aggestam, "Introduction: Ethical Power Europe," p. 4.

32. Although Manners, in "Normative Ethics," leaves the impression that he ascribes importance to the EU's foreign policy behavior as such, this theoretical development is not yet clarified, bearing in mind the strong emphasis placed on principles rather than on actions in his groundbreaking article "Normative Power Europe." The correspondence he put forward between what the EU says with "actions" alone is also somewhat puzzling. For this reason, in this discussion I refer to his initial emphasis on what the European Union "is" and "says."

33. Miliband, "Europe 2030," p. 3.

34. Javier Solana, speech by the High Representative for the Common Foreign and Security Policy to the College of Europe, October 19, 2005.

ELENA BARACANI

23

U.S. and EU Strategies for Promoting Democracy

The strategies of the United States and the European Union for promoting democracy are part of the "international dimension" of democratization, which refers to all of the external factors that can influence democratic changes in domestic political regimes, such as transnational and regional events, NGOs, states, and other international actors. Initially, democratization studies gave no importance to external factors in explaining the causes of the democratic transitions that occurred in southern Europe and Latin America between 1974 and 1989.[1] It was only with the fall of the Berlin Wall, the breakdown of the Soviet Union, and the end of the cold war that international actors, such as states, international organizations, NGOs, and independent foundations, engaged more actively and systematically in promoting democracy. As a consequence, democracy promotion has become "a norm of practice within the international system."[2] Several experts have affirmed that the international dimension, together with domestic variables, should be taken into consideration to explain democratization processes as an intervening factor.[3]

In this new international context, there is no doubt that, at least rhetorically, democracy promotion is at the center of both U.S. and EU foreign policy and their strategic partnership. In both cases democracy promotion, rather than being a foreign policy objective in itself, is an instrument for achieving their primary foreign policy goals, security and economic prosperity. For instance, in his inaugural speech of January 2005, U.S. president George W. Bush argued that promoting the freedom of other countries is now an "urgent requirement of our nation's security."[4] Likewise, President Bill Clinton's administration declared "promoting democracy" to be one of the three pillars of the national security strategy because "democratic states are less likely to threaten our interests and more likely to cooperate with the United States to meet security threats and promote free trade."[5] In 1995, former national security adviser Anthony Lake stated clearly, "We led the struggle for democracy because the larger the pool of democracies, the greater our security and prosperity."[6] Similarly, according to the European Security Strategy, "The best protection for our security is a world of well-governed democratic states."[7] This implies that in the case of conflict between democracy promotion and national security interests, both the United States and the EU will give priority to the defense of their security interests, even if this means tolerating or even supporting dictatorial regimes.

This chapter describes and compares the U.S. and EU strategies of democracy promotion, evaluating whether they have shared strategies or whether there is a "transatlantic divide over democracy promotion."[8]

Democracy Promotion in Historical Perspective

While the United States has a long history of democracy promotion that goes back to the presidency of Woodrow Wilson, the EU has become a democracy promoter only in recent decades, since the end of the cold war.[9] Democracy promotion is said to be "central to U.S. political identity and sense of national purpose."[10] On the contrary, the EU has become a democracy promoter "more by accident than by design," as a consequence of its enlargement policy.[11] In addition, according to a survey of European and U.S. attitudes on foreign policy in 2007, Europeans favored EU democracy promotion more than U.S. citizens favored similar activities by the United States.[12]

The United States

President Wilson defined the country's role in World War I as a mission "for democracy, for the right of those who submit to authority to have a voice in their own government, for the rights and liberties of small nations . . . and to make the world itself free."[13] During the cold war the primary accomplishments of the United States in promoting democracy were the creation of democratic regimes in Germany and Japan and support for the process of European integration. However, in this period, "America's principal objective was not to promote political freedom but to contain the Soviet Union."[14] Indeed, U.S. support for undemocratic regimes was considered an acceptable alternative to communist expansion.

It was only with Ronald Reagan that democracy promotion became a central objective of U.S. foreign assistance.[15] His administration articulated the democratic peace argument, according to which the regime type of other states matters, and if they are democracies they will be less threatening to the United States.[16] In addition, in 1983, Reagan's proposed "Campaign for Democracy" led to the creation of the National Endowment for Democracy (NED), "a Congressionally-funded, bipartisan, non-governmental organization dedicated to supporting democrats abroad."[17] However, it should be recalled that for the Reagan administration promoting democracy was only one component of its anticommunist policy.[18]

Before the creation of the NED, U.S. foreign assistance was managed through the United States Agency for International Development (USAID), created in 1961 by President John F. Kennedy to counter communism and Soviet foreign assistance. It did not explicitly aim to promote democracy, but rather focused on economic development.[19] Therefore, according to Thomas Carothers, the creation of the NED "represented the major first step toward the establishment of the broad program of U.S. democracy assistance."[20]

While initially democracy aid was mainly "a side element of anticommunist security policies," in the 1990s it found its place in U.S. foreign policy and rapidly increased in dollar amounts and geographic reach.[21] The administration of George H. W. Bush (1989–93) established democracy promotion as one of the three principal elements of its foreign policy, alongside economic concerns and national security. In practice, however, the emphasis placed on democracy promotion varied greatly from region to region, depending mainly on the configuration of U.S. interests. After the fall of the Berlin Wall, the Bush administration initiated a carrot-and-stick policy of "democratic differentiation" in eastern Europe in order to encourage movement toward democracy and a free-market economy.[22] Under the Support for East European Democracy (SEED) program, the United States allocated an average of $360 million to the region each year in the period 1989–94.

President Bill Clinton embraced the "enlargement of the democracy community" as a key element of U.S. foreign policy. According to national security adviser Anthony Lake, "The successor to a doctrine of containment must be a strategy of enlargement—enlargement of the world's free community."[23] However, according to Carothers, the Clinton administration did not substantially increase the U.S. emphasis on democracy promotion in any region, but continued to incorporate democracy promotion only where U.S. economic and security interests correlated with the advance of democracy.[24] It continued to eschew it where the U.S. interest required working relationships with nondemocratic regimes, as in the case of China.

President George W. Bush (2001–08) did not enter the White House with the mission to promote democracy around the world, but his administration was strongly affected by the terrorist attacks on September 11, 2001, which turned democracy promotion into a central objective of his foreign policy agenda.[25] Bush ordered the forcible ouster of autocratic regimes in Afghanistan and Iraq, and he also increased general foreign assistance funding, including support for democracy promotion.

The European Union

In the original founding treaties of the European Union there was no mention of "democracy."[26] It was only in January 1962, when the European Parliament approved the Birkelbach report, that the necessary political conditions were established for membership in and association with the European Economic Community (EEC).[27] In particular, it was decided that "only states which guarantee on their territories truly democratic practices and respect for fundamental rights and freedoms can become members of the Community."[28]

On this basis, the February 1962 application by Franco's Spain for association status with the EEC was dropped for political reasons and only a commercial agreement was reached in 1970.[29] Then, after the 1967 Colonels' Coup, which established a military dictatorship in Greece, the EEC decided to freeze its association with Greece.[30] The last years of the 1970s and the first part of the 1980s were characterized by the accession processes of Greece, Spain, and Portugal and by the Declaration on Democracy at the Copenhagen summit in April 1978. It stated that respect for and maintenance of parliamentary democracy and human rights in all member states are "essential elements of their membership in the EC [European Community]."[31] On the whole, the literature has shown that the role played by the European Community in the democratic consolidation of Greece, Spain, and Portugal during the 1980s was only an indirect one.[32] Its strategy of democracy promotion "was marked by a distinct lack of procedure and its operation by *ad hoc* approaches and a continuing tendency to react to events rather than trying to determine their outcome."[33]

With the creation of the EU at Maastricht in 1992, the "development and consolidation of democracy" became one of the objectives of its Common Foreign and Security Policy. The EU started to play a direct role in the democratization process of accession candidate countries from central and eastern Europe that joined the Union in 2004. The main turning points in the EU relationship with central and eastern European applicants were the 1993 Copenhagen European Council and the 1997 Luxemburg European Council meetings. In 1993, the heads of state and government of the EU agreed that those associated countries of central and eastern Europe desiring membership could become members of the EU, even though, for the first time, the promise of membership was accompanied by a statement of formal conditions, among which was "democracy."

In 1997 the Luxemburg European Council launched the enhanced pre-accession strategy to be applied to all central and eastern European applicants, which made it possible for the EU to implement political conditionality and move from indirect influence to direct leverage. The political conditions established in Copenhagen were translated by the EU into a demand for specific political reforms from each candidate. Moreover, the progress of each candidate in complying with these demands began to be monitored annually by the European Commission in specific reports. Finally, the EU began rewarding those candidates that complied with its requests with institutional links (such as the start of accession negotiations) and economic assistance.[34]

At the beginning of the twenty-first century, the EU is seeking to replicate this successful strategy of "democracy promotion through integration" not only with the current candidate countries (Turkey, Croatia, and the former Yugoslav Republic of Macedonia) and the remaining potential candidate countries of the western Balkans (Albania, Bosnia-Herzegovina, Serbia, Montenegro, and Kosovo), but also with those countries of eastern Europe, the southern Mediterranean, and southern Caucasus that fall under the European Neighborhood Policy launched in 2004 but that do not have the prospect of membership in the Union.[35] Indeed, according to the European security strategy, "Our task is to promote a ring of well-governed countries to the East of the European Union and on the borders of the Mediterranean."[36]

Strategies of Democracy Promotion

Strategies of external democracy promotion, defined as approaches that donors take to promote democracy, can vary on two main dimensions.[37] These two dimensions are the "degree of leverage" and the model of democracy that is promoted.[38] "Leverage" here is defined as external pressure for democratization, and not governments' vulnerability to external pressure."[39] Thus this definition is very close to what Larry Diamond calls "peaceful forms of pressure . . . to advance human rights and democracy."[40] The second dimension of democracy promotion—the model of democracy promoted—refers to the fact that different external actors can give priority to different policy areas.

External Leverage and Models of Democracy Promotion

External leverage for democratization may be viewed as a continuum of strategies adopted by the international actors. At one pole there is no active external leverage, but rather what has been called "diffusion,"[41] "contagion,"[42] or "example"[43] to describe a situation in which ideas and models of democratic change come from outside, but without any direct activity by external actors. The other pole represents the end of the use of peaceful forms of pressure in favor of "democratization by force,"[44] "military intervention,"[45] or what has been called "control."[46] This pole describes a situation in which an external actor promotes democracy through the use or threat of force.

Figure 23-1. *Degrees of External Leverage for Democratization*

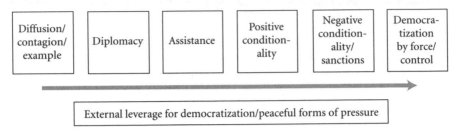

Between these extremes are different modalities of democracy promotion that involve different degrees of external leverage. The most important are: (1) diplomacy; (2) democracy assistance; (3) positive conditionality; and (4) negative conditionality or sanctions. Of course, there may be some overlap between them.

"Diplomacy" here refers to diplomatic pressures that push the target country toward democracy.[47] Democracy assistance comprises "all aid for which the primary purpose, not the secondary or indirect purpose, is to foster democracy in the recipient country."[48] It is both economic and technical: "The provision of advice and instruction, training programs, equipment and other forms of material support to institutional capacity building are typical examples, as are financial subventions to pro-democracy bodies and subsidies to cover the costs of certain democratizing processes."[49]

"Positive conditionality" refers to the fact that the target country has to satisfy the democratic conditions required by the external actor in order to be granted additional benefits or "carrots" such as economic assistance or closer bilateral relations.[50] Negative conditionality, or sanctions, are penalties imposed on a country that does not respect the required democratic conditions, such as the suspension of economic assistance or the "freezing" of bilateral relations (see figure 23-1).[51]

Both the United States and the EU have made active use of all the methods listed in figure 23-1 to promote democracy, with the exception of coercion in the case of the EU. Democratization by force and "democratization through integration" are the characteristic models of democracy promotion by the United States and the EU respectively, while democracy assistance is the model common to both.

There has been a constant debate over the United States' use of military force to promote democracy, even though it is not "the only instrument of regime change in the U.S. arsenal," but rather "the rarest used."[52] Democratization through integration is the preferred model of the EU to promote democracy.[53]

However, it can only be applied to a specific category of third countries: the accession candidate country. This means, as in the case of democratization by force by the United States, that it is not the most common model used to promote democracy. Indeed, the EU can only offer it to the accession candidate countries, in exchange for respecting its democratic principles in addition to its economic assistance. The incentive of membership in the organization is considered a much more important "carrot." Indeed, it means that the country that joins the Union can participate in the EU decisionmaking process at the same level as the other member states, and that, like other members, it can benefit from the EU's redistributive policies.

The most commonly used model of democracy promotion for both the United States and the EU is democracy assistance. Formally, this assistance is usually positively or negatively conditioned on the achievement of some democratic objectives. The decision to implement this conditionality is a political one and it is very rarely taken.

It is not easy to compare the levels of democracy assistance from the United States and the EU, for several reasons: (1) both the United States and the EU administer numerous democracy-related budgets; (2) it is not easy to distinguish democracy assistance from other sectors of assistance; and (3) it is not easy to find comparable data.[54] However, the OECD statistics on development make it possible to make this comparison within the EU as a whole—referring to the European Commission (EC)—and between individual member states and the United States.[55]

Based on these data, figure 23-2 shows an overall perspective of all official development assistance (ODA) for government and civil society provided by the United States and the European Commission to all recipients (197 countries) between 1990 and 2006. First, it can be observed that U.S. government and civil society ODA increased steadily from $628 million (all figures here are 2005 prices) in 1990 to a peak of $4.28 billion in 2004. In 2005 and 2006 it fell to $3.7 billion and $1.9 billion respectively. Similarly, in the case of the EC there was also an increase in government and civil society ODA: from $19 million in 1990 to $2.2 billion in 2006.

However, in spite of this increase in government and civil society ODA, it remained a small percentage of the total ODA provided by the United States and the European Commision between 1990 and 2006: 10.34 percent for the United States and 9.71 percent for the EC (see table 23-1).[56] In addition, data presented in table 23-1 show that ODA for "Support to NGOs," in the same period, was 0.03 percent of total ODA, in both the United States and the EC.

Figures 23-3 and 23-4 show the regional distribution of government and civil society ODA in the period 1990–2006. In the case of the United States, the

Figure 23-2. *Official Development Assistance (ODA) from the United States and the European Community for Government and Civil Society, 1990–2006*

Commitments in millions of constant 2005 dollars

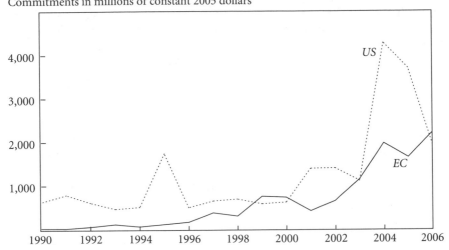

Source: Author's calculations based on aid activity data from OECD.

Middle East received the highest percentage of aid for government and civil society (25 percent), followed by South and Central Asia and by North and Central America (both received around 13 percent over the years). In the case of the EC, the region that received the largest amount of government and civil society ODA in the period under study was the South of Sahara (31 percent), followed by Europe (22 percent) and South and Central Asia (7 percent).

Finally, with regard to the modalities of U.S. and EU democracy assistance, it can be argued that the European Union, unlike the United States, prefers to concentrate on state actors rather than focusing its democracy assistance activity on civic groups, political parties, and other society actors. In addition, while the EU relies much more on direct grants to state institutions in order to implement its projects, the United States relies much more on training and technical assistance.

Models of Democracy Promoted

In both the United States and the EU the model of democracy promoted is the Western liberal democratic one. It has the following basic features: (1) regular, free, and fair elections; (2) a constitution that enshrines democracy and a full set of human rights; (3) a governmental system based on the separation of powers with an accountable executive, a representative legislature, and an independent

Table 23-1. *U.S. and EC Official Development Assistance (ODA)*
to All Recipients by Sector, 1990–2006
Billions of constant 2005 dollars (percent of total ODA)

Type of assistance or expenditure	United States	European Community
Education	$5.926 (2.84)	$5.715 (5.17)
Health	$8.856 (4.24)	$4.295(3.88)
Population programs	$16.374 (7.83)	$1.106 (1.0)
Water supply and sanitation	$5.467 (2.62)	$4.202 (3.8)
Government and civil society	$21.604 (10.34)	$10.735 (9.71)
Conflict, peace, and security	$4.136 (1.98)	$8.67 (0.78)
Economic infrastructure	$21.326 (10.2)	$17.178 (15.54)
Production sectors	$12.670 (6.06)	$11.094 (10.03)
Multisector	$15.483 (7.41)	$11.773 (10.65)
Commodity aid / general program assistance	$34.301 (16.41)	$20.830 (18.84)
Action relating to debt	$17.026 (8.15)	$197 (0.18)
Emergency assistance and reconstruction	$21.267 (10.18)	$15.186 (13.73)
Support to NGOs	$55 (0.03)	$29 (0.03)
Refugees in donor countries	$2.731 (1.31)	$9 (0.01)
Unallocated / unspecified	$704 (0.34)	$823 (0.74)
Other social infrastructure and services	$3.921 (3.55)	$3.921 (3.55)
Admininstrative costs of donors	$7.460 (3.57)	$2.611 (2.36)

Source: Author's calculations based on aid activity data from OECD.

judiciary; (4) local government structures, and (5) political parties that aggregate citizens' interests. In addition, in the past two decades the United States and the European Union have both moved from the promotion of a formal democratic model (with a liberal-democratic constitution and free elections) to the promotion of a more substantive model of democracy.[57]

In the case of the EU, this substantive model of democracy has been developed by the European Commission during the accession process of the central and eastern European countries that joined the Union in 2004. It includes the strengthening of institutional and administrative capacity, judicial independence and efficiency, the fight against corruption, civil control of the military, and a vast array of human and minority rights, not only civil and political rights but also social, economic, and cultural rights.[58] In the case of the United States the "democracy template" focuses on three main sectors—electoral process, state institutions, and civil society—and includes free and fair elections, strong national political parties, a democratic constitution, an independent and effective judiciary, a representative and competent legislature, responsive local governments, a pro-democratic military, active advocacy NGOs, a politically educated citizenry, strong independent media, and a strong independent union.[59]

Figure 23-3. *U.S. ODA to Government and Civil Society Recipients by Region, 1990–2006*

Commitments in percent of total ODA

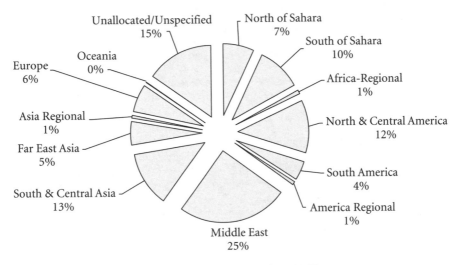

Source: Author's calculations based on aid activity data from OECD.

A slight difference in the U.S. and EU models of democracy promoted may be found in the fact that the United States pays much more attention to political party, NGO, and union building than the EU. The latter focuses much more not only on civil and political rights, but also on social, economic, and cultural rights.

Conclusion: Shared Strategies or a Transatlantic Divide over Democracy Promotion?

It has been shown that there are both similarities and differences in the U.S. and the EU strategies of democracy promotion. On the whole, it can be argued that they share the same strategy, with only slight differences. First, rhetorically, democracy promotion is at the center of both entities' foreign policy, and in practice, democracy promotion is in both cases subordinated to other national interests, security, and prosperity. Second, with regard to the model of democracy promotion, even if democratization by force and democratization through integration are the characteristic models of democracy promotion of both the United States and the European Union, they are also the rarest used, while democracy assistance is the model common to both. Third, in both cases, between 1990 and 2006 the ODA for democracy-related activities increased and

Figure 23-4. *EC ODA to Government and Civil Society Recipients by Region, 1990–2006*

Commitments in percent of total ODA

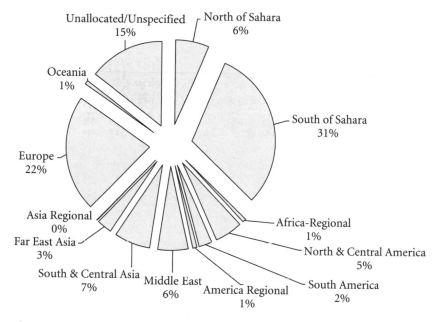

Source: Author's calculations based on aid activity data from OECD.

represented about 10 percent of total ODA.[60] Finally, in both cases the model of democracy promoted is the Western liberal one, which has shifted in the past two decades from formality to greater substance. Indeed, differences can be found only in (1) the United States' longer history of democracy promotion, versus the EU's more recent one; (2) the centrality of democracy promotion to U.S. political identity, while the EU has become a democracy promoter more by accident; (3) the fact that Europeans are more supportive of democracy promotion than Americans; (4) U.S. democratization by force versus EU democratization through integration; and (5) the U.S. focus on society versus the EU focus on the state.

Notes

1. Guillermo O'Donnell, Philippe C. Schmitter, and Laurence Whitehead, *Transitions from Authoritarian Rule: Comparative Perspectives* (Johns Hopkins University Press; 1986); Juan J. Linz and Alfred Stepan, *Problems of Democratic Transition and Consolidation:*

Southern Europe, South America and Post-communist Europe (Johns Hopkins University Press, 1986); Larry Diamond, Juan J. Linz, and Seymour M. Lipset, *Politics in Developing Countries: Comparing Experiences with Democracy* (Boulder, Colo.: Lynne Rienner, 1989); Leonardo Morlino, *Democracy between Consolidation and Crisis: Parties, Groups and Citizens in Southern Europe* (Oxford University Press, 1998), p. 166.

2. Carl Gershman and Michael Allen, "The Assault on Democracy Assistance," *Journal of Democracy* 17, no. 2 (2006): 36.

3. Philippe C. Schmitter, "The Influence of the International Context upon the Choice of National Institutions and Policies in Neo-Democracies," in *International Dimensions of Democratization*, edited by Laurence Whitehead (Oxford University Press, 1996), pp. 26–54; Laurence Whitehead, "Three International Dimensions of Democratization," in *The International Dimensions of Democratization*, edited by Whitehead, pp. 3–24; Geoffrey Pridham, "The International Dimension of Democratisation: Theory, Practice and Inter-regional Comparisons," in *Building Democracy? The International Dimension of Democratisation in Eastern Europe*, edited by Geoffrey Pridham, Eric Herring, and George Sanford (Leicester University Press, 1997), p. 7; Samuel P. Huntington, *The Third Wave of Democratization in the Late Twentieth Century* (Oklahoma University Press, 1991).

4. Office of the Press Secretary, The White House, "President Sworn-In to Second Term," January 20, 2005 (www.whitehouse.gov/news/releases/2005/01/20050120-1.html [October 2008]).

5. Quoted in Gideon Rose, "Democracy Promotion and American Foreign Policy," *International Security* 25, no. 3 (2000): 189. In particular, according to G. John Ikenberry, the American focus on democracy promotion must be seen as part of a larger American way of thinking about the sources of a stable, peaceful, and prosperous international order, or what he calls "America's Liberal Grand Strategy." According to this strategy "the United States is better able to pursue its interests, reduce security threats in its environment, and foster a stable political order when other states . . . are democracies rather than non-democracies." John G. Ikenberry, "America's Liberal Grand Strategy: Democracy and National Security in the Post-war Era," in *American Democracy Promotion: Impulses, Strategies, and Impacts,* edited by Michael Cox, G. John Ikenberry, and Takashi Inoguchi (Oxford University Press, 2000), p. 103.

6. Anthony Lake, "Remarks on the Occasion of the 10th Anniversary of the Center for Democracy," Washington, September 26, 1995.

7. European Council 2003, "A Secure Europe in a Better World. European Security Strategy" (www.consilium.europa.eu/uedocs/cmsUpload/78367.pdf [August 2008]).

8. Jeffrey S. Kopstein, "The Transatlantic Divide over Democracy Promotion," *Washington Quarterly* 29, no. 2 (2006): 85–98.

9. For a systematic survey of American democracy promotion in the twentieth century, see Tony Smith, *America's Mission: The United States and the Worldwide Struggle for Democracy in the Twentieth Century* (Princeton University Press, 1994). However, according to Steven W. Hook, "Contemporary initiatives in the pursuit of democracy promotion may be viewed as the continuation . . . of a virtually continuous 'democratist crusade' that has been underway throughout the nation's history." Steven W. Hook,

"Inconsistent U.S. Efforts to Promote Democracy Abroad," in *Exporting Democracy. Rhetoric versus Reality*, edited by Peter J. Schraeder (Boulder, Colo.: Lynne Rienner, 2002), p. 110. Similarly, Gideon Rose quotes Lincoln, according to whom the Declaration of Independence gave liberty "not alone to the people of this country, but hope to the world for all future time," in Rose, "Democracy Promotion," p. 186.

10. Jonathan Monten, "The Roots of the Bush Doctrine: Power, Nationalism, and Democracy Promotion in U.S. Strategy," *International Security* 29, no. 4 (2005): 112–56. See also Hook, "Inconsistent U.S. Efforts"; and David C. Hendrickson, "The Democratist Crusade: Intervention, Economic Sanctions, and Engagement," *World Policy Journal* 11 (Winter 1994–95): 3–20.

11. Valerie Bunce and Sharon Wolchik, "International Democracy Promotion: Players, Policies and Potential for Democratic Change," in *American Democracy Promotion and Electoral Change in Postcommunist Europe and Eurasia*, edited by Valerie Bunce and Sharon Wolchik (forthcoming).

12. According to a 2007 survey of the German Marshall Fund and Compagnia di San Paolo (2007, p. 4), 71 percent of Europeans believe the EU should promote democracy in other countries, while the U.S. support for such a project is 37 percent (45 percent in 2006, and 52 percent in 2005). German Marshall Fund and Compagnia di San Paolo, *Transatlantic Trends. Key findings 2007* (www.transatlantictrends.org/trends/doc/TT07KFR_FINAL.pdf [August 2008]). This trend in American public opinion had already emerged at the beginning of the twenty-first century; see Ole R. Holsti, "Promotion of Democracy as Popular Demand?" in *American Democracy Promotion*, edited by Cox, Ikenberry, and Inoguchi, pp. 151–80.

13. Quoted in Hook, "Inconsistent U.S. Efforts," p. 110.

14. Cox, Ikenberry, and Inoguchi, *American Democracy Promotion*, p. 4.

15. Francis Fukuyama and Michael McFaul, "Should Democracy Be Promoted or Demoted?" *Washington Quarterly* 31, no. 1 (2008): 23–45; Bunce and Wolchik, "International Democracy Promotion."

16. Ikenberry, "America's Liberal Grand Strategy," p. 125.

17. Marc F. Plattner, Introduction to "A Quarter-Century of Promoting Democracy," *Journal of Democracy* 18, no. 4 (2007): 111. The NED in the 1990s had an annual budget in the range of $25 million to $35 million, and gave at least half of its grant funds to the International Republican Institute (with ties to the Republican Party), the National Democratic Institute for International Affairs (with ties to the Democratic Party), the American Center for Labor Solidarity (with ties to the AFL-CIO), and the Center for International Private Enterprise (with ties to the U.S. Chamber of Congress), which were created after the NED. Political party institutes work primarily on elections and political party assistance, the American Center for Labor Solidarity supports labor unions, and the Center for International Private Enterprise promotes free enterprise abroad. The rest of NED's funds go to organizations in the United States and abroad to promote civic education, democratic awareness, independent media, human rights, often in nondemocratic countries; see Thomas Carothers, "Taking Stock of Democracy Assistance," in *American Democracy Promotion*, edited by Cox, Ikenberry, and Inoguchi, p. 190; Thomas Carothers, "The NED at 10," *Foreign Policy* 94 (1994): 123–39.

18. Thomas Carothers, *In the Name of Democracy: U.S. Policy toward Latin America in the Reagan Years* (University of California Press, 1991), p. 238.

19. In particular, in the 1950s U.S. aid consisted primarily of economic and military assistance to governments friendly to the United States; in the 1960s economic development became a priority of U.S. aid; and the 1970s were characterized by the "basic human needs" doctrine in foreign aid (for details see Carothers, "Taking Stock of Democracy Assistance," pp. 182–83).

20. Carothers, "Taking Stock of Democracy Assistance," p. 183.

21. Thomas Carothers, "A Quarter-Century of Promoting Democracy," *Journal of Democracy* 18, no. 4 (2007): 112.

22. Thomas Carothers, "Democracy Promotion Under Clinton," *Washington Quarterly* 18, no. 4 (1995).

23. Anthony Lake, "From Containment to Enlargement," Department of State Dispatch, September 27, 1993, p. 658. On the origins of the Clinton's doctrine of democratic enlargement see Michael Cox, according to whom President Clinton always viewed the promotion of democracy as a pragmatic strategy designed to enhance U.S. influence. Michael Cox, "Wilsonian Resurgent? The Clinton Administration and the Promotion of Democracy," in *American Democracy Promotion*, edited by Cox, Ikenberry, and Inoguchi, pp. 218–39. See also Douglas Brinkley, "Democratic Enlargement: The Clinton Doctrine," *Foreign Policy* 106 (Spring 1997): 111–27.

24. Carothers, "Democracy Promotion under Clinton."

25. Kopstein, "The Transatlantic Divide," p. 85; Fukuyama and McFaul, "Should Democracy Be Promoted or Demoted?" p. 23.

26. Indeed, the 1951 Treaty of Paris was more concerned with preventing the recurrence of war. However, the preamble to the Rome Treaty of 1957 noted that member states are "resolved by thus pooling their resources to preserve and strengthen peace and liberty and calling upon the other peoples of Europe who share their ideal to join their efforts." See Geoffrey Pridham, *Designing Democracy: EU Enlargement and Regime Change in Post-Communist Europe* (Palgrave Macmillan, 2005), p. 29.

27. "Report by Willi Birkelbach on the Political and Institutional Aspects of Accession to or Association with the Community" (www.ena.lu/report_willi_birkelbach_political_institutional_aspects_accession_association_with_community_december_1961-020000 6013.html [September 25, 2009[).

28. Pridham, *Designing Democracy*, p. 30.

29. MacLennan J. Crespo, *Spain and the Process of European Integration, 1957–1985* (London: Palgrave, 2000).

30. Van Coufoudakis, "The EEC and the 'Freezing' of the Greek Association, 1967–74," *Journal of Common Market Studies* 16, no. 2 (1977): 114–31.

31. Quoted in Pridham, *Designing Democracy*, p. 33 n27.

32. See Whitehead, "Three International Dimensions," p. 261; Morlino, *Democracy between Consolidation and Crisis*, p. 166; and Paul J. Kubicek, *The European Union and Democratization* (London: Routledge, 2003).

33. Pridham, *Designing Democracy,* p. 35.

34. See Elena Baracani, "EU Democratic Rule of Law Promotion," in *International Actors, Democratization and the Rule of Law: Anchoring Democracy,* edited by Amichai Magen and Leonardo Morlino (London: Routledge, 2008), pp. 53–86.

35. On this concept see Antoaneta Dimitrova and Geoffrey Pridham, "International Actors and Democracy Promotion in Central and Eastern Europe," *Democratization* 11, no. 5 (2004): 91–112.

36. European Council, "A Secure Europe."

37. Thomas Carothers, "Democracy Assistance: The Question of Strategy," *Democratization* 4, no. 3 (1997), p. 111.

38. Another relevant dimension of variation may be the time span, which refers to the fact that external actors' activities to promote democracy can be short term, as in the case of election monitoring missions, or long term when the activity of democracy promotion lasts several years, as is usual in the case of state-building missions.

39. See Steven Levitsky and Lucan A. Way, "International Linkage and Democratization," *Journal of Democracy* 16, no. 3 (1995): 21; Steven Levitsky and Lucan A. Way, "Linkage versus Leverage: Rethinking the International Dimension of Regime Change," *Comparative Politics* 38, no. 4 (2006): 382.

40. Diamond, Linz, and Lipset, *Politics in Developing Countries,* p. 111.

41. See, for example, Harvey Starr, "Democratic Dominoes: Diffusion Approaches to the Spread of Democracy in the International System," *Journal of Conflict Resolution* 35, no. 2 (1991): 356–81; Jeffrey Kopstein and David A. Reilly, "Geographic Diffusion and the Transformation of the Postcommunist World," *World Politics* 53, no. 1 (2001); Larry Diamond, *The Spirit of Democracy: The Struggle to Build Free Societies throughout the World* (Times Books, 2008).

42. See Whitehead, "Three International Dimensions," pp. 5–8; and Kubicek, *The European Union and Democratization,* pp. 4–7.

43. See Henry R. Nau, "America's Identity, Democracy Promotion and National Interest: Beyond Realism, Beyond Idealism," in *American Democracy Promotion,* edited by Cox, Ikenberry, and Inoguchi, p. 147; Amichai Magen and Leonardo Morlino, *International Actors, Democratization and the Rule of Law: Anchoring Democracy* (London: Routledge, 2009).

44. See Diamond, *The Spirit of Democracy,* p. 133.

45. See Carothers, "Taking Stock of Democracy Assistance," p. 186.

46. See Whitehead, "Three International Dimensions," p. 8; Kubicek, *The European Union and Democratization,* pp. 4–7; Magen and Morlino, *International Actors.*

47. See also Carothers, "Taking Stock of Democracy Assistance," p. 186; Diamond, *The Spirit of Democracy,* pp. 114–16.

48. Carothers, "Taking Stock of Democracy Assistance," pp. 187–88.

49. Peter Burnell, ed., *Democracy Assistance: International Co-operation for Democratization* (London: Frank Cass, 2000), p. 9.

50. Carothers, "Taking Stock of Democracy Assistance," p. 187.

51. Carothers calls this democracy policy tool "economic pressure," in ibid., p. 186.

52. See Fukuyama and McFaul, "Should Democracy Be Promoted or Demoted?" p. 34. However, even though the use of force to promote democracy is usually associated with the United States, it should not be excluded by the EU, at least to protect democracy, considering the increasing importance that the principle of the responsibility to protect is assuming in world politics.

53. See Dimitrova and Pridham, "International Actors and Democracy Promotion."

54. See Richard Youngs, "Trends in Democracy Assistance," *Journal of Democracy* 19, no. 2 (2008): 160–69.

55. However, I focus here only on data on the European Commission and U.S. aid activity.

56. These data are in line with the report by Finkel and others, which shows that democracy assistance provided only by USAID, in the period 1990–2003, steadily increased over the years, and that it was still a small percentage of the total aid provided by USAID, about 9 percent in 2003; Steven E. Finkel, Anibal Perez-Linan, and Mitchell A. Seligson, "Effects of U.S. Foreign Assistance on Democracy Building: Results of a Cross-National Quantitative Study," 2006, pp. 26–27 (www.usaid.gov/our_work/democracy_and_governance/publications/pdfs/impact_of_democracy_assistance.pdf [July 2008]).

57. See also Pridham, *Designing Democracy*, p. 25.

58. See Dimitrova and Pridham, "International Actors and Democracy Promotion," p. 97; and also Baracani, "EU Democratic Rule," p. 70. However, it should be noted that this substantive model of democracy is promoted by the EU mainly toward its accession candidate countries and the remaining potential candidate countries of the western Balkans, and that this is not the model of democracy promoted toward other third countries that do not have the prospect of membership in the Union; see, for example, the case of Morocco, in Elena Baracani, "From the EMP to the ENP: A New European Pressure for Democratization?" *Journal of Contemporary European Research* 1, no. 2 (2005): 54–67.

59. See Thomas Carothers, *Aiding Democracy Abroad: The Learning Curve* (Carnegie Endowment for International Peace, 1999).

60. However, it should be recalled that, between 1990 and 2006, the total amount of U.S. ODA for government and civil society ($21.6 billion at 2005 prices) was double that of EC ODA for the same purpose ($10.7 billion at 2005 prices).

MARTIN HOLLAND *and* NATALIA CHABAN

24

Perceptions of EU Foreign Policy outside Europe

With a foreign policy dimension being a relatively new addition to the arsenal of European Union actions and goals, scholarship on this topic is in its formative years, although already four distinct clusters of interlinked inquiries have emerged. The first combines insights into the Union's performance and capabilities in the international arena (including the EU's public diplomacy efforts).[1] The second explores the EU's international identity in various discourses.[2] The third researches the EU's roles and external expectations of these roles by its external interlocutors.[3] And the fourth concerns the "auto-" and "xeno-" visions of the EU's actions, roles, and goals, as well as its rhetoric and self-representations.[4] Positioning this chapter within the fourth paradigm, we claim in this study that systematic inquiries into the EU's external imagery will inform both the EU citizens and policymakers on how outsiders' perceptions might influence the EU's external actions and roles and subsequently how they can influence foreign policy discourse within the Union.

The first three research clusters are typically dominated by EU-centered and EU-originated research.[5] The fourth category counterbalances this "Euro-dominant" perspective by incorporating visions of the EU from outside its borders and external inquiries into the EU's foreign policy. Regretfully, there are several limitations to the current state of the art: most EU external perceptions studies are ethnocentric, deficient in comparative perspectives across both time and space and typically conducted on an ad hoc basis, often overemphasizing certain themes (such as elite perceptions) while overlooking others (such as media framing or public opinion).[6] Moreover, most of the studies of the EU perceptions merely focus on the content of images, leaving deeper consideration of the factors that shape these surfacing meanings unexplored.

A number of studies have attempted to overcome such limitations.[7] Preeminent among these is the transnational comparative project "The EU through the Eyes of the Asia-Pacific."[8] This pioneering, comprehensive study systematically compares the image of the Union across time in nineteen locations in the Asia-Pacific.[9] It provides insights into the media's framing of daily news coverage, public opinion, and attitudes and perceptions toward the EU held by national stakeholders (business, political actors, civil society, and media). Using the results of this empirically rigorous project, this chapter studies both the content of the EU media images and those factors that may shape the content in six Asian locations: Japan, South Korea, mainland China, the Special Administrative Region (SAR) of Hong Kong, Thailand, and Singapore. Testing the ubiquitous portrayal of the EU as "economic giant" and "military dwarf," we compare the EU political and economic media representations in eighteen reputable newspapers and five primetime television news programs monitored daily over twelve months in 2006.[10]

Image of the EU outside Its Borders: Endogenous and Exogenous Factors

The study of external views of the EU, according to Michito Tsuruoka, should engage two parallel directions: while it is important to investigate and identify perceptions of the EU in third countries, it is equally crucial to explore how these perceptions came into existence.[11] Tsuruoka argues that two types of sources may influence people's views—namely, exogenous factors (constituted by the EU's actual actions within and outside its borders) and endogenous factors ("unrelated to what the EU is doing in its own territory and in the world").[12] The interplay between the two types of sources shape images of the EU in each third-country case.

Among the most prominent endogenous factors, Tsuruoka cited third-country relations with the United States. Each of the six countries in Asia considered here has extensive political and economic loyalties to the United States (not to mention modern-day cultural connections, including popular youth culture and the desire to be educated in or to immigrate to the United States). These connections became deeply rooted in the history of the region in the second half of the twentieth century. Of course, it is not only Asia that sees America as its primary partner in international interactions.

Both the EU and Asia often prioritize their economic and political contacts with the United States, while deemphasizing and potentially overlooking issues in their dialogue with each other.[13] Yet little by little, the EU is turning to Asia, not only because of the mercurial rise of China, the high performance of Japan and South Korea, or the economic success of other nations in the region. In a parallel movement, Asia has increased its business contacts with the EU, viewing the Union as a lucrative partner thanks to the rapid growth of the single market, enlargement, and the success of the common currency. Two of the six locations, South Korea and Singapore, are contemplating the possibility of a free trade agreement (FTA) with the EU. The EU-27 is becoming a leading economic counterpart to the region (including the six Asian locations studied in this chapter). The EU is China's leading trading partner, ahead of both the United States and Japan.[14] Typically, for Hong Kong[15] and Singapore[16] the EU ranks as the second most valuable trading region (behind mainland China and Malaysia respectively), with South Korea[17] and Thailand[18] ranking the EU third in their trade statistics. The EU is the third-largest recipient of Japan's imports and the second-largest exporter to Japan.[19] Indeed, the lasting reputation of the EU as an "economic giant," "trading powerhouse," and "financial Gargantuan" seems to be supported by the exogenous factors of economic interactions the Union currently enjoys with Asia.

While economic considerations keep Asia's expectations of the EU afloat in the region, the EU's political influence remains disjointed and unclear. The EU's exogenous contributions to this status quo are its uncertain political profile (not a federal state, yet more than a loose intergovernmental organization), complex decisionmaking processes (on national, supranational, and even regional levels), and the cacophony of voices speaking on the international stage (the European Commission with its competing Directorate-Generals, the High Representative for Foreign Policy, and the European Presidency). Despite these limiting circumstances (and the frequently cited clichéd perception that it is a "military and political dwarf"), the EU aspires to engage in political dialogue with Asia on many levels.[20] According to Julie Gilson, such dialogue can be initiated multilaterally inside international organizations (such as the United Nations or World Trade Organization) and at international forums (dedicated to such issues as nuclear proliferation, security, human rights, or the environment, to name a few); through interregional interactions (such as the Asia-Europe Meeting (ASEM) or the EU dialogue with ASEAN or ASEAN+3 nations); bilaterally (between the EU and Asian nations individually); and at the country-to-country level (between individual EU member states and individual Asian states). The three areas where the EU exercises most of its political influence in Asia are human rights, developmental aid, and environmental protection. A security dialogue between the EU and Asia, although less visible, includes EU negotiations with North Korea, the EU peacekeeping mission in Aceh in Indonesia, interactions with ASEAN on maritime security, and more general antiterrorism initiatives.

Among the endogenous factors, Tsuruoka identifies the political orientation of a third country and a tendency for center-left governments to align their actions with those of Europe and its traditional welfare concerns, and for center-right governments to prefer the neoliberal agenda of the United States.[21] Political affiliations and preferences undoubtedly shape the direction of the EU's present-day dialogue with these Asian localities as well as the Union's image within those Asian societies. A sudden change of government (such as the 2006 coup d'état in Thailand) can overthrow traditional alliances and visions of the contacts with the outside world and cause difficulties in formulating positions towards Europe.[22]

The list of exogenous and endogenous sources influencing the EU's image should also include the experiences of European colonialism (where applicable). This is a factor that could be equally classified as exogenous (the EU comprises member states who were colonial powers in the past) and endogenous (the EU as an institution has never been a colonial ruler, yet it may still encounter Euro-skepticism and exaggerated nationalism in conjunction with anti-European sentiment). Japan and South Korea were never colonized by a European power and remained relatively isolated from European influence over centuries. Thailand, while never colonized, experienced a significant European influence throughout the nineteenth and twentieth centuries from Britain and France, which colonized the bordering territories of Vietnam, Laos, Cambodia, and Burma (Myanmar). Brian Bridges has called mainland China a "semi-colony," with its seashore territories being under Europe's control and its inland territories being relatively unexposed to Europe.[23] Hong Kong and Singapore are two port cities that experienced a prominent European presence in the past.

From this cursory description of various endogenous and exogenous factors in the EU performance, it seems that the exogenous, EU-induced sources are more obvious and thus easier to account for when analyzing the EU's external image. In contrast, the endogenous factors are more obscure and cryptic, and require additional cross-culturally sensitive and locally aware inquiries. The real challenge for the Union is to improve its awareness of endogenous dynamics, factors over which "the EU has little influence . . . and may end up [producing] not positive but negative perceptions of the EU."[24] This study addresses this call while looking at one particular discourse, that in the news media.

As Johan Galtung and Mari Holmboe Ruge noted, "the regularity, ubiquity and perseverance of news media will in any case make them first-rate competitors for the number-one position as international image-former."[25] The power of the media to lead in the construction of images of a nation's external partners is influenced partially by the limited degree of personal exposure to foreign lands and peoples among the general public, and partially by the lack of interpersonal communication on matters of foreign policy and external relations. Thus when it comes to the representations of national "Others," media have a heightened ability to tell the audience "what to think," as well as "what to think about" and "how to think about" it.[26] Undoubtedly, the content of news about the EU is an important element of its image; its patterns of information frame the EU for the news audiences outside the Union. This chapter systematically analyzes the content of media images of the EU as an economic and political actor in six Asian locations.

Methodology

The dataset used in this analysis comprises the daily coverage of the EU and its institutions—the European Commission (EC), the European Parliament (EP), the European Central Bank (ECB), and the European Court of Justice (ECJ)—as well as the Asia-Europe Meeting (ASEM) in the calendar year 2006. Giving priority to images and perceptions of the EU as a novel yet well-established political concept, the study did not search for news referring to individual member states. However, the analysis does take into account references to member states in news items that mentioned the EU (or the EC, EP, ECB, and ECJ). This research decision reflects the ambiguous reality of the EU. The coding protocol differentiated between news items that presented the EU as a major actor (with a member state acting in a secondary or minor role) or a member state as a major actor (with the EU being presented in this context from a secondary or minor perspective).

In each location, the study monitored four specific news media outlets: three daily newspapers and one primetime national television news program. The study recognizes that ownership patterns, resources, audience size, and news selection practices differ across locations and across the outlets inside each location. In order to guarantee comparability for content analysis, the sampling, aiming at higher consistency, was based on the criterion of the targeted audience.

The newspapers in each case included, first, a reputable popular national paper, targeting, together with a primetime news program, the broadest demographic on a national scale; second, a high-circulation business daily, targeting national business stakeholders who do or plan to trade and invest with the EU; and third, a local English-language daily newspaper, targeting foreigners outside and expatriates inside the locations, younger and educated locals who wish to improve their English, and international media searching for information (see table 24-1). The last choice also provided an additional common denominator for comparison for the multicultural and multilingual research team. In Singapore, the English-language newspaper was also the highest-circulation local paper. The newspapers chosen (especially "popular" and "business" ones) have among the highest circulation in the world.[27] The overall sample referenced the EU (if only once and in brief) in 9,502 articles (see table 24-2).

Table 24-1. *Media Outlets Monitored, January through December 2006*

Country	Popular Press	Business Press	English Press	TV
China	People's Daily	International Finance News	China Daily	CCTV
SAR Hong Kong	Oriental Daily	Hong Kong Economic Journal	South China Morning Post	TVB Jade
Japan	Yomiuri Shimbun	Nihon Keizai Shimbun	The Japan Times	NHK News
South Korea	Chosun Daily	Maeil Business	Korea Herald	KBS
Singapore	Lienhe Zaobao	Business Times	Strait Times	Channel 8
Thailand	Thai Rath	The Manager	Bangkok Post	ITV

Source: Authors.

Economic and political reporting constituted 46 percent and 35 percent of the total coverage of the EU respectively (the remainder was devoted to social and environmental themes).

The content analysis employed a set of elaborated identical categories to evaluate the visibility, thematic priority, and EU image presented in the field of economic and political activities. Economic representations were classified into categories such as the state of the economy in general, business and finance, industry, agriculture, and trade. Political representations were grouped into "external" and "internal" actions of the EU.

Analysis: Media Images

Descriptions of the EU in the Asian media overwhelmingly characterized the EU in either economic (46 percent) or political (35 percent) terms, but with growing reference to a more nuanced EU global role as both a social and an environmental reference point (see table 24-2). While the economic importance of the EU is hardly surprising, the emergence of the EU as a recognized political actor is an interesting development: the traditional criticism of the EU as suffering from an "expectations-capability gap" in its international relations may need to be rethought.[28] While depictions of the EU as a political actor were common, Thailand was unique in this being the dominant reporting frame (although the 431 news items were largely reflected through the English-language press); elsewhere the economic frame was the main focus of EU reporting. South Korea recorded the lowest level of political news both in absolute terms (213 items) and as a percentage of all EU news stories (22.8 percent).

A closer examination of those reports where Europe was presented as a political actor reveals a significant common perspective: around three-quarters of

Table 24-2. *Distribution of Topics across All Media Outlets*
Number of topics

Country	Political	Economic	Social	Environ-ment	Total
China	821	852	378	27	2,078
SAR Hong Kong	519	1,154	333	155	2,161
Japan[a]	387	391	72	5	855
Singapore	956	1,094	349	79	2,478
S. Korea	213	482	181	57	933
Thailand	431	395	151	20	997
Total number of stories	3,327	4,368	1,464	343	9,502
Percent	35	46	15	4	100

Source: Authors.

a. Data for Japan cover six months. Data for all other countries cover a twelve-month period.

these news items related to an external view of the EU in the world and only about one-quarter focused on internal European questions. This emphasis was particularly clear for China, where 84 percent of reports involving the EU as a political actor were externally focused (see table 24-3).

This similarity in the different Asian contexts extended to the dominant EU international involvements that were reported. While these topics reflected the international events of 2006, it is noteworthy that the EU is now being presented in the Asian media as an international political actor. Some 57 percent of all such external political news stories across the region concerned just three EU actions: the EU's intervention in the Iran nuclear issue (686 items), involvement in the Middle East (407), and EU-China relations (349). There was a clear pattern among the media in China, Hong Kong, Singapore, and Thailand, as illustrated in table 24-4. In Hong Kong, Thailand, and China, more than 30 percent of the coverage of the EU's external actions was related to Iran (in Singapore, 25 percent). Coverage of the Middle East, and Iran in particular, outstripped other topics in Singapore (21 percent) and Thailand (23 percent); not surprisingly, EU-China relations was among the topics most frequently covered by media on the Chinese mainland and in Hong Kong (26.4 percent and 15.5 percent, respectively)

South Korea and to a lesser degree Japan were exceptions to this topical consensus. Rather than Iran, South Korea's nuclear concerns were understandably focused much closer to home, and the EU's mediation in this issue was the second most widely covered story involving EU foreign affairs. Interestingly, EU-China relations was a topic widely ignored by the Korean media (just 5 items out of 172 identified in the external political frame), while attention to EU policy in the Middle East was the most commonly cited news topic (34 items).

Table 24-3. *The EU as a Political Actor: Internal and External Frames of Reference in the Media*
Number of news items

Country	Internal	External	Total	Percent external
China	131	690	821	84
SAR Hong Kong	179	340	519	66
Japan[a]	110	277	387	72
Singapore	230	726	956	76
South Korea	41	172	213	81
Thailand	115	316	431	73
Total	806	2,521	3,327	76

Source: Authors.
a. These figures have been modified from those used in the chapter on Japan, in M. Holland and others, eds., *The EU through the Eyes of Asia* (University of Warsaw, 2007), which recorded a 68–32 percent internal/external split.

South Korea and Japan shared a preference for discussing the EU in conjunction with the United States, a perspective largely missing elsewhere and reflective of their closer ties with the United States on foreign policy issues.

Turning to the smaller of the two political frames—those stories internal to the EU itself—the leading theme common to the six locations was EU enlargement (which represented one in five of the 806 intra-EU political news items analyzed). There were two distinct groups camouflaged by this average figure: over one-third of the internal EU political news items in both South Korea and Singapore were about enlargement; coverage of this issue in Hong Kong, Thailand, and Japan, however, was closer to just one in ten. And when the Asian media reported on enlargement, the focus was not on the 2004 process, or on Romania, Bulgaria, and Croatia, but usually on Turkey.

In support of the media emphasis on the EU as a political actor in other parts of the world, it was not surprising (albeit a relief to those still trying to construct a single EU international personality) that in all regions the dominant political face of the EU was Javier Solana, the High Representative for CFSP; interestingly, the EU Presidency was rarely featured, and in Japan the European Central Bank was the most widely cited EU actor. More positively, the press is now comfortable using the abbreviation "EU" without any explanation that this refers to the European Union, putting Europe on par with the commonly accepted substitution of "USA" for the United States of America, for example. This may sound like a trivial point, but the fact that the term "EU" has been so accepted is indicative of widespread public awareness. No longer is the EU confused with either trade unions or insurance unions! Interestingly too, in the media the term

Table 24-4. *Topics of External Political News Items*
Country or region and number of times referenced

Country	Rank		
	No. 1	*No. 2*	*No. 3*
China	Iran (208)	EU-China (182)	Middle East (82)
SAR Hong Kong	Iran (107)	EU-China (53)	Middle East (25)
Japan	Iran (68)	United States (12)	EU-China (46)
Singapore	Iran (186)	Middle East (153)	EU-China (53)
South Korea	Middle East (34)	North Korea	United States (71)
Thailand	Iran (98)	Middle East (73)	China (10)
Overall	Iran (686)	Middle East (407)	China (349)

Source: Authors.

"EU-3" (France, the United Kingdom, and Germany) is often taken as synonymous with the EU (a reflection perhaps of the 2006 interaction with Iran, where it was the EU-3, not the EU Presidency troika, that led).

However, this potentially reassuring response to Henry Kissinger's now 35-year-old question "Who speaks for Europe?" has to be somewhat moderated by the continuing presence of key member states (the EU-3) in news reports about the EU's international political character.[29] While theoretically it might be supportable to argue that this Janus-like quality of the EU's international image is an accurate reflection of institutional and treaty realities, it does nothing to clarify or promote the EU as a single actor in the eyes of the Asian media.

While the emergence of the EU as a global political actor in the Asian media is a welcome sign of multidimensionality in EU news reporting, as noted already, traditional perceptions have not disappeared, with the EU still presented as primarily an economic actor in almost half (46 percent) of all EU news reports in 2006 (see table 24-2). While Japan (53.4 percent) and South Korea (51.7 percent) had the highest volume of EU economic stories, last-place Thailand still had a high level of coverage (39.6 percent) of the EU as an economic player in its EU news items. This general preoccupation with the EU as a mercantilist entity matches the trading realities in all of the analyzed locations. To what extent, then, do the Asian media reflect these trends in their coverage of the EU?

First, an obvious but important observation: in each individual medium (television, popular press, English-language press, and business press), the business press recorded the highest volume of EU items with an economic focus. While this was most dramatically the case for Singapore and China, the average for all six business papers was a remarkably high level of around 70 percent. Here the regional similarity ends, however: in three cases the English-language

Table 24-5. *The EU as an Economic Actor: The Most Visible Themes*
Percent

Country	Trade	Business/ finance	Industry	State of economy	Agri- culture	Other
China	51	21	20	5	2	1
SAR Hong Kong	31	48	6	12	2	1
Japan	29	52	13	4	1	1
Singapore	41	36	14	9	0	0
South Korea	38	15	17	22	1	7
Thailand	56	23	11	4	6	0

Source: Authors.

press is in second place (*China Daily, Japan Times*, and *Bangkok Post*); in Hong Kong it was the popular newspaper *Oriental Daily*; and in South Korea and Singapore television was the second most important source of EU economic news stories (though these two countries reported a particularly small number of news items).

Within the dataset two separate economic themes are apparent: the EU as a trading partner and the EU in relation to business and finance (see table 24-5 for details). These two topics combined accounted for around half (South Korea) and over three-quarters (Thailand and Hong Kong) of all news stories on the EU as an economic actor. Under the heading "Trade," the issues discussed in relation to the EU covered bilateral trading issues, the WTO's Doha Round of trade talks, antidumping duties, free trade areas, and trade protection. For example, in Thailand the majority of all *Thai Rath* stories (the most widely read Thai-language daily paper) that framed Europe as an economic actor dealt with trade restrictions or antidumping measures that the European Union had imposed on Thai exports.

News reports on the euro, European interest rates, merger regulations and competition rules, foreign direct investment, and taxation dominated the "Business and Finance" category. Within these topics there was a diversity of positive stories (trade surpluses, strong economy, economic cooperation) and negative ones (trade restrictions, lack of progress at Doha, energy crises, problems with the European economy). From a European perspective, there was a striking lack of interest in the EU's Common Agricultural Policy (CAP), a topic that is something of a media favorite (critically) within Europe. Even in Thailand, which has experienced a series of agricultural disputes with the EU, this subject accounted for only 6 percent of the coverage of the EU as an economic player. In contrast to consistent *Eurobarometer* findings on European attitudes, for Asia, the CAP seems no longer newsworthy.

Table 24-6. *Distribution of EU News on Primetime Television News*

Country	Number of EU news items	As a percentage of EU news items across all four media outlets
China	148	7.5
SAR Hong Kong	16	0.7
Japan	n.a.	n.a.
Singapore	16	0.7
South Korea	36	3.7
Thailand	25	2.5

Source: Authors.
n.a. = Not available.

The face of Europe in economic affairs was less clear-cut than that in the political arena, where Mr. Solana, representing the EU Council, dominated. The media used both the governor of the European Central Bank (Jean-Claude Trichet) and the commissioner for trade (Peter Mandelson) to symbolize the EU as an economic entity (and thereby extended the institutional complexity and opaqueness of the EU). Consequently, both the ECB and Directorate-General (DG) for Trade were the leading institutional bodies mentioned in these news reports, with the more usual addition of the European Parliament appearing through its Community budget oversight responsibilities. The terms "euro" and "euro-zone" were regularly used to complement EU brand awareness. However, once again these common EU symbols were in conflict with the ever-present member state presence: just as we found in the analysis of the political frame, France, the United Kingdom, and Germany were frequently used to represent the EU's collective economic message.

To conclude the analysis, if the EU news data that appeared just on prime-time television news broadcasts are extracted, a somewhat different pattern emerges, primarily one of almost complete neglect. As table 24-6 demonstrates, television constituted the smallest coverage by far, only 2.5 percent of the EU news items' annual total in Thailand, but television is undisputedly the most influential medium for disseminating information. The official China Central Television (CCTV-1) has an audience of 1 billion; Hong Kong's TV Jade has 90 percent of the local audience; and in Singapore, South Korea, and Thailand the selected stations were the most widely watched non-English channels.

When considering the television data, the dominance of China has the effect of skewing the findings. Thus when the domestic focus was examined in evaluating how the EU was presented, the EU was mentioned predominantly in relation to third countries: this was emphasized in the Chinese case, where the

majority of news items fell into this category. Surprisingly, the frame of reference with the lowest score overall was where the EU was mentioned in relation
to a local focus (for example, fewer than ten stories on CCTV-1 were about EU-
China topics). The clear preference on television was to describe the EU as an
external international actor, involved somewhere else in the world. This pattern
was confirmed across the television coverage in the six locations, where just over
half of EU television news items were about the European Union in the wider
world. The findings for the focus of centrality were consistent with this perspective: half of all EU television news items were categorized as minor, locating the
EU as peripheral to the main focus of the story.

The findings for the framing of the EU on the primetime news as an economic or political actor were surprising. Interestingly, the dominant perspective
of the EU as a political actor in the television news was as a "political dwarf," not
as an "economic giant." What was particularly striking is the similar emphasis
given by television to the EU as a social and economic actor. Although rarely
featured on primetime news in the Asian region, when the EU did appear,
any previously myopic views of the EU had been replaced by a comparatively
sophisticated differentiation of EU roles and influence in Asian eyes.

Following the pattern found in the print media, in television reports where
Europe was presented as a political actor, three-quarters of these related to an
external view of the EU in the world. This pattern was particularly clear in both
China and Thailand. It is noteworthy that the EU is now being presented on
Asian television as an international political actor.

The framing of the EU as an economic actor also revealed some significant
patterns. In television reports on economic issues there was not a single story
about European agriculture; the dominant economic frames related to trade
and industry. This striking absence of agriculture on Asian primetime television
news is intriguing and suggests a perception of European concerns that would
be very unfamiliar within the EU itself.

In summary, in both print and television media, coverage of the EU is unques-
tionably modest. Where the EU was reported, it was described predominantly as
an economic global power and as an external actor elsewhere in the world, and
not as necessarily locally relevant to bilateral issues in the region. It was striking
that the EU is no longer presented as a monolithic economic entity: its different
roles are beginning to become effectively differentiated by the media. The EU's
economic prowess is still recognized, but this is now balanced by recognition
of an active emerging political international role, even when that role is with a
third country elsewhere.

So, if the EU is largely peripheral in the media, is that necessarily problematic?
There are certainly risks that can be associated with inaccurate or inappropriate

perceptions generated through the media. The data suggest that there is a potential expectations deficit: if the EU is not given prominence and its role in the region is underreported, the inevitable consequence may be reduced expectations of Europe's involvement. A self-fulfilling logic—lower demands leading to reduced media interest leading to lower demands—could ensue. Given that the EU is a significant trading partner for all the regions covered in this research and has growing political and security relationships, misperceptions based on media choices pose significant policy challenges, such as a possible undervaluing of the EU-ASEAN/ASEM relationship and an overvaluing of other relations.[30] Any such downgrading runs the risk of missed opportunities for both the EU and Asia. While underreported, the positive development unearthed by the findings is the emerging perception of an EU that is more economically and politically balanced: Europe's image is no longer just that of "Fortress Europe"; rather, the EU as an international, benign, international actor is being observed and reported more often and more accurately. If this media trend continues (and the EU's global role continues to expand), new opportunities for matching Asian needs and objectives with what the EU might be in a position to provide are possible.

Discussion

What makes it onto the news agenda is a separate field of inquiry and not tested here. However, the broad determinants of foreign news coverage about the EU have been identified to be the following: the importance of countries (in terms of their population and gross national product), their proximity (geographic, commercial, and cultural), drama (negative news), ideology (including the values of news agencies), and ease of access to a country.[31] Other factors are trade volume, the presence of international news agencies, military and political clout, and whether major incidents have occurred.[32] Importantly, even if the EU is not a state, it is still extensively treated as a state in categorizations; Manners and Whitman have claimed that the EU is usually addressed and understood by its external partners as having a capacity similar to that of a state.[33] According to this template, the EU should be newsworthy in the six Asian locations studied. The EU constitutes the world's largest trader and richest market, contains close to half a billion people, and advocates policymaking transparency with clear values and norms all facilitated through effective international media networks such as Reuters and Agence France-Presse.

This study has explored two significant questions: does the EU matter to the world, and how is the Union recognized overseas? To answer these questions, we looked at the interplay of endogenous and exogenous factors in shaping the external image of the EU. We have assumed here that media images reflect and feed back collective beliefs of foreign counterparts and paint for audiences a particular picture of the world.

The comparative content analysis of the six news media discourses revealed several commonalities in representing the EU as an economic and political actor, despite the numerous differences in newsmaking processes and unique political, economic, cultural, and demographic situations in each location. For example, the EU was reported predominantly as an economic player visible in trade, business, and finance, but relatively invisible in industry or agriculture. In the political realm, the media portrayal of the EU featured the EU acting in a third-country context, rather than in domestic or regional contexts. The EU's internal actions, the EU acting politically inside its own borders, were substantially less visible than its external performance.

While variety in reporting and interpreting the EU was to an extent predictable, the commonalities were less so, and intriguing parallels emerged. Arguably, the interdependence of regions and countries in a globalizing world economy translates in media terms into the creation of transnational media conglomerates, globally shared news production constraints on news "commoditization" (treating news as a product for sale), dominance by Western news wires, and even dominance of Western communication and information policies.[34] These features would suggest that the information fed to very different locations around the world is becoming less and less differentiated. In this context, certain similarities in the media framing of the EU in Asia, despite the ultimate diversity of the region, are to be expected. This chapter has argued that, additionally, exogenous factors (resulting from the EU's own activities) are also among the shapers of a parallel media image in the six Asian locations: the EU's performance as an influential economic actor (for example, activities of the ECB, the euro's progress, the state of the EU economy, EU actions in the WTO, the EU's FTAs in the region) and the EU as a global actor (in its negotiating role in the Middle East or Iran).

With media professionals being officially among the key targets of EU public diplomacy, these findings on EU news coverage could be useful in developing this new and challenging area in the Union's policymaking.[35] If the EU is serious about being a valiant public diplomacy actor, it needs to reinvent its strategy for dealing with international media and develop more coherent international communication strategies. The DG for Communication focuses on EU internal media, not on how media in other parts of the world may perceive the EU. To complicate the situation, each DG within the Commission, as well as each EU Presidency, each EU member state's embassy, and each state's CFSP representatives have their own resources for dealing with international media. Yet the outcome of this enormous corps of professionals transmitting messages to media gatekeepers worldwide is often disjointed and not coordinated. Studies such as the one presented here can provide some missing insights in the field.

Notes

1. H. Smith, *European Union Foreign Policy: What It Is and What It Does* (London: Pluto Press, 2002); C. Bretherton and J. Vogler, *The European Union as a Global Actor* (London: Routledge, 1999); P. Fiske de Gouveia and H. Plumridge, *European Infopolitik: Developing EU Pubic Strategy* (London: Foreign Policy Centre, 2005); D. Lynch, "Communicating Europe to the World: What Public Diplomacy for the EU?" European Policy Center Working Paper 21 (2005) (http://epc.eu/TEWN/pdf/251965810_EPC%2021.pdf [June 2009]); D. Korski, "Making Europe's Voice Louder," European Council on Foreign Relations, 2008 (www.ecfr.eu/content/entry/commentary_making_europes_voice_louder [June 2009]).

2. L. E. Cederman, ed., *Constructing Europe's Identity: The External Dimension* (Boulder, Colo.: Lynne Rienner, 2001); S. Lucarelli, "Interpreted Values: A Normative Reading of EU Role Conceptions and Performance," in *The European Union's Roles in International Politics: Concepts and Analysis*, edited by O. Elgström and M. Smith (London: Routledge, 2006); S. Lucarelli and I. Manners, eds., *Values and Principles in European Union Foreign Policy* (London: Routledge, 2006); H. Sjursen, "What Kind of Power? European Foreign Policy in Perspective," *Journal of European Public Policy* 13, no. 2 (special issue 2006): 169–81; M. Ortega, ed., "Global Views on the European Union," Chaillot Paper 72 (Paris: EU Institute for Security Studies, 2004) (www.iss-eu.org/chaillot Jchai72.pdf).

3. O. Elgström and M. Smith, eds., *The European Union's Roles in International Politics: Concepts and Analysis* (London: Routledge, 2006).

4. N. Chaban and M. Holland, eds., *The European Union and the Asia-Pacific: Media, Public and Elite Perceptions of the EU* (London: Routledge, 2008); M. Holland, P. Ryan, A. Nowak and N. Chaban, eds., *The EU through the Eyes of Asia* (University of Warsaw, 2007).

5. See Michito Tsuruoka, "How External Perceptions of the EU Are Shaped: Endogenous and Exogenous Sources," paper presented at the conference "The EU in International Affairs," Brussels, April 24–26, 2008.

6. David Shambaugh, Eberhard Sandschneider, and Zhou Hong, eds., *China-Europe Relations: Perceptions, Policies and Prospects* (London: Routledge, 2007); Michito Tsuruoka, "How External Perspectives of the European Union Are Shaped: Endogenous and Exogenous Sources," paper prepared for the 20th World Congress of the International Political Science Association (IPSA), Fukuoka, July 13, 2006; Karine Lisbonne-de Vergeron, *Contemporary Indian Views of Europe* (London: Chatham House, 2006); Karine Lisbonne-de Vergeron, *Contemporary Chinese Views of Europe* (London: Chatham House, 2007); P. Murray, "Australian Perspectives on the European Union," *European Information* 8 (1999); P. Murray, "Australian Voices: Some Elite Reflections on the European Union," *CESAA Review* 29 (2002): 5–18 (www.cesaa.org.au/publications. htm [May 2009]); P. Murray, "What Australians Think about the EU: Elite Perceptions and the Current Context," paper presented at the conference "The EU in International

Affairs," National Europe Centre (NEC), Canberra, July 2002 (www.anu.edu.au/NEC/ MURRAY-updated1July.pdf); Final Report, "Survey Analysis of EU Perceptions in South East Asia," Framework Contract AMS/451-Lot 7, A.R.S. Progetti S.r.l. Ambiente, Risorse e Sviluppo (January 2003); Final Report, "Perceptions of the EU's Role in South East Asia," Framework Contract Commission 2007, EuropeAid/123314/C/SER/multi, Lot no. 4, 2007/144031, Gruppo Soges.

7. O. Elgström, *Leader or Foot-Dragger? Perceptions of the European Union in Multi-lateral International Negotiations*, Report 1 (2006) (www.sieps.se/publ/rapporter/bilagorf 2006 I.pdf); Bertelsmann Stiftung survey, *World Powers in the 21st Century*, Bertelsmann Stiftung, Berlin, June 2006 (www.cap.lmu.de/download/2006/2006_GPC_Survey_ Results.pdf); U.S. German Marshall Fund survey, September 2007, reported in *EUobserver* (http://euobserver.com/9/24717/?print=1); "The External Image of the European Union," GARNET Working Paper No. 17/07 (www.garnet-eu.org/index.php?id=27); also reported in "Beyond Self-Perception: The Other's View of the EU," special issue of *EFA Review* 12, no. 3 (2007).

8. Conducted by the National Centre for Research on Europe (NCRE), University of Canterbury, New Zealand, since 2002.

9. As of 2009, the study had been conducted in the Australasian countries (Australia and New Zealand), Asian locations (Japan, South Korea, mainland China, SAR Hong Kong, SAR Macau, Singapore, Thailand, Vietnam, the Philippines, Indonesia, India, and Malaysia), and Pacific nations (Fiji, Papua New Guinea, Samoa, the Solomon Islands, and the Cook Islands). For more information, see www.euperceptions.canterbury.ac.nz.

10. The data for this chapter come from a specific transnational research endeavor conducted under the umbrella of "European Studies in Asia" (ESiA) supported by the Asia-Europe Foundation (ASEF) in conjunction with the NCRE. See www.esia.asef.org.

11. Tsuruoka, "How External Perceptions of the EU Are Shaped."

12. Ibid., p. 3.

13. J. Camilleri, "Restoring the Silk-Road: Perceptions, Perspectives and Policies," paper presented at the international conference "EU-Asia Relations: A Critical Review," CERC, University of Melbourne, Australia, March 27–28, 2008.

14. EU-China Trade Relations, Delegation of the European Commission to China (www.delchn.ec.europa.eu/euch_Trad_rala1.htm).

15. Department of Trade and Industry, *European Union and Hong Kong SAR: Some Important Facts* (www.tid.gov.hk/print/english/aboutus/publications/factsheet/eu2007. html).

16. Delegation of the European Commission to Singapore, *EU in Singapore—Trade and Investment* (www.delsgp.ec.europa.eu/en/eu_in_sg/trade_sg.htm).

17. Delegation of the European Commission to the Republic of Korea, *EU-ROK Relations* (www.delkor.ec.europa.eu/home/relations/rokrelations/rokrelations.html).

18. "Top 30 Trading Partners of Thailand," special publication of the *Bangkok Post*, August 1, 2007.

19. European Commission, *EU and the World: External Trade. Japan* (http://ec.europa. eu/trade/issues/bilateral/countries/japan/index_en.htm).

20. See Julie Gilson, *Asia Meets Europe: Inter-Regionalism and the Asia-Europe Meeting* (Cheltenham, UK: Edward Elgar, 2002), pp. 109–10.

21. In this case study, the range of internal political arrangements included a presidential republic in South Korea, a constitutional monarchy with a parliamentary government in Japan and Thailand, a SAR in Hong Kong, an oligarchy in Singapore, and a communist regime in China.

22. In Thailand in 2006 this study's researchers encountered many difficulties conducting stakeholder interviews since the local decision- and policymakers were very reluctant to talk about EU-Thai relations immediately after the coup.

23. Brian Bridges, *Europe and the Challenge of the Asia Pacific: Change, Continuity and Crisis* (Cheltenham, UK: Edward Elgar, 1999).

24. Tsuruoka, "How External Perceptions of the EU Are Shaped," p. 10.

25. Johan Galtung and Mari Holmboe Ruge, "The Structure of Foreign News," *Journal of Peace Research* 2, no. 1 (1965): 64–91.

26. B. Cohen, *The Press and Foreign Policy* (Princeton University Press, 1963); M. McCombs and D. Shaw, "The Agenda-Setting Function of Mass Media," *Public Opinion Quarterly* 36 (1972): 176–85.

27. World Association of Newspapers (www.wan-press.org/article2825.html?var_recherche=chosun).

28. Christopher Hill, "The Capability-Expectations Gap, or Conceptualising Europe's International Role," *Journal of Common Market Studies* 31, no. 3 (1993): 305–28.

29. The much-cited reference to Henry Kissinger's complaint about foreign policy under the European political cooperation procedure of the early 1970s remains a useful shorthand for criticizing the EU's multiple personalities in external political relations.

30. The Asia-Europe Meeting (ASEM) is an informal process of dialogue and cooperation. It brings together Austria, Belgium, Brunei, Bulgaria, Cambodia, China, Cyprus, the Czech Republic, Denmark, Estonia, Finland, France, Germany, Greece, Hungary, India, Indonesia, Ireland, Italy, Japan, Laos, Latvia, Lithuania, Luxembourg, Malaysia, Malta, Mongolia, Myanmar, the Netherlands, Pakistan, the Philippines, Poland, Portugal, Romania, Singapore, Slovakia, Slovenia, South Korea, Spain, Sweden, Thailand, the United Kingdom, Vietnam, the ASEAN Secretariat, and the European Commission. See http://aseminfoboard.org.

31. Jorgen Westerståhl and Folke Johansson, "Foreign News: Values and Ideologies," *European Journal of Communication* 9, no. 1(1994): 73–75.

32. Ian Manners and Richard Whitman, "Towards Identifying the International Identity of the European Union: A Framework for Analysis of the EU's Network of Relationships," *European Integration* 21, no. 2 (1998): 237.

33. H. D. Wu, "Systematic Determinants of International News Coverage: A Comparison of 38 Countries," *Journal of Communication* 50, no 2: 110–30.

34. Teun A. van Dijk, *News Analysis: Case Studies of International and National News in the Press* (Hillsdale, N.J.: Lawrence Erlbaum, 1988), p. 32.

35. David Lynch, "Communicating Europe to the World: What Public Diplomacy for the EU?" European Policy Center Working Paper 2 (2005) (epc.eu/TEWN/pdf/25196 5810_EPC%2021.pdf).

PART

V

Conclusion

FEDERIGA BINDI *and* JEREMY SHAPIRO

25

EU Foreign Policy: Myth or Reality?

The main message of this book is that although the foreign policy of the European Union has evolved and broadened in scope over the years, it remains a peculiar institution; it is neither a nation-state nor an intergovernmental organization. Even after much evolution, EU foreign policy cannot be assessed according to the terms of a national foreign policy. This chapter defines what EU foreign policy has come to mean and the terms on which it can be assessed. The point is to evaluate its efficiency and its capacity to deliver results for its member states and Europe's population. Finally, the chapter discusses the extent to which foreign policy has contributed to establishing the EU domestically and abroad as an independent actor in international affairs.

The Nature of the European Union's Foreign Policy

Part of the issue in understanding the European Union foreign policy is that its very existence is part of the wider debate about European integration, even when its content is not. At least three distinct views on the possibility and desirability of a European foreign policy coexist within Europe. The harshest critics of Europe insist that there is no such thing as a European foreign policy, that there never will be, and more to the point, that there never should be. A more nuanced view holds that Europe's foreign policy does not matter much now, but that it should if the states of Europe want to realize their foreign policy goals. Finally, the contributors to this volume generally believe that a European foreign policy does exist but that Europe's leaders often resist using the term for fear that it will frighten their publics or reduce their influence.[1] In this view, the key to recognizing and understanding the European foreign policy is to go beyond the narrow definition of the European Security and Defense Policy (ESDP) and the Common Foreign and Security Policy (CFSP) to encompass all of the broader policy areas in which the EU operates at the international level.

We understand foreign policy broadly as the strategy or approach chosen by a national government to achieve its goals in relation to external entities. In this sense, the EU clearly has a foreign policy. The confusion comes because most studies of foreign policy focus on the decisionmaking process itself as part of the explanation. As Chris Hill put it, "Foreign policy analysis enquires into the motives and other sources of behavior of the international actors, particularly states. It does this by giving a good deal of attention to decision-making. . . . In doing so it tests the rather plausible hypothesis that the outputs of foreign policy are to some degree determined by the nature of the decision-making process."[2] Applying this method to studying the EU's foreign policy is more complicated than applying it to nation-states. As the chapters in this book amply demonstrate, the nature and institutional setting of EU decisionmaking is complex even by the rather exacting standards of national governments.

The EU's complexity has made it the object of many studies and attempts to define it. Alberta Sbragia shares the view of most analysts in asserting that "the European Community is . . . unique in its institutional structure, it is neither a state nor an international organization."[3] For Robert Keohane and Stanley Hoffmann, "If any traditional model were to be applied, it would be that of a confederation rather than a federation. . . . However, confederalism alone fails to capture the complexity of the interest-based bargaining that now prevails in the Community."[4] Wolfgang Wessels and Andreas Maurer sum up the difficulties in definition: "Whatever the language used, political scientists and lawyers classify the EC/EU as a system for joint decision-making in which actors from two or more levels of governance interact in order to solve common and commonly identified problems."[5] This doesn't sound exactly like what a state does, but it describes an institution that plays an important role in solving policy problems in Europe, including, as this volume has demonstrated, the problem of foreign policy. Even if studying the EU's foreign policy is quite hard by usual methods, any serious analysis of how Europe relates to the outside world cannot ignore it.

The Evolution of the EU's Foreign Policy

It is clear that the EU's foreign policy has evolved as a patchwork, an ugly amalgam of different issue areas that were thrown together with little thought to overall strategy, and thus no parallels can be made with the foreign policies of its member states. It is fairly easy to define, for example, the foreign policy of the United States, and one can even find a reasonably accurate expression of it in official documents such as the "National Security Strategy of the United States." The European Union, in contrast, has not defined the goals of its foreign policy, to a large degree because it cannot agree on them. There is a "European security strategy" document, published in 2003, that reads much like that of the United States, but it is in fact not a representation even at the broadest level of what the European Union actually wants to do in the world. In fact, it is quite clear when looking at the diversity of opinion on the EU's role in the world among its member state populations and governments that the EU as a collective does not know what its foreign policy goals are. As the failed attempt to update that strategy in 2008 demonstrated, there is no longer even sufficient consensus to articulate a fairly meaningless new strategy document.

There is a long history of European efforts to establish a common foreign policy. The nations of Europe first tried to pool resources in the field of defense, even before the European Economic Community (EEC) existed. That proved a step too far: the European Defense Community was initiated to respond to both domestic and international challenges: namely the problem of German rearmament and the Korean War. But when it became clear that that conflict was a local war, Europeans lost interest, abandoned the EDC, and looked inward. Developments in the 1960s were merely the international extension of domestic policies and problems. For example, the customs union brought with it a commercial policy, with a major boost coming from the General Agreement on Tariffs and Trade (GATT) because it provided the EEC with a forum for negotiating as one entity. In the same years the EEC development policy responded to the need to deal with (primarily) French colonies within a European framework—that is to say, to act together where France had failed individually with the Communauté Française. After the 1973 enlargement, development policy received a considerable boost as it also came to include former British colonies.

In the 1970s, the world changed yet again, and the European Community found itself unequipped to deal with that change: the oil crisis and the Arab-Israeli wars are two notable examples. Relations with the United States also changed, and not for the better. Henry Kissinger, then the U.S. secretary of state, bluntly told the Europeans a truth that they did not want to hear: that they have only regional interests. Offended, the Europeans tried to form a European political identity in order to express their global interests. In concrete terms that meant that for the first time they gave themselves a few specific instruments for dealing with foreign policy: the European Political Cooperation (EPC) and the European Council. By the end of the 1970s, international events conspired to remind Europe that it could not ignore the wider world and could not simply rely on the United States to define its interests in the world. The refusal of the Europeans to go along with American sanctions against Iran after the revolution in 1979 or to join the U.S. boycott of the Moscow Olympics in 1980 in response to the Russian invasion of Afghanistan are two prominent examples that showed that the Europeans do exist and that they do not always agree with the United States.

In the 1980s, with the accession of Greece, Spain, and Portugal, the European Community essentially comprised all of Western Europe. There was a general sense that as a geographic entity the European Community needed a qualitative leap forward in its capacity to act geopolitically. The Single European Act of 1986 gave the EPC a permanent secretariat and entrusted the EC Presidency with representing Europe abroad. In the same years, with the accession of Spain and Portugal, the EEC became interested in Latin America, launching the San Jose dialogue to create links with the Latin American countries and to send a signal to the United States that Latin America would no longer be its exclusive sphere of influence. The EEC also pushed the new democracies in Latin America to create regional groupings in the image of the EC. The most notable result was the creation of Mercosur, an imitation of the EEC that Europe regards as a sincere compliment.

In the 1990s, the fall of the Berlin Wall redefined the very meaning of Europe, while the wars in the Balkans demonstrated the dangers of a weak Europe. Internally, the end of the Soviet Empire meant a reunited Germany, which posed a challenge to existing arrangements of European governance. In 1992 the Treaty on the European Union sought to anchor a bigger Germany in a stronger Europe, with a common European currency and a stronger foreign and defense policy. Eventually the only result in the field of foreign policy was the so-called CFSP, which was actually an institutional upgrade of the EPC rather than a coherent foreign policy. The European failure to act decisively in the Balkans meant that the 1990s was also the period in which the Europeans started talking seriously about defense. The results were similarly relatively weak institutions (the ESDP) rather than a true common defense policy. Only after the civil wars ended in the Balkans was the EU able to make a difference on the ground.

All in all, however, the main priority of the 1990s was the relationship with the central European countries. With an eye toward granting these countries membership, the EU negotiated enhanced Association Agreements with them. The fall of the Berlin Wall also naturally led to an attempt—not always successful—to enhance relations with Russia and with the other states of the former Soviet Union, which would soon become the EU's neighbors. Last but not least, the early 1990s saw an attempt to become a major actor in the Mediterranean with the Barcelona dialogue (though it did not go much further than dialogue) and to go global by relaunching relations with Asia and the United States.

After 9/11, internal security also became an issue, in response to the specter of terrorism as well as the massive influx of immigrants to Europe. The big bang enlargement to the east in 2004 made Europe and the European Union nearly synonymous, at least as geographic expressions. The EU's continental scope implied a global role, but the burdens of integrating the new members, the even more cumbersome decisionmaking processes, and the divisions introduced by a new bloc of members meant that the expanded Europe was even less capable of formulating a foreign policy.

In sum, the EU's foreign policymakers have usually reacted to events rather than forming a proactive agenda. The EU and its member states have responded tactically to events, adding competencies in foreign policy at the EU level when there was an urgent need or a specific opportunity rather than according to some finely elaborated strategy. The rather unsurprising result of this approach has been an EU foreign policy that is often disappointing to its members, its publics, and perhaps especially the EU institutions themselves. But while piling up this record of disappointment, the EU has also developed an ideological basis for foreign policy as well as institutions and capacities that have the potential to serve as the foundation for more significant achievements.

A true European Union foreign policy would require a more strategic outlook to realize that potential. The elaboration of a European security strategy (ESS) in 2003 was an important step in that regard, but creating a strategy document is not the same as having a strategy. The formulation of a security strategy is (or should be) a political process, an effort to build consensus around a broad approach to securing a polity's interests. It is much more than just a document; it is a process that seeks to negotiate the limits of what the polity can agree on, to smooth out the most logically incompatible edges of that consensus, and to produce a document that can command widespread respect and agreement. The resulting strategy document, even if it gets the headlines, is the least important part of that process—it is the result of a political negotiation, not the impetus for a strategic change. The ESS was not created through such a political process; rather the ESS process was heavily centralized in the staff of the EU's High Representative for the Common Foreign and Security Policy, Javier Solana. Indeed, the European Union lacks the institutional infrastructure to carry out such a process.

The Institutional Setting of EU Foreign Policy

A European Union foreign policy is dependent on the creation of an institutional framework that can support a political process of policy formulation. Currently, the negotiation of an EU foreign policy reflects the peculiar nature of the EU as neither purely domestic nor purely intergovernmental. EU foreign policy is mostly, though not exclusively, negotiated by diplomats and foreign ministers in a classic intergovernmental setting. It follows that a multiplicity of actors with often widely varying and sometimes conflicting ideas are involved in the process. Every six months a new country takes over the EU Presidency with a different agenda, creating a striking lack of continuity in foreign policy priorities. Furthermore, there is the problem of varying abilities by the Presidency to develop consensus among the EU partners and to adequately represent the EU abroad. The French and Czech presidencies in the fall of 2008 and the spring of 2009 were examples of this.

There are also multiple actors representing the EU abroad—the Presidency in office, the High Representative, the Commission president, and the commissioner charged with external relations—who often present conflicting views. The Lisbon Treaty would clearly help streamline representation by reducing the number of actors, though it remains to be seen how many of the new actors will work in practice. The Lisbon Treaty would also bring two further benefits to EU foreign policy: the creation of an EU diplomatic service and the attribution of a "legal personality" to the EU. This would allow the EU to enter into binding treaties, which should clarify and streamline the EU's ability to make external agreements.

Even if Lisbon takes effect, the requirement for unanimity or consensus will continue to make it difficult to take action, even in situations where the treaties technically allow for majority decisionmaking. This is the case, for example, with the establishment of areas for enhanced cooperation among subsets of member states. Indeed, the enhanced cooperation procedure, despite long, painful negotiations over its formulation, has never actually been used.

Last but definitely not least, the EU does not have a foreign policy because at some level it does not want one. The member states, the ultimate constituents and deciders in the European Union, still view themselves as having independent foreign policy goals. This situation results not only from disagreements over policy, although there are plenty of those, but also and more commonly from conflicts over the priority that should be given to different goals. Thus, for example, in the extremely damaging internal European dispute over Iraq in 2003, there was little disagreement within Europe over the best Iraq policy. The significant disagreement emerged over whether Europe's Iraq policy or Europe's relations with the United States should take precedence. The result was European incoherence and inconsistency. But consistency and prioritization are the essence of formulating policy—without them a policy in a very real sense does not exist.

The Ability of the European Foreign Policy to Deliver

The EU's lack of institutional coherence is reflected in its failure to give birth to a unified foreign policy actor. Still, the EU is not a nation-state, and the success or failure of its foreign policy should not be judged by the same standards. Indeed, if we lower the bar somewhat and assess the EU foreign policy against the standard of intergovernmental organizations, it is clear that the EU has had a fair amount of success.

The most successful EU foreign policy, although it is not often thought of as such, has been enlargement. The EU has proven able to attract former neighbors and, most important, to support their internal democratization processes and economic recovery. In this sense, this book demonstrates that when the EU was able to agree on coherent, purposeful action (with regard to the central and eastern European countries) it was successful. In the case of previous enlargement to the south, however, there was less causality between (at that time) the actions of the EEC and political and economic developments in Greece, Spain, and Portugal. In this case, it was rather the power of attraction of the EEC that functioned best. Yet enlargement is a card that cannot be played forever. It has proved expensive, not only monetarily but also institutionally and culturally. The EU's capacity to achieve consensus and reach decisions within its cumbersome institutional structure has clearly been weakened by the addition of so many new members, many of whose perspectives and cultures differ from those of the existing members. Turkey, which would be one of the largest members of the Union and its first majority Muslim country, would clearly be one of the trickiest cases.

Another domain where the EU has proven remarkably successful is in its commercial policy. In this area the EU clearly acts effectively as the undisputed agent of its member states, which consequently now put little effort into conducting independent commercial policies. Key economic partners, including the United States and China, recognize the EU as the interlocutor in this area and have largely given up on "divide and conquer" strategies. This does not mean that there are no disputes in commercial policy between the EU and its partners. To the contrary, such disputes are commonplace, starting with the well-known case of the EU-U.S. dispute over bananas. Paradoxically, such disputes are a symbol of success because they demonstrate that the EU is an effective advocate of European interests, that it stands up to partners such as the United States and China when necessary, and that through the relatively orderly resolution of disputes it is capable of reaching compromises that are useful to both sides and the global trading system.

In the domain of antitrust (often called competition policy), the EU has also often been able to effectively represent its members at the international level and even take the lead during the Bush years when the United States was largely inactive in this area. It is a good example of the EU's potential for capitalizing on a policy area that was given to it for technical reasons (to facilitate efficient internal market operations), and, through its capacity to create a coherent European structure and mobilize European power, mature the policy into a foreign policy tool ("a strategy for international relations," as Alberto Heimler defines it in his chapter).

In certain cases, membership in the EU has also provided an effective megaphone for member states' national foreign policies. Relevant cases are Latin America for Spain and Portugal, Timor Leste for Portugal, and Africa for Belgium and France.

But despite these important successes, the EU's record on foreign policy is a decidedly mixed one. In certain areas that one might consider key for Europe and for specific member countries, the EU has not been very effective. This is largely because the EU has no real mechanism for resolving internal disputes. Therefore, if there is no consensus, there is no policy. Examples abound and range from very large issues such as disputes over U.S. policy in Iraq to deep divides over Russia's intentions, to smaller-bore but embarrassing issues such as the failure to formulate a common position for the Durban Review Conference against racism.

In more recent crises, such as the Georgian crisis in the former Soviet republic of Georgia in August 2008, the EU has been able to reach some consensus, but on a very narrow and immediate issue: creating a ceasefire between Georgia and Russia. But even in that case the EU did not have the capacity to ensure its enforcement and in the end achieved much less than what was necessary.

We also see variable success among the EU states at using their membership in the EU as a megaphone for national foreign policy, depending on their capacity to manipulate the EU machinery and to generate consensus on their issues with the other states. It is not a matter of size: both large and small states have used the megaphone, though in different ways—large states by forcing consensus, small states by penetrating the EU institutions, especially through the Presidency. For instance, France was able to create consensus on the Common Agricultural Policy (CAP) and on commercial policy in ways that promoted French interests abroad, and Portugal shaped EU policy on Africa more through the penetration of EU institutions.

Also on the shortcomings side, the EU's neighborhood policy is a promising vehicle, but the chapters of this book show that it not very effective without the prospect of membership. There are abundant examples of how conditionality is not effective without the membership carrot: from the Mediterranean to Eurasia, and even in Turkey, where the prospect of membership remains uncertain. Likewise, even on issues such as human and civil rights and democracy promotion, which are at the very heart of the EU foreign policy discourse, the EU has no real leverage if future membership is not at stake. A concrete example of this is provided by Maurizio Carbone in his assessment of the effectiveness of different agreements with the African, Caribbean, and Pacific (ACP) countries.

Looking forward, the EU may soon also have difficulty maintaining standards among its new members because it has little enforcement capacity once a country has joined the EU.

Immigration, an important matter for many EU member states and for the EU itself, is another area where the EU's inability to influence neighbors and to arrive at a common policy is striking. Given the Schengen zone's lack of internal borders, the need to decide on many aspects of immigration policy at the European level is self-evident. But because immigration touches at the heart of domestic political disputes, the EU has not been able to reach any community consensus on this policy, and it remains a field of conflict among member states. The absence of EU competence on this issue is particularly paralyzing for foreign policy because questions of internal security and immigration are now present in virtually any agreement with third entities.

Finally, the most contentious and arguably the least successful part of EU foreign policy is defense policy. Since 2000, the European Security and Defense Policy (ESDP) has generated quite a lot of heat, but not much light. Even though there have been twenty-odd missions carried out under the ESDP banner, most have been very small, at least twelve were completely civilian, and most remain largely ineffective. The headline goal decided in 1999, to have a fully capable force of 60,000 soldiers by 2003, has not been realized. In general, member states' security policies remain stubbornly national, particularly on the most important security issues, and certainly when it comes to the all-important procurement policy. Many member states are not really interested in a common security policy—some because they treasure independence, some because they do not want to be involved militarily beyond their borders, and some simply for reasons of fiscal prudence. The result is that while the member states of Europe collectively spend over $300 billion on defense and field nearly 2 million men and women in uniform (500,000 more than the United States), 70 percent of the total cannot operate abroad, and the EU as a collective has very little ability to use its military capacity to promote its foreign policy goals.

International Recognition

The last question this book addresses is whether the EU is considered a reliable partner outside of the EU. What is the non-EU public opinion of the EU? And has the EU's foreign policy contributed to creating a European identity domestically? The picture here is mixed. There is certainly a strong recognition of the EU as an outstanding commercial actor throughout the world. Yet there is a much more confusing picture in other policy aspects. In foreign policy there have been great expectations in much of the world, including the United

States, that the EU will act like a country; but often the EU's actual capacity to deliver has led to disappointment and frustration. Examples include the Balkans, Afghanistan, China, and Russia. The EU's role as a geopolitical actor is also often jeopardized by internal divisions. Examples here are relations with Russia and the situation in Iraq, where the domestic priorities of some of the member states (France and Germany) have dictated their international behavior, despite the possibility for the EU to have a stronger role were it to have a unified and fully supported position. If the EU wants to play a global role that is perceived as such outside its borders, it will have to find a way to contain the divisions and the global aspirations of some of its member states.

Notes

1. B. White, *Understanding European Foreign Policy* (London: Palgrave, 2001), p. 37.

2. C. Hill, *The Changing Politics of Foreign Policy* (London: Palgrave, 2003), p. 10.

3. A. Sbragia, *Euro-politics: Institutions and Policy-making in the "New" European Community* (Brookings, 1992), p. 257.

4. In W. Wallace, ed., *The Dynamics of European Integration* (London: Pinter, 1990).

5. W. Wessels and A. Maurer, "The Evolution of the EU System: Offers and Demands for National Actors," paper prepared for European Community Studies Association (ECSA) conference, Madison, Wisc., June 2001, p. 5.

Contributors

IRINA ANGELESCU
Graduate Institute of International
and Development Studies
(IHEID), Geneva

ELENA BARACANI
Italian Institute for Human Sciences

FEDERICA BINDI
Brookings Institution and University
of Rome Tor Vergata

MARA CAIRA
IULM University, Milan

MAURIZIO CARBONE
University of Glasgow

TOM CASIER
University of Kent

NATALIA CHABAN
University of Canterbury

MARTA DASSÙ
Aspen Institute Italia

KHALID EMARA
Egyptian Foreign Ministry

LAURA C. FERREIRA-PEREIRA
University of Porto

SERENA GIUSTI
ISPI (Instituto Superior Politécnico
Internacional) and Catholic
University of Milan

LUCA GORI
Italian Foreign Ministry

ALBERTO HEIMLER
SSPA—Italian Public Administration
Graduate School

MARTIN HOLLAND
University of Canterbury

JOSEPH S. JOSEPH
University of Cyprus

STEPHAN KEUKELEIRE
Katholieke Universiteit Leuven
and College of Europe

FINN LAURSEN
Dalhousie University

FRANCESCA LONGO
University of Catania

ROBERTO MENOTTI
Aspen Institute Italia

ANDREW MORAVCSIK
Princeton University

PHILOMENA MURRAY
University of Melbourne

STEFANIA PANEBIANCO
University of Catania

TOMISLAVA PENKOVA
ISPI (Instituto Superior Politécnico
   Internacional), Milan

LARA PICCARDO
University of Genoa

JOAQUÍN ROY
University of Miami

JEREMY SHAPIRO
Brookings Institution

ALFRED TOVIAS
Hebrew University and Leonard
   Davis Institute for International
   Relations

NICOLA VEROLA
Italian Foreign Ministry

BERNARD YVARS
University of Montesquieu

Index

ACP group. *See* Africa, Caribbean, and Pacific (ACP) group
Acquis communautaire, xi; acceptance of, as condition of membership, 30, 160; and ENP conditionality, 107; incorporation into EU, 35; insistence on, as legal colonialism, 178; and visa procedures, 104
Action Plans (ENP): *vs.* accession process, 174; characteristics of, 101–2; conditionality in, 106–9, 112; EMP nations' disappointment with, 109; EU-centric nature of, 105, 107–8, 179; lack of procedures and timetables in, 192; purpose of, 187–88
Advantage, comparative *vs.* absolute, and globalization, 279–80
Afghanistan, Soviet invasion of, 22
Afghanistan War: Canada and, 236; and recognition of EU military deficiency, 58
Africa, Caribbean, and Pacific (ACP) group: efforts to integrate into global economy, 244, 248; EU's renewed interest in, 249
Africa, EU foreign policy on, 246–49; differing agendas of African and EU partners, 247, 249; EU-centric nature of, 249, 250; history of, 249–50; new joint Africa-EU strategy, 248–49, 250. *See also* Cotonou Agreement
Africa-EU relations: in 1990s, 34; context of, 246–47; before Cotonou agreement, 240. *See also* Cotonou Agreement
Africa-EU summits, 239
African peer-review mechanism (APRM), 248
African Union (AU): and Africa-EU relations, 246; EU as model for, 292
Africa Peace Facility, 247
AFSJ. *See* Area of freedom, security, and justice

Agricultural policy. *See* Common Agricultural Policy
Agricultural trade, and Euro-Mediterranean Partnership, 174, 180–81
Agriculture in EU, Asian perception of, 328, 330
ALBA (Bolivarian Alternative of the Americas), 226, 227
Alba (operation), 32
ALBAN, 220
Albania, as potential candidate country, 155
Albright, Madeleine, 57
ALFA, 220
AL-INVEST, 220
Allied Harmony (operation), 57–58
Amsterdam Treaty, 34–35, 55
Andean Community: and CAFTA, 227; Chilean membership, 225; EU relations with, 222
Andean Pact, 222, 274
Anderson, Robert D., 87, 89
Anna Lindh Foundation, 185, 200
Antitrust law: development in Eastern Europe, 86–87; effect-based approach, 87; international, Fox proposal for, 94; international, opposition to, 89; international cooperation and consultation on, 90–92; and rule transfer, 83, 86–87, 91–96; spillover effect in, 92–93; WTO efforts to incorporate, 87–90. *See also* Competition; Competition policy
Approximation of laws. *See* Rule transfer
APRM (African peer-review mechanism), 248
Area of freedom, security, and justice (AFSJ): Amsterdam Treaty and, 35; application of, in Mediterranean, 77–80, 80–81; Association Agreements and, 38; in European security strategy, 77; as goal of ENP, 104

351

THE CHILDREN'S HOUR

MARCIA WILLETT

McArthur & Company

TORONTO

First published in Canada by
McArthur & Company
322 King St. West
Suite 402
Toronto, Ontario
M5V IJ2

Published 2003 by McArthur & Company

National Library of Canada Cataloguing in Publication

Willett, Marcia
    The children's hour/Marcia Willett

ISBN 1-55278-394-4

    I.   Title

PR6073.I277C45 2003   823'.914   C2003-903633-2

Typeset in 11½/15pt Garamond Book by
Falcon Oast Graphic Art Ltd.

Printed in Great Britain by
Mackays of Chatham, Chatham, Kent

1 3 5 7 9 10 8 6 4 2